A History of United States Coinage

Also by Ted Schwarz

The Business Side of Photography
How to Make Money with your Camera
Coins as Living History
How to Start a Professional Photography Business
The Successful Promoter
The Five of Me (with Henry Hawksworth)
Tell Me Who I Am Before I Die (with Christina Peters)
Workshop in Photographic Lighting
Beginner's Guide to Coin Collecting
How to Have Fun and Make Money Photographing Models
Minds in Many Pieces

A History of United States Coinage

TED SCHWARZ

SAN DIEGO • NEW YORK
A. S. BARNES & COMPANY, INC.
IN LONDON:
THE TANTIVY PRESS

The Tantivy Press
Magdalen House
136-148 Tooley Street
London, SE1 2TT, England

First Edition
Manufactured in the United States of America
For information write to A. S. Barnes and Company, Inc.,
P.O. Box 3051, San Diego, CA 92038

Library of Congress Cataloging in Publication Data

Schwarz, Theodore.
A history of United States coinage.

Includes legislation.
Bibliography: p.
Includes index.
1. Coins, American—History. 2. Mints—United States—History. 3. Coinage—United States—History. I. Title
CJ1830.S38 1980 737.4'9'73 77-69642
ISBN 0-498-02210

1 2 3 4 5 6 7 8 9 84 83 82 81 80

Contents

Acknowledgments

Special assistance with this book was provided by Laura Clark, who did research for me in the National Archives and by the staff of the American Numismatic Association in Colorado Springs, Colorado, who let me photograph their extensive coin holdings and provided free access to their large library.

Introduction

History is more than the recitation of dates and events. It is the story of the strivings, the passions, and the accomplishments of individuals. History is as varied and exciting as life itself. It is a panorama of the life situations and emotions experienced by those who came before us.

And so it is with the history of United States coinage. The first colonial coin was actually an act of defiance against the king. The morale and economy of thousands of Confederates were undermined by the money produced by Union counterfeiters during the Civil War. And as World War I approached, the nation was shocked to discover the mint had released a new quarter that could only be judged obscene by the standards of the day.

A History of United States Coinage is different from other books about money. It was written to tell the "human" side of the history of our nation's coinage. Instead of concentrating on the mechanics of coin production, it tells of the intricate role coinage has played in the development of the nation. There are stories of the gold-rush and silver-rush towns, where money substitutes were used by the brothels, bars, and merchants before private mints began producing their own coins. There are stories of counterfeiters and con men as well as intimate glimpses into the lives of our nation's greats. For example, in learning how the Franklin half dollar came into existence, you discover such sidelights of Franklin's character as the fact that he was the first newspaperman in America to use sex-and-violence to sell more copies.

A History of United States Coinage also tells of the establishment of branch mints and gives the stories behind our nation's commemorative silver and gold coins. It is the most comprehensive volume of its type ever written and, I hope, the most entertaining as well.

For those of you who may have special interests within the field, the comprehensive bibliography at the back of the book should be of interest. The mechanical details of coin production, for example, are treated in depth in such books as *The U.S. Mint and Coinage* by Don Taxay and *Counterfeit, Mis-struck and Unofficial U.S. Coins* by the same author. All the legal documents relating to the establishment of the Charlotte Branch Mint (North Carolina) are found in *The Establishment of the Charlotte Branch Mint—A Documented History* by Anthony Stautzenberger. And the mechanical equipment used by the branch mints is described in such volumes as *Mint Mark: "CC"* by Howard Hickson.

But such books are for the advanced hobbyist with an interest in studying, in depth, one small aspect of United States coinage. *A History of United States Coinage* is meant for the collector, the casual reader, and the lover of history. It is a comprehensive study of all aspects of our nation's coinage, including an overview of pertinent laws, which will be found in the appendixes.

A History
of United States Coinage

1

In the Beginning—The First American Mint

It might be said that the American Revolution began not with a rifle shot but with a coin. The first act of defiance against the crown occurred in 1652, more than 100 years before the acknowledged start of hostilities. It was a "crime" committed by the Masachusetts Bay Colony whose Great and General Court (the colony's legislature) ordered the illegal striking of desperately needed coinage.

To understand the Massachusetts action, it is important to understand the problems the early settlers were facing. When the colonists left England for the new land, they did not worry about having money for trade. The small ships on which they traveled were limited in the weight they could hold. Families carried only the necessities for survival—food, tools, weapons, and similar items. Few coins were brought at first because the earliest travelers expected to have to be self-sufficient, making and growing everything they needed.

In a few years after the colonists' arrival the land had been cleared and homes built. Since the farms were producing more food than a single family could eat, some of the men were able to abandon the fields and set up other businesses. A man might work as a cabinetmaker or silversmith rather than just as a tiller of the soil. But such businesses require a medium of exchange, and the lack of coinage made that a problem.

At first the colonists worked with barter. A man who raised chickens would go to the shop of a man who made shoes. He would offer to exchange a certain number of chickens for shoes for his family. If the shoemaker liked chicken, he would agree to the trade. The exact number of chickens to be exchanged would be based on the time and expense of raising them versus the time the shoemaker spent making the shoes.

When the shoemaker had his fill of chickens, he might still accept such a barter if he knew that someone else would accept them. Perhaps he wanted a new chair for his shop. He might hold the chickens in a coop behind his building until he could arrange to trade them to a cabinetmaker who would provide him with the chair he desired.

Anything of value might become a barter object. Animal pelts, livestock, grain, and even tobacco were utilized, the latter being most popular in the Virginia colony, where it was grown extensively. The price of a "good wife" in Virginia was between 100 and 150 pounds of tobacco. It can be assumed that a lesser amount was paid for a woman who was not so good.

Another popular coin substitute was wampum, a "money" system developed by the American Indian. Here is Roger Williams' description of wampum. "It is of two kinds which the Indians make of the stem or the stock of the periwinkle [a type of shellfish] after all the shell is broken off. Of this kind, six of the small beads, which they make with holes to string up their bracelet, are current with the English for a penny. The other kind is black, inclined to a blue shad, which is made of the shell of a fish which some of the English call henspoquahoc [quahog, a type of clam] and of this description three are equal to an English penny. One fathom of this stringed money is worth five shillings."

Wampum actually served multiple purposes for the Indians. Of greatest importance was the fact that it was a money of consistent value. The value of barter objects varied from area to area and time to time depending upon current need for a given item. But wampum maintained its value because the time required for its production was always the same. It took about one hour to smooth a piece of shell into a quarter-inch bead, which would then be pierced for stringing. White wampum was more common than black wampum but the time needed to prepare both types of shells was the same.

In addition to its monetary value, wampum was ornamental. It might be woven into belts and other adornments so it could be given as gifts or worn to display one's wealth in much the same manner that diamonds or pearls are worn today.

At first the colonists found that wampum made an ideal trading device. Unfortunately, it was only a short while before the Indians and the settlers began to cheat one another. It was possible to dye the white wampum black in such a way that the settlers could not spot the ruse. Dishonest Indians would pass the dyed wampum to the whites and then refuse to accept it in future transactions. Their more experienced eyes could always spot the artificial coloring.

The whites, on the other hand, took to crudely manufacturing their own white wampum. Enough was produced to create an over abundance, causing all the wampum in circulation to become devalued. Prices soared out of control as the first inhabitants of America were introduced to inflation.

Other financial approaches were tried. The Great and General Court of Massachusetts Bay Colony authorized the use of musket balls as money. It ordered "that muskett bulletts of a full boare shall passe currantly for a farthing apeece, provided that noe man be compelled to take above XIId [twelve pence] att a tyme in them." The musket balls had consistent value because of their universal use for hunting and defense.

But the efforts of the Massachusetts colonists to find a substitute for coinage seemed destined to failure. The lack of coins became so serious that class problems developed as well. John Winthrop, Massachusetts' first governor, told a humorous story about a man named Rowley who was having difficulty maintaining his social position because he lacked the funds to pay his servant. He didn't want to lose the servant but he didn't know how to pay his wages either. Winthrop wrote: "the master was forced to sell a pair of his oxen to pay the servant's wages and so told the servant he could keep him no longer, not knowing how to pay him the next year. The servant answered him that he would serve him for more of his cattle. But how shall I do, said the master, when all my cattle are gone? The servant replied, why, then you shall serve me and you shall then have your cattle again."

There were more problems facing the New England colonists. For several years the earliest settlers relied upon new waves of immigrants to support their businesses. People were limited in the possessions they could carry on the ships arriving from England. They needed furniture and other large items, and these they purchased from the merchants already settled in the colonies. But by 1640 the influx of new colonists had almost ceased. Craftsmen found that the demand for their wares had dropped to such a level that they could no longer support their families.

Even farmers found that the market for agricultural produce was so limited that prices sometimes dropped below the cost of production. Many families returned to England, which was then in the throes of a civil war. Others went to the West Indies. Even Governor Winthrop was disheartened. According to his diary, he would never have left England had he realized the hardships he would one day experience.

Those colonists who stayed in the New England settlements often went into radically different lines of work. Fishing and international trading, especially with the West Indies, began to occupy the time of the men. The Massachusetts colony became a major shipping center and this brought new coinage problems for the people.

Merchants selling goods abroad had to accept payment in whatever coinage was current in the countries visited. The most common coin was the Spanish dollar, an eight-real coin also called piece of eight—beloved of fictional pirates. It had been minted in the silver-rich lands of Mexico and Peru since the 1500's and was also made abroad. It was fairly consistent in quality, and with almost two billion "dollars" in Spanish coins made during the first 250 years of settlement in North and South America, it became a common item for trade. Worth eight reales, the Spanish dollar was frequently cut into eight equal parts or bits, each worth twelve and one-half cents. It was this division of the Spanish coin that resulted in the American slang expression "two bits," meaning a quarter.

The British colonists had no trouble adjusting to the Spanish coins, which held a constant value in relation to the British denominations they had used in their homeland. The people knew the quality and quantity of silver in the Spanish eight-real coins were maintained at a constant level, unlike the coins of other nations, which were frequently worth far less than their face value. Many rulers reduced the silver in their coins in order to make additional profits, and other countries had constantly to test the coins to determine what value they would have in international trade.

Soon the American colonists were receiving French, Portuguese, and Dutch coins, among others, and having to set values for them. The only coins that almost never reached the shores of Massachusetts were the English ones the people were accustomed to using before their emigration.

The reasons British coins failed to circulate in great numbers were numerous. The first reason was that the king of England was fighting a civil war. Men and arms had to be bought for gold and silver, a fact which was of highest priority. The king saw no reason to turn any of the precious metal into coins for shipping to the colonies when this could not benefit him in any immediate way.

Even if there were no civil war, the king would not have been enthusiastic about helping the colonists with their coinage problems. The majority of the people who settled the new land were held in disrespect. Many were rebels against the norms of English society. Still others were former prisoners shipped to America to work as servants for the wealthy. Men and women were often deported to save the crown the expense of maintaining them in jails. If the crown wouldn't pay the price of housing criminals in England, it had no intention of supporting them in a far land.

To make matters worse, the balance of trade with England went against the colonists' interest. The colonists imported far more goods than they exported. Many times, barter arrangements were worked out. But usually the British merchants demanded gold and silver coin before they would ship anything to America. What little hard money could be found in the colonies seemed to make its way inevitably back to England.

The influx of coins from different countries also brought numerous problems. Perhaps the greatest problem was determining coin values in relation to British money. Each community set its own standards, and these differed greatly from area to area. A French coin might be worth a British pound in one colony and perhaps three-fourths of a British pound in another colony.

Then there was the problem of counterfeit coinage and coins with improper metal content. Most of the colonists had little knowledge of the legitimate coinage of foreign countries. If a merchant was handed what was supposedly a Dutch coin, he would have no idea whether it was genuine. Even if it was genuine, the amount of silver or gold used in a coin struck by one ruler might not equal the amount used by his successor for a coin of identically marked value. Since the real value in international trade was determined by the value of the metal in the coin and not the marked value, this was an important detail.

Many merchants within a community varied the price of the items they sold according to the way they were paid. Thus a chest might sell for one price in wampum, a second price in Spanish dollars, a third price in cattle, and a fourth price in French coin. The people resented the arbitrary standards but they had no alternative. They were not provided with any British coinage and it was illegal for them to produce their own.

By 1652, the Massachusetts Bay Colony leaders felt they had to do something to correct the coinage problem. They knew that to start their own mint would be an act of defiance against the king, one which conceivably could result in troops being sent to take control of their affairs. But the king had been deaf to their pleas for too long. They needed a money standard to which all the people could relate and this meant producing their own coins.

On May 27, 1652, the General Court passed a law that read . . .

> enacted by the Authority of this Court; that all persons what soeuer haue liberty to bring in vnto the mint howse at Boston all bulljon plate or Spanish cojne there to be melted, & brought to the allay of sterling Silver by John Hull, master of the sajd mint and his sworne officers, & by him to be cojned into 12d: 6d: & 3d peeces, which shall be for forme & flatt and square on the sides & stamped on the one side with NE on the other side with XIId VId and IIId = according to the valew of peeces which shall bee together with a privy marke = which shall be Appointed euery three months be the Gouernor, & known only to him & the sworne officers of the mint. And the mint master for himselfe & officers, for their pajnes and labour in melting Refining and Coyning is allowed by this Courte to take one shilling out of euery twenty shillings which he shall stampe as a aforesajd.

John Hull, the man who was authorized to strike these coins in defiance of the king was one of the more colorful characters in the

Massachusetts Colony. He was a study in contrasts—a man who made business deals that brought him great wealth and with it a reputation not unlike that of the late Howard Hughes. Yet he was also a skilled artisan and so patriotic that he was willing to use his personal fortune to help finance a war when there was little chance he would ever see his money again.

John Hull was born at Market Harborough, Leicestershire, England, in December of 1624. His father was a blacksmith by trade, but his dabbling in real-estate investment made the family wealthy. He had a love of adventure and was intrigued by reports coming back from the new world. He decided to take his family abroad, bringing John to the Massachusetts Colony when he was ten years old.

The elder Hull became a farmer, and his son helped him in the fields. At eighteen, however, young Hull decided he wanted to learn a trade. He went to work for his half brother, a goldsmith who was willing to take him on as an apprentice. The term "goldsmith" was used loosely in the colonies. In England such artisans worked in gold as well as silver and other precious metals. But little gold was brought to the colonies. Men like Hull worked in silver, pewter, and similar materials.

Hull went into business for himself during the depression years of the 1640s. The flow of immigrants had almost ceased, and most families had little money for anything other than the necessities of life. However, he managed to survive until new business, such as international trade, brought renewed prosperity to the people.

Many of Hull's creations were for church use. He melted Spanish pieces of eight for their silver, then molded the metal into chalices and other items. He copied designs from pieces brought from England, for he had little creative ability. He was a skilled craftsman who could produce quality pieces, though they lacked both originality and ornamentation.

By the time Hull was twenty-three he was well on his way to being successful. He married a woman named Judith Quincy, and had Governor Winthrop perform the religious ceremony. However, he was not a particularly religious man and did not make an effort to join the church until the following year.

Hull joined the Massachusetts militia, an action he considered more important than any he had previously taken in his life. This was probably because of the community spirit involved in the organization. The Puritans had resurrected the medieval idea of universal military training so that every one in the community would be prepared in an emergency. They took turns at night watch and had training drills every month. The men were basically a home-defense guard but they could be drafted to fight in an Indian war, should one erupt.

John Hull's military ability was probably average at best, but his popularity was so great that he was asked to join the elite Honorable Artillery Company where he rose to its highest rank, captain. He was given a special uniform of russet coat, white lace collar, and scarlet swordsash. Although reluctant to go into battle, he proudly drilled his troops in the uniform that he felt was the height of personal splendor.

Hull used his popularity to enter into a variety of unrelated businesses. He spent most of his time working at his trade, but he bought ships and hired crews to engage in international commerce on his behalf. Each vessel was laden with whatever cargo Hull felt he could sell. The ships went to different ports throughout the world, selling their wares and filling their holds with foreign products in demand in the colony. These were brought to Boston, where handsome profits were realized from their sale, and the whole procedure was then repeated.

Having learned the value of land from his father, Hull made investments in that area as well. He bought farms, sometimes selling them for a profit and other times hiring people to work them for him. He went into the timber business, raised horses, and entered the field of finance, loaning money to individuals and businesses and taking mortgages.

Personal ethics always took second place to the necessities of money-making for Hull. He felt that slavery was wrong and warned his captains that if they ever took slaves, their ships would be struck down by the Lord. However, when his craving for red Madeira wine became uncontrollable, he abandoned his "principles" and authorized that two slaves be taken to Madeira in trade for a quantity of the wine. He had been told that such a trade was the only way he could obtain the wine and his thirst took precedence over his expressed feelings about human rights.

It was only logical that when money was to be coined, Hull received the commission to make it. His goldsmith trade made him a natural choice since he was used to working with silver and other metals. His extensive business experience made him sympathetic to the plight of all the merchants trying to turn a profit with a limited supply of coinage. And his popularity was so great that no one minded the excess profits he eventually made.

The colony did everything it could to help Hull. He was given a special building in which to strike the coins as well as all the tools needed to melt, refine, and coin silver. He was also authorized to take one shilling three pence for every 20 shillings he struck. This fee represented outrageous profit for him and was far higher than the coinage fees charged by any mint in Europe.

Hull went into partnership with Robert Sanderson, a fellow goldsmith who had trained in England. They were under oath to coin all specie by "the just allay of the English coine" and to give it its true weight. These orders were followed faithfully.

The first coins struck were almost blank, crudely cut planchets "stamped on the one side with NE and on the other with the figure XIId VId and IIId." They were coins of desperation meant to serve as the fastest way to alleviate the money shortage. However, it was quickly seen that they were causing more problems than they were solving.

The crude coins were easy to counterfeit and easy to "clip." Clipping was a term applied to the removal of small amounts of silver from a coin by shaving or cutting an edge of it. Properly done, a clipping could not be readily detected when a coin had just been prepared for circulation. The planchets were crude but everyone trusted Hull so they were taken at face value. However, after several people tried their hands at clipping the same coin, the abuse made it obviously smaller than standard issues and it was soon refused by merchants.

The silver left over from the clipping was saved. When a fair amount had accumulated, the person who had done the altering would take it to the mint and have it melted and remade into coins. Even though a fee had to be paid to Hull for providing this service, the clippers gained a considerable profit.

The General Court quickly ordered a change in the coin so that even the slightest clipping could be detected. This meant using a design that took advantage of the entire surface of the coin. The act of October 19, 1652 was intended ". . . for the prevention of washing or Clipping of all such pieces of mony as shall be Cojned w in this Jurisdiction. It is Ordered by this Courte and the Authoritje thereof, that henceforth all pieces of mony cojned as afore sajd shall have a double Ring on either side, with this Inscription—Massachusetts, and a tree in the Center on the one side, and New England and the yeere of our lord on the other side, according to his draught heere in the margent." The act, written in the Massachusetts Records, was accompanied by a crudely drawn version of the coin being authorized.

The colonists were well aware of the dangers in the step they had taken. The Hull coins were certain to anger the British government and they were undoubtedly going to be ordered to cease striking them. They were equally certain the Hull coins were necessary for trade and would continue to be for several years. They therefore decided that regardless of the fact that the coins were supposed to bear "the yeere of our lord," they would continue dating them "1652," the original issue date. Then, when they were ordered to stop the coinage, they would claim that no more were being produced since coins with more recent dates could not be found in circulation.

There were three different varieties of new designs. The first is believed to have depicted an oak tree. Then came the Pine Tree and Willow Tree variations. The choice of the Oak Tree design appears to have been a chance occurrence. It was apparently selected without thought to any special meaning the oak might have. However, it

The Oak Tree threepence of 1652, created by John Hull. This coin was more elaborate than the very first coins tried, which were easily counterfeited. However, counterfeiting and clipping of the edges to obtain bits of silver was still a popular way to make extra money.

The Pine Tree shilling of 1652.

proved to be the wisest choice the colonists could have made.

In 1662, England's internal strife had been settled and Charles II was safely on the throne. He now had time to consider matters other than the retention of power, and he began studying reports coming to him from the Massachusetts colony. He learned that there was an unauthorized mint in operation and he was as angry as the colonists had feared he might be. He immediately summoned one of his advisors, Sir Thomas Temple, who was fortunately a friend of the colonists. The king ranted at Temple, charging that the Massachusetts mint was a direct challenge to the crown. It had been built in defiance of British law and he was going to have it put out of business.

Temple tried to calm the king. He told him that the colonists were a simple people with only a slight knowledge of the law. He said they would not knowingly defy the crown and that the only reason they had constructed the mint was the severe financial crisis they faced. He then took one of the Oak Tree pieces and had the king study it closely. He explained that the coin showed the Royal Oak.

The reference to the oak related to an incident that took place when Charles was fleeing some enemies in Boscobel during the turmoil that had recently plagued England. The king had climbed an oak tree and hidden in its branches, saving his life. Although the colonists had given no thought to the incident (and may not even have known of it), the king was deeply touched by the supposed honor.

Temple further explained that with the civil war raging in England, the colonists felt it was unwise to use the king's portrait as was common in Britain. However, they felt that the oak tree could be used in its place and that the coins would thus honor his name.

The king was delighted. He disregarded his advisors who felt that regardless of the colonists' intentions, they should be punished for violating the letter of the law. He said that he wouldn't authorize continued production of the coins as official issue but that he also wouldn't stop the operations of John Hull's mint for the time being.

The mood of the British government began to change in 1665. That was the year the colonists requested a copy of the laws which pertained to them. These laws very clearly stated that the coining of money was illegal, so the colonists could no longer plead ignorance. They were forced to make a formal request for the law to be changed so they could continue to operate their mint.

Reaction to the plea was slow in coming but early reports filtering back to the colony indicated that it was not going to be favorable. The colonists felt that the only answer was to use a business device that has since become a tradition for some corporations—they sent a bribe. A shipload of masts, prepared from the abundant colonial trees, was sent to the King.

The bribe seemed effective, for it temporarily reduced the pressure the crown was applying to make them stop coining. However, as is often the case in such matters, a second bribe had to be given just two years later. This time the bribe consisted of "tenn barrells of Cranburyes, two hogsheads of speciall Good Sampe, and three thousand of Cod ffish", according to an order recorded on October 22, 1677, in the Massachusetts Records.

Naturally the bribes were never called by such a derogatory term. They were merely presents from a loyal colony wishing to show the king a token of their warm feelings for all he had done for them. The mint was never mentioned, though they made certain the bribes were sent whenever the mint's activities were under discussion in England.

Hull and Sanderson were becoming quite wealthy from their mint operation. The terms under which they operated gave them profits beyond any that were proper according to the strict codes of the time. Business people were supposed to charge only as much as would yield an honest profit. But to many this meant 50 to 100 percent, well beyond that which the public felt was just. However, the laws against such profiteering were vague at best, and everyone seemed to try to get as much as he could for his merchandise. Thus enforcement was a haphazard affair.

In 1660 the General Court wanted Hull to agree to a lowered fee for coining. Hull explained that he found the current fee most satisfactory and saw no reason to have it lowered. However, to placate the colony's leaders, he began quietly contributing a "gift" to the treasury every year. This gift was only a fraction of the excess profits he was making but the treasury was in such desperate need of money that the gift was always accepted. No further effort was made to get Hull to lower his coinage charges.

The extent of Hull's profits might be shown by the rather humorous situation that arose when his daughter was married. Betsy Hull was an short young woman, less than five feet tall, whose diet consisted of large quantities of pies, puddings, and other fattening sweets. When her suitor, Samuel Sewall, later a judge at the Salem witch trials, asked for her hand in marriage, Hull was supposed to have commented: "Yes, you may take her and you'll find her a heavy burden enough".

The ceremony was an elegant affair climaxed by one of the most unusual dowry presentations in history. Huge scales were brought out and Hull had his daughter sit on one side. Then a large chest of freshly minted Pine Tree shillings was brought forth and the coins were scooped into the other side of the balance. When the two scales were again level, Hull told young Sewall: "There, son Sewall, take these shillings for my daughter's portion. Use her kindly and thank Heaven for her. It's not every wife that's worth her weight in silver".

The dowry amounted to the British money equivalent of 30,000 pounds sterling. That was far more money than was "earned" during the weighing stunt. It is guessed that Betsy's weight was 125 pounds. With one British pound sterling weighing four ounces, no more than 500 pounds sterling could have been placed in the balance. The remaining endowment was the gift of an obviously doting father.

The minting of coins did not solve all the problems the Massachusetts' colonists were facing. Many of the coins were going overseas just as the British coins had done. Sailors would get them in change in the port of Boston, then take them with them when their ships left for other ports. This perpetuated the coin shortage, and several laws had to be enacted ordering the confiscation of coins found in the possession of any ship or individual leaving the colony. It was the only way to keep the coins in local circulation where they were so desperately needed. But enforcement of the law against coin removal was difficult.

To make matters worse, fewer and fewer coins were being struck because most people had stopped bringing their foreign silver coins to the mint for melting and striking into the authorized Massachusetts coins. At first the pieces of eight were regularly brought to the mint by traders. However, they soon found they made more money using the Spanish coins abroad, since Hull took such a large commission for his work. The General Court finally decided to allow foreign coins to circulate in the same manner as Massachusetts issues once they had been assayed and stamped with the mark "NE". Specific values were assigned to each piece with the eight-real coin passing as six shillings, for example.

John Hull's life, which had been devoted to making as much money as possible, took an unusual twist in 1676 during King Philip's War. There was an effort to remove warring Indians who had refused to leave the western shore of Narragansett Bay. The territory had been granted to the whites in 1657 when the Pettaquamscut Purchase Agreement was made with the Narragansett Indians. However, no one could settle there because of renegade attacks.

Hull was in his fifties in 1676, too old to be asked to take an active part in the battles. However, his services were used by making him treasurer of the colony. It was to prove the most expensive post he could possibly have assumed. The Massachusetts colony had no funds for fighting the war, so a series of taxes were levied against the various towns. These levies were ordered one after the other, fourteen being issued in one year alone. It was Hull's job to see that they were paid.

As has been seen, money was quite scarce and collecting the tax was a difficult chore. Many of the towns were forced to use barter methods, paying in the form of fish grain. Those who did not feel much enthusiasm for the war, and there were many, paid with rotting corn and spoiled fish. Hull used his own money to supplement what he had collected when the levies failed to equal the amount needed by the colony. Four years after he took the office he was owed more than 1,500 pounds. To make matters worse, after he finally had left the post, the colony had a chance to buy Maine for 1,250 pounds. Again Hull was asked to help. This time Hull went to wealthy Boston merchants for funds, eventually raising 700 pounds. The rest of the money he obtained by borrowing funds against his personal line of credit in England.

All the work proved too taxing for the aging Hull. As his son-in-law Samuel Sewall wrote in November of 1683, Hull "labored under the weight of this accompt with his own hand, until weakeness of body and the bulke thereof necessitated him to take in Captain Daniel

Henchman to his assistance . . . and besides his own paines, one of his relations and two of his apprentices did labour much in this service for all which he hath not charged one penny".

On October 1, 1683, Hull died. The Colony still owed him over 2,125 pounds for his many services and personal financial support. His labors on behalf of the people had cost him a small fortune. His total estate proved to be just a little over 6,000 pounds, a fraction of what it was prior to his entering public service.

About the time that Hull lay dying, the British government finally ordered the stopping of coinage in the Massachusetts colony. The people attempted to reason with the crown asking to be allowed either to continue what they were doing or to start a new mint under official sanction. Neither request was granted.

There was nothing for the people to do but try to ensure that the coinage thus far produced would remain useable. The General Court passed a law stating that the coinage already in existence should continue to pass for the value stamped on it at the time it was minted. It also took a severe stand against counterfeiting the coinage which had become a problem. The act, passed in 1692, stated:

"And whosoever, from and after the publication of this act, shall attempt and practice the counterfeiting, or clipping, rounding, filing, or otherwise diminishing or debasing any of the monies and coins currant within this province, being thereof lawfully convicted before the justices of assize, shall forfeit double the value of the money so counterfeited, clipped, rounded, or filed, one half to their majesties towards the support of the government and the other half to the informer; and shall also stand in the pillory in some open place in the shire town of that county where the offence is committed, and there have one of his ears cut off."

Some time in 1682 or 1683 the mint that had been operated by the John Hull for thirty years went out of existence. The inability to keep adequate numbers of the coins in circulation in the colonies, coupled with the growing hostility of the British Government, brought an end to the first major act of defiance taken by any of the colonies.

2

Colonial Coins and Money Systems

As was noted in the first chapter, barter of one sort or another was considered an essential practice among the colonists. John Hull's mint went a long way towards alleviating the coin shortage in Massachusetts, but the other colonies were still trying to find their own answers to the problem.

Virginia's answer to the coin shortage was to develop an elaborate system based on tobacco. John Rolfe, the man who married Pocahontas, cultivated the first commercial crop of the plant in 1612. It quickly became so important and so widely accepted that seven years later, in 1619, the first general assembly at Jamestown decided that tobacco would be the official currency of the colony. It was a valued barter object and the labor necessary to bring a plant to maturity was known and consistent from grower to grower. The value of tobacco was thus set at three shillings a pound for the best grade and eighteen pence a pound for the lesser grade.

Soon almost everything was bought and sold for tobacco, a fact that delighted the poorest members of the colony. They realized they could have instant wealth if they planted whatever land they could obtain with tobacco. Each day they would stand watching their crop, dreaming of the goods they would buy with the closest thing to a "money tree" Americans have ever devised.

What the people failed to consider was that tobacco, albeit the monetary standard, had no value in terms of basic survival. When they stopped planting corn and other crops meant for eating, they were running the risk of starving to death in the midst of their supposed riches.

Gradually a crude form of inflation began to occur. The few people who had supplies of grain, corn, and other necessities refused to part with them for the old prices. Cornmeal, for example, soon cost 30 times the tobacco needed to buy it a few years earlier. A side of venison rose to three times its former value. Then the price of tobacco plummeted. From three shillings a pound in 1619, it dropped to one-and-one-half pence a pound in 1645. Twenty years after that the price reached a penny a pound.

Runaway inflation outraged the general public. The people of Virginia decided that if overproduction of their "tobacco money" had destroyed its buying power, the way to stem inflation was to destroy the crops. In January of 1640 all the bad tobacco and half of the good were put to the torch. The people were literally burning their money in order to make whatever was left over more valuable. In addition, the people demanded that the legislature set new, fixed rates for the value of the crop. It was to be a shilling a pound for the highest grade the first year, and that figure was to be doubled for the highest grade of the following year's crops.

By March 1643, enough Spanish, British, and other coins had made their way into the Virginia colony that at least some coinage could have been used, reducing dependence upon the inflated tobacco. But the legislature would not hear of it. The only exceptions to the tobacco rulings were owners of horses, mares, and sheep. They had the option of demanding cash when making a sale of their livestock. All others were forced to accept tobacco if the purchaser refused to use anything else.

Despite the dramatic gesture of burning the fields, tobacco continued to be overproduced. Finally, the House of Burgesses met in James City on November 20, 1645. They recognized that the tobacco money had failed and that a system of coinage had to be adopted. They decided to utilize the Spanish eight-reales coins manufactured in the new world. These were coins similar to our silver dollar and were among the most common in international trade. They were of consistently high quality silver and were readily accepted by everyone.

The act stated: "That all peeces of Eight in Spanish money be valued and taken in payment, att the rate of sixe shillings and all other Spanish silver quoines proportionably which shall be brought into the collony. . . ."

Eventually Virginia, like the other colonies, established tables of value for every type of coin circulating within its boundaries. French, Spanish, Peruvian, Arabian and other coins were valued in relation to the English pound. Unfortunately, each colony had different standards for the same coins, a fact that would result in serious trade problems when goods were brought from one colony to another.

The one barter object that seemed to hold its value as well as the coins that gradually came into circulation was the common nail used in construction. It was only in the late 1700s that a machine was made to mass-produce nails. Prior to that, nail cutting and heading was the job of the blacksmith who made them one at a time. The labor necessary for this production was consistent throughout the colonies and a value was placed on each nail accordingly. Thus we developed a description of nails based on English money earned for the labor and this description has lasted into modern times. We still have tenpenny nails, twentypenny nails and the like.

Nails were so expensive that the majority of houses were built with wooden pegs. When nails were used, the resale value of the house was not as great as the cost of buying new nails for another structure. As a result, when a wealthy colonist decided to move to a different area, he would burn down his house to retrieve the nails used in construction. When burning became extensive and the danger of fires spreading to surrounding buildings and trees became great, the Virginia colonial leaders worked out a compromise. The legislature would pay the home owners the cost of the nails used, and the homes would be left standing when the owners moved on.

Running a business became a complex problem as different types of payment had to be accepted. Someone might want to barter or use coins or some other device. Just how confusing this became is obvious when you read some of the descriptions provided by early diarists. For example, in the 1704 journal of Mrs. Knight of New Haven, there is the following description:

> They give the title of "merchant" to every trader, who rates his goods according to the time and species they pay in; viz., "pay;" "money;" "pay as money;" and "trusting." Pay is grain, pork and beef, etc., at the prices set by the General Court. Money is pieces-of-eight, ryals, Boston or Bay shillings, or "good hard money," as sometimes silver coin is called; also wampum, viz., Indian beads, which serve as change. Pay-as-money is provision aforesaid, one-third cheaper than the Assembly set it; and Trust, as they agree for at the time. When the buyer comes to ask for a commodity, sometimes before the merchant answers that he has it, he says, "is your pay ready?" Perhaps the chap replies, "yes." "What do you pay in?" says the merchant. They buyer having answered, then the price is set; as supposed he wants a 6d knife, in "pay" it is 12d; in "pay-as-money" 8d., and "hard-money," its own value, 6d. It seems a very intricate way of trade. . . .

Beaver skins were popular items for money, and they had fairly fixed values. Each skin was worth two shillings, a price approximating fifty cents today. The major advantage of beaver skins was that the northern colonists knew exactly how they could be used. Silver coins might or might not pass for their face amount but a good beaver pelt never varied in its desirability.

Interestingly, the Indians adopted beaver-skin trade for roughly the same reason that whites adopted wampum use in many areas. The Indian knew where to trap the beavers far better than the white man. He could obtain them easily and looked upon them as worthless. But the Indian trapped in such quantity that it was very much like the white man producing wampum. Each felt he was gaining the advantage of the other.

Among coins circulating in the colonies, the Spanish pieces were the most readily available. A mint had been built in Mexico City in 1536 to utilize the vast quantities of silver found in the Aztec cities. The coins were struck in the names of the Spanish rulers, Charles I and Joanne. Before Mexico gained independence from Spanish domination in 1821, more than two billion "dollars" in silver coins had been struck by its mints.

The types of Spanish coins were varied. The earliest Spanish coins made in the New World were chunks of silver sliced from a bar and stamped with designs. They are known as "cobs" and are cruder than almost any other coin in history. Eventually the coins were rounded and milled with corrugated edges. The designs became more sophisticated and many were quite attractive. They also had a consistent intrinsic worth that was controlled carefully enough for the coins to become universally accepted in trade.

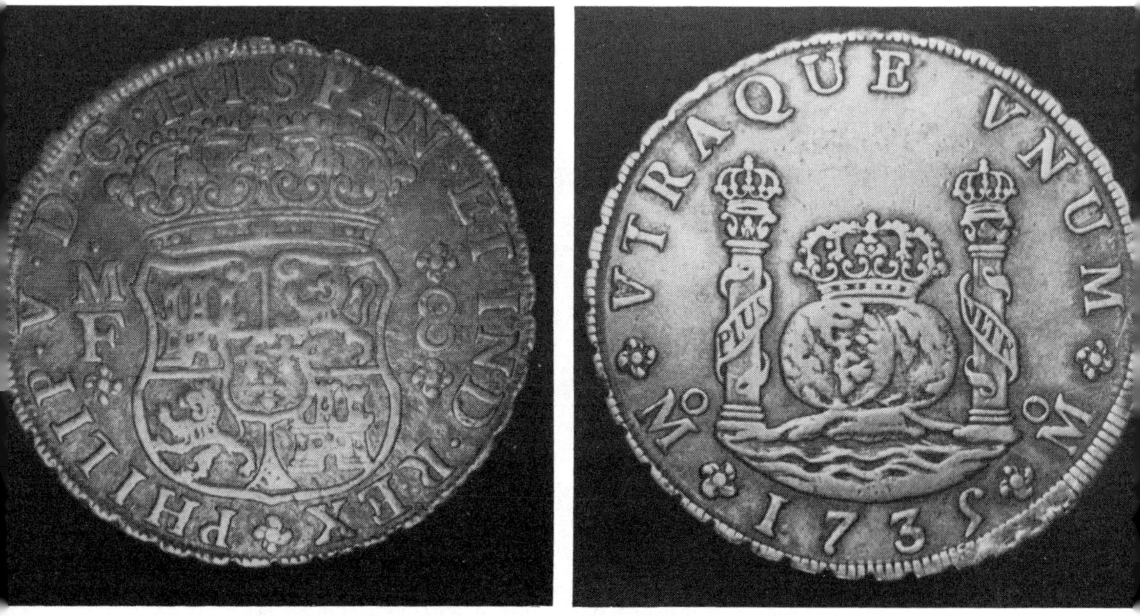

This is the obverse and reverse of one of the most famous coins in the New World. It is the Spanish milled dollar, which was valued at eight reales. When this coin was cut into slices, like the pieces of a pie, each piece was known as a "bit" or a "piece of eight." Even after the United States developed its own system of coinage, people referred to prices in terms of "bits." There is a popular chant that goes "Shave and a hair cut, two bits," meaning that the price was actually a quarter under the new system.

While the Spanish were the most widely used foreign coins, numerous other types were also used. Among the most unusual were those of Mark Newby, an Irish immigrant who arrived in New Jersey from Dublin on November 19, 1681. He was one of the few people to travel to the colony with a substantial quantity of coins. These were called St. Patrick's half-pence and, though not familiar to the colonists, were readily adopted as being better than no coins at all.

The official action regarding Newby occurred on May 8, 1682. Under Section VI of "Grants, Concessions and Original Constitutions of the Province of New-Jersey" there appeared:

"Be it Enacted . . . that Mark Newbie's half-pence, called Patricks half-pence, shall, from and after the said Eighteenth Instant, pass for half-pence Current pay of this Province, provided he, the said Mark, give sufficient Security to the Speaker of this House, for the use of the General Assembly from Time to Time being, that he the said Mark, his Executors and Administrators, shall and will change the said half-pence for pay Equivalent, upon demand: and provided also, that no Person or Persons be hereby obliged to take more than five Shillings in one Payment."

The coins themselves are rather unusual. The reverse has a bishop, St. Patrick, with a staff in his left hand and a shamrock in his right.

The obverse of the coin has a kneeling king playing the harp. A crown is above the harp and an angel in front. Each halfpenny has a

The obverse of the St. Patrick halfpenny that circulated in New Jersey. This coin and the St. Patrick Farthing were created by Mark Newby of Dublin, Ireland. The coin was widely circulated in the New Jersey province.

brass plug inserted in the crown to give the impression it is gold.

The origin of the coins is uncertain though there is good evidence that they were struck in the 1640s during the reign of Charles I of England. The reason for the coins probably relates to the revolt of the Irish against the British who were depriving them of religious and civil rights. The revolt occurred on October 23, 1641. The violence resulted in almost ten thousand English and Irish being killed. The following year England experienced civil war and the British army had to abandon the conflict in Ireland to return home and restore order.

The civil war ended with the death of Charles I in 1649, but the Irish declared that they still supported his overthrown family. They announced that they would support Charles II, an action which outraged Oliver Cromwell, Lord Protector of England and victorious enemy of both Charles I and Charles II. He led an army into Ireland, subjecting the Irish to great abuse. When he returned to England he authorized his son-in-law to continue the pillage of Ireland, an action that destroyed for the time the Irish hope of obtaining freedom.

The coins in question may have been struck during the period when Ireland's forces were still in some measure in control of the situation. On November 21, 1642, the Irish confederate assembly meeting in Kilkenny passed an act stating:

> That a seal should be made for the kingdom; that every person discoursing, in writing or otherwise of the enemies, shall not call them by the name or names of English or protestants but shall call them by the name of puritanical or malignant-party. That coin and plate shall be raised and established in this kingdom, according to the rates and values hereafter-mentioned, and that there shall be forthwith coined the sum of four thousand pounds, to pass current in this kingdom, according to a proclamation or act published by direction of this assembly in the city of Kilkenny, and not otherwise; that the right honourable the earl of Castlehave, and such others as his lordship shall call to his assistance, shall present unto the supreme council of this kingdom an institution and order of knighthood, concerning the honour of St. Patrick, and the glory of this kingdom.

Many of the design features on the coin are identical to those used by the engraver at the English royal mint during the reign of Charles I. It is guessed that the mint may have struck the coins for the Earl of Glamorgan if not for the confederate assembly. Whatever the case, the change in political fortunes brought about by the civil war in England undoubtedly led to the suppression of the coins. This would account for the limited number that have been found and the ability of Newby to bring them to New Jersey.

Some colonial coins were actually tokens with no legal status but which were used by the people as though they had actual worth. For example, in 1694, the Elephant token appeared in New England and circulated with the value of a halfpenny. The elephant on the obverse symbolized the reported fact that the copper for the coins had been obtained in Africa by the Royal African Company, which had the tokens made. The reverse had such mottoes as GOD PRESERVE NEW ENGLAND and GOD PRESERVE CAROLINA AND THE LORDS PROPRIETERS.

In 1737, a man of rather wide-ranging interests struck a number of copper tokens which were valued at threepence. This was Dr. Samuel Higley of Granby, Connecticut who was a doctor, blacksmith, and amateur metalurgist. He owned land near the Granby copper mines and exported copper to England. Coins were in short supply, so he used some of the copper to make tokens for trade. (Some experts say that Samuel Higley couldn't have made the coins because he died before they were struck. The best available evidence seems to indicate that he made and used a number of the tokens before his death in May 1737, which occurred while he was on a trip to England. His brother John continued striking the pieces.)

One story about the Higley tokens is that they were originally used to buy liquor in a local public house. The tokens were accepted by the bartender, at least at first. Eventually some dispute developed over the real value of the tokens, which had been rated at threepence. The later issues of the tokens have the rather humorous motto VALUE ME AS YOU PLEASE.

About the closest the British government ever came to striking coins specifically for use by the colonists was when it authorized individuals to have coins made for circulation. Such coins were struck

The obverse and reverse of the Rosa Americana twopence, which was coined by William Wood, an Englishman, for use in both Ireland and the American Colonies.

The obverse and reverse of the halfpenny created by Wood in 1723.

at the London mint rather than at private mints where their legal status was seldom more than that of the tokens discussed.

One manufacturer of authorized coins was a man named William Wood who received a patent dated July 12, 1722 that gave him permission to produce three hundred tons of coins for the American colonies in denominations of half-pence, pence and twopence. The patent had come to Wood in a roundabout way. The original patent to produce coins for the colonies was granted to the Duchess of Kendall,

A halfpenny created by Wood specifically for Ireland in 1722. It is known as one of the Hibernia coins series.

Another Hibernia piece. This is a farthing created in 1723. The obverse for both the 1722 and 1733 coins was very similar to the 1723 halfpenny obverse.

The obverse of the halfpenny struck in copper for use in Virginia in 1773.

mistress to King George I. She had no interest in using the patent but delighted in the ten thousand pounds she received when she sold it to Wood, an English metal worker.

Wood's permission to produce the coins was to be valid for fourteen years. The bulk of the coining, two hundred tons, was to be completed

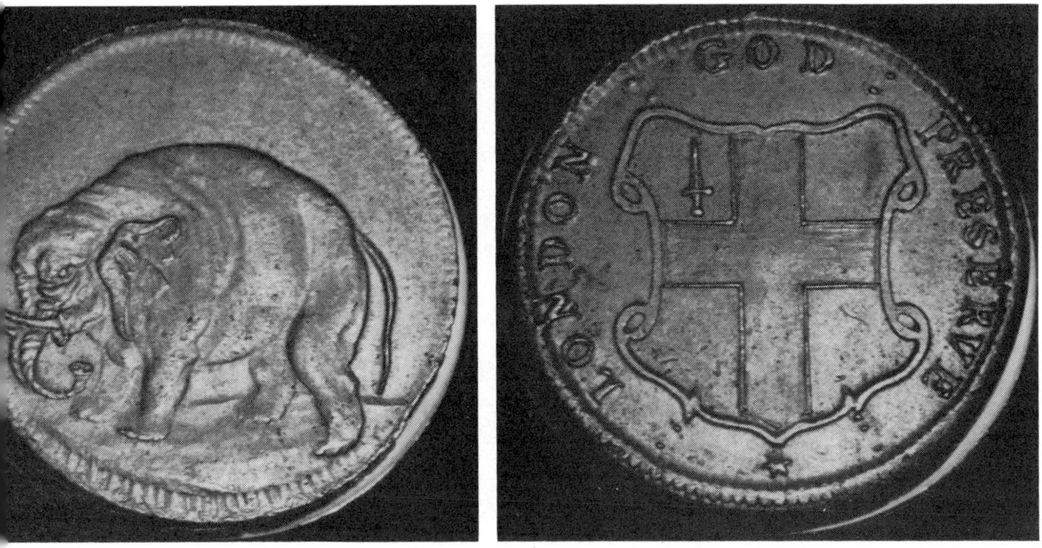

The obverse and reverse of a token were advertising pieces. These may have seen some use as coins in areas that were lacking in money. They circulated in Carolina among other areas. The tokens illustrated were apparently produced during the great plague that devastated London in 1665–66. It also circulated in Tangier, Africa, according to some reports.

The Hibernia-Voce Populi halfpenny produced for use in both Ireland and colonial America. It was made in 1760 by a man named Roche of Dublin. He was known to be a manufacturer of buttons for the uniforms of soldiers.

Another Hibernia-Voce Populi halfpenny of 1760.

The reverse of a ship token that circulated in Rhode Island. It was struck in brass, copper, tin, and pewter.

during the first four years. Each succeeding year he would be allowed only ten thousand pounds of coin production. He also had to pay an additional two hundred pounds to the Clerk Comptroller and one hundred pounds to the crown as a tribute every year he struck coins. Wood worked out a similar agreement to produce coins for Ireland. Fewer pieces were involved, however, and both types eventually circulated in the colonies.

This is a Chalmers sixpence. A silver token, it was produced by a goldsmith in Annapolis, Maryland in 1783. It was produced to circulate during a coin shortage.

A 5 sols piece of 1670 designed for use in the French Colonies. It was struck in 1670 by order of King Louis XIV.

sober, not very flattering depiction of George I with a Latin legend that translates to "George, by the Grace of God, King of Great Britain, France, and Ireland." The American issues had a rose on the reverse with the legends ROSA AMERICANA and UTILE DULCI, which meant "American Rose—The Useful with the Pleasant."

The Irish resented the new coinage and refused to accept it in

The 1766 halfpenny struck by William Pitt. Again, it was not officially a coin but was used to alleviate a coin shortage.

A *Sou Marqué* was used in the French colonies during the period of 1738 thru 1760.

A copper sou or nine deniers piece struck by order of Louis XV and dated 1721. These were also used in the French Colonies.

These are additional Sous that were used in the French colonies. The "RF" stands for Republique Française.

change. It was identical in size and metallic content to their own coinage but the fact that it was made by an Englishman upset them. Anger over British rule was rampant and they wanted nothing to do with the Wood production. He was eventually forced to withdraw the coins and ship them to the American colonies where they did circulate.

The coins specifically made for the American colonies were of lesser quality than those made for Ireland. Wood decided to make extensive profits from the American issues so he made them lighter in weight and lower in metal content than their face value stated. They circulated out of necessity but were rejected whenever an alternative coin was available.

There were numerous other coins prepared for colonial use but to detail them all would take a book in itself. Every colony had some form of coin or token in circulation that was unique to the immediate area. As a result, coinage remained a haphazard affair. Stability of sorts had to wait until after the colonists had won their independence from England and were united under their own central government.

3

The Revolutionary War and Continental Currency

As frustration with British rule in America led to revolution, the coin shortage still continued to plague the colonists. War was inevitable yet there wasn't nearly enough gold and silver to meet the debts that would be incurred in forming and supplying an army. As a result, the colonial governments were forced to switch to a less practical medium of exchange that had been occasionally used by individual colonies in the past: paper money. It was to lead to economic chaos.

The use of paper money had been endorsed by numerous colonial leaders over the years, including one of the most respected minds in the New World, Benjamin Franklin. In 1729, he had written a pamphlet explaining why the issuance of paper money would in no way hinder the fiinances of a government. His reasoning was that:

> money is a medium of exchange; and whatever men agree to make the medium is, to those who have it, the very things they want, because it will buy for them the very things they want. It is cloth to him who wants cloth. It is corn to him who wants corn. Custom has made gold and silver the materials for this medium of exchange. But the measure of value for this medium is not gold and silver, but labor. Labor is as much a measure of the value of silver as of anything else. Suppose one man employed to raise corn, while another man is busy refining silver. At the end of a year the complete produce of corn and the complete produce of silver are the natural price of each other. If the one be twenty bushels and the

other twenty ounces, then one ounce of silver is worth the labor of raising one bushel of corn. The riches of a country are to be valued by the quantity of labor its inhabitants are able to purchase, and not by the quantity of silver or gold they possess. Trade in general being nothing but the exchange of labor for labor, the value of things is most justly measured by labor. Money, therefore, as bullion, is valuable by so much labor as it costs to produce that bullion. . . .

Franklin went on to stress that bullion was heavy and that paper money seemed the natural substitute. He felt the bullion should be stored and bills of credit, paper money, issued in its place. His argument was basically sound though a contrast to earlier beliefs he had held. The change may have been influenced by his owning a print shop, where the paper money, if authorized, might be printed at considerable profit to himself.

The paper money was never very popular. People put their greatest faith in the gold and silver that had been used as a medium of exchange for centuries. However, when coins were in short supply, paper money was accepted as a necessary way of doing business. During the Revolution the Continental Congress felt that the colonists would again accept it, since hoarders had removed almost all precious metal from circulation.

There were serious coin shortages in the states following the Revolutionary War. Numerous states produced various coin designs that were not truly authorized and were circulated only because other coinage was not available. This coin was circulated in New York in 1787. The obverse showed a standing Indian and the reverse, illustrated, shows an eagle on the globe.

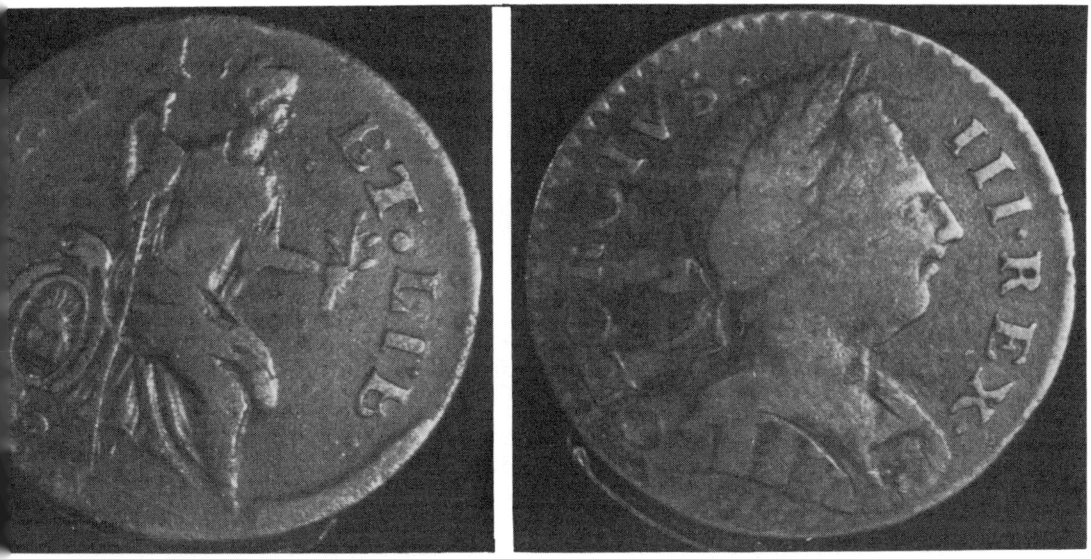

This coin is known as the Nova Eborac. It is an imitation of the British halfpenny. The illustration shown is of the figure of Britannia. It was used in 1787.

These coins were used in New Jersey in 1786. They were authorized by the New Jersey Colonial Legislature and were copper coins based on the British system. They circulated at a rate of fifteen to each British Shilling.

On May 1, 1775, Massachusetts became one of the first colonies to issue unauthorized paper money to meet its debts. Since a formal break with Britain had yet to occur, the paper-money issue was an act of defiance against the laws of the crown. It was reminiscent of the earlier Massachusetts action that resulted in the opening of the first mint in America. The enabling resolution stated:

> Whereas, many of our brethren of the Colonies of Connecticut and Rhode Island are now with us, to assist us in this day of public and general distress, in which we are all deeply concerned; and whereas our brethren of said Colonies have brought with them some of the paper currencies of their respective Colonies, which have not, of late, had a currency with us, and for want of which our common interests may greatly suffer, Resolved, that said paper currencies shall, from and after the date hereof, be paid and received within this Colony, in all payments, to all intents and purposes, in the same proportion to silver, as the same are paid and received within the respective colonies by which the same have been issued.

The colonies were uniting financially for their mutual benefit. The Continental Congress was already meeting and the colonial leaders were facing the fact that they had to have common links in order to effectively battle the crown.

The paper money that came to be issued by the colonies, and accepted at the same value from area to area, were actually interest-bearing notes. They were produced with full knowledge of the fact that the people preferred coins to paper and so, to make it more appealing, the notes promised a bonus to those who held them past a certain date. Typical was one of the Massachusetts Bay Colony notes issued on May 25, 1775. It read:

"The possessor of this note shall be entitled to receive out of the public treasury of this Colony the sum of twenty shillings, lawful money, on the twenty-fifth day of May, A. D. 1776, with interest, at the rate of six per cent per annum. and this note shall be received in all payments at the Treasury, at any time after the date hereof, for the principal sum, without interest, if so paid before the 25th day of May 1776, which notes shall be received in all payments in this Colony, and no discount or abatement shall be made thereon, in any payment, trade, or exchange whatsoever."

The issuing of money that was acceptable from colony to colony was quickly followed by an issue authorized by the Continental Congress. The leaders of the colonies had made the decision to formally separate from England, a move that had come very quickly. Thomas Jefferson, for example, wrote that prior to April 19, 1775, the Continental Congress had been interested in improving conditions in the colonies rather than separating from England. He wrote: "The Colonies had not yet cut asunder the ties of their allegiance to the Crown. The Continental Congress had sent a petition to the King denying any intention of separation from England."

But the issuing of money was a defiant act whose intentions were clear to everyone. On May 10, 1775, the Continental Congress began

The Immune Columbia copper coin was produced in 1785 by Reuben Harmon, Jr., of Rupert, Vermont.

Another design of Harmon's copper coins, this one produced in 1786.

issuing paper money redeemable in Spanish milled dollars, or gold or silver of a set value. This was meant to finance preparations for war at a time when coinage was fast becoming unavailable. The notes were issued without proper backing but it was felt that the government would somehow obtain needed coinage once it was totally independent of British domination.

These are tokens made in England between 1792 and 1794. Each star on the reverse represents one of the states. The tokens have been called the Kentucky tokens because the top star has the "K" for Kentucky in it.

This is the Middelton token of 1796. It was made in the mint of Boulton and Watt, just outside of Birmingham, England, and was meant for use in the United States. The token was struck in both copper and silver.

The Continental Congress actually had no legal authority. The paper money the congress created could not be forced on the people. It was not the official currency of an actual government, and the Continental Congress didn't have the power to levy taxes to gain additional gold and silver to serve as backing for the notes.

Paper money issued by the Continental Congress made its first appearance in May of 1775 with additional issues appearing ten more times at different dates through January 14, 1779. The notes were in rather odd denominations. They included fractional notes worth dollar values of one sixth, one third, one half, and two thirds; in addition notes were issued in the following whole-dollar amounts: 1, 2, 3, 4, 5, 6, 7, 8, 20, 30, 35, 40, and 45, and so on in five-dollar increases up to 80 dollars.

The reason for the strange issues is that all money was still being related to the English system and all purchases were rated the same way. One third of a dollar was equal to nine pence in British money. Such a sum would buy a pound of flour, a yard of calico, three glasses of rum, or a pound of pork. A farm laborer's wages, not including keep, were from six to eight dollars a month depending upon his skills and the type of work he did. Army pay scales were similar. Horses, cows, and other livestock sold for twenty dollars or more, the price increasing in ten-dollar increments. Thus the denominations fit in very nicely with the prices of goods the colonists were used to buying.

Among the many problems the colonists encountered with the issues of paper money was counterfeiting. The printing was crude enough that it was easy for the British to duplicate; this they did to undermine the colonial war effort. Pro-British papers like the *New York Gazette* advertised counterfeit paper money in their pages. Typical was a Gazette notice for April 14, 1777, that read: "Persons

This coin is known as the Bar cent because of a series of bars on the reverse (not shown). It made its appearance in New York in 1785 but the coin is undated and its origin is uncertain. It may have been first issued at the same time as the Nova Constellatio copper coins produced by Thomas Wyon of Birmingham, England.

These copper coins were made in England at the request of Talbot, Allum & Lee, a New York firm. The company engaged in trade with India and, due to serious shortages, used the coins out of necessity.

going into the other Colonies may be supplied with any number of counterfeit Congress notes for the price of the paper per ream. They are so nicely and exactly executed that there is no risk in getting them off, it being almost impossible to discover that they are not genuine. This has been proved by bills to a very large amount wich have been successfully circulated. Inquire for Q.E.D., at the Coffee House from 11 P.M. to 4 A.M. during the present month."

The public suffering due to the inflationary currency was immense. On December 31, 1775, Nathanael Greene wrote to Rhode Island's Governor Samuel Ward: "This is no time for giting riches but to secure what we have got. Every shadow of oppression and extortion ought to disappear, but instead of that we find many articles of merchandise multiplied four fold their original value, and most cent per cent [100 percent]. The farmers are extortionate where ever their situation furnishes them with an opportunity. These are the people that I complain mostly of; they are wounding the cause."

Similarly, Joseph Eggleston, Jr., wrote to his father from Delaware on September 2, 1777: "The prices of every kind of article here would astonish you. You desire I would procure you a good beaver hat and some other articles. In answer to which part of your letter I would inform you that goods are 200 per cent dearer than they were in Virginia when I left it. I was obliged to buy a hat a few days past, and paid 18 dollars for one of an inferior kind. Boots sell for the moderate price of 21 dollars; broad cloth 12 pounds a year. Rum is 20/ the quart; whisky 10/. Every other article bears a proportionate price."

This is the famous Franklin Press token, which is actually a British token that saw little circulation in America. However, because of its connection with Benjamin Franklin, it is collected avidly by American collectors.

Robert Morton's diary for the first three days of December 1777, says that:

> The English merchants that came in the fleet will not dispose of their goods without hard money, alleging that no bills are to be bought, no produce to be obtained, and no method can be adopted by which they can send remittances. Numbers of the most respectable inhabitants are using all their influence to support it, and numbers of others who have no regard for the public good are giving out the hard money for what they want for immediate use, thus purchasing momentary gratifications at the expense of the public, for if the circulation of this money should be stopt, many who have no legal money but paper and have no means of obtaining gold and silver, will be reduced to beggary and want, and those who are so lost to every sense of honor, to the happiness of their fellow citizens, and eventually their own good, as to give out their hard money, either for the goods of those who are newcomers, or in the public market where it is now exacted for provisions, will, by their evil example, oblige those who possess hard money to advance it and ruin the credit of the other money for the present. The consequence of which must be that we shall be shortly drained of our hard cash, the other money rendered useless, no trade by which we can get a fresh supply; our ruin must therefore be certain and inevitable.

As the prices for goods rose, some merchants tried to hoard staples to get even better prices later on. This often led to violence. A case in point, dubbed the "Boston Coffee Party," is described by Abigail

This is a medal dated 1796. It refers to the French Settlement of Castorland in what is now Carthage, New York. The settlement was started about the time of the French Revolution.

Adams writing to her husband John on July 31, 1777.

> I have nothing new to entertain you with, unless it is an account of a new set of mobility, which has lately taken the lead in Boston. You must know that there is a great scarcity of sugar and coffee, articles which the female part of the state is very lath to give up, especially whilest they consider the scarcity occassioned by the merchants having secreted a large quantity. There had been much rout and noise in the town for several weeks. Some stores had been opened by a number of people, and the coffee and sugar carried into the market and dealt out by pounds. It was rumored that an eminent, wealthy, stingy merchant (who is a bachelor) had a hogshead of coffee in his store which he refused to sell to the committee under six shillings per pound.
>
> A number of females, some say a hundred, some say more, assembled with a cart and trucks, marched down to the warehouse and demanded the keys, which he refused to deliver. Upon which, one of them seized him by his neck and tossed him into the cart. Upon his finding no quarter, he delivered the keys, when they tipped up the cart and discharged him; then opened the warehouse, hoisted out the coffee themselves, put it into the truck and drove off.
>
> It was reported that he had personal chastisement among them: but this, I believe, was not true. A large concourse of men stood amazed, silent spectators of the whole transaction. . . .

The public reaction towards the continental paper currency was

This is the famous Continental Dollar, which was struck as a pattern issue. Patterns, which will be discussed later, are coins that are meant to test designs but not meant for circulation. Often a coin design is preceded by a number of patterns that are either radically different from the final coin adopted or are slight variations of the design. The Continental Dollar was struck in pewter, brass, and silver.

reasonably favorable during the first issue, a fact which helped the notes maintain their face values. On June 22, 1775, two million dollars in continental notes went into circulation, and the public accepted each paper dollar as being equal to a dollar in coinage. But by January 14, 1779 when the last ten million dollars in notes were put into circulation, it took $25.31 in paper money to buy what could be obtained for a dollar in coins. Altogether $242,060,780 in Continental Currency was issued, none of it properly backed. To make matters worse, by February 1781 the exchange rate reached a point where seventy-five dollars in paper money was needed to buy goods selling for just a dollar in gold or silver.

It is believed that the members of the Continental Congress not only recognized the need for coins when they issued the paper money but also considered striking one as early as 1776. That was the year of what is known as the Continental Dollar. This large unusual coin was prepared in brass, pewter, and silver. The obverse of the coins shows the sun's rays striking a sundial; the reverse has an endless chain, each link encircling the name of one of the colonies. The obverse legends read: CONTINENTAL CURRENCY 1776, FUGIO, and MIND YOUR BUSINESS. The reverse states: AMERICAN CONGRESS: WE ARE ONE.

The striking of the Continental Dollar was rather unusual too. There are only three silver and about a dozen brass coins known. The coin is most frequently found in pewter, often completely free of any evidence of wear.

The initials "E.G." appear on the obverse die of one of the Continental Dollars and these are believed to stand for the designer, most likely Elisha Gallaudet. He was the designer of some of the paper money issued by the Continental Congress and was the likely person to have done the work.

There is a chance that the Continental Dollars were meant to replace one-dollar notes, which were not made between 1776 and 1778. However, not enough of these coins were ever struck for this to have become a reality. The severe shortage of precious metals would have made the task a near impossibility.

The first serious effort to develop a native coinage for the united colonies seems to have begun in 1779. Edward Brigden, a British coiner who sided with the Americans in the struggle for freedom from the crown, contacted Ben Franklin with ideas for an American coinage. Franklin was one of the American ministers to France at the time, and Brigden may have hoped that the statesman would help him get a contract for the production of the coins. He certainly seemed to go out of his way to impress Franklin for he suggested coins that would have mottoes of the type Franklin delighted in printing in his almanacs. The coiner even went so far as to send samples to Franklin who replied in a letter dated October 2, 1779, posted from Passy, France.

> I received your favor of the 17th past, and the two samples of copper are since come to hand. The metal seems to be very good, and the price reasonable, but I have not yet received the orders necessary to justify my making the purchase proposed. There has indeed been an intention to strike copper coin, that may not only be useful as small change, but serve other purposes.
>
> Instead of repeating continually upon every half-penny the dull story that everybody knows (and what it would have been no loss to mankind if nobody had ever known), that George the Third is King of Great Britain, France, and Ireland, etc., etc., to put on one side, some important proverb of Solomon, some pious moral, prudential or economical precept, the frequent inculcuation of which, by seeing it every time one receives a piece of money, might make an impression upon the mind, especially of young persons, and tend to regulate the conduct: such as, on some, The fear of the Lord is the beginning of wisdom; on others, Honesty is the best policy; on others, He that by the plough would thrive, himself must either hold or drive; on others, Keep thy shop, and thy shop will keep thee; on others, A penny saved is a penny got; on others, He that buys what he has no need of, will soon be forced to sell his necessaries; on others, Early to bed and early to rise, will make a man healthy, wealthy, and wise; and so on, to a great variety.
>
> The other side it was proposed to fill with good designs drawn and engraved by the best artists in France, of all the different

species of barbarity with which the English have carried on the war in America, expressing every abominable circumstance of their cruelty and inhumanity that figures can express, to make an impression upon the minds of posterity as strong and durable as that on the copper. This resolution has been a long time forborne; but the late burning of defenceless towns in Connecticut, on the flimsy pretence that the people fired from behind their houses when it is known to have been premeditated and ordered from England, will probably give the finishing provocation, and may occassion a vast demand for your metal.

I thank you for your kind wishes respecting my health, I return them most cordially fourfold unto your own bosom.

As the war came to an end and the congress was attempting to formulate plans for a national coinage, the states were having problems with poor-quality coins being shipped in from England. Large numbers of British half-pence made from inferior materials and worth far less than the official issue circulating in England were appearing in areas such as Philadelphia. The problem was extremely serious as this excerpt from volume 7 of *American State Papers* indicates.

The coinage of copper is a subject that claims our immediate attention. From the small value of the several pieces of copper coin, this medium of exchange has been too much neglected. The more valuable metals are daily giving place to base British half-pence, and no means are used to prevent the fraud. This disease, which is neglected in the beginning, because it appears trifling, may finally prove very destructive to commerce. It is admitted that copper may, at this instant, be purchased in America at one-eighth of a dollar the pound.

British half-pence, made at the Tower, are forty-eight to the pound. Those manufactured at Birmingham, and shipped in thousands for our use, are much lighter, and they are of base metal. It can hardly be said that seventy-two of them are worth a pound of copper; hence it will follow that we give for British half-pence about six times their value. There are no materials from which we can estimate the weight of half-pence, that have been imported from Britain since the late war, but we have heard of sundry shipments being ordered, to the nominal amount of one thousand guineas; and we are told that no packet arrives from England without some hundred weight of base half-pense. It is a very moderate computation which states our loss, on the last twelve months, at 30,000 dollars, by the commerce of vile coin.

Among the many leaders of the Continental Congress, two of the most important were Robert Morris, the Superintendent of Finance, and Gouverneur Morris, his assistant. Despite their common last names, the two men were not related.

Gouverneur Morris worked out a coinage system that was extremely elaborate and Robert concurred with his approach. Officially, Robert was the one who developed the system but a study of diaries and other writing seems to indicate that Gouverneur was probably the one who did most of the work. The plan was elaborate. It was based on the idea that American coinage should be unique but nevertheless compatible with the British and Spanish systems since the money of those two countries circulated so widely. The plan also took into account the fact that each state set different values for the same coins.

The Morrises found that each state valued Spanish dollars differently. One state said a Spanish dollar was worth 5 shillings. Others valued it at 6 shillings, 7 shillings 6 pence, or 8 shillings in British money. Thus a dollar was worth 60, 72, 90, or 96 pence, depending upon where it was spent.

The men decided that the government should make a three and one half percent profit over the bullion's worth when striking coins. Under this plan the dollar would be divided into 1,440 parts, a number which is the common multiple of the 60, 72, 90, and 96 pence figures. Thus the smallest coin, which they called a "unit" or "quarter," would be equal to 1/1,440 of a dollar.

Basically, there would be five different coins most commonly found in trade. Three would be silver and two would be copper. The largest would be the "mark" which would be 1,000 "quarters." Then would come the "quint" which would be 500 quarters and the "cents" or 100 quarters. There would also be copper "eights" and "fives" worth eight and five quarters respectively. The actual value of the mark would be about seventy cents in today's coinage system, with the cent worth about seven of our current cents.

The system, while confusing, was brilliant in terms of international finance. All English pence directly translated into quarters as did all Spanish coins. Even the different values the states put on English and Spanish money could be adapted into the new system. Thus the eight would be equal to a halfpenny in six of the states. The remaining states would value the same coin as either a third, fourth, or fifth of an English penny.

The coinage plan presented by the Morrises was a compromise. Gouverneur Morris' writings indicate he desired a true decimal plan, which the final concept did not represent. Robert Morris felt that while the decimal system was ideal, he also thought the concept should be altered so that the new American coinage would be compatible with the British and Spanish coins already in circulation.

Thomas Jefferson also had devised a coinage plan which he based on the Spanish dollar. A coin, the "unit," equal in value to the Spanish dollar, would be broken into decimal units with one one-hundredth of the unit being the smallest coin. The coins would be struck in gold, silver, and copper, according to their values. There would be a half-dollar or "five-tenths" coin; a "fifth" coin or "pistreen"; a "tenth" or "bit"; and a "twentieth" or "half-bit," all made in silver. A "hundredth" would be made in copper and a coin of "ten units" or "ten dollars" would be made in gold.

Jefferson's objections to the Morrises' plan were written after his appointment to the chairmanship of the congressional currency committee in June 1783. He commented:

> It is inconvenient in its application to the ordinary money transactions. 10,000 dollars will require 8 figures to express them, to wit, 14,400,000. A horse or bullock of 80 dollars value will require a notation of six figures, to wit 115,200 units. As a money of account this will be laborious even when facilitated by the aid of decimal arithmetic. As a common measure of the value of property it will be too minute to be comprehended by the people. The French are subjected to very laborious calculations, the livre being their ordinary money of account, and this but between the 1/5 & 1/6 of a dollar. But what will be our labours should our money of account be 1/1440 of a dollar?

Jefferson justified his own system thus:

> The unit or dollar is a known coin and the most familiar of all to the mind of the people. It is already adopted from South to North, has identified our currency and therefore happily offers itself as an Unit already introduced. Our public debt, our requisitions and their apportionments have given it actual and long possession of the place of Unit. The course of our commerce too will bring us more of this than of any other foreign coin, and therefor renders it more worthy of attention. I know of no Unit which can be proposed in competition with the dollar, but the pound: But what is the pound? 1547 grains of fine silver in Georgia: 1289 grains in Virginia, Connecticut, Rhode Island, Massachusetts and New Hampshire; 1031¼ grains in Maryland, Delaware, Pennsylvania and New Jersey; 966¾ grains in North Carolina and New York.
>
> Which of these shall we adopt: To which State give that preeminence of which all are so jealous? And on which impose the difficulties of a new estimate for their coin, their cattle and other commodities. Or shall we hang the pound sterling as a common badge about all their necks? This contains 1718 3/4 grains of pure silver. It is difficult to familiarize a new coin to a people. It is more difficult to familiarize them to a new coin with an old name. Happily the Dollar is familiar to them all, and is already as much referred to for a measure of value as their respective State pounds.

The Continental Congress had appointed a grand committee on coinage that reviewed all the plans. By May 1785, Jefferson's proposal had met with the most favorable response, though modifications were recommended. Jefferson's pistreen was dropped in favor of a quarter-dollar coin, for example. (All coinage laws can be found in detail in the Appendix at the end of this book.)

It was July 6, 1785, when Congress finally made specific plans for a

An experimental copper coin of 1785 called an Immune Columbia Copper. It was probably created by James Atlee. It was not authorized by law and never was adopted as a coin.

A Nova Constellatio copper coin of 1783. It was struck when the United States was under the Articles of Confederation. It was ordered by Gouverneur Morris, who was Assistant Financier of the Confederation. The tokens were made in Birmingham, England, by Thomas Wyon and were imported as a private business venture; they had no official status.

decimal coinage system, a first anywhere in the world. New names were also created for the coins. For example, "eagle" was the name to be given to a gold ten-dollar coin which would have an eagle on the design. The "tenth" coin Jefferson had created would be replaced by what would be known as a "disme." (That name was eventually changed to "dime.") The quarter dollar would be called a "double-disme" and a "cent" would take the place of Jefferson's "hundredth." There would also be a "half-cent" or "two-hundredth" and a "mille" or one one-thousandth of a dollar. The mille was such a tiny unit and had so little commercial value that no coin of this size was ever prepared.

On October 16, 1786, Congress passed the Mint Ordinance confirming the coinage plan already approved by special committee. Detailed provisions for copper coinage were spelled out, as were regulations for the use of gold and silver. A mint was established and various rules were made into law.

During the period when coinage plans were being made, several pattern coins were struck in Birmingham, England, from dies made

The very first coins issued by what was known as the United States were Fugio cents. They were approved by Congress on April 21, 1787. The coins have also been called the Franklin cents because the inscription is similar to some of the mottoes which he valued. According to the Act of July 6, 1787: "Resolved, that the board of treasury direct the contractor for the copper coinage to stamp on one side of each piece the following device, viz: 13 circles linked together, a small circle in the middle, with the words 'United States,' around it; and in the centre, the words 'We are one'; on the other side of the same piece the following device, viz: A dial with the hours expressed on the face of it' a meridian sun above on one side of which is the word *'Fugio,'* and on the other the year in figures '1787' below the dial, the word 'Mind Your Business.' " The word *Fugio* means "time flies."

by Thomas Wyon. These were the Nova Constellatio copper patterns or tokens. The obverse had an eye in the center surrounded by a large thirteen point star with thirteen small stars between the points. The motto NOVA CONSTELLATIO encircles the outside. The reverse has the letters US encircled by a wreath and the legend LIBERTAS * JUSTITIA 1783. This was apparently a private venture of Gouvernor Morris and there were die changes in 1785 and 1786. These were not legally authorized by Congress, however, and the coinage act made it impossible for such private coinage to continue in existence.

The Nova Constellatio coins were the only ones struck based on the Morris system. They are found with the numbers 1,000, 500, and 100 for the mark, quint and bit, respectively. But they were never accepted for circulation.

The first official United States coinage, authorized under the Articles of Confederation several weeks before the Constitution was sent to the different states for ratification, were the Fugio coppers. These coins were planned under contract to one James Jarvis, who was to produce three hundred tons of copper coin "of the federal standard." The report of April 21, 1787, added: "That it be coined at the expense of the contractor, but under the inspection of an officer appointed and paid by the United States. . . ."

The design for the new coins was specifically determined on July 6, 1787. At that time the board of treasury insisted that the coins appear with ". . . thirteen circles linked together, a small circle in the middle, with the words 'United States,' round it; a meridian sun above, on one side of which is to be the word 'Fugio.' and on the other the year in figures '1787' below the dial, the words 'Mind your Business.' "

The coins have often been called Franklin cents because their mottoes (*fugio* has been translated "I [time] fly," the reference being to the sundial depicted on the coin) are the type of homilies that Franklin so enjoyed. However, they might be more accurately attributed to David Rittenhouse the fiirst director of the United States Mint at Philadelphia.

The reason Rittenhouse is believed to have been connected with the design is because of a clock he had constructed many years before. According to an account in Barton's *Memoirs of David Rittenhouse:*

> In the year 1756, he made an eight-day clock, for his brother-in-law, Mr. Barton; over the dial-plate of which, was engraven this mementory motto—Tempus fugit; and underneath, this blunt but too often necessary precept—Go about your business.
>
> On one description of the continental bills of credit, issued by Congress during the American war, were represented a sundial and a meridian sun over it: above, the word " 'Fugio;" and beneath, these words—"Mind your Business." And on the reverse of a copper one cent piece, struck in the year 1787, in pursuance of a resolve of congress of the 6th of July in that year, are impressed the same device and mottoes as those last mentioned; corresponding with

those adopted by our Philosopher, when only twenty-four years of age: a circumstance that shows; how early in life he had formed a just estimate of the value of time.

It may not be improper here to observe, that the various devices affixed to the continental money, as it was called, were much admired for their appropriate significancy; and that they were generally supposed to be the production of the late ingenious Judge Hopkinson, an intimate friend of Mr. Rittenhouse.

The actual coining of the Fugio cents proved more complicated than originally expected. Jarvis had used deception to obtain a contract and managed improperly to gain 12,809 pounds of government-owned copper four months before he received formal authorization to begin coining. There were also conflicting statements made by Jarvis concerning the premium he was to pay congress for the coinage privilege.

Jarvis quickly found that he could not deliver coins in the quantities he had promised, nor could he meet the due dates agreed upon. He frantically attempted to subcontract the work to the well established private minting firm of Mathew Boulton in England, but to no avail. Jarvis lacked the funds to provide security for such a venture and Boulton did not want to get involved.

Jarvis' total obligation to Congress was to deliver twenty-five tons of copper cents on December 1, 1787; a like amount the following March 15; fifty tons more on August 31, 1788; and two hundred tons more to be delivered in two equal sums on August 31, 1789, and May 11, 1790.

On May 21, after defaulting on the specific terms of the mint contract, Jarvis delivered just under 400,000 Fugio Cents to the Treasurer of the United States. This represented less than one fifth of the obligation he was supposed to have met the previous December.

Just where the Jarvis cents were struck is unknown. Accounts of the time said New York but that may have been because they were issued from that city, which served as the seat of government. Jarvis' father-in-law, Samuel Broome, operated a mint in New Haven, Connecticut, where he turned out some of the Connecticut state coinage. He would have been equipped to produce the Fugio cents, but whether or not he did remains unclear.

It is interesting to note that Jarvis did not produce the number of coins possible with the copper supply he was known to have. Even if his personal credit had been too poor to purchase additional supplies of copper once he got his contract, he had surreptitiously obtained 12,809 pounds of copper back on January 16, 1787, almost a third more copper than was used to produce of coins he actually delivered. He did not account for the missing metal.

By the time Jarvis had gotten around to delivering the small amount of coins, the value of copper had decreased and it was doubtful that the coins could be circulated as cents. Their intrinsic worth was but a fraction of their face value. A committee of congress began studying the matter and decided that it would be best to end the contract with Jarvis, a contract of which he was already in default.

Jarvis replied with a plea for understanding. In a letter found in the *Papers of The Continental Congress and the Constitutional Convention,* he said:

> Since my personal respects to you of Thursday, it appears an incumbent duty to the Public as well as to myself to state the reasons, why the deliveries of my Contract heretofore due have not been regularly made: and to endeavor to prove that no real injury has arisen in consequence of my delay to the Public. Should I be so fortunate as to clear up these two points to the satisfaction of Congress, I flatter myself they will extend a liberal and generous conduct to me; and will rather accept of a beneficial accomodation, than pursue any measures which may not only materially injure me, but eventually tend to the disadvantage of the Public.
>
> It was ever understood that the idea of procuring a sufficiency of Copper in the Country, within the proposed period was a fallacy too notorious to be attended to; and that therefore it would be necessary to Import it from Europe: This had not only been part of the plan on which my first calculations were founded but my declared intention to many of the Honorable Members of Congress, as well as to your Honble Board.

Jarvis explained that there were several months' delay between the signing of the contract with the United States government and the receipt of official directions concerning weight, design, and other specifications. Only after receiving the specifications could he go to Europe to arrange for the necessary copper and by then he said it was almost deadline time. He had credit problems, since the new American government's credit was not considered all that good.

After a long-winded explanation that seemed to skirt the truth of the matter, he concluded:

> It now remains to inform your Honorable Board that I have made such Arrangements in Europe, as to enable me to ascertain the periods of my deliveries and to execute the Coin in such stile as will not only be reputable to myself but as much facilitate the circulation, if some attention is paid to the relative value of Copper.
>
> Should the Honorable Committee of Congress allow me to present myself before them I doubt not but I shall be able to remove from their mind any impressions to my disadvantage. . . .

On September 16, Congress decided they had had enough of Jarvis and his coinage. They canceled the copper contract and authorized a committee to study the department of finance's dealings in the matter. Meanwhile Jarvis and his father-in-law took off for Europe with a new promotion scheme—the establishment of a subsidiary private mint for Boulton in Paris.

Little action was taken concerning Jarvis until 1791 when Secretary of the Treasury Alexander Hamilton brought suit against Jarvis for breach of contract. The New York Supreme Court heard the proceedings and decided, on February 24 of that year, that Jarvis was guilty and should pay a fine of twenty thousand Spanish milled dollars plus damages.

On January 29, 1792, Jarvis was arrested when he was unable to meet his obligation as determined by the court. Meanwhile, the copper value of the coins had dropped to just slightly over half their face value. The entire episode proved an embarrassment for all involved.

On September 17, 1787, the idea of states' supplying their own coins came to an end with the adoption of the Constitution of the United States (ratified and in effect on March 4, 1789). Under Section 8 it was noted that: "The Congress shall have Power . . . To coin Money, regulate the Value thereof, and of foreign Coin, and fix the Standard of Weights and Measures. . ." And Section 10 stated: "No State shall enter into any Treaty, Alliance, or Confederation; grant Letters of Marque and Reprisal; coin Money; emit Bills of Credit; make any Thing but gold and silver Coin a Tender in Payment of Debts. . ."

Perhaps the most important contribution to the new coinage being planned was made by Alexander Hamilton, the Secretary of the Treasury. The House of Representatives requested that he prepare a report that would present a workable approach to the creation of a national mint. The report, issued on January 21, 1791, was of immeasurable value to the new nation. Detailed segments will be found in an appendix to this book, but a brief overview is given here to provide an understanding of his achievement.

Hamilton recommended that neither silver nor gold be chosen alone as a monetary standard. His preference was to have both metals used, with a fifteen to one value ratio of silver to gold. A basic unit would be equal to the Spanish dollar then circulating in the United States. However, the weight of pure silver in the Spanish dollar that would be the basis for the amount of silver in the American coin was to be determined by educated guess.

An assay of a typical coin was of little value since so many of the coins were badly worn. Instead he took several samples with differing amounts of wear from circulation and found an average silver content of 371 grains. This conflicted with an earlier study by Morris which had determined that the coins had 373 grains. Hamilton was unconcerned, however, about such minor differences. He did check the current gold value of the Spanish dollar as set by merchants and found it to be 24 ¾ grains. Taking fifteen times that figure, he arrived at a figure of 371 ¼ grains as the recommended weight of silver for the new coin. It would thus be a unique coin, different from the Spanish dollar yet very close in weight.

Hamilton wanted to have just six denominations of coins, two each in gold, silver, and copper. He felt there should be gold dollar and ten-dollar coins, a silver dollar, and silver "tenth" or disme, as well as copper cents and half-cents. His reason for wanting so few coins was economy of production. He conceded that additional denominations might be needed, but felt that these could be made in silver when demand became great enough.

Hamilton felt that little or no profit should be made from the production of coins. He though that each coin's metal, coupled with the expense of manufacture, should equal the face value or come very close to it. He felt that this would make the coins more acceptable to the public.

Although Hamilton's proposals generally showed a highly sophisticated knowledge of money, some of his beliefs seem rather naive. He supported the creation of a half-cent because he thought such coins enabled the poor to buy cheaply and that thus they could "labor for less." Yet small coins did nothing to lower prices. All they could do was allow merchants to sell smaller quantities. The half-cent denomination would have no effect on the base price of an item.

Hamilton's plan also called for the elimination of foreign coins but only as the mint was able to replace them with United States' issues. For the first year the mint would be in operation, all foreign coins would circulate freely. During the second year of mint operation the legal foreign coins would be restricted to Spanish silver and the gold issues of three other countries. Then, in the third year the same coins would circulate, their value based on their intrinsic worth rather than the figure stamped on the coins. This would result in a gradual phasing-out of the foreign coinage, which would no longer be legal tender under any circumstances from the fourth year forward. However, recognizing the universal acceptance of Spanish silver and possible United States Mint production delays, he said that it would be a good idea to have the law give the President the option of letting Spanish coins circulate longer than three years.

Hamilton's desire to make both gold and silver coinage legal tender was to have repercussions in the years ahead. He felt that bimetallism would increase the amount of coinage in circulation. He evaded considering the problems that would arise if the values of gold and silver ever deviated from the fifteen-to-one ratio.

Hamilton seemed to prefer gold alone as legal tender, since it was historically the most stable metal in terms of its value. And Robert Morris preferred silver since it was the most common metal used for the world's coinage systems. But, they both compromised in favor of the joint system, and Hamilton's report was approved by Congress. On March 3, 1791, the establishment of a mint was officially ordered.

The vote relating to the mint was extremely close. There were arguments about the desirability of having the Federal government issue coins and not the states, about the lack of paper money, the cost of the mint, and other issues. The House vote in favor of the measure was a very close twenty-five to twenty-one.

The Mint Act was exceedingly vague, however. Congress simply resolved "That a mint shall be established under such regulations as shall be directed by law.

"That the President of the United States be, and he is hereby authorized to cause to be engaged, such principal artists as shall be necessary to carry the preceding resolution into effect, and to stipulate the terms and conditions of their service, and also to cause to be procured such apparatus as shall be requisite for the same purpose."

In October of 1791, the Senate asked Robert Morris to head a committee that would make the final plans for a mint utilizing Hamilton's coinage concepts. The bill created in that committee was passed on January 1, 1792, and sent to the House of Representatives. There it met considerable opposition because of a clause discussing the use of Washington's head on the coins.

George Washington had been elected President of the United States in 1789 and was idolized by much of the nation for his military achievements. The clause in question stated:

> That, upon said coins, respectively, there shall be the following devices and legends, namely: Upon one side of each of the said coins there shall be an impression or representation of the head of the President of the United States for the time being, with an inscription which shall express the initial or first letter of his Christian or first name, and his surname at length, the succession of the Presidency numerically, and the year of the coinage; and upon the reverse of each of the gold and silver coins there shall be the figure or representation of an eagle, with this inscription, "UNITED STATES OF AMERICA" and upon the reverse of each of the copper coins, there shall be an inscription which shall express the denomination of the piece, namely cent, or half cent, as the case may require.

At some point prior to December of 1791, Morris had arranged for sample coins to be privately struck. The engravings were done by Peter Getz, a twenty-three-year-old silversmith whose skills were far greater than one would expect in a self-taught artist.

Getz designed both copper cents and silver half-dollars, which were struck in December 1791, though dated 1792. They were made in the basement of a saw factory owned by John Harper at the corner of Cherry and Sixth Streets in Philadelphia. In either January or February of 1792, additional strikes were made on a press that had

With the Revolutionary War completed, a series of tokens was made in various countries honoring George Washington. The Washington pieces appeared from 1783 to 1795, and most of them were probably made in England. Some of the tokens are valued at one cent and others use the English denomination halfpenny. In photograph A, the head resembles George the Third and has the inscription *Georgius Triumpho* (Triumphant George). However, it is believed that the head is a stylized version of Washington's head and that the Triumphant symbolizes Washington's triumph over the King.

The token shown in photos B and C illustrates this similarity to the King. The reverse shows Brittania. As is seen by photo D, the head is more in line with American design. However, photo F demonstrates the reversion to what has been called the "Roman Head."

The coin shown in photo L was produced in North Wales and is a Halfpenny.

A.

B.

C.

D.

UNITED STATES OF AMERICA

E.

PRESIDENT

F.

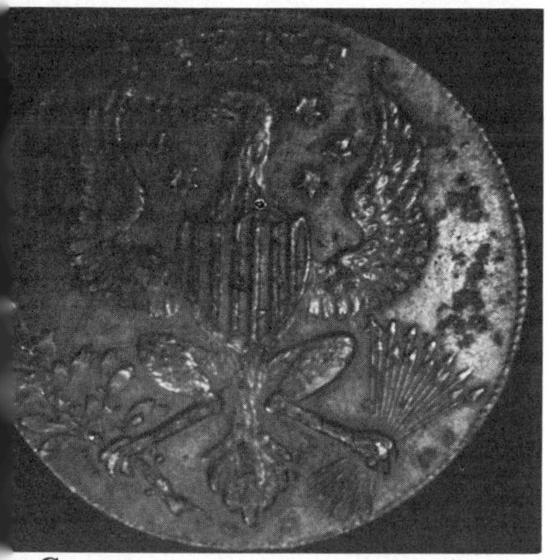

G.

FRIEND TO PEACE

H.

WORMWOODS
LONDON
1795

I.

LIBERTY AND SECURITY

J.

K.

L.

been built by Adam Eckfeldt, who would eventually become chief coiner for the mint.

There are other coins bearing Washington's portrait, and many were struck at about the same time as the Getz coins. But his are the only ones that were made in the United States. Others were made in England, primarily, by private coiners hoping to handle United States' coinage on a contract basis.

The cents were probably distributed to members of the House of Representatives as a means of persuading them to adopt the design. It had quite the opposite effect, however, because the members seemed to feel the coins too similar to those struck in the past to honor British royalty. Since the country had revolted against the idea of being governed by a king, critics felt the coins should not even hint of royalty.

Congressman John Page spoke most eloquently against the presidential coin design in a speech he gave in the House on March 24, 1792:

> We have all read that the Jews paid tribute to the Romans, by means of a coin on which was the head of their Caesar. Now as we have no occasion for this aid to history, nor any pretence to call the money of the United States the money of our Presidents, there can be no sort of necessity for adopting the idea of the Senate. [The congressman endorsed the idea that a depiction of Liberty replace the presidential likeness proposed.] I am certain it will be more agreeable to the Citizens of the United States, to see the head of Liberty on their coin, then the heads of Presidents. However well pleased they might be with the head of the great man now their President, they may have no great reason to be pleased with some of

> his successors; as to him, they have his busts, his pictures everywhere; historians are daily celebrating his fame, and Congress have voted him a monument. A further compliment they need not pay him, especially when it may be said, that no Republic has paid such a compliment to their Chief Magistrate, and when indeed it would be viewed as a stamp of Royalty on our coins, would wound the feelings of many friends, and gratify our enemies.

Page's arguments won over the House, which slashed the section relating to the president's image from the measure, then sent the bill on to the Senate. But the senators liked the idea of the head of Washington and rejected the change. Once again the members of the House debated the issue, and the proponents of Washington's image on the coins argued that it was the best way to honor the man who had made them free.

But Page was to prove a most articulate and convincing speaker on this issue. He again took to the floor to say

> I confess that, as long as the people are sensible of the blessings of liberty, and have their eyes open to watch encroachment, they will not be enslaved; but it they should overshut them, or become inattentive to their interests and the true principles of a free government, they like other nations, might lose their liberties. It is the duty of the members of the House to keep the eyes of their constituents open, and to watch over their liberties. It is therefore unbecoming a member to treat with levity and to ridicule any sentiment which had that tendency. For my part, I think it the peculiar duty of the Representative of a free people to put them upon their guard against anything which could possibly endanger their liberties. With this view I warn my constitutents of the danger, not merely of imitating the flattery and almost idolatrous practice of Monarchies with respect to the honor paid to their Kings, by impressing their images and names on their coins, but I wish to add as few incentives as possible to competition for the President's place. I warn my Country against the cabals, the corruption and animosities, which might be excited by the intrigues of ambitious men, animated with the hope of handing their names down to the latest ages on the medals of their country. But this indiscriminate honor is unworthy of the President's acceptance. A Nero, a Caligula, a Heliogabalus, it has been observed, many enjoy it as well as a Trajan. To apply it to the present Chief Magistrate, alone, would be less exceptionable. But this would be highly improper for if he should pass an act for this purpose, it might blast his reputation. I am of the opinion that the Senate knew his delicacy would not permit him to pass such a one. They have therefore extended the compliment to all his successors. We are under obligations to the great man now our President; but a lover of liberty and friend to the rights of man, would be cautious how he showed his sense of that obligation. As a friend to the President, I am unwilling to offer him a compliment which, if accepted, might

> damn his reputation. Were I in his place, I would cut off my hand rather than it should sign the act as it now stands. Were I his greatest enemy, I should wish him to pass it as it was passed by the Senate. . . .

The speech was successful in its intent. The House again passed the measure removing the presidential honor and this time the Senate agreed. The mint act became law as of April 2, 1792.

4

The New Mint

On April 14, 1792, President Washington appointed David Rittenhouse the first director of the United States Mint. Rittenhouse was in extremely poor health at the time but interested in the challenge. He was one of the foremost scientists in the United States and the nation's leading expert on astronomy. He had constructed an observatory with the first telescope in America as early as 1756. He invented the collimating telescope, the metallic thermometer, and other devices. He was a clockmaker, occasional political figure, and professor of astronomy at the University of Pennsylvania.

The new mint would be producing ten-dollar gold pieces (eagles), five-dollar gold (half eagles) and two and one-half dollar gold (quarter eagles) as well as dollars, half-dollars, quarter-dollars, dismes and half dismes, all in silver, and copper cents and half cents. The mint would be established in Philadephia and the director was required to hire those people necessary for the operations of the mint, subject to presidential approval.

One of the provisions of the new mint law was to cause a few operating expense problems. Anyone who had gold or silver bullion could take it to the mint and have it made into coins of equal value at no additional cost. The mint had to absorb the cost of conversion, an unrealistic approach if self-sufficiency was to be achieved. If the owner of bullion did not want to wait until the metal could be coined, he could leave the bullion and accept coins made from other bullion for a fee of one-half percent. Only with this circumstance was it possible for the mint to meet production costs.

Gold and silver coins were to be legal tender at face value when unworn. However, heavily worn pieces would be weighed and valued at a proportion of their full weight at striking.

In order to start coin production in earnest, it was necessary to have a place to build the mint. Rittenhouse studied the matter and suggested the purchase of a former distillery that was the property of Frederick Hailer. The land in question was 37–39 North Seventh Street and the adjoining lot at 631 Filbert Street. President Washington approved the land selection on July 9, 1792. At that time he also agreed to the hiring of Henry Voight (or Voigt), a mechanic and watchmaker, as chief coiner of the Mint.

Voight's appointment was supposedly a temporary one. Thomas Jefferson, now secretary of state, had been trying to find a European coiner with more experience than Voight. Jefferson wrote to Thomas Pinckney, the United States minister to England, on June 14:

> The U.S. being now about to establish a Mint, it becomes necessary to ask your assistance in procuring persons to carry on some parts of it; and to enable you to give it, you must be apprised of some facts.
>
> Congress, some time ago, authorized the President to take measures for procuring some artists from any place where they were to be had. It was known that a Mr. Drost, A swiss, had made an improvement in the method of coining, and some specimens of his coinage were exhibited here, which were superior to anything we had ever seen. Mr. Short was, therefore, authorized to engage Drost to come over, to erect the proper machinery, & instruct persons to go on with the coinage; and as he supposed this would require about a year, we agreed to give him a thousand louis a year and his expenses. The agreement was made, two coining mills, or

The first half cent struck in the United States. It is dated 1793 and was designed by Adam Eckfeldt.

screws, were ordered by him; but in the end, he declined coming. We have reason to believe he was drawn off by the English East Indian Company and that he is now at work for them in England. Mr. Bolton had also made a proposition to coin for us in England, which was declined. Since this the act has been passed for establishing our mint, which authorizes, among other things, the employment of an Assayer at Fifteen Hundred Dollars a year, the chief coiner at the same, and an engraver at Twelve Hundred Dollars, but it admits of the employment of one person both as Engraver and Chief Coiner, this we expect may be done, as we presume that any engraver, who had been used to work for a coinage must be well enough acquainted with all the operations of coinage to direct them; and it is an economy worth attention, if we can have the services performed by one officer instead of two; in which case it is proposed to give him the salary of the chief coiner, that is to say Fifteen Hundred Dollars a year. I am therefore to request that you will endeavor, on your arrival in Europe, to engage and send us an assayer, of approved skill, and of well attested integrity, and a Chief coiner and Engraver, in one person, if possible, acquainted with all the improvements in coining and particularly those of Drost and Boulton. Their salaries commence from the day of their sailing for America. If Drost be in England, I think he will feel himself under some obligation to aid you in procuring persons, how far Boulter will do it seems uncertain. You will doubtless make what use you can of the good dispositions of either of them or of any other person. Should you find it impracticable to procure an Engraver capable of performing the functions of Chief-coiner also, we must be content that you engage separate characters. Let these persons bring with them all the implements necessary for the carrying on the business, except such as you should think too bulky and easily made here; it would be proper therefore that they should consult you as to the necessary implements and their prices that they may act under your control, the method of your paying for these implements and making reasonable advances to the workmen shall be the subject of another letter, after the President shall have decided thereon. It should be a part of the agreement of these people that they will faithfully instruct all persons in their art, whom we shall put under them for that purpose. Your contract with them may be made for any term not exceeding four years. . . .

Jefferson and the other Americans who were trying to engage a European coiner eventually failed in their task. Voight was given a commission by Washington in January 1793, and began to operate the mint. Rittenhouse's health was so poor that Voight was effectively in control. Voight remained in his position until his death at age seventy in February 1814.

Washington was anxious for coinage to begin. He authorized the purchase of metal enough to begin producing cents, half cents and silver dismes and half dismes in a letter dated July 9, 1792. But first, there was the matter of building the mint.

On July 19, workmen began tearing down the old distillery, and by July 30, five loads of mortar sand was hauled to the site. Mint Director Rittenhouse, concerned with the morale of the employees, sold some of the trash found in the old distillery the following day. The dollar he earned from the sale was used to provide punch for the thirsty workmen busy laying the foundation stone of the mint.

The very first coins of the mint were made about October 1792. These were the disme, half disme, and what is known as the Birch cent. The two silver coins have an interesting history because they are intimately connected with George and Martha Washington. The obverse of the 1792 disme was probably designed by Adam Eckfeldt who had been hired as part of the administrative staff. (He is listed as a die forger and turner in the 1795 employment roster.) The facts are uncertain but the design is almost identical to that used on the 1793 half cent, which is known to have been his creation.

The portrait on the disme is said to be that of Liberty, but the model was actually Martha Washington. Apparently the image was based on a painting of Martha; she did not pose for the coin. But whether she was told of the honor in advance is not known.

For many years it was believed that the coins were struck from silver plate owned by George Washington. A silver tea service or similar items were supposed to have been taken to the mint for melting and coining. The story is quite probably true, although only circumstantial evidence exists to confirm it. Washington's letters indicate a long-term interest in the mint and coinage. He was anxious to see the coins made and was proud to announce, in a speech given November 6, 1792 (before the start of large-scale coining): "There has been a small beginning in the coinage of half-dismes, the want of small coins in circulation calling attention to them. . . ."

An intriguing fact was uncovered by numismatist Walter Breen and reported in a booklet he wrote in 1954. He found that the only known tableware George Washington owned at his death was of Sheffield plate. This is silver-clad copper rather than solid silver. Sheffield plate was becoming popular in America in 1792, but socially prominent individuals like the Washingtons always had sterling silver as well. Yet Breen found that no sterling silver tableware can be traced to Washington's estate. This fact lends credence to the belief that the Washington's sterling was sacrificed to make coins.

Another bit of evidence supporting this belief is the fact that Washington was a neighbor of the gold- and silversmith Ephraim Brasher on Cherry Street in New York during 1790. The surviving domestic account books show that several silver utensils were purchased from Brasher at this time. Since they are unknown today, they were perhaps given away as gifts; more likely, they became the first dismes and half dismes.

These early half dismes were ugly coins with one of the worst renderings of an eagle ever seen. The bird is scrawny and, though defiant, looks physically as though he might easily be defeated by a hummingbird.

The obverse of the coin bears the Martha Washington portrait and the motto LIB. PAR. OF SCIENCE & INDUSTRY. At least fifteen hundred of the half dimes were coined according to a notation in Thomas Jefferson's account books uncovered by researcher Don Taxay.

The Large cent designed by Robert Birch during this same period has a figure of Liberty (probably modeled on Martha Washington) with long, stringy hair being blown by the wind on a muggy summer day. The motto is similar to that of the half dismes but with more complete spelling: LIBERTY PARENT OF SCIENCE & INDUST. The reverse has the words ONE CENT encircled by a wreath, UNITED STATES OF AMERICA, and 1/100.

Work progressed fairly quickly on the mint, which was built in two stages. The first building was erected at the front of the lot and was completed by early 1793. The second building was completed the following year.

Thomas Jefferson, though secretary of state, played a direct role in the development of the mint. It would seem logical that the mint would be connected with the treasury department as it is today. But Washington thought otherwise. The National Archives contain a letter Washington wrote to Jefferson on October 20, 1791, which reads:

. . . "The Post office (as a branch of Revenue) was annexed to the Treasury in the time of Mr. Osgood; and when Colo. Pickering was appointed thereto, he was informed as I find by my letter to him dated the 29th. of August 1791, that he was to consider it in that light. If from relationship, or usage in similar cases (for I have made no enquiry into the matter, having been closely employed since you mentioned the thing to me, in reading papers from the War Office) the Mint does not appertain to the Department of the Treasury I am more inclined to add it to that of State than to multiply the duties of the other."

Jefferson's first concern when he became involved with the mint was to find adequate supplies of copper for coinage. The mint officials advertised in *Dunlap's Daily Advertiser* saying: "The highest price will be given for old copper at the Mint No. 29 North Seventh Street." Similar items appeared in *Bache's General Advertiser*. The advertising began on September 3, 1792, and the first copper purchase was made nine days later. It was six pounds of old metal brought in by Henry Voight at a price of one dollar. By November 22, the mint had purchased copper worth $269.86.

But even the larger copper purchases did little to meet the need. Jefferson recognized that something more would have to be done to ease the shortage. On November 28, 1792 he wrote to Washington:

> The rise in the price of copper, & difficulty of obtaining it from other quarters, has induced the Director of the Mint (as I had the honor of mentioning to you yesterday) to turn his attention to Sweden as the country from which according to his information it may be obtained on the best terms. He wishes that some means could be adopted of importing same on the public account. There is so little direct commerce between this country & Sweden that we shall be obliged to resort to some intermediate port & I have imagined that (our resident in Holland being absent) our Minister in London could be the bestperson to confide the business to for the present occasion. You will see by mr. Rittenhouse's letter inclosed that he proposes an importation of 30. or 40. tons from Sweden at present, the former quantity by his estimate will cost between nine & ten thousand dollars. If you approve of this mode & quantum of supply, a bill from the Treasury of 10,000 Dol. on the Holland bankers payable to mr. Pinckney shall be desired to adopt the best means he can of having 30. tons of copper shipped from Sweden for the Mint. . . .

Washington agreed to the Swedish purchase. The mint was further authorized to continue to buy wherever the price was best.

While copper was still in short supply the mint was experimenting with the best way to produce cents. Voight had developed a method for making a small cent that would be part copper and part silver to make the intrinsic worth equal to the face value. His idea was to make a smaller copper cent and insert a silver plug valued at three-fourths cent. The total copper would have a value of one-fourth cent and the cost of coining would apparently be absorbed by the govermment. Several of the silver-centered cents were made. Also struck were all-copper coins of the same size as the latter and several large copper pieces containing four times the copper in the silver-centered coins.

The experimental copper and copper-silver coins were interesting but unwanted. Congress had already endorsed plans which would not support them. Only the proposal of a large all-copper coin was to survive.

With regard to the conditions under which the mint employees worked, it is interesting to read the rules and regulations laid down for workers. These were first promulgated in 1795, when the mint was finally put into full operation. Here are a few of them:

> ARTICLE 1. Every workman shall attend to his business as follows: From the 10th day of March until the 10th day of September begin at five o'clock in the morning and work till 8. From 8 to 9 is allowed for breakfast when business shall commence and continue till one. From one till three is allowed for dinner when business shall again commence and continue until 7 o'clock in the evening.
>
> From the 10th day of September until the 10th day of March they shall begin work at 7 o'clock in the morning and work till 9. From 9 till 10 is allowed for breakfast, when business shall re-commence

and continue till 1. From 1 to 2 is allowed for dinner when business shall again commence and continue until 7 o'clock in the evening.

The first article also stated that Mint workers should be on the job eleven hours each day. The year was divided into four seasons, with each season having different starting, stopping, and eating hours, probably to take advantage of changing daylight patterns.

ARTICLE 2. No workman shall absent himself from the Mint without leave. Any offender shall for the first offense forfeit one day's pay, for the second two days' wages, and for the third all that shall be due him and be discharged.

ARTICLE 3. Any employee intending to leave the Mint shall give one week's notice and if satisfactory shall be given a certificate according to his merit and abilities. If he shall quit through caprice or any frivolous motive he shall forfeit one week's wages and be discharged without a certificate.

ARTICLE 4. No workman shall on any pretense without consent first obtained from his employer (head of department) bring or admit any acquaintance or other person into the Mint who is not employed there, under penalty of dismissal and forfeiture of all wages due.

ARTICLE 5. Any workman who shall come to the Mint drunk or shall get drunk while there shall forfeit as in Article 2.

ARTICLE 6. Every workman shall attend closely to the particular business assigned him and shall not meddle with or touch that of any other unless requested to do so.

ARTICLE 7. No workman shall presume to leave the Mint nor open any of the doors which lead into the street or alley during working hours without the permission of some one of the principal officers of the Mint. Any one transgressing this article and taken in the attempt shall be treated as guilty of a dishonorable act. He shall be stripped naked, his pockets be searched and if anything shall be found upon or about him belonging to the Mint, he shall forthwith be turned over to the civil power and prosecuted as the law directs.

ARTICLE 8. Every workman employed at the Mint shall leave one week's wages in arrears as long as he shall continue there.

ARTICLE 9. In order to avoid suspicion no workman shall carry about him any of the same coin which at that time is striking in the Mint under penalty of forfeiting all such coin found upon him and likewise all the wages due him and be discharged.

ARTICLE 10. The Pressmen who shall have the keys of the presses shall never leave them without locking them with the chain in such a manner that the balances or levers cannot be moved in their absence so as to strike or squeeze any piece of money or coin, and when the business of the day is finished shall deliver to the Treasurer or his clerk the keys thereof.

ARTICLE 11. Every man employed in the Mint shall be careful to let no scraps or pieces of metal lie about to waste but shall keep his working place or bench clean and his tools in good order, and every

Saturday there shall be a general cleaning throughout the Mint by the joint assistance of all hands.

ARTICLE 12. The foreman shall have authority to see these articles fulfilled by all hands without fear or affection.

An interesting contrast is found when one compares those early mint rules with those in effect just thirty years later. In 1825, for example, the Mint workers arrived at 5:00 A.M. and worked until 4:00 P.M. with the exception of Saturday when the mint closed two hours earlier. The new rules also said:

> The allowance for drink money is discontinued. No spirituous liquors to be brought into the Mint by any workman. Intoxicated workmen will be discharged. Profanity and smoking not tolerated. . . . The watchman shall ring the yard bell every hour precisely by the Mint clock after ten o'clock until relieved by the doorkeeper and send the dog through the yard immediately after ringing the bell. If an attempt is made on the Mint, he shall act conformably to his secret instructions which he must not disclose. He shall keep in a proper arm chest securely locked a musket and bayonet, two pistols and a sword, all to be kept in perfect order and inspected once a month by a Mint officer. When necessary to carry a light from one part of the Mint to another, the watchman shall carry a dark lantern but not an open candle. He shall have necessary keys of access to rooms and departments.

The production of coins in those first few years was a haphazard affair. When the first Large cents appeared, the copper coins became the subject of nationwide outrage. Typical of the reactions was an item that appeared in the *Pennsylvania Gazette* for March 20, 1793: "The American cents (says a letter from Newark) do not answer our expectations. The chain on the reverse is but a bad omen for liberty, and liberty herself appears to be in a fright—May she not justly cry out in the words of the Apostle 'Alexander the coppersmith hath done me much harm; the Lord reward him according to his works.' "

The chain design, which was considered suggestive of slavery and thus improper for a newly independent nation, had been quite acceptable on the Fugio cents. The hostility seems unreasonable, though it may have resulted from the "artistic" combination of the chain and the extremely crude representation of Liberty. Whatever the case, a new design with a modified Liberty obverse and a wreath for the reverse was adopted. The work was probably done by Adam Eckfeldt because the obverse is similar to his design for the 1792 disme and the reverse is similar to his half cent design for 1793. However, this is only speculation.

The coin production was to be hindered by a number of causes including an epidemic of yellow fever that ravaged Philadelphia for several years. Almost nothing was known about the disease and the "advanced" medical treatments of the time were contributing factors in numerous deaths.

This is America's least-loved coin. It is the Chain America cent, which possesses the inscription Liberty in Fright.

The reverses of the coins were also being changed. The first alteration was used in 1794 and the second was tried in 1796.

A leading Philadelphia physician at the time of the yellow fever epidemic was to become intimately involved with the mint as one of its first treasurers. His name was Dr. Benjamin Rush and his views about the proper treatment of the disease are interesting in the light of modern medical knowledge. On September 12, 1793, a few weeks before the mint was forced to close due to the illness of so many of its employees, Rush issued a statement to the citizens of Philadelphia.

> Dr. Rush regrets that he is unable to comply with all the calls of his fellow citizens who are indisposed with the prevailing fever. He begs leave to recommend to such of them as cannot have the benefit

of medical aid to take the mercurial purges, which may now be had with suitable directions at most of the apothecaries, and to lose ten or twelve ounces of blood as soon as is convenient after taking the purges, if the headache and fever continue. Where the purges cannot be obtained or do not operate speedily, bleeding may now be used before they are now taken. The almost universal success with which it hath pleased God to bless the remedies of strong mercurial purges and bleeding in this disorder enables Dr. Rush to assure his fellow citizens that there is no more danger to be apprehended from it, when those remedies are used in its early stage, than there is from the measles or the influenza.

Dr. Rush assures his fellow citizens further that the risk from visiting and attending the sick, in common cases, at present is not greater than from walking the streets. He hopes this information will be attended to, as many of the sick suffer greatly from the want of the assistance of bleeders and of the attendance of nurses and friends.

While the disease was so generally mortal, or the successful mode of treating it only partially adopted, Dr. Rush advised his friends to leave the city. At present he conceives this advice to be unnecessary, not only because the disease is now under the power of medicine, but because the citizens who now wish to fly into the country cannot avoid carrying the infection with them. They had better remain near to medical aid and avoid exciting the infection into action, which is now in their bodies, by a strict attention to former directions.

Dr. R. does not believe it will be prudent for those persons who are in the country to return to town until after frost or heavy rains have taken place, both of which alike weaken or destroy the contagion of the yellow fever.

The item, which appeared in the *Philadelphia Federal Gazette* might also be considered a thinly disguised advertisement for Rush. If one visited his local druggist, he could obtain "Doctor Rush's Mercurial Sweating Powder for the Yellow Fever, with printed directions for taking the same, prepared and sold by permission." Thus if one did not put money into the good doctor's hands for treating him directly, he would pay him indirectly by buying his remedy. Unfortunately neither his healing touch nor his medication were of any value. More people died of the bleedings, critics charged, than would have died from the effects of the disease had they gone untreated.

Rush's medical practice began to decline when it was found that his "sure cures" were of little or no value. His income was greatly reduced, yet he tried to support his family solely through his private practice. He was offered the directorship of the mint on April 9, 1795, at a salary of 750 pounds a year, but he declined since it would take him away from medicine.

Two years later Rush welcomed a mint appointment, this time as treasurer because the position of director had been filled. While a decision was being reached concerning his appointment, Judge Richard Peters sent a letter on his behalf to Secretary of State Timothy Pickering. The letter stated "Rush has a large & expensive Family to whom he is very indulgent. As to the present Depression of his Business I think Nothing of it & am sorry he gives Way to Resentment or Chagrin on that score. His Patients are mostly among opulent People & Strangers who are generally out of Town. He should not have shown himself irritated or hurt by the Newspaper Abuse thrown on him."

The newspaper abuse was in regard to his yellow fever treatments, which had failed to live up to their promise. The Peters' letter helped win the appointment for Rush, though among the reactions, a typical comment came from South Carolinan William Loughton Smith who was serving as United States' minister to Portugal. He wrote, on February 25, 1798: "I have been much amused in reading over some files of American papers by the last vessel. I see the old dispute revived with great violence for bleeding for fever and ague, and that Dr. Rush is charged with bleeding many hundreds to death. . . . I was not very much surprized at this charge, but I confess I was surprized to see him appointed treasurer of the mint. I hope he won't bleed that to death also."

On September 18, 1793, a newly designed Large cent was released into circulation, following which the mint closed down due to the yellow fever. The new coin, probably produced by Joseph Wright, showed a much improved Liberty head in what is known as a Liberty Cap design. Wright's work also is seen on the half cent of that year. He

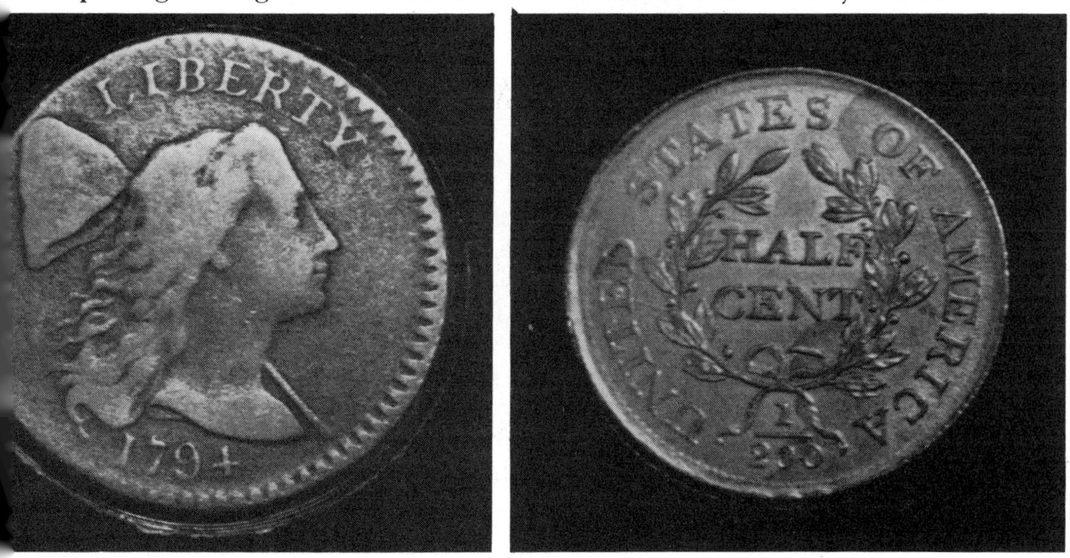

Coin designs were changed constantly during those early years. Engravers were developing skills not previously needed in the United States and artists such as Gilbert Stuart were contributing modifications for design. This coin represents an alteration made by Robert Scot in 1794.

This is another Robert Scot coin. This coin was the 1795 Half Dime. Similar designs were used for other silver coins produced the same year.

died shortly after the coins went into circulation.

The position of mint engraver was taken over by a man named Robert Scot (also spelled "Scott"). He was from Edinburgh, Scotland and had worked as an engraver for the State of Virginia from 1780 to 1782. Scot was well known for his artistic work with line engravings but is not known to have handled the prepration of dies for coins and medals.

Scot's first work was the preparation of dies for copper coinage. More than 40,000 pounds of copper had been delivered to the mint during the last two months of 1793, so there was an ample supply. He modified Liberty's head, giving her a fuller face, and created a more effective overall design for the copper coins.

Gold and silver coins had yet to be produced at this time because of the size of the bond, ten thousand dollars, that both the chief coiner and the assayer were expected to post. An appeal was made to Thomas Jefferson for a change in the law. He took the appeal to Congress, which agreed that the regulation was too severe. The bonds were lowered, so that the chief coiner needed only to post half the original bond and the assayer to post just one thousand dollars.

Scot immediately went to work developing designs for the new coins. He started with some pattern half dismes that were never placed in general circulation. He also produced a second design that was used for half dimes, in addition to designs for half-dollars and dollars in silver which were used. While these had a reasonably well drawn head of Liberty, the eagle appeared rather sickly.

An idea of how the public reacted to those early coins can be had from a letter written by Carlisle Pollock of New York City to General Williams of Salem, New York. The letter, dated January 26, 1796, was quoted in the *Coin Collector's Journal* of February 1877 and typifies the reaction to the silver pieces during these first few years.

> Heaven forbid that future ages should judge of the taste and talents of the present citizens of America by so mean and pitiful a sample of their works. I have seen all the coins already issued, and nothing can be more wretched; an unmeaning fool's-head on one side, and something that resembles a turkey cock on the other. Oh, shame, shame, shame! The Eagle of America mantling the arms of the United States, as you see it on the City Hall, would have been a dignified impression, and on the other side, if the President's head should be too aristocratic, a plough and a sheaf of wheat would be better than an Idiot's head with flowing hair, which was intended to designate the head of an Indian squaw. Since I began with this subject, I shall beg leave to mention an error in opinion that prevails with respect to the arms of America, and which the new coin justifies me in stating. In the coins the bald eagle is the representative of America, and is there placed as her arms. This is not the case, the arms of America are stripes of blue, red and white on a shield; the blue denotes dominion, the red implies power of force, and the white represents purity. To decorate and embellish the arms, the bald eagle was introduced, as a mantle or supporter to the shield, but making no part of the arms, according to the rules of heraldry; no more than the lion and the unicorn make a part of the British arms; they are supporters of the arms, but not the arms themselves. . . .

There were opposing views, of course. The *New Hampshire Gazette* for December 2, 1794, for example, praised the new dollar enthusiastically. However, the majority opinion seemed to be that the coins could have been far better than they were. In fact, the famous portrait artist, Gilbert Stuart, stopped by the mint and suggested a number of changes for the design of Liberty on the dollar. According to a mint director, James Ross Snowden, writing more than sixty years later, Stuart's comment on the Liberty design during that 1795 visit was: "Liberty on the other coins has run mad." He added a reference to her wildly streaming hair saying, "We will bind it up, and thus render her a steady matron."

The specific changes Stuart made are unknown. It is believed he made a pencil sketch, which has not survived. But the story shows the early mint's concern for improved artwork.

The earliest silver dollars, struck on October 15, 1794, were originally taken by the mint director, David Rittenhouse. Many were so poorly struck that they became planchets for the striking of the following year's coins. The coin press was made for producing cents and half cents only. It could not exert the pressure needed to make the larger coins. The coins that were of decent quality were eventually spent by Director Rittenhouse and later were found in many parts of the country.

An unusual occurrence was reported regarding the silver dollars and half-dollars struck during 1794 and most of 1795. They were superior in intrinsic worth to what the law required. They contained more silver than they were supposed to have according to the mint law of 1792, a situation that was not illegal but proved expensive and embarrassing.

The reason for this was that those who left quantities of silver with the mint for coinage received fewer dollars than the quantity of silver would normally permit. One major depositor, President Washington's friend John Vaughan, received a quantity of coins worth $2,260 less than the number to which he was entitled by a strict adherence to the proper silver content. He later went before Congress with his case in order to get his money back. The difference between the amount of silver specified by law for each coin and the amount actually used meant that depositors spent roughly one percent more than they should have.

In 1795, the members of Congress felt it necessary to look into the workings of the mint. Coins were not getting into circulation as well as anticipated, and a committee was appointed to learn why. It was found, though, that the delays were the result of problems any new mint might encounter given its circumstances. The report said:

> No work of this kind, requiring equal force and equal precision, ever having been made in this country, workmen, those expected to be obtained from Europe, by some means, having failed in the different branches, were hard to be got, and men, when engaged, were not masters of their business; the materials were difficult to be obtained, and often proved insufficient for the force required, even bar iron, from the large size required, as well as the casings, caused great delay before they could be had; often times when the machinery was finished and set to work, it gave way, and all was to

The dime of 1797.

This was the Draped Bust design of the 1795 Silver dollar. Again it is typical of the type used on all the silver coins.

> be done over again. All the tools necessary for their execution have been done at the mint. This could not be effected by a union of all the proper artisans, each a complete workman in his own department, but, from necessity, was confined to the principal officer of the coining department. The buildings were all to be completed before the works could be begun. The lots on which the same are built, from a principle of economy, were so restricted in size, that they are now found to be much too small. It was also a considerable time before an engraver could be engaged, during which, the cheif coiner was obliged to make the dies for himself, and yet the dies are subject to frequent failure by breaking. Great delays have also taken place for the want of a melter and refiner.

David Rittenhouse resigned his position as mint director during 1795 and was replaced by Henry William DeSaussure, who immediately set to work to begin production of gold coin. There was already gold on deposit, and the first coins were delivered on July 31, 1795. The delivery consisted of 744 five-dollar gold pieces, known as half eagles. Eagles, ten-dollar gold pieces, were not struck until September of that year.

Another major change came in 1795. As has been seen, the original law allowed anyone to deposit silver and silver goods (such as Washington's tea service) to be made into coin. Many of the silver items left with the mint were French billon coins—coins made from a mixture of silver and other metals. The amount of silver in billon coins varied, but it never exceeded fifty percent of the coin's intrinsic worth. The mint refined silver at no charge to the depositor, a courtesy that cost it thousands of dollars.

In 1795, the law was changed. Only refined silver was accepted for coinage without charge. Any silver items that had to be refined would cost the depositor a fee for coinage.

The next few years of the mint's existence were extremely frustrating for the people involved with it. Sometimes it seemed that no sooner had a workman developed his skills, then yellow fever would take his life. Shortages of silver and copper were constant problems. The nation had a severe money shortage and the United States treasury was unable to assure the mint of adequate metal supplies. A quarter dollar was introduced in 1796, again designed by Scot, but no additional coins of that denomination could be struck between 1796 and 1804 due to lack of silver.

By the turn of the century, the mint was in turmoil. It was nowhere near so productive as it should have been, and many thought the federal mint should be abolished entirely, as will be seen in the next chapter.

5

Limping Into the New Century

The desire to reduce the federal budget by eliminating the expense of an unproductive mint employing many unskilled workers was first expressed in 1795 when Congress investigated its operations. By March of 1800, though, an effort had begun in earnest to close the mint's doors permanently. It was led by Senator James Hillhouse, who stated that the mint's cost was disproportionate to its services and criticized the fact that most of its production circulated only in the vicinity of the mint. This effort failed.

Two years later, however, it seemed as though the mint truly would be abandoned. Elias Boudinot, mint director, prepared a letter for Secretary of the Treasury Albert Gallatin in which he inventoried all property of the mint ranging from the buildings and lots to such minor items as "Three horses, good for little but for the use of the mint." The letter went on:

> It is impossible to ascertain the value of these articles, as most of them are of but little consequence, except for the use of the Mint or to persons who may intend to put them to the like uses, and if sold at public sale, probably will not bring half their real value. The machinery of the Mint, may last a year longer with small repair, but after that, will cost about 300 dollars to put them in good repair. The horses may also last another year, but must then at farthest be replaced by others.
>
> If it should be thought best to continue the Mint, the establishment should be rendered permanent, and the machinery should be moved by steam instead of horses, which would in some measure reduce the annual expenses of labor, as almost the whole of it could

be carried on with the same original force. Our lots are much too small, by which we are greatly cramped as to room. They are now very valuable, being in the heart of the city; their price would purchase a very advantageous lot in a less public place, and buildings might be now planned, so as to reduce the expenses of a Mint. But I am perfectly satisfied, that no modification of the Mint could be contrived to lessen them below 17 or 18,000 dollars per annum, though if a larger quantity of bullion could by any means be provided, a greater quantity of coin could be annually made with the same expense, although I am, individually of the opinion, that its present issue of about 500,000 dollars annually, in addition to the current coin of the Union, is sufficient for the present welfare of the United States.

It is the absolute necessity of strict and regular cheques, throughout the whole establishment, that makes the expense of the Mint so great, and this cannot be dispensed with, under any modification that can be proposed. I verily believe, that under no given circumstance, can the necessary coin of the United States be produced with safety to the Government at a much less expense than it is at present, and I believe, that, in the consideration of the subject, it would not be safe, to estimate the expense, at any rate, much under 20,000 dollars.

In the above estimate of expenses, it should be remembered, that the copper cents may produce a profit of 5000 dollars per annum, that ought to be credited against the expenditures of the Mint in future, which reduces the amount considerably.

Robert Scot was equally convinced that the Mint would soon be abandoned. He felt that the responsibility for production of coins would fall back into private hands; he was anxious to benefit should that eventuality be realized. On March 4, 1802, he wrote Gallatin asking that he be given an exclusive contract to produce the governments' coin. Still no action was taken.

On April 27, 1805, after Boudinot decided to resign as Mint Director, Thomas Jefferson wrote to Dr. Robert Patterson to offer him the job of mint director. He cautioned, however, "I should be sorry to withdraw you from the College; nor do I conceive that this office need do it; it's duties will easily admit your devoting the ordinary College hours to that institution, indeed it is so possible that the Mint may some time or other be discontinued that I could not advise a permanent living to be given up for it."

It was not until 1828 that Congress decided that not only was the mint truly practical but also that it should be expanded. On March 2, 1829, appropriations were made for enlarging the Mint's operation. On April 30, new land was purchased, and that same month efforts were set afoot to obtain new equipment. The mint had at last become a permanent, fully accepted institution of the young nation.

The original mint, never very adequate, was found to be useless after the expansion. On July 2, 1832, *Paulson's American Daily Advertiser* featured the following advertisement.

United States Mint Property under authority from the President of the United States, will be sold at Public Sale on Thursday, the 19th of July, 1832, at 8 o'clock in the evening at the Merchants Coffee House.

The site of the old Mint, together with the improvements thereon, and a quantity of valuable machinery. The premises embrace a lot of ground situated on the east side of Delaware Seventh Street between Market and Arch Streets in the City of Philadelphia, containing in front or breadth on said Seventh Street 36 feet, 10 inches, and in length or depth 99 feet, together with a continguous lot of ground in the rear of the above containing in front 17 feet on a 14 feet passage way called Sugar Alley and in length or depth 56 feet 10 inches, and also another lot of ground fronting said alley 20 feet 6 inches and extending in depth 88 feet dividing from the last described by a 4 foot passageway.

The improvements are a large double house on Seventh Street 36 feet 10 inches in front, 3 stories high, conveniently divided, affording accommodations to the various offices and vaults and a part of the operating machinery and also a range of shops extending about 17 × 80 feet across the rear of the premises.

The machinery comprises a steam engine of 10 horse power, together with a complete system of rolling apparatus for hot or cold rolling, together with a drawing table connected with the steam power, all now in daily use, with a variety of other implements, furnaces, etc.

Subject the first two described lots to an annual ground rent charge of 21 dollars and the last described lot to an annual ground rent charge of 6 dollars and 50 cents.

The premises and machinery will be offered either separately or together, as may be considered most advantageous to the United States and to those persons inclined to purchase.

Terms, etc. at sale.

But the sale could not be held right away. The offer was withdrawn due to delays in the construction of the new Mint. It wasn't until October 8, 1835 that the mint finally went to auction, realizing a price of just $10,000.

It was supposedly during this period the controversial 1804 silver dollar appeared. This is one of the most famous rarities of American coinage, a mere handful being known. It was one of the first United States coins to realize more than $100,000 in a single sale, and it still is setting price records when it appears on the market.

The production of silver dollars was stopped in 1804 and not resumed until the 1830's. But mint records indicate that 19,570 silver dollars were struck during the first quarter of 1804. Thus the question arose as to what happened to the coins since so few are known today.

For years "experts" offered answers to the question of the 1804 dollars. One story has them being used to pay sailors in Africa. According to this notion, the coins circulated on that continent but very few ever found their way back to the United States. Another account has the 1804 dollars being used for international trade. Unfortunately, on their way to China, a typhoon sank the ship on which they were loaded.

One of the more plausible stories says that the 1804 dollars were melted by the mint shortly after they were struck. But with the constant shortage of silver coins experienced by the nation, it would have been quite unlikely that the mint would melt newly made coins. Since no written record of a melt order has been found, if the coins were melted it would have to have been done without authorization.

The reality, as far as careful research can determine, is that the 1804-dated silver dollars must have been made many years later. The fact that more than nineteen thousand coins were struck in 1804 does not mean that they bore the 1804 date. It was common practice never to waste old dies. Most likely there were dies left over in 1803, bearing the date 1803 and that of an earlier year, and these were used to make the coins produced in the first quarter of 1804.

The 1804-dated dollars extant today were made no earlier than 1834. They bore the 1804 date because the man who authorized them also thought that the silver dollars struck in 1804 were dated that same year. The full details, including the highly technical reasons why the coins could not have been made in 1804, can be had from the book *The Fantastic 1804 Dollar* by Eric Newman and Kenneth Bressett. What follows is a brief description of the events that led up to the unauthorized production of this rarity.

In 1832, the United States was actively involved in trade in the Far East. Edmund Roberts had been designated a special agent of the Department of State and had as his task the negotiation of treaties with a number of countries including Japan, Muscat, and Siam. He was appointed outside of normal channels, since the appointment of a special agent did not require congressional approval.

The 1804 Silver dollar. This coin was not minted until the 1830's. ***(Photo courtesy of Krause Publications.)***

There were numerous design changes for the coins during the early years of the mint's operations. Usually the copper half cents and copper cents shared similar design concepts over the years. The same was true with the silver coins, though they differed in design on the copper pieces. The coins illustrated are a random selection from those early years. The first is the half cent of 1803.

Provided with a sheaf of blank passports, Roberts filled them in for whatever country he felt he should visit next. His mission was to be totally secret because the agreements he reached with the countries were intended to give the United States an edge in international trading. If the British, French, or other nations learned of his mission and itinerary, it was felt they would themselves attempt to conclude agreements with the various nations that would exclude the United States. The secrecy was so essential that Roberts traveled disguised as a captain's clerk on the naval vessel *Peacock.*

Roberts learned the Asians expected those doing business with them to bring gifts for their leaders. Going before an Asian king without presents was not done.

Roberts' first voyage proved successful. He worked out trade agreements with the Imaum of Muscat and the P'hra Klang of Siam. These treaties were presented to the United States Senate, which ratified them on June 30, 1834. At this time Roberts prepared to resume his mission. Once again it was necessary to bear gifts, but the Department of State was having budget problems. They wanted him to keep the cost of the gifts to a reasonable level. Roberts was told to propose presents that would be acceptable to the Asian leaders yet not cost very much. This was a problem because cheap-looking gifts would be seen as tokens of little respect, and this could result in the agreements' being canceled.

This is the design of 1828 and shown are two variations of the reverse. The first variation uses what are known as "large berries" as a design supplement and the second employs what are known as "small berries."

The half cent design of 1853. Actually, this coin was issued from 1849 through 1857.

On October 8, 1834, Roberts made his suggestion in a letter saying, "I am rather at a loss to know what articles will be most acceptable to the Sultan, but I suppose a complete set of new gold & silver & copper coins of the U. S. neatly arranged in a morrocco case & then to have an outward covering would be proper to send not only to the sultan, but to other Asiatics."

John Forsyth of the State department approved the idea as did other government officials. On November 11, 1834 Forsyth wrote Mint Director Samuel Moore and ordered the preparation of such a set:

> The President has directed that a complete set of the coins of the United States be sent to the King of Siam, and another to the sultan of Muscat. You are requested, therefore, to forward to the Department for that purpose, duplicate specimens of each kind now in use, whether of gold, silver, or copper. As boxes, in which they are to be contained, may be more neatly and appropriately made at Philadelphia, under your direction, than they could be here, you are desired to procure them, if it will not be too much trouble, and have the coins suitably arranged in them before they are sent on. They should be of as small a size as is consistent with the purpose in which they are intended; and should be of wood, covered with plain marocco. The color of one should be yellow, and the other crimson.
>
> You are authorized to draw upon the Department for the value of the coins, and the expense of the boxes.

The order was quite clear and, at first, there seemed to be no problem. All official United States coins were being made in 1834 with two exceptions—the silver dollar and the eagle or gold ten-dollar coin. Both had ceased being made in 1804, and neither coin was still being held by the mint. All the coins of earlier years had apparently gone into circulation.

The result was that a quasi-legal counterfeit was prepared. There were 1804 eagles available and uncirculated specimens were obtained by the mint for the presentation cases. All the other coins were dated 1834 except for the silver dollar. New dies were prepared bearing the 1804 date since it was assumed such coins really existed though no one had seen them. These dies were used to strike the first 1804-dated silver dollars to be seen in the United States. The coins were prepared by the mint workers under direct orders of top management but legally had no right to exist. They became "authorized counterfeits" and a major curiosity for coin collectors. Even worse, additional strikes were made for private sale by mint employees, so the problem was compounded. The coins have thus one of the most curious histories of any piece ever to emerge from the mint.

Another coin with an unusual history was produced during those early years. Large cents that the mint was regularly and abundantly producing seemed to be popular for just about everything but spending. Since they were not legal tender for debts, any one with large quantities of them had trouble exchanging them for silver or gold. Merchants with sizeable holdings would fill kegs with them, then sell the kegs for a price per pound that was less than the total face value of the coins. The merchants seemed to feel it was better to take a small loss than a big one.

Other merchants used the coins for advertising. They would fill massive jars with them, then place the jars in their shop windows to arouse the curiosity of passers-by.

The large cent of 1814.

Large cents aided housewives in the production of pickles. They were tossed in the crock in order to give the pickles that rich green color that is so desirable. Unfortunately, the women didn't realize that the chemical reaction between the coins and the other ingredients resulted in a poison; this killed a number of pickle-eaters. Hundreds of others became ill before the public became aware of what was causing the poisoning.

An apparently less dangerous use for the coin was the tossing of one or more of them into kettles of apple butter, which were slow-cooked for several hours. The coins supposedly prevented the kettles from scorching.

A Large cent was tacked to the ridgepole of a new house barn in New England to insure good luck. Perhaps somewhat less lucky were the corpses whose eyes were held shut by the coins.

Large cents also served business and mechanical uses. Hotel keepers shaved off one side and added a room number. Then a hole would be placed through the coin and a key for that room attached to it. The coins were also notched for use as gun sights and cut to serve as gears.

Apparently the idea that wearing copper objects is of help in treating arthritis goes back to the early part of the nineteenth century. The coins were worn on necklaces and, in at least one case, as a belt. A sound medical practice was the placing of one of the Large cents in a saucer into which just enough vinegar was added to barely cover the coin. The chemical reaction produced copper sulfate, which doctors applied to ringworm lesions on their patients.

The list of nonmonetary uses for the coins seems almost endless. Yet despite the public's dislike of the cents as a means of exchange, the

A variation in the obverse head design.

Note that by 1832 the skill in engraving had greatly improved and the changes in the head of Liberty make her more human in appearance.

government continued producing the coins for many years.

The changes in coin design during the early years of the nineteenth century were often of limited artistic merit. John Reich created a turban-headed figure of Liberty which was first used in 1807. It was to prove a far more controversial design than anyone anticipated.

The first problem was with the turban itself. It was similar to the Phrygian Cap of ancient times. The Romans gave the cap to their slaves when the slaves were given their freedom. The implication seemed to be that the Americans had been in bondage only to be given their freedom either by the British or the early Revolutionary War leaders.

Another criticism was of the model of Liberty. The artist was accused of using his fat mistress as model for the engraving. However, his defenders averred that Reich did not use his mistress. They claimed instead that the model was a "blowsy barmaid."

It was not until the 1830's that the United States had its first radical change in coin design. A new engraver, Christian Gobrecht, was hired by the mint and his work marked a sharp departure from the design of the earlier coins.

Gobrecht's background was unusually varied for a coin designer. He was born in Hanover, Pennsylvania, on December 23, 1785. His father was a clergyman in the German Church and had been in the United States only since 1753.

Gobrecht showed mechanical aptitude and was apprenticed quite young to a clockmaker in Manheim, Pennsylvania, a town in Lancaster County. But the clockmaker soon died and the boy moved to

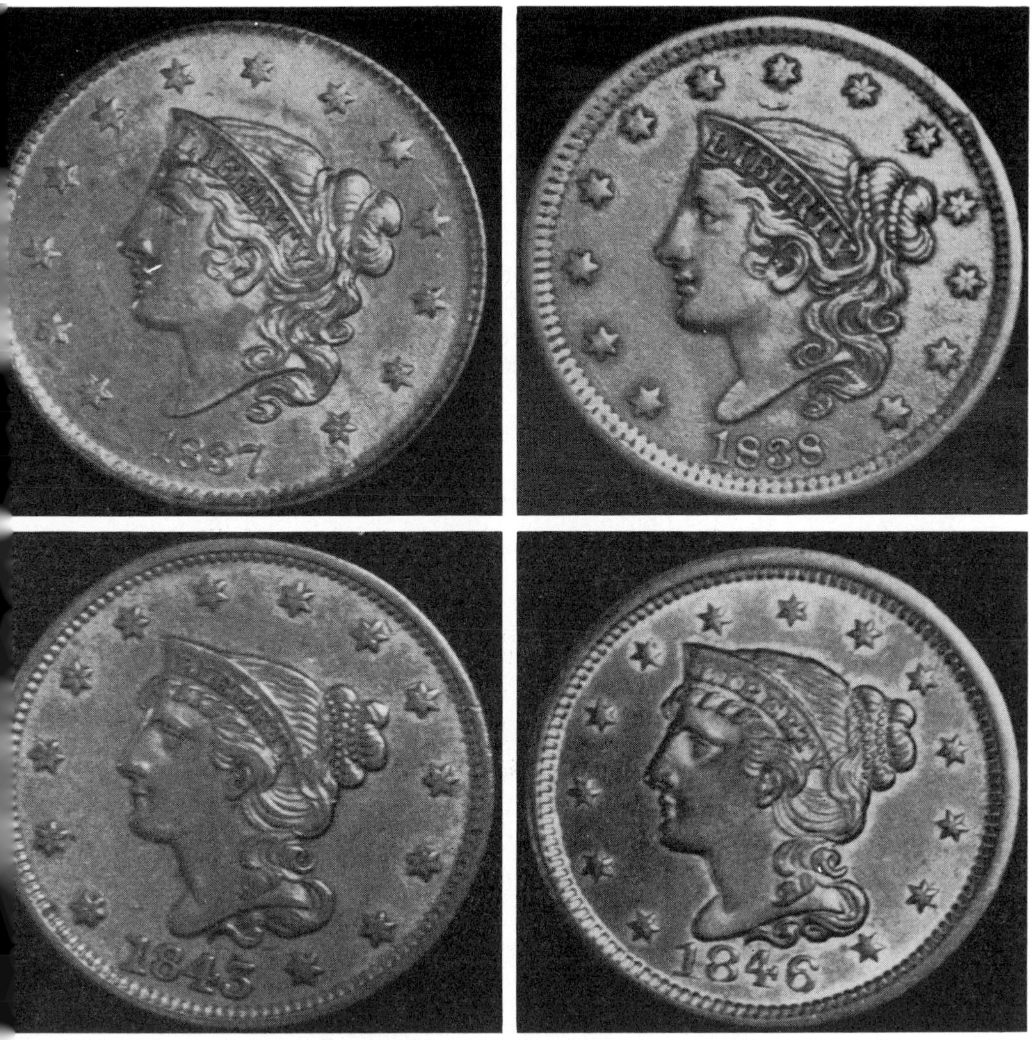

These four coins show additional variations.

Baltimore, where he managed to teach himself the skill of engraving custom-designed, ornate clock faces. Gobrecht tired of making clocks and took a job as engraver for newspaper type punches and cutting headings. He also learned to produce seals and eventually added die making to his skills.

Gobrecht's involvement with the production of money began in 1811 when he moved to Philadelphia to become an engraver of bank notes, seals, callico printers' rolls, and other items. Six years later he invented a medal-ruling machine that proved a major aid to medal engravers. In addition, his mechanical tinkerings led him to invent a talking doll, a camera lucida, and two musical instruments. The camera lucida is a device that projects the image of an object onto a piece of paper, where it can be traced. It is a drawing aid for artists.

Gobrecht first expressed interest in coinage on December 1, 1823, when he applied for employment at the Mint. The chief engraver had died in November, and Gobrecht requested President James Monroe that he be allowed to take his place. Gobrecht most likely was becoming bored with his work and the idea of coinage must have intrigued him. He was a man who seemed to seek new outlets for his talents as soon as he had mastered one particular aspect of his profession.

However the position was awarded to William Kneass. Kneass undertook an overhaul of United States coin designs. He modified the quarter dollar in 1831 and redesigned the gold coinage in 1834. That same year he also introduced a new Liberty Head half dollar.

By June of 1835 the mint's operations had expanded and the first of the branch mints was opened. In a letter to the secretary of the treasury retiring director Samuel Moore expressed the opinion that the secretary should hire a second engraver, and that his choice was Gobrecht. Moore felt that the second engraver was essential ". . . in order to furnish, in due season, the dies required for the Branches of the Mint." In the same letter Moore says,

> Soon after the passage of the Branch Mint act, an opportunity was taken of conferring with Mr. Gobrecht, in order to learn on what terms he could now be attached to the public service; and this subject has been very recently renewed in a more particular conversation with him. He is at present, it appears, under engagements as a Bank Note Engraver which produced to him nearly $2000 per year. I perceive however, a disposition to accept a connexion with the Mint, at a Compensation of less Amount,

The Capped Bust design of William Kneass as used on the half dime.

provided it be relied on as more than a transient arrangement. I have no expectation, however, that he would give his time to the public for less than $1500 per annum, nor does it seem reasonable that he should.

It did not take long for a decision to be reached. Kneass suffered a stroke that left him with limited physical movement. It became essential to hire Gobrecht.

At the same time that Gobrecht came to the mint, the famous artists Thomas Sully and Titian Peale also went to work for the government. Sully and Peale had been hired to create new designs for the obverse and reverse of the coinage. Sully was a noted portrait painter and Peale specialized in the drawing of birds.

The obverse of the new coin was the result of several different suggestions as to what a coin design should be. The new mint director, Robert Patterson, wanted to avoid having a bust of Liberty as in the past because it seemed personal and lacking in symbolism. He preferred a full-figured representation of Liberty similar in appearance to the design of Britannia used on English copper coins. Kneass came up with a preliminary idea prior to his stroke, and Sully developed the concept more fully.

Patterson had Gobrecht make a copperplate engraving from one of the three sketches Sully developed for the coins, and this was sent to the secretary of the treasury. It was accompanied by a note explaining Patterson's esthetic position:

> For "the impression emblematic of Liberty," you know that our coins have heretofore used a bust, &c. It appears to me that it would be better to introduce an entire figure. When a likeness is to be given on the European coins, the head alone is very properly used,

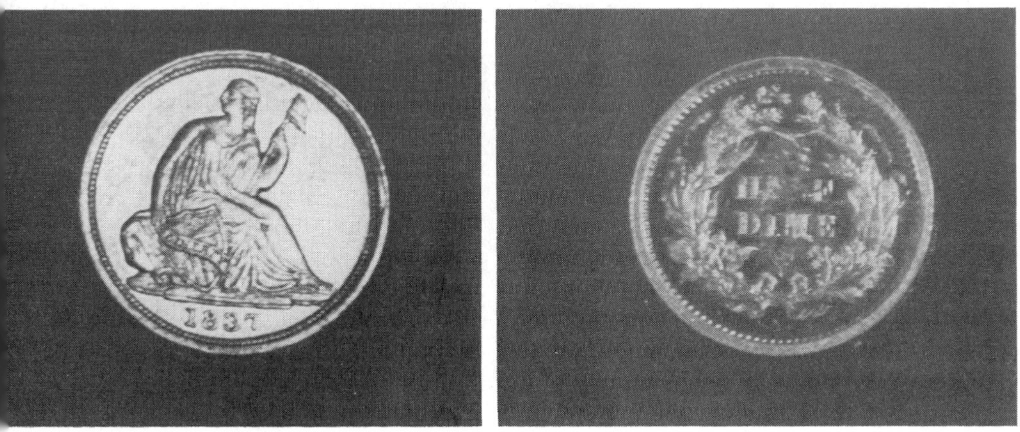

The Seated Liberty design of Christian Gobrecht as used on the half dime.

The Draped Bust design on an 1850 dime.

The Capped Bust dime introduced in 1809 and modified slightly over the next few years.

in order that the features may be distinctly represented. But, when an emblem only is called for, it would seem rather desirable to avoid this individuality in the features. Besides, there is certainly more reason for a display of taste and beauty of form when the full figure is used.

The round form of the coin, and the small size, and the practical necessity of covering as much of the face as possible, seem to require that the figure be in a sitting posture,—sitting, for example, on a rock.

The Christian Gobrecht design of 1837. Changes were made in the following year as well as in 1853.

> To be distinctly "emblematic of Liberty," I would propose that the figure hold in her right hand the liberty pole surmounted by the pileus,—an emblem not unclassical, and which is universally understood.
>
> I would also suggest, that the left hand be made to rest on the United States shield, on which the word "Liberty" required by law, may be inscribed.

The design was to be put to a humorous use that no one could have anticipated. In the 1850's, a counterfeiter took great delight in the way in which Liberty was seated. The counterfeiter, to keep his hand in, managed to obtain tools during one of his frequent stays in prison. While he did not feel it wise to try to produce coins from behind bars, he saw no reason to keep from altering them as a test of his skill. Thus a number of Seated Liberty coins were changed to display Miss Liberty seated on a chamber pot.

The first Gobrecht engraving made from the Sully design was not quite satisfactory. Patterson saw it this way:

> It is true that in our first attempt the pole is not thrown sufficiently back from the figure, and this is in part due to a fault in the left arm and shoulder, the latter of which, as you have probably observed, is too low, and too far from the neck, and the former of which is too prominent, requiring to be subdued and thrown back by being made flatter. A similar fault exists in the face, which we find to be very much improved by flattening the cheeks. The right arm is too muscular, and the articulation at the elbow is not properly marked. The right hand was at one time beautiful, but was

The third variation of the Christian Gobrecht design, this one introduced in 1853.

injured by yielding to an injudicious criticism. The index finger of the left hand is too much in the position of pointing. There is too much confusion of drapery about the left breast, and near the right hand. The knees are too lumpy, the articulations not being shown with sufficient distinctness.

The inspiration of the reverse design of the coin has been the subject of all manner of speculation. Some stories say the bird was intended to be representational, but considering Peale's desire for accuracy in bird drawings, this is highly unlikely. Others say it was based on an eagle that had become a pet of the mint. This latter story was repeated in an issue of *Harper's Young People* and quoted in the *American Journal of Numismatics in 1893*. The story read:

> On the Dollars of 1836, 1838, and 1839, and the nickel Cents coined in 1856, is the portrait of an American eagle which was for many years a familiar sight in the streets of Philadelphia. "Peter," one of the finest eagles ever captured alive, was the pet of the Philadelphia Mint, and was generally known as the 'Mint bird.' Not only did he have free access to every part of the Mint, going without hindrance into the treasure vaults, where even the treasurer of the United States would not go alone, but he used his own pleasure in going about the city, flying over the houses, sometimes perching upon lampposts in the streets. Everybody knew him, and even the street boys treated him with respect.
>
> The government provided his daily fare, and he was as much a part of the Mint establishment as the Superintendent or the

A variation of the reverse.

The Draped Bust quarter reverse. Notice that the Eagle is rudely drawn and seems almost a cartoon caricature.

Chief-coiner. He was kindly treated and had no fear of anybody or anything, and he might be in the Mint yet if he had not sat down to rest upon one of the great flywheels. The wheel started without warning, and Peter was caught in the machinery. One of his wings was broken, and he died a few days later. The Superintendent had his body beautifully mounted, with his wings spread to their fullest extent; and to this day Peter stands in a glass case in the Mint cabinet. A portrait of him as he stands in the case was put upon the coins named.

The story is an interesting one, and the fact that Peter did exist is unquestioned. However, the bird depicted on the Gobrecht coins, as well as in the later design mentioned, was definitely not Peter. This is shown in a letter about the reverse design which Patterson wrote on April 9, 1836.

> The die for the reverse is not yet commenced, but I send you the drawings which we propose to follow,—the pen sketch being that which we prefer. The drawing is true to nature, for it is taken from the eagle itself,—a bird, recently killed, having been prepared, and placed in the attitude which we had selected. The eagle is flying, and, like the country of which it is the emblem, its course onward and upward. I propose to follow the letter of the law as to the legend on the reverse, and to introduce nothing but the words 'United States of America' around the margin, and the denomina-

The Capped Bust Quarter and its reverse and variations over the years.

Another variety of the Capped Bust design with a modified reverse.

> tion of the coin. The absurdity of the shield sticking to the breast of a bird is avoided,—the shield, with its thirteen stripes, being placed with the figure of Liberty, on the face of the coin. The arrows and branches are also removed from the eagle's claws, as contrary to nature and good taste. A constellation of stars, equal to the number of states, is distributed irregularly over the sky supposed to be seen beyond the eagle, instead of having 13 equal stars stiffly arranged in line around the edge.

The eagle adopted on the coin was not what Titian Peale desired, however. Numerous sketches have survived showing that he was anxious to have a bird shown as naturally as possible. But the design finally selected was closer to an eagle of heraldry than reality.

And so new era in coin design had begun. The Gobrecht engraved coins designed by Sully and Peale were the first to show the potential quality that could come from the new mint.

Before proceeding with the story of United States coinage, let's stop and take a look at the events that had been unfolding during these years with regard to silver and gold.

The concept of bimetallism had been a coinage problem from the start. Internationally, gold and silver tended to fluctuate in relative value from country to country. Its value also varied with time: one ounce of gold might be worth sixteen ounces of silver one month and fifteen ounces the next. At times the countries maintained similar standards; at other times they varied slightly. But always the relative values of gold and silver were allowed to float. They were not fixed by law as they were in the early coinage acts of the United States (see appendix).

The original silver-to-gold relationship established by the United States government was fifteen to one, which compared with Euro-

The Christian Gobrecht quarter introduced in 1838.

The Draped Bust half-dollar introduced in 1801.

pean values at that time. But by 1799, the value abroad was sixteen to one. This meant that it did not pay to take gold to the United States Mint to exchange for silver. It was either hoarded or sent abroad for the extra premium, thus ceasing to circulate within our borders.

Silver dollars had also ceased to circulate, as has been discussed earlier. Copper coins were unpopular and so the country had to rely on United States coins ranging from half dimes to half dollars for change, a totally unsatisfactory way to do business. To make matters worse, many of the small denomination silver pieces were shipped

The Capped Bust design for the half-dollar introduced in 1807.

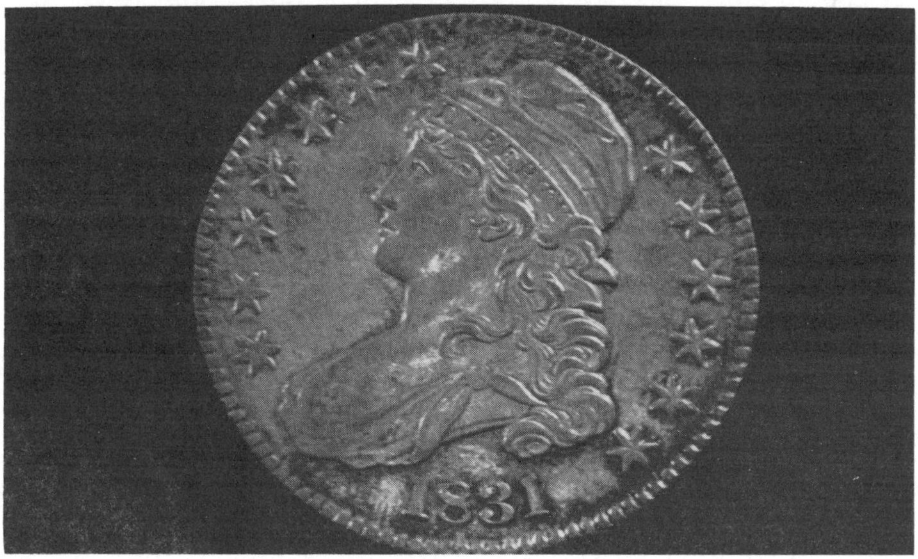

A variation in the design of the half-dollar.

abroad or used as bullion. A Senate study revealed that by 1830 there had been twenty-five million dollars in silver coins struck by the mint with almost half that amount (eleven million dollars worth) shipped abroad. Of the remaining fourteen million dollars, approximately two million was held by the Bank of the United States and did not circulate.

Numerous methods were used to counter the coin shortage. Foreign coins were frequently spent, both legally and illegally. At

The reverse used at the beginning of the 19th Century.

The variation of obverse and reverse introduced in 1836 for the half-dollar.

least five million dollars in Spanish silver coins of varying denominations were in use in 1830. However, even with the Spanish coins adding to the specie, the estimated number of small coins (less than a half-dollar in size) available to the public had dropped to twenty-five cents per person by 1830.

The use of foreign coins was so widespread that many Americans had yet to make a transition to the decimal system. Instead they continued to think in terms of foreign and primarily British values.

Merchandise was as likely to be found priced at a "shilling" or a "real" as it was at the equivalent American rate of 12½ cents. Many merchants regularly priced their goods at an awkward six and one-quarter and twelve and one-half cents rather than use the five- and ten-cent American coins.

Oddly enough, even the United States Government encouraged the use of foreign coins in the 1830s. The postal system had set its rates in fractions that related to the Spanish coin values, not those of the American system.

Coinage reform was constantly on the minds of congressmen but there were numerous influences affecting their judgement. Of prime consideration was the pressure of special interest groups. The westward movement was resulting in gold and silver strikes unlike any the world had yet known. If a state produced gold, its representatives naturally wanted gold to become the basis of our monetary system. If a state had silver, that metal was favored. The more ore purchased by the government, the more the mine owners would prosper and be likely to financially reward their state's lawmakers.

The special-interest gorups on all sides were too strong for common sense to prevail. Bimetallism was continued, although the value ratio of gold to silver was changed to almost sixteen to one. Again this varied from the European standards, making it profitable for Europeans to send gold to the United States since they could get more silver for it than in their own countries. (Specifics of the various coinage acts are found in the Appendixes.)

The two coins intended to be the legal standards were the silver dollar and the ten-dollar gold piece. Other coins were legal tender only in amounts strictly limited by law.

Perhaps the best summation of the coinage problem was made many years after the coinage act of 1834, which set the new gold-to-silver ratios. In a report made to the Secretary of the Treasury in 1876 Comptroller John Knox stated,

> The act of June 28, 1834, which reduced the gold standard about six and one-fourth percent., practically demonetized the silver coinage. Previous to the date of the passage of that act American gold and silver coins of all denominations were equally a legal tender, and the silver coins of less denomination than one dollar were chiefly in use, only $1,369,517 in silver dollars having been issued from the mint at that date. The Act of 1834 overvalued the gold coinage, driving from the country the full-weight silver coins previously in circulation; and it may be confidently stated that from 1834 to 1873 no silver dollar pieces have been presented at any custom-house in payment of duties.
>
> From 1793—the date of the first issue of silver coin by the United States—to 1834, the silver and the gold dollar were alike authorized to be received as legal tender in payment of debt, but silver alone circulated. Subsequently, however, silver was not used, except in

fractional payments, or, since 1853, as a subsidiary coin. The silver dollar, as a coin of circulation, had become obsolete and useless. The reason why, prior to 1834, payments were made exclusively in silver, and subsequent to that date in gold, is found in the fact that prior to the legislation of 1834 the weight of fine silver in the silver dollar was fixed at fifteen times the weight of fine gold in the gold dollar; but after that date, owing to a reduction in the weight of gold required for the standard gold dollar, the silver dollar was made to contain of fine metal almost precisely sixteen times that of the new gold dollar; the actual market value of gold during the entire period having been greater than fifteen and less than sixteen times the value of silver of equal weight. During the earlier period, therefore, the standard silver coins were relatively the cheaper, and consequently circulated to the exclusion of the gold; while during the later period the standard gold coins were cheaper, circulating to the exclusion of the silver.

Gold, silver, and copper coins were not the only means of meeting one's obligations. Paper money abounded throughout the country. States had the right to let their banks issue paper money whose value was based on the soundness and good will of the issuing banks. The only real control came from the Bank of the United States, which also issued its own notes.

The Bank of the United States had been modeled after the Bank of England. It was, in effect, a national bank with the legal right to authorize establishment of branches in different parts of the nation. To a very limited degree it might be compared to today's Federal Reserve System. The Bank of the United States deposited govern-

Some improvements on the reverse of the Eagle introduced in 1838 on the half-dollar.

This is the 2½ dollar gold piece. Gold coin designs were often similar to one another. This one was designed by William Kneass.

Christian Gobrecht's design for the two and one-half Dollar Gold piece introduced in 1840 was quite different from the design he used on the silver coins.

ment funds in certain favorite banks in different states, strengthening the competitive positions of those institutions and enabling them to issue more paper money. Not only did this result in more and more paper money getting into circulation—money not controlled by reserves of gold or silver—but it also laid the government open to attack for playing favorites. This charge was probably quite true.

In the early 1830s, when Andrew Jackson assumed the presidency, the life of the Bank of the United States was almost over. Jackson

The Classic Head half-dollar. It is similar to the design of the quarter dollar during this same general period.

Christian Gobrecht's design for the Half Eagle. Reverse introduced in 1839.

disliked the concept of the bank and its ability to issue paper money. He believed in "hard money"—gold and silver. The bank's charter came up for renewal, and Jackson fought its continued existence.

By 1833 the Bank of the United States was in such serious danger that the director, Nicholas Biddle, took actions designed to place the bank in a more favorable light. He cut back on loans and generally tightened credit policies.

The Eagle or ten-dollar gold piece with Capped Bust design of Robert Scott.

Jackson had his way, though. The bank was not rechartered.

Jackson and his followers wanted to have the government funds deposited in a central treasury with various subtreasuries used around the country for the collection of revenues. All revenue would be payable only in hard money. It was felt that this would lessen the use of paper notes and place the country on a sounder financial footing.

Rather than reducing the issue of paper money, the immediate effect of the failure to recharter the Bank of the United States was an increase in the issue of paper money by state banks. To make matters worse, a major crop failure occurred in 1835, and farmers were unable to meet their financial obligations to merchants and land speculators. These people, in turn, could not pay their loans at the bank.

The crop failure affected the country in other ways, too. Food had to be imported into the United States, and this resulted in an unfavorable balance of payments. Naturally the other countries would not take state bank notes, so gold and silver coin went abroad at a record rate.

To make matters worse, on July 11, 1836, Jackson issued his Specie Circular. It ordered that all future payment for public land be made in gold and silver. Since this was not available in necessary quantity, land buying slowed greatly, and many previous buyers had to default on payments.

The depression that resulted from the Panic of 1837, as the money crisis came to be called, was to have a profound effect on the coinage system as well. Coin substitutes were created on a wide scale for the first time. These substitutes—merchants' tokens actually—would appear again and again over the years as the need arose.

The reverse of the Gobrecht design for the Eagle. Introduced in 1838.

A variation on the Gobrecht design, this one produced in 1866 by the newly built San Francisco Mint. Note the mint mark—the letter "S"—below the Eagle's claws and above the "e" and "n" in the word "ten."

The tokens were actually issued for two reasons. Of prime importance was the need for small change. The tokens were usually made of copper and served as cents for the most part. They became known as "Jackson tokens" or "Hard Times tokens" because of the depression. A number of them had sayings that were either pro-

Jackson or attacks on his policies. Others served as advertising vehicles. Thousands of the tokens were issued by hundreds of merchants throughout the country—far more than were needed to supplement the lack of coins. They proved an inexpensive way to make change and get an advertising message into wide circulation.

The problems with bimetallism continued to be a factor in United States coin history for many more years. But let us now explore the westward expansion of the nation, which resulted in the discovery of

The first variety of the Christian Gobrecht half-dollar. The reverse, however, follows the second design variation.

The fifth variety of Gobrecht half-dollars.

gold and silver in previously unknown quantities. It was this expansion that led to the creation of the branch mint system and some of the most colorful coinage ever created out of necessity.

The first type of Christian Gobrecht dollar.

6

The Founding of the Branch Mints

The story of the branch United States mints is primarily the story of westward expansion and the discovery of gold and silver in various parts of the American continent. Word of each new strike brought hundreds and thousands of prospectors into an area almost overnight. Housing was thrown together with whatever materials were available to the people, and makeshift communities were frequently built in twenty-four hours. Instant towns meant instant commerce and a need for coin to use in exchange. But the miners arrived with the tools of their trade and very little money. As a result, haphazard methods of commerce became necessary.

Before examining such areas as San Francisco and Denver and the stories behind their branch mints, let us look at the first of the branches, which were placed in already settled areas. These are the mints of Dahlonega, Georgia; Charlotte, North Carolina; and New Orleans, Louisiana. They were built in relatively well established areas where gold had been discovered in quantity.

The Charlotte branch mint's story begins in 1799 when Conrad Reed, a twelve-year-old boy, was playing in a small stream called Meadow Creek. He had taken a bow and arrow and was attempting to shoot fish when he noticed a yellow substance in the water. He picked it up and took it home but his father had no idea what it was. Gold had never been known in this part of the country so the elder Reed and others who later found similar bits of the metal assumed it was something else.

John Reed, Conrad's father, had his curiosity aroused, however.

He took the metal to a silversmith in another town but the silversmith also assumed it couldn't be gold, considering the circumstances of its discovery. It was only in 1802, when Reed chanced to take the metal to Fayetteville, that a jeweler identified it as gold.

Reed was intrigued. He had new found respect for the small piece of metal he sold to the Fayetteville jeweler for $3.50. Although the price paid was well below the real market value, it was sufficiently high that Reed and several other men began exploring the creek. In 1803, they found a piece of gold that weighed twenty-eight pounds. Soon their mining operation was uncovering large quantities of gold.

It is interesting that people in other sections of North Carolina and Georgia were having experiences similar to Reed's. The presence of gold was so unexpected that everyone assumed it was something else. Chunks of gold were used as doorstops, and gold dust was utilized to reduce rust in rifles. People were casually tossing away hundreds of dollars in gold before they finally learned what they had.

Gold mining quickly became well organized in a multi-state region of North Carolina, South Carolina and Georgia. Unfortunately, once the men had uncovered the gold they were at a loss to know what to do with it. A quantity of the bullion found its way to ships bound for other countries. But to have exchange value, most of the gold needed to be officially assayed and made into coin. This meant that it had to be sent to the Philadelphia mint, a necessity that presented serious problems.

A miner sending gold to the Philadelphia mint had personally to pay the cost of transportation and protection. Even if it arrived without damage or loss, money was not immediately forthcoming. It might be several months before he would be given his coins.

The stagecoach provided a somewhat better way to transport small quantities of ore. Usually the miner would accompany it, taking considerable time away from his mining work. Moreover, the cost was prohibitive since it could be as much as ten cents a mile. A man riding alone on horseback could make almost as good time for less expense, though with greater risk since there wouldn't be other armed men accompanying him.

A third approach was to sell the gold locally. Many rich individuals made an excellent business of buying the gold at substantial discount from its real value. While the miners received immediate cash for their gold, the buyers made a splendid profit when they shipped it to Philadelphia. This was an unfair situation and was to be mentioned in the debate over the establishment of a branch mint. The point was raised in Congress in December of 1832 by Georgia Congressman Augustin Clayton.

> . . . we wish the laboring man to have it in his power to carry his gold himself to the mint, and get its true value, instead of its passing into second hands, the hands of the speculator, who, by reason of his

Among the coins struck by August Bechtler in 1842 was this one dollar gold piece. This coin was struck for use in Carolina.

This coin might be considered the first fifty-dollar gold piece authorized by the United States. It was prepared by the United States Assay Office, which was actually the reorganized firm of Moffat & Company in San Francisco.

superior wealth, can wait for its proceeds and carry it there at his leisure, full well knowing his profits will pay him for his delay. Again we wish our people to be placed in the condition of those who might happen to have mines immediately in the neighborhood of the mint. If, for instance, the good people residing upon the banks of the Delaware and Schuylkill, in the vicinity of Philadelphia, should have the good fortune to discover gold mines upon their lands, every one would at once perceive of what great advantage

This is a twenty dollar gold piece from the United States Assay Office. It was struck in 1853.

The Colorado firm of Clark, Gruber & Company struck this ten dollar gold piece in 1860.

their proximity to the mint would be to them. They could carry to that establishment, at the close of every day, the fruits of their labor, and realize immediately that which would command certainly the support, if not the higher comforts of life.

Transportation wasn't the only problem. As more and more people moved to the gold mining areas, towns expanded and coin shortages occurred. The only method for making payments that could be found by those having gold was to carry dust in one or more bird quills. The quill would be kept in the pocket until needed, then the dust would be shaken onto a scale until the weight and value equaled the price of the merchandise.

The first person to find a large-scale, workable alternative to the carrying of gold dust in quills was a German immigrant named Christopher Bechtler (misspelled "Bechler" in some early newspaper accounts). Bechtler came from the German Duchy of Baden. He was born in 1782 and emmigrated to New York, arriving October 12, 1829. Both he and his son, Augustus, became naturalized citizens in 1832. Bechtler is little known today. He was a gunsmith and a goldsmith. The jewelry he manufactured included necklaces, chains, cuff links, rings, and other items. Thus he knew gold, having worked with it to frequently.

In 1830 Christopher Bechtler and his son journeyed to Rutherfordton in the heart of the North Carolina gold mining territory. They traveled with Charles Bechtler, another son, and Christopher's nephew, who was named Christopher, Jr. The elder Bechtler immediately recognized the problem the miners were facing with their gold and the fact that the federal government had done nothing to remedy the matter. He decided that he would start his own mint for the production of gold coin.

The exact date that Bechtler began minting is uncertain. However, on August 27, 1831, an advertisement appeared in the *Carolina Spectator and Western Advertiser,* published at Rutherfordton.

> To Gold Miners and Others:
>
> "The undersigned, having coined a great quantity of North Caroline gold into pieces of $2.50 and $5 values, of 20 carats fine, and being well prepared to increase the business to any extent, is established 3½ miles on the road leading from Rutherfordton to Jeanstown, invites the attention of miners in South Caroline and Georgia, as well as North Carolina, to the advantage which would result from having the product of their mines coined or made into ingots bearing their just value rather than disposing of it in its fluxed state without an essay, and therefore liable to produce an improper value: gold in a fluxed state of 22 and 23 carats is generally sold for 84 cents per dwt. in the bank, whereas its intrinsic value, if coined, is 90 or 94 cents, consequently an actual saving of 6 cents per dwt. will be made by having it coined after paying all expense of coining, etc. Should encouragement be given, new dies will be made especially for stamping South Carolina and Georgia gold.
>
> "He would also make known here the plan which he has adopted and will pursue: On receiving a bar of fluxed gold to be coined, the same will be divided, a portion assayed (by a fire ordeal) for the

Typical of the coins struck by the Branch Mint is this five dollar gold piece produced in San Francisco. Note the letter "S" between the Eagle and the letter "v" in the word "five."

The "O" below the Eagle and directly above the space between "one" and "Dol." stands for the New Orleans Mint.

purpose of ascertaining its exact fineness, and he will be accountable for the amount of the value of the whole so ascertained—at the same time returning to the owner ½ dwt. of each assay, which he may keep for his own satisfaction or for the purpose of having it assayed elsewhere to find its value, that no deception or fraud may be practiced, and, in case there should be, that he might have the means of detecting the same—for all which he holds himself responsible. The following are his prices: For fluxing 400 dwts. or less, $1; for assaying (by fire ordeal) 1000 dwts. or less, $1; for coining, 2½ per cent. When the gold is to be coined no charge is made for assaying.

He has on hand a handsome assortment of jewelry, watches, etc. Any particular kind of jewelry will be executed to order in the neatest and most skilful manner. . . . [signed] C. Bechtler.

The notice was the first known advertisement of what was obviously an on-going operation.

The Bechtler operation proved something of a tourist attraction, also. G. W. Featherstonhaugh wrote as follows of his visit to the mint on September 20, 1837, in his book *A Canoe Voyage up the Minnay Sotor,* published in London in 1847.

After breakfast I walked a few miles to visit a German of the name of Bechler, who issued a gold coinage of which I had seen several pieces. He received me very civilly, and I passed a great part of the day with him at his cottage in the woods. . . . He had resided seven years in this country, and had established for himself a character for integrity, as well as skill in his profession.

The greater part of the small streams in this part of the gold region have more or less gold in them, so that all the settlers upon the streams were engaged, more or less, in washing for gold. Each of them possessing but a small quantity, and there being no general

During the Depression of the late 1830's the coin shortage was severe, and many companies produced tokens to be used as change. Some of them attacked President Jackson. This coin is typical of the politically oriented tokens.

Another token from these years. This one was unusual in that it was an anti-slavery token. Sentiment concerning slavery was extremely high and some of the token manufacturers expressed their feelings through the use of these coin substitutes.

purchaser, it was an article not easily disposed of without taking the trouble to go great distances. Bechler had also obtained some in the usual manner, and having made a die, coined his gold into five dollar pieces, of the same intrinsic value as the half eagles of the United States, which are worth five dollars each. He also coined pieces of the value of two dollars and a half, and stamped the value, as well as his own name, upon every piece that he coined. These after a while found their way to the mint of the United States, were assayed, and found to be correct. This becoming known, all the gold finders in his vicinity, and indeed from greater distances, began to bring their gold to his mint to be coined. At the period of my visit, his gold coinage circulated more freely than that of the United States, which was very scarce. He told me that his book showed that he had coined about two millions of dollars from the gold found by the settlers, putting his name, with its weight and quality to every piece. On receiving the gold from the country people, which in this part of the gold region is allowed with silver, he first reduced it to a common standard, them made the five dollar pieces equal to those of the United States in value, and when coined delivered it to the respective proprietors, deducting two per cent for the seignorage. It would be in his power to take improper advantage of the confidence placed in him, but I heard no instance of his having attempted this. Some of the gold in this region is alloyed with platina (platinum), the specific gravity of which, compared with that of gold, is as 21 to 19. He might, therefore, have made the difference in weight up with platina, which would have put fourteen per cent. into his pocket. As a metallurgist, he

These are all variations of the coin substitute tokens. These were known as Hard Times tokens and Jackson tokens.

had all the skill necessary to do this, but when I mentioned the possibility of this, he answered that it was what an honest man would not do, and that if any man were to do it, he would soon be found out, for the gold did not remain long in circulation, since it found its way very soon to the United States mint, where it was necessary for him to keep a good character.

Bechler's maxim was that honesty is the best policy; and that maxim appeared to govern his conduct. I never was so pleased with observing transactions of business as those I saw at his house during the time I was there. Several country people came with rough gold to be left for coinage. He weighed it before them and entered it in his book, where there was marginal room for noting the subsequent assay. To others he delivered the coin he had struck. The most perfect confidence prevailed betwixt them, and the transactions were conducted with quite as much simplicity as those at a country grist mill, where the miller deducts the toll for the grist he has manufactured. . . .

The Bechtler honesty was not a family trait. When Christopher died in 1842, his son and then his nephew took over the mint, running it on a more limited scale for at least seven more years. The coins he produced were frequently of poor quality in terms of fineness and weight.

In addition to the five-dollar and two-and-one-half dollar coins mentioned, the Bechtlers also produced the first "gold dollars" in the country's history. (The United States Mint didn't strike gold dollars until 1849). Although seldom mentioned in the writings about Bechtler, the dollars probably were struck as early as 1831.

There is a difference in color among the Bechtler coins. The ones of a bright yellow color were struck from gold found in Georgia and parts of central North Carolina. Gold from the mountain region of North Carolina and most of South Carolina was dark yellow.

The total value of gold coined by the Bechtlers is unknown, though it exceeds $3,600,000. It was so important to the people that it continued circulating long after a branch United States mint was established to service the area. In fact, Bechtler coinage continued circulating at least through the 1870s. During the Civil War it was favored over both Confederate and Union money.

While the Bechtler mint was in full operation, Congress continued to debate the branch mint issue. The expense of transporting gold to Philadelphia was the prime consideration. The congressmen had to be convinced that the quantity of gold received in the port city of New Orleans as well as the gold mined in Georgia and North Carolina was of such a quantity that the cost of transportation to Philadelphia for coinage was far more than the cost involved in setting up branch mints in those areas.

Finally, on March 3, 1835, a law was passed stating:

that branches of the mint of the United States shall be established as follows: one branch at the city of New Orleans for the coinage of gold and silver; one branch at the town of Charlotte, in Mecklenburg county, in the State of North Carolina, for the coinage of gold only; and one branch at or near Dahlohnega, in Lumpkin county, in the State of Georgia, also for the coinage of gold only. And for the purpose of purchasing sites, erecting suitable buildings, and completing the necessary combinations of machinery for the several branches aforesaid, the following sums, to be paid out of any money in the treasury not otherwise appropriated, shall be, and hereby are, appropriated: for the branch at New Orleans, the sum of two hundred thousand dollars; for the branch at Charlotte, fifty thousand dollars; for the branch at Dahlohnega, fifty thousand dollars.

The act in its entirety appears in the Appendix.

Construction of the mint began slowly and the director's report two years later indicated that completion was still a few weeks away. But finally, at the end of March 1838, the newspapers were delighted to announce that coinage of half eagles at the Charlotte mint had begun. The first branch mint was finally in operation.

Before leaving the gold fields of the South, let's take a brief look at the work of one other private coiner, who in fact preceded Bechtler in the area. This was Templeton Reid of Georgia.

Reid, who will be mentioned again in the discussion of San Francisco's branch mint, was a goldsmith and assayer in Lumpkin County, Georgia. His mint was located in Gainesville according to some accounts or in Granville according to others. Little is known of him except that his Mint coined and stamped as much as seven hundred dollars per day by some accounts, giving him a 7% profit of approximately fifteen thousand dollars a year while he was in production. He struck two-and-one-half dollar, five-dollar, and ten-dollar gold pieces.

Reid's mint did cause the legal question to be raised as to whether or not the existence of private mints violated the Constitution. It was decided that they were legal since under the wording of the Constitution only states were expressly forbidden to make coin. No one had anticipated that individuals might take it upon themselves to do so.

Perhaps the most dramatic story of any branch mint is that of the San Francisco facility. The California gold rush resulted in some of the most exciting and unusual stories in the history of the American West. But what few people realize is that it was illness, more than any other factor that made the Calfornia settlement possible.

For many years western expansion had been thwarted by the Indians of California. A few forts had been established, such as Fort Vancouver in the Oregon territory, but the soldiers seldom ventured

Even the houses of prostitution had to find a way for customers to pay and receive change.

very far from the protection of the walls. The traders in the area were few in number. Only large numbers of people moving into the area en masse could possibly survive the attacks of the native Indians. And such a movement was inconceivable because the attractions were simply not great enough.

For many years the Indians were victorious in almost every conflict with the white man. But the whites had brought a new weapon with them into the territory some twenty years before the California gold rush. A weapon more far terrible than the rifles and cannons that protected the forts, it was invisible to the naked eye and so lethal that no man—red, white or black—could hope to defeat it. The weapon was disease.

The disease was first reported in July 1830 in Fort Vancouver, where several of the inhabitants developed an intermittent fever combined with alternating chills and burning sensations. The disease was crippling while it ran its course but was seldom fatal for its victims. The soldiers had quinine which seemed to keep it under control.

The unfortunate victims could hardly have been aware that their illness would prove the key to the opening of the West to settlement by whites. All the damage ever done by guns and sabers seemed as nothing by comparison to the havoc the disease created.

The infection has never been positively identified though it is reasonable to assume that it was malaria brought to the area by sailors. Many have thought it to be smallpox, cholera, typhus or measles, but these assumptions can be disproven.

Cholera is an ailment that spreads quickly only when there is a common water supply. Such a supply did not exist for the Indians living along the San Joaquin and Sacramento Rivers although the illness in these areas reached epidemic proportions. Furthermore, cholera's symptoms were known to the white settlers in the area, and they would have been able to make a positive diagnosis.

If the disease had been typhus or plague, it would have had to be spread by rats or other rodents. Either the rodents would have to have been infected quickly and over large areas of the territory or a massive invasion of infected rodents would have had to occur. In the latter case, the rodents would most likely have moved from the coastal regions eastward while the disease spread first north and then south. This did not occur.

Measles would also have been recognized. It plagued the missions during the first years of the nineteenth century and was readily diagnosed.

For these reasons, and because of the symptoms recorded, it is likely the ailment was malaria. The fact that malaria can be effectively treated with quinine strengthens this belief.

Malaria had long been a scourge of the Hawaiian Islands and it would have been easy for sailors traveling to the California coast to bring the infected mosquitoes with them. Malaria did in fact prove to be a problem in the gold-mining camps. It also reached epidemic proportions among army troops stationed in the Sacramento valley in the 1850s. But by that time it had left its permanent scar on the Indian population of Oregon and California.

The malaria, when it struck the Indian tribes of the West Coast, was unlike anything they had ever encountered. They experienced violent headaches and every bone ached. Many shook uncontrollably, alternating between freezing and burning sensations. They were too weak to take care of themselves and many starved, unable to reach the ample stores of food often not more than a few yards from where they lay.

Dr. John Townsend, one of the most credible eyewitnesses to maintain a diary during that period, wrote,

> The Indians of the Columbia were once a numerous and powerful people; the shore of the river, for scores of miles, was lined with their villages. . . . The spot where once stood the thickly peopled village . . . is now only indicated by a heap of indistinguishable ruins. The depopulation here has been truly fearful [i.e., near Fort Vancouver]. A gentleman told me, that only four years ago [1830], as he wandered near what had formerly been a thickly populated village, he counted no less than sixteen dead, men and women, lying unburied and festering in the sun in front of their habitations. Within the houses all were sick; not one escaped the contagion; upwards of a hundred individuals, men, women, and children, were writhing in agony on the floors of the houses, with no one to render them any assistance. Some were in the dying struggle, and clenching with the convulsive grasp of death their disease worn companions, shrieked and howled in the last sharp agony.
>
> Probably there does not now exist one, where five years ago, there were a hundred Indians.

Witnesses traveling the area below the falls of the Columbia River noted that the Indian population had been almost totally destroyed within four years. The shores of the river were littered with the rotting corpses of unburied dead. Entire villages were without a surviving member. In some communities a few managed to avoid the disease, but these fled to new areas, fearful to the lurking danger in their old homes.

The Multnomah Indians who lived on Wappatoo Island, situated where the Columbia and Multnomah rivers joined, vanished completely. The Indians of Deer Island, thirty-three miles below Fort Vancouver, also disappeared. One witness who visited Wappatoo wrote: ". . . a mortality has carried off to a man its inhabitants and there is nothing to attest that they ever existed except their decaying houses, their graves and their unburied bones, of which they are heaps."

The Cascades region, north of Mount Hood, was apparently the easternmost area affected by the epidemic. A few survivors were found in the villages, but since many homes had been stripped of possessions, other survivors may have fled. In some villages, witnesses found the dead half buried, this indicates that there probably had been survivors who had fled.

At the height of the epidemic, one-fourth of all the Indians in the area were dying yearly. The illness moved swiftly through whole tribes and there were many stories similar to the one told of the Klackatacks who lived near Fort Vancouver. In 1827, Cassanove, chief of the Klackatacks, could raise 400–500 warriors. But when the illness struck, it took only three weeks to kill every member of the tribe.

The disease spread more slowly into California. It was not until 1833 that the devastation so common further north was noticed in southern areas. John Work, who led a party of men from Oregon down the Sacramento to the lower Feather River, reported seeing large native populations in villages he passed from August 1832, to January, 1833. However, after spending some time along the lower San Joaquin, he noted: "Some sickness prevails among the Indians on the feather river. The villages which were so populous and swarming with inhabitants when we passed that way in Jany or Febry [sic] last now seem almost deserted & have a desolate appearance. The few wretched Indians who remain . . . are lying apparently scarecely able to move. It is not starvation as they have considerable quantities of their winter stock of acorns still remaining. . . ."

In larger villages the disease spread so quickly that all attempts to cope were fruitless. Witnesses report that the healthy inhabitants would first bury the dead. Then, as the number of dead increased, the bodies were piled on top of each other for burning. The ashes were deposited in tombs near the village. Finally, when few survivors remained, all attempts to dispose of the dead were abandoned. Many went to the surrounding woods to sit under the trees, either alone or

Additional tokens.

with their families, to await the illness and death that had taken the lives of their fellows.

The reason for the severity of the malaria epidemic among the Indians was probably their lack of medical knowledge concerning the ailment. They had never encountered it and did not use quinine. The quinine available in the area had been brought by settlers, trappers and soldiers who kept it for themselves.

By the time the epidemic finally abated, at least twenty thousand Indians had died (and this is a conservative estimate). Witnesses stated that no less than three out of every four had perished. Indian strength on the West Coast had dwindled to the point where only token opposition to white takeover of the land could be offered. The country was ripe for settlement and the unfolding of the events led to the founding of the San Francisco branch mint.

The California gold rush began on the land of John Sutter, who never ceased to curse the luck the gold brought him. Sutter was a man who had always teetered on the brink of success. His family was Swiss, but he was born in Germany. He undertook a number of business enterprises in that country. He had grandiose schemes but no luck in carrying them out. Suffering bankruptcy, he fled his creditors by coming across the Atlantic when he was thirty-two. In 1834, he went to the Hawaiian Islands, where he lingered for five years. He tried a new business, failed, and removed to California after the malaria epidemic had eliminated Indian opposition to settlement.

Sutter never had any trouble obtaining financing or assistance for his various projects. He managed to persuade Juan Bautista Alvarado, the Mexican Governor of California, to grant him the use of fifty thousand acres of land for agricultural developing. The land was in the valley east of San Francisco.

Sutter's land made him feel affluent and he decided a man in his position should be called by a special title. "Captain" Sutter seemed to sit well, so he invented a personal history that included service in the Swiss Guard of Charles X of France. It was during this supposed military duty that he claimed to have received the title "captain" by which he was known when he built his fort. He underscored his pomposity, calling the land "New Helvetia." Most others called it "Sutter's Fort."

Captain Sutter developed various enterprises on his land, all of which flourished. He had extensive land under cultivation, and ran 10,000 sheep, 12,000 head of cattle, 1,000 hogs and 2,000 horses and

In many communities the coin shortages continued even after a private Mint had been established. During one such period in San Francisco this token was issued.

mules according to various accounts. He had his own saw mill to provide wood for his numerous projects and he employed many white, Indian, and Mexican workers. He was on his way to becoming the biggest and most prosperous rancher and farmer in that part of the country.

Although he did not know it at the time, Sutter's plans were shattered on January 24, 1848. It was Monday, and James Marshall, a partner he had gained the year before, was making an inspection of the saw mill. Here is his account: "I went down as usual and after shutting off the water from the race I stepped into it, near the lower end, and there upon the rock about six inches beneath the water I discovered the gold. I picked up one or two pieces and examined them attentively. I then tried it between two rocks and found that it could be beaten into a different shape but not broken."

Marshall was immediately convinced that he had found gold. He ran what tests he could on the spot, then took the material to Sutter's Fort, where there were equipment and chemicals for more extensive testing. The tests showed conclusively that the metal was gold.

Sutter realized the end was near for him. Had he discovered the gold himself he might have kept it a secret. But Marshall had told several of the other workmen and gradually everyone in the immediate area came to know of the find.

The reason for Sutter's pessimism was because the gold would make him poor, not rich. He was on his way to making a fortune with his ranch, farm, and other enterprises. But the land he was using did not technically belong to him. He had no claim to any mineral wealth that lay below the surface. It might belong to Mexico or it might belong to the victor of the Mexican War, the outcome of which was unknown to him at that time. Whatever the case, it would probably be public domain and that would mean gold seekers would soon swarm over the area.

Sutter had to face failure once again. He talked with the Indian workers and arranged to lease his land to them. He took what money and possessions he could and left.

The story of the gold discovery was released to the world by Henry Bigler, a Mormon who worked at the mill. Bigler began gold hunting almost from the day the first bits of metal were found and his letters shared the discovery with his Mormon friends in other areas.

On March 15, 1848, the California gold rush might be said to have begun. The San Francisco Californian had a one paragraph item: "Gold Mine Find. In the newly made raceway of the saw-mill recently erected by Captain Sutter, on the American fork, gold has been found in considerable quantities. One person brought thirty dollars-worth to New Helvetia, gathered there in a short time. California, no doubt, is rich."

The face of California changed radically in the next few months. In some areas as many as 460 wagon loads of men and supplies passed through settlements each day, all of them headed for California. More than twenty-two thousand men passed over one route in 1849. Nine thousand came by way of Sante Fe that same year; ten thousand left St. Joseph, Missouri; and thousands more came by every possible land and water route. Soldiers at nearby forts deserted, for the men earned $1 a day as soldiers and $30 a day panning gold when they were lucky.

Some became rich. Others lost everything or found barely enough to keep alive. Many became discouraged and either left the gold fields or went into business selling whiskey, food, and other items to luckier miners.

Goods of all types were in great demand, and it was impossible adequately to supply the newly arrived miners. As a result, everything skyrocketed in value. Men who brought needed equipment and materials with them to California, resold the equipment at enormous profit. One merchant paid top price for 1,500 dozen eggs that were on a schooner docked in the harbor and sold them at thirty-seven and one-half cents a dozen, realizing a handsome profit. To the merchant's astonishment, the man who purchased them from him sold them at four dollars per dozen. The merchant immediately paid the same price for the schooner's remaining 1,499 dozen eggs, took them to Sacramento, and resold them for the incredible price of six dollars per dozen.

Bayard Taylor visited San Francisco in 1849. In his book *Eldorado,* he comments on the rampant inflation: "Money bought fourteen per cent monthly, on loan. A gentleman of Baltimore who came out in the Panama, sold for $15,000 a steam engine which cost him $2,000. Some drawing paper which cost about $10 in New York brought $164. . . . Town lots were continually on the rise; fifty-vara lots in the Happy Valley half a mile from town brought $3,500. I met with a number of my fellow passengers, nearly all of whom had done well, some of them having already realized $20,000 and $30,000."

The restaurant prices reflected the affluence of the time. This was a period when an income of a dollar a day was fairly common throughout much of the United States. Yet in San Francisco, Delmonico's menu offered:

Soups

Mock Turtle	$0.75
St. Julien	1.00

Fish

Boiled Salmon, Trout, Anchovy Sauce	1.75

BOILED

Leg Mutton, caper sauce	1.00
Corned Beef, Cabbage	1.00
Ham and Tongues	0.75

ENTREES

Fillet of Beef, mushroom sauce	1.75
Veal Cutlets, breaded	1.00
Mutton Chop	1.00
Lobster Salad	2.00
Sirloin of Venison	1.50
Baked Maccaroni	0.75
Beef Tongue, sauce piquante	1.00

A typical dinner at the restaurant could easily cost five dollars, or about what most people were earning in a week outside the gold fields. Yet the restaurant flourished in San Francisco.

An interesting aspect of the San Francisco gold rush is its effect on the financial language of our times. The terms "bull" and "bear" used to describe market conditions on Wall Street had their origin at this time. A bull market is the sign of rising prices and a healthy economy. A bear market means the economy is on a downward trend. These terms originated in a pastime that delighted many of the San Francisco miners.

The "sport" the miners enjoyed involved placing a bear in the middle of an arena, his leg tethered by a long chain. The chain allowed the animal considerable movement but kept it from escaping the arena. The bear, a giant grizzly, weighed approximately 1,400 pounds and was extremely dangerous.

Once the bear was securely chained, a large bull, its movements also limited by a chain, was released into the arena. The bull would charge the bear, goring it and knocking it down. The bear fought by grasping the bull around the neck, tossing it upward and biting viciously with its strong jaws. The winner was the animal who managed to stay alive. However, because the bear went *down* when attacked and the bull was tossed *upward,* the terms came into our language with similar meanings for finance. "Bear" markets go down. "Bull" markets go up.

The gold miners suffered numerous abuses and difficulties because of the lack of adequate coinage. They often had to sell their gold for well below the roughly sixteen dollars an ounce that it was worth. Anyone with goods to sell knew he could ask whatever he wanted for them, accepting gold for several dollars less than the Eastern price, then shipping it to Philadelphia when a sizeable quantity had been obtained.

One alternative was to pay for goods by the "pinch" of gold dust. A bartender, for example, would sell whiskey in exchange for gold dust. After serving the drink, the bartender would reach into the bag of gold dust carried by his customer. He took as much gold as he could "pinch" or hold between his thumb and first finger. In order to get the most gold for their liquor, bartenders usually let their fingernails grow long, then kept their fingers wet and a little sticky. The excess gold gathered under the nail was carefully scraped into a container

These are all additional tokens used in different parts of the country. Most were advertising vehicles.

before taking the next pinch. It was always the merchant, not the customer who did the pinching.

The lack of coinage was felt more keenly in San Francisco than in other gold-rush towns because it was a port city. Merchandise entering and leaving the port on a regular basis, required payment of customs duties. At first California's Governor R. B. Mason ordered the customs collector to accept gold dust in payment, rating the dust at sixteen dollars an ounce, which was two dollars an ounce less than the highest Eastern price being paid but still a reasonable amount. However, the Governor soon learned that United States law required the duty to be paid in gold and silver coinage only. He had to deny the payments of those who could only bring gold dust even though it was of intrinsically high value.

The governor did make an attempt to ease the situation slightly by agreeing to let merchants deposit gold dust at the customs house as a pledge that they would pay the duty when they got the coin. The gold was accepted based on an arbitrary value of ten dollars an ounce. Thus ten ounces of gold, worth as much as one hundred-eighty dollars at the Philadelphia mint, would have to be deposited in pledge for a one hundred dollar duty. The merchant would then have sixty days in which to come up with the coin. If he couldn't get coin to redeem his pledge, the gold dust would be sold to the highest bidder having coin to pay for it. In some cases the dust was sold for as little as six dollars an ounce to a shrewd operator with the means and time to send it to the East, where extremely high profits would be made.

By July 1848, the merchants of San Francisco had come to realize the seriousness of their situation. They met to see what might be done to alleviate their problems. One suggestion was that the time allowed for the merchant to raise coins to pay customs bills be increased from two to six months. However, the governor's only concession was to let the merchants have ninety days to redeem half of their pledge and an additional six months to redeem the remainder.

Merchants who imported goods quickly learned to hoard every coin they could find in anticipation of current or future customs payments. No coins were given out in change which made doing business extremely difficult.

The international money coming in through the port of San Francisco made doing business chaotic. Coins arrived from all over the world, and no one was certain about the true value of any of them. Eventually many of the coins came to be accepted by size—which was not, of course, an accurate measure of value. For example, French francs, Spanish pesetas, and similar coins were silver pieces intrinsically valued at less than twenty cents each. But since they were the size of the American quarter, they passed at twenty-five cents.

The only solution to the problem seemed to be the creation of a state assay office which could form the gold into ingots accurately stamped with value and fineness. But when the merchants tried to get such an assay office opened, they were rebuffed. They finally decided to seek private coiners like those who had eased coin shortages in other areas.

One of the first private assayers to operate in San Francisco was the firm of Moffat & Co. John Moffat had come to San Francisco from New York early in 1849. He went into business with three other men, and on September 6, 1849, placed an advertisement in the newspaper *Alta California* to announce he would be smelting and assaying gold dust.

Moffat & Co. did not at first produce coins, but rather rectangular ingots of gold of varying values. The intrinsic worth stamped on the rectangles ranged from $9.43 to $264.00.

Moffatt & Co. might have continued making ingots for several years had it not been for the arrival of Albert Küner on July 16, 1849. He was an immigrant adept in the art of cameo-cutting, a skill that could easily be applied to coin engraving. He took a job with Moffat & Co. where he prepared the dies for a ten-dollar coin.

The ten-dollar gold piece designed by Küner was an obvious imitation of the United States ten-dollar gold coin. It was not a counterfeit, though, because the name Moffat & Co. replaced the word "Liberty" on the obverse and the words "S.M.V. California Gold" replaced "United States of America." The initials "S.M.V." stood for Standard Mint Value. This was meant to show that the coins, while not government issues, were intrisically every bit as valuable as genuine coins.

The Moffat & Co. claim that their ten-dollar gold pieces were the equal of United States Mint coinage was an apparent exaggeration. Samples that reached Philadelphia were tested and found to be overvalued by slightly more than two cents per coin. It was a minor difference, though, and the people of San Francisco were delighted to at last have coins even if they were less than perfect. Later it was learned that some of the coins were as much as twelve cents short in value, yet the people still did not complain. They seemed to feel this was a problem of the limited coining facilities available to Moffat & Co. rather than a deliberate attempt by the company to cheat the public.

Two other types of private gold coinage made their appearance in 1849, though they were seen only briefly. Templeton Reid, who had minted in Georgia in the 1830s, produced ten-dollar and twenty-five dollar gold pieces clearly marked "California Gold" during that year. The coins are quite rare and little is known about his having moved to that state. There exists the suspicion that Reid never actually made the trip to California. He may have worked with only a small quantity of gold that he had sent to him from California. The coins are so rare that this is quite possible.

Probably the first privately minted coins seen in California were those of Norris, Greig & Norris. They were the subject of a newspaper

Every year the United States Mint is likely to experiment with coin designs and medals that are different from those currently in circulation. Often a number of different designs will be made into coins for study and possible use. When they are not adopted, they may be destroyed or privately sold (as did frequently occur in the nineteenth Century), or placed in the Smithsonian Institute, which has what amounts to the national coin collection. These pieces are known as "patterns" and are avidly collected by people familiar with them. Patterns have been made repeatedly throughout the years but only those made before 1916 can be legally owned. The Lincoln cents made in plastic, aluminum, glass and other materials fits into this catagory. Many coins are designed that are never adopted.

The standard guide to patterns is one that was originally created by J. Hewitt Judd, M.D. It is called *United States Pattern, Experimental and Trial Pieces.* It is periodically updated and published by Western Publishing Company, Inc., Racine, Wisconsin. A number has been assigned to each pattern recorded in the book and these numbers are utilized by collectors to describe a coin. For convenience, I am including the Judd book number for each item illustrated. The coin shown here is J-2. It was a copper cent considered in 1792. A much larger coin than this was eventually adopted for use. The details on this coin are barely visible due to extensive wear. However, because this is one of only five in existence, it is considered extremely valuable.

account of May 31, 1849. The coins were all five-dollar gold pieces and very few were struck. Only Moffat & Co. produced coin in sufficient quantity to make a difference in the miners' business transactions.

Several other coins appeared during the months following the start of the gold rush but they were frequently discredited. Among them were Utah issues of the Mormons which were probably the worse coins to be offered in terms of intrinsic worth. A twenty-dollar gold piece made from "Great Salt Lake City Pure Gold" had been so mixed with other metals that the real value was approximately seventeen dollars. A coin could be a few cents off and still be accepted. But a three-dollar difference was obviously deliberate debasement and the coins were rejected by everyone.

The problem of private coin abuses was taken up by the California legislature during the winter of 1849. A bill was proposed to stop the

The size and weight of the Large Cents made them extremely unpopular. The government began experimenting with a smaller coin and created this cent in 1853. It was never released into circulation. (J-149.)

manufacture of private coins because of the problems their debasement was causing. The bill stated that among other abuses many of the private coiners would not exchange their product for United States coins of supposedly equal value. It was therefore assumed that the private coins were counterfeits for all practical purpose and that the coiners must cease their actions.

Newspaper commentary regarding the bill was quite hostile towards the private coin makers. The issue of January 26, 1850, of the *Alta California* editorialized:

> It is well known that a great variety of pieces, presumed to be gold, have been issued in San Francisco and the river towns, of various denominations or value, from $5 to $10, or stated to be of that value, and thrown into active circulation. When they were first coined no serious objection was entertained against them, but they were rather regarded as a matter of convenience, the amount of current coin in the country being extremely limited, while 'dust' was abundant. It was also given out by the parties issuing these pieces that they would be redeemed, upon presentation, with current coin of the United States at par. Subsequently it was announced that they would be redeemed with dust only. They were regarded at the Custom House as an illegal tender, and were refused in payment of duties, and at the Post-office were not received in payment of postage. Many mercantile firms have denied them, and none of the brokers would take them at their par value. This state of things exists at the present time. They are looked upon with suspicion and distrust. Issued by individuals or self-constituted banking institutions, the public have no evidence, other than the asseveration which they bear upon their face, of their value or of their purity. That they are perfectly illegal is clearly manifest, if not absolutely counterfeit coins. It has been

This is another cent experiment. This time the coin was made with the Christian Gobrecht design. The pattern was produced in 1854 and is J-156.

contended by many persons that according to the strict construction of the law they are absolutely counterfeits of the United States coins, as it is not necessary that theyshould be of the exact similitude of the legalized coin of the United States Mint. They purport to be of the same value and weight, and are of the same size and general appearance as the standard coin. We coincide with this view of the matter, and are decidedly of the opinion that they come wit in the full meaning of the law. That the 'tokens' that have been issued are of the value they profess to be we do not mean to question. We believe them to be so, but we cannot countenance a system which, if suffered to exist any longer, will be the cause of defrauding the community to the greatest extent.

Representatives of Moffatt & Co. were irate both over the proposed law and the newspaper editorial. A reply was sent to the paper. The argument presented was sound, though the company officials carefully omitted mention of the fact that their five- and ten-dollar gold pieces were very closely patterned after those of the United States government and thus might be classed as counterfeits. The company's rejoinder to the editorial was the following:

Private mints have been in operation for many years in the United States, and have been the subject of consideration and complaint by the Director of the Government Mint in his reports to Congress. The establishments for this purpose have been that of Templeton Reid of Georgia, now discontinued, and that of Christopher Bechtler in North Carolina, still in operation. This mint is located at Rutherfordton, N. C., and is of considerable importance. Its operations were commenced in 1831, and are still carried on, although there is a Branch Mint of the United States less than eighty miles distant. Mr. Bechtler has stated the amount of his coinage to February, 1840 (nine years), at $2,241,890.

An assay of the coinage of Mr. Bechtler by the Mint of the United States developed the fact that his $5 pieces on the average were worth but $4.84, and this practice is still going on in the United States, not only where the necessity does not exist for want of a circulating medium, but directly at the portals of the Mint of the United States; and nothing is done to prevent it by the public authorities because no law forbidding it exists. The Director of the Mint, in his Report to Congress for the year 1840, after a brief statement in relation to Mr. Bechtler's coinage, observed: "It seems strange that the privilege of coinage should be carefully confined by law to the General Government, while that of coining gold and silver, though withheld from the States, is freely permitted to individuals, with the single restriction that they must not imitate the coinage established by law." We cannot but believe that had there existed any law against the coining operations of Mr. Bechtler or other individuals, the Director of the Mint, and those upon whom it developed to see that so important an interest of the United States should be protected, would have enforced it. But we do not place ourselves in the category designated in the Resolutions referred to. We aver that we have violated no law of the United States in regard to coining money; that we have defrauded no man of one cent by the issuing of our coin; that we have in no instance refused or failed to redeem in current coin of the United States all of such issues without detention or delay, and we hold ourselves ready now and at all times hereafter to do so. We have too high an opinion of the wisdom and good sense of the Legislature of this State to believe that they will pass any Act in pursuance of the Resolutions referred to, as the subject belongs only to Congress,

Another cent pattern of 1854. (J-160.)

> and is not usurped or interfered with by any of the State authorities. In regard to the value of our coin, we assert, and submit it to the test of any assaying establishment, that each piece is worth more than it purports to be, and will pay a handsome profit to any one who will take them to the Government in bullion.

On April 20, 1850, a new law finally settled the private mint problem in California once and for all. Rather than attempting to regulate the private mints, the legislature sought to eliminate the need for them by creating a "state assayer." The state assayer, according to the law, would among other duties ". . . carefully refine and assay any and all gold-dust or bullion placed in his hands by the Director for that purpose, and to cause the same to be made into ingots or bars, in the form of an oblong square, and of such weight as shall be desired by the depositor. Provided, that no such ingots or bars shall be made or issued of less weight than two ounces."

A further section of the law added:

> The State Assayer shall regularly number and stamp upon the ingots or bars thus made the true value in dollars and cents, and the correct weight and carat fineness thereof, in accordance with the United States Mint standard; also the letters "CAL.", the date, and his own initials in plain letters over the words "State Assayer," and upon each end and side of any ingot and bar so issued, some uniform stamp or impression, and shall as soon as thus prepared, place it in the hands of the Director, taking his receipt in a book kept by the Assayer for that purpose, and the Director shall hand it over to the depositor, if demanded, within four days after the deposit of the dust, unless the time shall be prolonged by the depositor by a written agreement, when the weight given shall be returned to the Director, who shall cancel and keep the same.

Frederick D. Kohler was appointed state assayer. Kohler had been assaying gold privately but abandoned that business, selling his equipment to Baldwin & Co.

It is interesting to note that while the official "coins" issued by the state assayer were a boon to business, not all businessmen were happy with the situation. When the public had to pay in gold dust, unscrupulous merchants could accept it at well below true value, then send it on to Philadelphia for an extremely high profit. The official ingots that circulated were not items on which anyone could make a profit and so they hurt some people's incomes. As a result, a number of unethical businessmen got together and agreed to refuse to accept the ingots at stampted value, knowing full well that the marked worth was accurate.

The *Sacramento Daily Transcript* was one of the strongest critics of the unethical businessmen and fought to help the public. An article of July 15, 1850, said:

When a cent was finally decided upon, various models were made with different designs. This pattern was produced in 1855 utilizing an Eagle that would eventually be found, with slight modifications, on regular issue coins of 1856 through 1868. (Judd J-167.)

Various reverses were tried for the 1856 coin. This reverse pattern is J-180.

Another reverse pattern from 1856. (J-184.)

But the bankers and others in San Francisco interested in keeping gold below its real worth to further their own ends, were not to be so easily checked in their lucrative operation. Previous to the appointment of the Assayer they called a public meeting, formed an association, and by combined efforts succeeded in defeating the good end which the law aimed to secure. Strange to say, that up to this time the people—merchants, miners, mechanics, and laborers—have permitted this combination to hold the sway, decrying the value of the ingots, refuse to receive them at their par value, and thus prevent their general circulation and the good results which would necessarily have followed. . . .

First, then, the miner parts with his gold at $16 the ounce. If he has fifty ounces it nets him in gold coin $800; but suppose ingots are circulated at their par value, as they should be, the miner then takes his fifty ounces to the Assayer's, where he pays for assaying it, say, $1 per ounce, and it yields him in ingots, after the expense is paid, say $1, $17 per ounce. Fifty ounces at $17—$850—Making a difference of over 6 per cent. in his favor.

But a still greater saving might be effected on quicksilver gold than 6 or even 8 per cent. Quicksilver gold brings only $14 per ounce. Does the miner and do the people generally know that this gold is worth more intrinsically than any other? If they do not, the Assayer will tell them so. The particles of gold taken up by the quicksilver are doubly refined and pure, and those who ship it to the States make the enormous profit of from $4 to $5 on every ounce shipped, all of which comes out of the pocket of the miner and laborer. The question may now be asked, what is the true value of the ingot, and it will probably surprise some of our readers to be informed that these ingots which are refused by this combination are worth more than American gold coin and yet such is the case; every ingot stamped $37 will realize $40 in gold coin at the United States Mint. . . . Shall the whole community suffer in order that those who are engaged in this gold shipping business may be aggrandized? We say emphatically No! Let us receive the ingots.

In September 1850, California came a step closer to having a branch Mint. Moffatt & Co., the most respected private mint despite the newspaper criticisms, was granted a contract by the United States Secretary of the Treasury to assay gold brought to it. The company was to stamp the gold with its value and affix the stamp of the United States on each ingot it made, along with the fineness and value. Augustus Humbert, formerly a maker of watch cases in New York, was given the position of United States Assayer with Moffat & Co. Thus, the company was producing official gold pieces even though they were not actually United States coins.

The establishment of the official United States Assay Office proved a mixed blessing. The Moffat & Co. issues were suddenly acceptable at the customs house since they were authorized by the federal government, and thus no longer simply the product of an independent business. But none of the other coins in circulation produced by private minters were acceptable to the merchants any longer. The various small-denomination gold pieces made by the Mormons and others were rejected or accepted at a high discount from intrinsic worth. Once again there was a serious coin shortage because the once spendable substitutes were no longer taken.

Moffat & Co. could have begun making small-denomination gold coins to ease the problem, but the federal government did not permit this. Instead they concentrated on the large coins needed for major business transactions. The result was a $50 gold piece—a massive chunk of gold which appeared towards the end of January 1851. The coin was discussed in the February 21, 1851, edition of San Francisco's newspaper, The *Daily Alta California.* The editorial stated:

> The new fifty-dollar gold piece, manufactured under the Act of Congress appointing a United States Assay Office in California, and made under the supervision of the United States Assayer, was issued by Moffat & Co. yesterday. About three hundred of these pieces have already been struck off. The larger ones, of one and two hundred dollars, will be of the same stamp and size, differing only in thickness. Those over $200 will contain the same stamp, but will be struck in the form of bars. These coins are of course a legal tender, and are the coins of the United States Government to all intents and purposes. The coin is peculiar, contining only one face, an eagle in the centre, around which are the words "United States of America." Just over the eagle is stamped "887 Thous." signifying the fineness of the gold. At the bottom is stamped "50 Dolls." The other face is ornamented with a kind of work technically called engine-turning, being a number of radii extending from the common centre, in which is stamped in small figures, "50." Around the edge is stamped the name of the United States Assayer. We trust our readers may learn the character of this new coin by ocular demonstration.

The public was both delighted with the new fifty-dollar gold pieces and a little wary of them. It was only when T. Butler King, collector of the port, announced that the fifty-dollar gold pieces would be acceptable payment for customs duties that the public relaxed.

The fact that the ingots produced by Moffat & Co. were acceptable as customs duty payments did not mean they were legal tender coins. But the value placed in them was shown by an April 7, 1851, article in the *Pacific News.*

> It will be gratifying to the business community to learn that the bankers have agreed to receive on deposit the fifty-dollar ingots stamped by the United States Assayer. They have come to this determination simultaneously with the resolve not to receive any of the coins issued except those of Moffat's. The reason assigned for

> this is that Moffat does not now issue any more of these coins, and redeems with silver all those in circulation whenever presented, while some of the others redeem theirs. The bankers therefore will only treat these coins on the same footing as gold dust—that is, purchase them at $17 per ounce.
>
> While this resolution will cause severe inconveniences and loss to holders, the former will be an immense public benefit. The fifty-dollar pieces, though not handsome in appearance, are very useful, and can now be used in general business operations, while the United States are pledged always to receive them for their face value.

Moffat & Co. was limited in the denominations it could produce for use in California once it became a federal government assay office. The firm sent a letter to Secretary of the Treasury Thomas Corwin on April 14, 1851, discussing the effect their fifty-dollar gold ingots had had on the local economy and the fact that new coins were needed.

> . . . Those private mints (four in number) encouraged, if not established by bankers, had for some time been flooding the country with their coins. All this coin was manufactured from the gold of the country without any process of refining; and although of full United States standard weight, yet under mint value because the average fineness of California gold is much below the mint standard. Careful assays of the coin had been made by the United States Assayer, and the fact demonstrated that it was on the average some 3 per cent. below its purported value. A correspondence between the United States Assayer and one of our bankers, showing the result, was published. The effect was instantaneous and overwhelming; the private mints were at once compelled to

In 1858 yet another reverse was tried for the one cent piece. (J-191.)

suspend operations, and their issues amounting, we have reason to believe, to a million and a half, have since been purchased at a discount of from 5 to 10 per cent., and it is not at all likely that another private coin will ever be struck in California. In the meantime the issues of the Assay Office were popular with the merchants and the people generally. They had the impress of authority, bore the United States stamp, were considered to all intents and purposes a United States coin, and bankers began to find that to discredit it was beyond their power. They have, therefore, made a virtue of necessity, and from enemies have become its friends. They not only now receive it and pay it out as they do other coins of the United States, but they have become the largest depositors of dust at the Assay Office. It will be seen from the report that all the issues of the Assay Office have been of the denomination of $50; such too has been the case in the present time. This is owing to the absence of a sufficient supply of legal currency; they are not shipped but go into circulation here, and the chief complaint against the office has been that it has not been authorized to make its issues of still less denominations. The necessity for such authority is augmented by the sudden withdrawl from circulation of so large an amount of private coin. . . .

The government would not go along with Moffat & Co.'s desire to coin small-denomination gold pieces. The *Daily Alta California* of July 25, 1851, lamented the fact, saying:

More large fish are to be produced and sent forth through our channels of trade to put the small fry to flight in all directions. The machinery at the slug mill of Moffat & Co. has at last been repaired, and re-commenced operations yesterday. The monstrous fifty-dollar chunks are becoming a decided nuisance, unless

An 1858 experimentation with the Flying Eagle obverse for the cent. (J-193.)

privately taken in large quantities. It is fast becoming one of the greatest favors you can ask of a storekeeper to accomodate you by changing one of them, such is their sluggishness in the market. We hear, in fact, of various instances where various individuals have purchased a pair of gloves or some other small article for which they have no earthly use, merely for the purpose of getting one of these pieces changed. No longer ago than on the occasion of the departure of the last steamer one of them was changed at our counter for a person who was excessively anxious to make a cash purchase of a steamer paper. Price of paper $0.25.

Local pressure began to mount for a real branch mint to serve San Francisco and the gold fields of the West Coast. Newspapers began detailing the problems everyone was encountering. On October 21, 1851, the *San Francisco Picayune* editorialized,

Of silver coin also the supply is too small to meet the wants of the community. This, to be sure, partially arises from the fact that the gold is being absorbed or shipped away, as we have just stated. But even though there were the same amount of silver coin in the State now that there was a year since, it would not be found sufficient to supply the vacuum in the convenient currency created by the withdrawal of the smaller gold coin. The great bulk of our silver currency has been composed of Mexican and Peruvian silver dollars, with a considerable sprinkling of five-franc pieces. For smaller trade we have had a most varied assortment of fractional silver, comprising representations of the currency of well nigh every nation in the world. Mexican dollars have always stood first in favor, because of their well known purity of standard, their convenience for all, and their necessity for some of our Pacific trade. Therefore we find that this coin has for a long time

Another obverse variation from 1858. (J-202.)

commanded 2 per cent. premium for the China and East India trade. The supply at the same time has continued to diminish. Like the doubloon, they can now be more profitably invested elsewhere. Instead of being shipped here for the purchase of gold-dust they are sent direct to the Atlantic States and Europe, where there exists a pressing demand, and they at present command high rates of premium.

This monthly inconvenience, now in fact almost amounting to a currency crisis, will not probably continue much longer. Only the prospect of speedy relief, and the fact of the recent increase in the value of gold-dust has hindered the re-commencement of private coinage, not-withstanding the existence of the statute prohibiting the same, and the knowledge of the evils certain in the end of result from it.

But we entertain no doubt that a relief of a satisfactory and durable nature will soon be afforded. Several months since, we believe, a request was forwarded to the Treasury Department by the United States Assay Office in this city asking for authority to issue gold coins of all the Federal denominations. It is probable that such power will be granted him, and that so far as gold currency is concerned a full supply of the desired denominations will be introduced. With another year we anticipate seeing a regularly organized United States Mint in operation here, receiving our twin staples, gold and silver, and issuing coin sufficient not only to supply our own State, but to rule the currency and trade of the Pacific.

By the end of 1851, Moffat & Co. was desperately attempting to get permission to produce gold pieces in denominations smaller than fifty dollars. There was very little need for the larger coin and the shortage of small coins was at a crisis point. A new private mint, Wass, Molitor & Co., began producing five-, ten- and twenty-dollar gold pieces. The coins were similar to official United States coinage, a design approach common to other private San Francisco mints like Dubosq & Co. and Baldwin & Co., which produced small amounts of coinage around 1850. Wass, Molitor & Co. also produced a small number of fifty-dollar gold pieces in 1855.

In January 1852, the leading merchants of San Francisco petitioned Moffat & Co. to begin making small denomination coins. Although it was technically illegal for the firm to do so, the directors agreed to begin producing ten- and twenty-dollar gold pieces to satisfy the desperate need for small change. Fortunately the problem ended in mid-February of 1852, when the company finally received government authorization to produce the smaller coins.

The new coins were greeted with relief, though by then the public was convinced that the true answer to the coin shortage was the establishment of a branch mint. However, the problem was no sooner eased than Moffat & Co. was dissolved (February 16, 1852) and a new firm, Curtis, Perry & Ward, took over the "Contract for Smelting and

Assaying Gold in California." The company was authorized at the start to produce coins of ten-dollar, twenty-dollar and fifty-dollar denominations as well as gold bars worth five hundred and one thousand dollars. But a setback occurred on September 4 of that year when Assistant Treasury Secretary William Hodge said that the custom house could no longer accept any funds other than official United States Mint issues and certain foreign coins.

On July 3, 1852, Congress finally got around to admitting that the West Coast needed a branch mint to meet the coinage needs of the people. Then on March 3, 1853, a serious effort was made to obtain proposals for the erection of a mint building. It was finally decided that the area on Commercial Street near Montgomery Street in San Francisco, the location of the old United States Assay Office, should be the spot for building the new mint. Curtis, Perry & Ward obtained the contract and constructed the three story building. It was finally finished in the spring of 1854 and was open for business on April 3 of that year.

Because of the plans for the new mint, Curtis, Perry & Ward ceased operating the assay office on December 14, 1853. That meant there were several months in which the coin shortage was even more severe than usual.

In February 1854, the firm of Kellogg & Richter was formed by two men who had formerly been connected with the assay office. The men began striking twenty-dollar gold pieces to counteract the shortage that the mint would be several years in easing. According to an item in the February 16, 1854, edition of the *Alta California,* "Messrs. Kellogg & Richter have established a private coining house on Montgomery Street, in the basement of the building adjoining Adams & Co.'s old banking house. They issued their first coin on the 9th. It is like United

The Indian cent obverse was also tried in 1858 and later adopted in 1859. (J-208.)

States coin, except that in place of LIBERTY on the head are the words KELLOGG & CO. They expect to be able to issue $20,000 per day."

The San Francisco mint began operations slowly. Supplies were limited and numerous delays kept the number of coins struck to a minimum. As a result, the private mint issues remained in use, despite the general hostility towards them. Groups of merchants hotly debated whether private issues should be accepted in change, their main concern being the intrinsic worth of the coins. When the mint lacked the chemicals needed to refine the gold to government standards, coinage was suspended while the supplies were obtained. When the private mints couldn't produce the quality coins they wished to issue, they simply released debased coins. It was only in 1856 that the San Francisco mint's coin production became large enough and regular enough to assure an adequate supply of hard money for the community at large. Three years after opening, the mint was at last meeting the needs of the West Coast.

The gold rush came to Denver, Colorado, rather as a slow trickle than a mighty stampede. Among the first people to find gold was a Delaware Indian named Fall Leaf who brought flakes of gold from the Rocky Mountains in the fall of 1857. Then, in the summer of 1858, more than one hundred men began looking for gold in earnest, starting at the mouth of Cherry Creek, near Denver. They found only small amounts. Two weeks later, James Pierce took a hundred dollars worth of gold from the South Platte River.

The discoveries came with enough frequency that news of the strikes spread far and wide. The fact that little gold had been found meant nothing to the hundreds of eager men who sold all their worldly possessions to outfit themselves for a gold prospecting trip to Colorado. They all felt Colorado would have the next big bonanza, and they each felt certain of striking a rich lode of ore.

During this period two brothers, transplanted Ohioans named Austin and Milton Clark, were operating a wholesale business on Cherokee Street in Leavenworth, Kansas. They sold tea, sugar, oats, and other foods as well as crockery and building supplies. Their business was near a river leading to St. Joseph, Missouri, an ideal location for catching the gold hunters and other people moving west.

The Clark brothers watched with interest the way the Denver area was growing as more and more people used the city as a base for prospecting in the surrounding hills. Their own community had grown from a single settler's house to a thriving "metropolis" of ten thousand persons in just under five years, so they could see Denver's potential as a boomtown. Adding to the growth, regular transportation to and from Denver began in 1859, when the Leavenworth and Pike's Peak Express Company was formed by John Jones and William Russell.

At first the gold strikes were few and far between. Many miners ran out of food, supplies, and hope. They turned around and went home or starved to death along the way. Others settled into businesses serving the new miners who continued arriving in large numbers. Then, on May 6, word reached Denver that a massive strike had finally been made in the area that came to be known as Central City. The presence of gold in quantity was at last a certainty.

The people of Denver quickly encountered the same frustrations experienced in other boom towns. They had vast quantities of gold that needed refining and coining. But the only mint to which they could send it was at Philadelphia, and shipping by stage coach cost ten percent of the value of the gold—five percent for freight and five percent for insurance. To make matters worse, much of the gold was lost along the way. One shipment worth slightly over a thousand dollars arrived with one hundred dollars worth of gold missing, for example. Many shipments ran into the hundreds of thousands of dollars, making them tempting targets for thieves.

While all this was happening, the Clark brothers entered into business with Emanuel Gruber, a banker who had come to the area from Hagerstown, Maryland. The three men decided to embark on a banking venture to be known as Clark, Gruber and Company, in Leavenworth, Kansas. Naturally, they became major buyers of gold dust and ore and were additionally "burdened" with the gold being used to pay for merchandise at the Clarks' wholesale business.

Gruber was well aware of the private mints that had sprung up in other gold rush areas and thought it would be a good idea for Clark, Gruber and Company to start such an enterprise. The legal aspects were checked and the men found that as private citizens they could legally coin gold if it was of a weight and fineness to match the quality of United States coins.

Clark, Gruber and Company could have stayed in Leavenworth,

This time the Flying Eagle was used for an unusual coin that had an Indian Head on one side and the Eagle on the other. (J-220.)

but they felt that opening a branch in Denver would be a wise move. They would establish coining facilities in that city and provide a long-needed service to the miners, who were frequently cheated when they had their gold refined.

Emanuel Gruber was interviewed by the *Denver Times* in 1904, and he recalled the problems of those early days. "My firm was one of the heaviest purchasers of gold dust in the early days. And when we bought a large quantity of dust, we had to ship it to the states to have it coined into money. This was a rather expensive proceeding, as there were only stage coaches and pony expresses reaching this city in those days, and we had to pay 5 per cent of the value of the dust as an insurance against loss in transit and another 5 per cent expressage. Our dust was out of our hands anywhere from three weeks to three months, and often times the cash we would have in transit would total nearly $300,000."

The move to Denver was reported by the *Leavenworth Daily Times* on April 20, 1860:

> Messrs. Clark, Gruber & Co., bankers of this city, last evening sent out to the mining region the entire machinery requisite for an assay office and mint for the coinage of eagles, double, half and quarter eagles. The apparatus is very complete and will be used in connection with the branch of their banking house, which these gentlemen are about establishing in Denver. A splendid safe and other appurtenances for the transaction of the latter department of the business was also forwarded at the same time. The whole goes out in charge of M. E. Clark, Esq., the senior member of the firm.
>
> This is a project of no little consequence to the inhabitants of the gold country and it is fortunate for them that it has been undertaken by a firm whose standing is as high as that of Clark, Gruber & Company. We trust the enterprise will be entirely successful.

The operations in Denver were established by July. "Our pieces differed little from those of Uncle Sam," Gruber remembered years later. "We had the Goddess of Liberty on the face of them, but in the fillet that bound her hair, instead of the word 'Liberty,' we placed the words 'Pike's Peak,' and on the obverse side, instead of the words, 'United States of America,' we stamped 'Clark, Gruber & Co.' In this year (1860) we coined only ten dollar and twenty dollar gold pieces. We made them of virgin dust, without any alloy, and they were really worth more than those of the government, which were alloyed."

When the operation first began, the area newspapers responded quite favorably. The editor of the *Rocky Mountain News* stated, "A specimen of their $10 pieces which we have seen, is exceedingly neat and tasty. Upon the obverse it exhibits the eagle of the government coin, with the words 'Clark, Gruber & Co., 1860.' The reverse bears a view of Pikes Peak, natural as life and twice as sharp, with the inscription of 'Pikes Peak Gold. Denver. Ten D.'. . . . We are gratified that this enterprise so important to the interest of our people, is in the hands of honorable gentlemen who will do a legitimate business and deal liberally and justly."

By the end of August, the coinage operation was receiving an estimated two thousand dollars in gold dust every day. The two-and-one-half, five- and ten-dollar gold pieces they produced from the dust were considered the best privately minted coins ever produced. In fact, the intrinsic quality was such that the coins were worth one-half percent more than the United States coins of similar denominations. A Philadelphia mint assay made in July 1861, revealed that though the coins were not of proper fineness, they were heavier than corresponding United States government coins so they had sufficient quantity of gold to compensate for the low fineness. As a result, the report said: ". . . the pieces are found to be of professed value, or slightly over."

The public reaction to the introduction of the coins can be learned from an article in the *Rocky Mountain News* of August 29, 1860.

> Our mint, Clark, Gruber & Co., melted and coined last week about $18,000 in $10, $5, and $2.50 pieces. As specimens of coinage these pieces are far superior to any of the private mint drops issued in San Francisco, and are nearly as perfect as the regular United States mint issues. The faces of the $5's and $2.50's are a good imitation of the government coinage, the head of the Goddess of Liberty, surrounded with thirteen stars, with the firm

Patterns do not always demonstrate different designs. In this case a Gobrecht half dollar was struck in copper even though the regular issue was to be silver. Only one coin was struck this way and it was stamped to deface it. This coin, though battered, is the only one in existence and is therefore quite valuable. (J-223).

name of "Clark & Co." occupying the head tiara. The reverse of the coin is occupied, of course, with "our noble bird" encircled by the words, "Pike's Peak Gold, Denver, 2-½D." Altogether it is a creditable piece of work, and we hope to see hosts of it in circulation before the snow flies. The fineness of this coin is 828½; and the excess of weight over U. S. coin is twenty-three grs. in a ten dollar piece. The value in gold is the same as government coin of like denomination, with an additional value in silver alloy equal to near one per cent. Deduct the cost of coining at the U. S. Mint, about one half per cent, and the actual worth of Clark & Co.'s coin is one half per cent more than any other coinage.

Other companies were also coining money during this period. Georgia Gulch, Colorado, had the firm of J. J. Conway and Company producing $2.50, $5 and $10 coins; and Tarryall, Colorado, had John Parson who produced $2.50 and $5 coins.

Other types of money were also being made. Clark, Gruber and Company began issuing paper money to go along with its coinage. $1, $2, $3 and $5 were printed, all backed by the gold holdings of the company. Since small change was also needed. C. A. Cook and Company of Denver followed the Clark, Gruber and Company lead and issued paper money in denominations of 10 cents, 20 cents, 25 cents, 50 cents, and one dollar.

Money substitutes also made an appearance; they would continue to circulate for more than thirty years—long after the United State branch mint was established. Perhaps the most humorous tokens were those issued by bars, restaurants and, apparently, houses of prostitution. The tokens of the latter carried such mottoes as "Good

Variations of the Indian Head design currently in existence were tried in 1859. (J-226.)

Another variation of the Indian Head. (J-228.)

For One Screw," though whether they were genuine brothel issues has been questioned over the years. The bar and restaurant tokens were genuine, though, and served both as small change and as an advertising medium. Since many of the saloons were involved with prostitution, it is quite possible that both establishments really did use these money substitutes.

By July 1861, Colorado had achieved official territorial states, and the Republican party held a territorial convention in Golden, Colorado. The area had previously been part of the Kansas Territory, but now that Colorado was a territory in its own right, everyone knew that statehood would soon be a reality. At the convention, the Republicans at the meeting felt that under the circumstances, it was important to push for a branch mint.

Clark, Gruber and Company proved to be an enthusiastic supporter of the Denver branch mint idea. They were not coining money to make high profits as the other private mints had done. They were performing a service they felt was essential and would have been delighted to concentrate solely on their banking endeavors.

Unfortunately the Civil War was raging when the Republican convention was being held in Golden. Congress had more things with which to concern itself than the addition of another mint to the system. In the spring of 1862, for example, a congressional committee of ways and means criticized the private mints without offering an alternative.

Their report stated: "The impropriety of such establishment [private mints] would be very obvious, even without the aids of experience derived from their operations in other parts of the country. It is nothing more or less than counterfeiting the legal coins; and although not done with a criminal intent, lends increased facilities for fraud and villainy; beside inflicting upon the country the evils of metallic currency, with no means of correctly ascertaining its value."

On April 21, 1862, a bill, originated by Congressman Hiram Bennett, to authorize a Denver branch mint was finally passed. A fund of $75,000 was established and a committee created to decide whether the government should build a new mint or buy out the Clark, Gruber and Company facility.

Clark, Gruber and Company said they would sell their facility to the government for twenty five thousand dollars, a substantial savings over the cost building a new Mint. But the committee couldn't seem to make up its mind what to do. Days turned into weeks, and the miners of the Denver area became disgruntled over the delays. They expressed their feelings in a resolution:

> And Whereas, at least five millions of dollars per annum are now being taken out of our mines, of which amount about one and one-half millions of dollars are bought by bankers and gold dust traders at a discount of at least seven per cent on its real value, amounting in the aggregate to one hundred and five thousand dollars yearly, and at least one-half million of dollars more is in circulation as currency, on which there is a loss of 10 or 12 per cent in handling, equivalent to fifty thousand dollars per annum, making on two millions loss to the people of one hundred and fifty thousand dollars annually, or twelve thousand nine hundred and seventeen dollars per month.
>
> And whereas, on the remaining three millions that is not shipped east, at least five per cent is lost to the shipper in expressage and time, making an additional loss of one hundred and fifty thousand dollars, footing up a total loss of three hundred and fifty thousand dollars annually, or twenty-five thousand four hundred and fifteen dollars loss, which the people are now sustaining every month by reason of the fact that the Mint is not in operation.
>
> And whereas, believing that the private Mint of Clark, Gruber and Co. is sufficient to answer all the present wants of the Government; and believing that it can be purchased at a fair price and put into operation at once, thereby saving the great loss above mentioned to the people every month, and without which we may have to be deprived of the benefits of a mint for two years or more, therefore.
>
> Resolved, that it is the opinion of this meeting that if the Mint is not put into operation before the next meeting of Congress, there is great danger of losing the entire appropriation, by a defeat of the act of Congress by which it is granted. . . .

Finally, in late October, Dr. O. D. Munson was appointed United States Assayer for a Denver mint. The government had agreed to buy Clark, Gruber and Company, and Munson immediately went to work in their facility. The terms of the transfer were confirmed on

November 25, 1862, and the final transfer was made in April.

On January 8, the *Weekly Commonwealth and Republican* printed this editorial tribute to Clark, Gruber and Company, whose work had led to the founding of a government branch mint at Denver.

> Messrs Clark, Gruber & Co., have shown an indomitable energy and perserverance in the conduct of their establishment. They have met and overcome obstacle after obstacle, opposition after opposition, and have entirely succeeded in their enterprise. They have done more than any others have done to prove to the world the richness of our mining districts and the excellence of the gold produced. They have by the circulation of their coin which from the first has been quoted at par with U. S. coins of the same ostensible value, extended widely over this country and Europe the knowledge of Colorado, and finally to Col. A. M. Clark, of this firm, we are largely indebted for the passage of the bill which gives us a branch mint in Colorado. The firm still remains as the agents of the United States Government until the officers appointed to conduct the operations of the mint shall arrive. . . .

Sadly, after all the expenditure of effort and money, the Denver mint did not go into immediate operation. It was not until February 1906, that the Denver Mint actually started producing coins. Until that time it served as an assay office for purchasing bullion and a depository for public funds.

The last of the branch mints was founded in Carson City, Nevada, following the discovery of the Comstock Lode. This time it was silver which brought the miners—silver in greater quantities than had ever been discovered before. Gold, in small quantities, was found, too, as early as the spring of 1859, but that find was overshadowed by the tremendous silver strike.

Carson City had the unique distinction of being founded for no other reason than the wrath of one man. Abe Curry, the first settler, was fed up with overpriced property available to him in other parts of the country.

Curry was a New Yorker who had traveled across country seeking a new home in California. He thought he might settle in one of the gold-rush boom towns but he found he would either have to live miles from any settlement or pay a fortune for land, in which everyone was speculating. Disgusted, he headed back east, stopping in Utah Territory. Once again the only available land in the settlement in which he was interested was owned by speculators seeking top dollar.

During his travels, Curry teamed up with three other men. They were Frank Proctor, J. J. Musser, and B. F. Green. Together they journeyed to the site of what was to become Carson City.

The land the men selected for settlement had originally been owned by a group of Mormons who had moved on to Salt Lake City after selling their property to one John Mankin for a tiny fraction of its worth. Mankin had no use for the land and was glad to unload it to Curry and his partners for five hundred dollars.

Carson City saw its first growth when the Nevada Territory was formed. Curry managed to sell a small plot of land to the territorial government for use as a prison. He was paid eighty thousand dollars for the parcel; an immense profit making him instantly wealthy.

By 1859, gold and silver hunters were ranging in the Nevada Territory in search of riches. The first major silver-ore strike was made by Peter O'Riley and Patrick McLaughlin in an area around Johntown, Nevada, near what came to be called Silver City. They met a man named Henry Comstock a few hours later and shared the news of their find with him.

Little is known about Comstock for he had a reputation for "never letting the truth interfere with his conversation." Comstock had either staked claims for several parts of the country in which silver had been found or managed to convince O'Riley and McLaughlin that he had done so. In any case, he became an equal partner in the discovery and the silver strike eventually carried his name—the Comstock Lode. However, rather than trying to work the claim, Comstock sold his share for a tiny fraction of its eventual worth and was soon broke. In fact, only O'Riley prospered at all, eventually making $500,000 from the sale of his share. But even O'Riley fell on hard times. He undertook a mining venture based on the advice of a spiritualist, who told him where to dig. She claimed she got her information from the spirits of dead miners who told her of their "lost" strikes. But her information proved false, and the loss of his money drove O'Riley insane.

By 1860, the news of the silver strike had become widespread and boom towns began to spring everywhere. Virginia City was visited by a reporter, J. Ross Brown, in March 1860. His book, *A Peek at Washoe and Washoe Revisited*, offers the following description.

> On a slope of mountain speckled with snow, sagebushes, and mounds of upturned earth, without any apparent beginning or end, congruity or regard for the eternal fitness of things, lay outspread the wondrous city of Virginia. Frame shanties, pitched together as if by accident; tents of canvas, or blankets, of brush, of potato-sacks and old shirts with empty whisty-barrels for chimneys; smoky hovels of mud and stone; coyote holes in the mountain side forcibly seized and held by men; pits and shafts with smoke issuing from every crevice; piles of goods and rubbish on craggy points, in the hollows, on the rocks, in the mud, in the snow, everywhere, scattered broadcast in pell-mell confusion, as if the clouds had suddenly burst overhead and rained down the dregs of all the flimsy, rickety, filthy little hovels and rubbish of merchandise that had ever undergone the process of evaporation from the earth since the days of Noah. The intervals of space, which may or may not have been streets, were dotted over with human beings of such

In 1863 more experimentation was done. This is J-302. It was made in copper-nickel.

sort, variety, and numbers that the famous ant-hills of Africa were as nothing in comparison.

Carson City also developed quickly that year, settlers moving in so they could have a base from which to go exploring for ore in the hills to the east of town. Soon there were hotels, saloons, stores and all the other businesses a community needs to prosper. Curry had become a rich man from his land holdings. Had he not made one mistake, he would have been even wealthier. Prior to the Comstock discovery, he had owned a small mine that he never took the time to develop properly. He sold it for a small profit, then watched the new owner remove more than fifteen million dollars in silver ore.

Carson City never had a private mint of the type that sprung up in other boom towns around the country. But there was a change shortage, and many people used Spanish coins. Mexican silver-mining experts had been brought into the Nevada Territory to help with production and, they apparently had an influence on the coinage situation. Prices in many areas were set to reflect Spanish coinage rather than the United States system. For example, there were "bit" and "two bit" bars that were extremely popular. At a one-bit bar, a man could get a drink for twelve and a half cents or one bit. A two-bit bar charged twenty-five cents a drink. The drinks at both bars were the same size and the prices never varied, yet they each had a loyal clientele. The "two bit" bars never seemed to want for business despite their charging double the price.

The biggest attraction of the bars in the Comstock area was the free meals they offered. Ample food was available to go with one's drinks and there was never any charge. However, a man couldn't just go into the bar, order a bit drink and gorge himself. That would have been "crude" and would have advertised the fact he was in financial straits. Instead a drink would be ordered and a small amount of food would be placed on a plate. More food would be consumed with each drink and there was never any obvious gluttony. However, after two or three hours of this, the patron would have managed to eat enormous quantities of food.

Almost from the time the Comstock Lode was discovered, the merchants and businessmen wanted to have a branch mint located in their city. They were regularly shipping their silver and the small quantities of gold to the San Francisco branch mint for processing and the director of the mint in Philadelphia, James Pollock, thought this approach was best. However, it was pointed out that not only were transportation costs high but also that much of the ore was immediately shipped overseas after reaching the coast. Traders in the Orient had to use silver for their business transactions and delighted in obtaining the new quantities of ore. If this silver was made into coins in Carson City, the money would go into circulation in the country and the United States government would avoid the loss of ore worth $500,000 per year.

In March 1863, the supporters of a Carson City mint were able to pass a bill through both houses of Congress authorizing its establishment. Congressman H. P. Bennett was appointed to investigate the Caron City area to see where a mint could be built and what costs would be involved.

Bennett proposed a site, but little was done about it. The Civil War took precedence over all other business. Even the miners were subdued in their efforts to gain the new mint. They were more concerned with impending statehood, which was finally achieved by Nevada on October 31, 1864.

It wasn't until February 1865, that Congress authorized the purchase of a full block in Carson City to have adequate land for the new Mint. However, a few congressmen felt the government officials spent so much time debating the purchase, that they exceeded the period during which they were authorized to take action. Debate over the issue continued for several months, during which time the people of Carson City remained greatly inconvenienced.

In July 1867, the mint plans were finalized and accepted by all. Land was purchased, architects began work, and by the end of September, a cornerstone was laid. Unfortunately construction workers were hard to find. Orientals were brought into the city but they were disliked by the town's people, who harrassed them mercilessly, driving many of them away.

It was not until 1870 that the Carson City mint became a reality. Bullion went on deposit in January, and dies were received at the end of the month. On February 10, the first 2,303 silver dollars left the mint.

One of the more unusual coins. How do you reduce the amount of metal needed for striking a coin without reducing the size—when the price of metal has skyrocketed? Punch a hole in the center. This cent was tried in 1884. (J-1721.)

And so the mint system was fully developed. There were branches in Dahlonega, Charlotte, San Francisco, New Orleans, Denver, (as an assay office at first), and Carson City. No matter where precious ores might be found, a mint facility now was close at hand to turn gold and silver into coin.

7

Turbulence and War

The period from 1850 to the beginning of the Civil War was a turbulent one in the history of United States coinage. Radical changes were taking place in our coinage, and the American attitude towards silver pieces was changing. It was during this time that the United States limited the legal-tender status of silver coins worth less than a dollar, something that had never been done before.

One of the first changes in our silver coinage was the introduction of a three-cent piece, a coin that had been proposed in 1849. In the same year Congress authorized the striking of a one-dollar gold piece, a coin meant to ease the continuing coin shortages around the country. Gold dollars could be used in place of half-dollars and, for many transactions, in place of quantities of quarters. Gold was coming in quantity from California, while the large silver strikes of Colorado had yet to be made.

The creation of a three-cent piece had long been considered as a convenience for the Post Office. The coin denomination would match the new price of mailing a letter being considered by Congress. The postal system had advanced to a point where its high rates could be reduced. The uniform three-cent mailing rate would soon be initiated, replacing a system of charges based on the number of papers mailed and the distance they were sent.

In 1850, Senator D. S. Dickinson formally proposed the creation of two new coins. The first was a one-cent piece that would be far smaller than the then current Large cent. It would contain one part silver to nine parts copper, a ratio that would result in a drastic size reduction.

The three-cent silver coin was the smallest United States coin that had ever been authorized when it was coined in 1851. There was a total of three variations in design. The one illustrated is the first design. All design variations were moderate, with little change from the basic creation.

This ratio would maintain the one-cent intrinsic value of the coin. It was the senator's idea that the coin have a hole in the center to facilitate counting by stringing or placing the coins on a spike. The cent would be legal tender up to a maximum of ten cents. The second coin proposed was a three-cent piece that would be legal tender in quantities up to thirty cents. A new one-cent coin was favored by Congress because, as has been said, the Large cent was never well received. However, the silver-copper hole-in-the-middle design was rejected.

The three-cent piece was quite a different matter. Congress was anxious to do away with the Spanish coins, which continued to circulate. They were old, and worn to the point where their accepted value and their intrinsic worth were quite far apart. Since most of the coins were either reales worth twelve and one half cents or medios worth six and one-quarter cents, the three-cent denomination would fit nicely into transactions where Spanish pieces had formerly been used.

In January 1851, a bill was introduced in the House to lower the postage rate to three cents and to provide for the issuing of a coin of that denomination. So certain was the mint director that the bill would pass, he set mint engraver James Longacre to the task of developing a new design. He was careful to follow the congressional proposals, assuming that the law would be enacted.

Longacre went so far as to strike trial coins. He sent one to Thomas Corwin, secretary of the Treasury, along with a note that described the pieces: "For the obverse I have therefore chosen a star (one of the heraldic elements of the National crest) bearing on its centre the shield of the Union, surrounded by the legal inscription and date. For the reverse I have devised an ornamental letter *C* embracing in its

The Christian Gobrecht design for the half dime. It constitutes the third variation that was made in the coin. In all, four variations appeared, each using the Seated Liberty form.

This coin of 1859 was made from a new die, and each of the stars has a hollow center.

centre the Roman numeral III, the whole encircled by the thirteen stars—I think I have obtained the object of the law—but it would be very gratifying to me to have your candid opinion, provided your health should be such as to allow for your making a response to my communication in a private way. . . ."

The design was liked by most who saw it but was later changed under pressure from some of the other mint workers. Meanwhile the debates continued in Congress.

While debate was going on, merchants and the public were becoming increasingly desperate for subsidiary silver coinage. The fluctuating silver market meant that the coins brought more than face value when shipped abroad. Those coins that weren't shipped were frequently hoarded. Both situations meant there was a great need for small change.

On March 3, 1851, the law was finally changed to allow for the minting of a three-cent silver coin. The design was to have ". . . such devices as shall be conspicuously different from those of the other silver coins, and of the gold dollar, but having the inscription United States of America, and its denomination and date; and that it shall be a legal tender in payment of debts for all sums of thirty cents and under." The new coin proved immensely popular and more than twenty million were put into circulation by 1852. It was the first United States non-decimal coin and was physically the smallest coin in circulation, facts that didn't seen to bother the public at all.

Something new had been planned for the three-cent silver coin, something that was to have major repercussions. The coins were to be debased. A dollar's worth of the three-cent silver coins had an intrinsic worth of just eighty-six cents. This did not affect how they were spent, but it did discourage their being melted. Other silver coins had, from time to time, been worth more in silver content than face value. This drove them from circulation. The three-cent silver coins were more likely to remain in circulation because the public came out ahead when spending them rather than melting or shipping them abroad.

The only problem was that the silver in all other coins was worth more than face value, due to a change in silver prices on the world market. Other countries kept the intrinsic worth of their coins so low that they had no value when melted. However, United States law fixed the silver content at such a high level that a slight fluctuation could result in more than a dollar's worth of silver being used in every dollar coin. As a result, the only coins that circulated were those so badly worn that their intrinsic worth had become less than face value.

Debate in Congress revolved around the idea of producing silver coins worth far less than face value. This "debasement," as the detractors called it, had been used effectively in Great Britain and other countries to keep ample coinage in circulation. There had never been any complaints, and the Europeans had been relatively free from the problem of hoarding. The debasement scheme was strongly pushed by Secretary of the Treasury Corwin in a report to Congress made on January 15, 1853.

On February 7, 1853, one of the first public remarks concerning Corwin's efforts was seen in a *New York Tribune* editorial. Horace Greeley wrote:

> We give way to this debasement as inevitable but we protest against any further, and we insist that Congress guard now against the possibility of further progress on this downward path. Let it now be solemnly enacted that gold is the national standard of value,

The fourth full variation of the half dime.

The Gobrecht dime variations. This is the fourth variation.

> and that our present gold coinage shall never more be debased or interfered with. Let every promise to pay imply so much gold as would fulfill that promise according to our present legally established standard. Then if silver becomes more or less plentiful, let the silver coinage be altered to conform to the fact, but let the standard of gold be unvarying evermore—silver being used as change or counters, and never being a legal tender for debts, except for sums below five dollars. If a dollar means anything in particular, it is high time for decisive settlement as to precisely what it does mean.

Two weeks after the newspaper protest, an act was passed (see Appendix) reducing the value of the silver in half-dollars and other minor coins. The new law limited the legal-tender status of the silver coins to just five dollars, a fact that proved shocking to those who wanted silver coins to be legal tender in any amount as they had been in the past. In effect, the law put the United States on the gold standard, since only gold coins were acceptable as payment for any debt, not just for one of five dollars or less.

Congressman C. L. Dunham, speaking for what proved the majority, gave his opinion of the change:

> What advantage is to be obtained by a standard of the two metals, which is not as well, if not much better, attained by a single standard, I am unable to perceive; whilst there are very great disadvantages resulting from it, as the experience of every nation which has attempted to maintain it has proved. The constant, though sometimes slow change in the relative values of the two metals has always resulted in great inconvenience, and frequently in great loss to the people. Wherever the experiment of a standard of a single metal has been tried, it has proved eminently successful. Indeed, it is utterly impossible that you should long at a time maintain a double standard. The one or the other will appreciate in value when compared with the other. It will then command a premium when exchanged for that other, when it ceases to be a currency and becomes merchandise. It ceases to circulate as money at its nominal value, but it sells as a commodity at its market price. This was the case with gold before the act of 1834; it is now the case with silver. Gentlemen talk about a double standard of gold and silver as a thing that exists, and that we proposed to change. We have had but a single standard for the last three or four years. That has been, and now is, gold. We propose to let it remain so, and to adapt silver to it, to regulate it by it.

During the debates the gold interests in Congress managed to add a new coin to our nation's system. Authorization for a three-dollar gold piece was tacked onto a bill that passed February 21, 1853. The idea

This coin was of the second variety of Gobrecht coins with arrows on each side of the date.

The fourth variety of Gobrecht Quarters. The arrows have been removed from the date and the eagle now has a banner on the reverse.

was to have a coin that could be used to buy 100 stamps or a roll of 100 new three-cent silver coins.

The three-dollar gold piece was a difficult coin for mint engraver James Longacre to design. Because the amount of gold was very close to the quantity used in the two-dollar-and-fifty-cent quarter eagle, the new coin had to be made thinner so that it would be noticeably wider than the quarter eagle piece.

Don Taxay, author of *The U. S. Mint and Coinage,* found a paper written by the engraver in which he explained his problem: "I have rarely, if ever felt more perplexity in determining on the nature of a device appropriate to the issue, than in respect to the intended coin of the value of three dollars—Its approximation in size & weight of necessity, to the coin already in use, and extensively so—of the value of two and one-half dollars, known as the 'quarter eagle,' makes it important that it should bear a distinctive character, in the device and inscription, which should be peculiarly striking, and obvious in order to prevent, or guard against the danger in circulation of passing or receiving one piece for the other."

Longacre's design is an interesting one and would be repeated in the years to come. He started with the head of Liberty and then decked her in an Indian headdress, a tiara, and other headpiece variations. The face of Liberty is apparently that of a Greco-Roman statue, assumed to be the Venus Accroupie, which Longacre had been using for his design model since 1849.

The regular-issue coins began entering circulation in 1854. A pair of dies went to the Dahlonega, Georgia branch mint, where a small number of these coins were produced. Other dies went to the Charlotte mint (which didn't use them), and to New Orleans, where a large number of the coins were struck.

Later, the coins were produced in Philadelphia through 1889. The San Francisco Mint also struck some of these coins put only in 1855, 1856, 1857, 1860 and 1870. They were never popular and served little purpose other than to allow the miners to sell a little more of their bullion to the federal government.

The gold dollar had been a problem since its introduction. The gold coin was so small—just thirteen millimeters in diameter—that it was easily lost. A decision was made to enlarge it in 1854, and the design was altered slightly. Longacre created a variation of his three-dollar gold piece Indian Head design. However, this proved difficult to strike, and two years later he returned to the exact design used on the three-dollar coin.

During this period, the mint was encouraging the removal of all foreign coins from circulation. A totally American circulating coinage was desired, so the mint officials offered more money for foreign coins than they were worth when used to pay taxes and other governmental obligations. A person selling his Spanish silver to the mint, for example, would receive twenty-three and one-half cents for two bits or a double real. He would get ten and nine-tenths cents for a bit or single real and five and one-fifth cents for a half bit or medio. The same coins, when used to pay taxes, were accepted at values of twenty-three cents, ten cents and five cents, respectively.

On February 21, 1857, Congress passed a law (see Appendix) withdrawing legal-tender status from all foreign coin. In addition it authorized the issue of a new cent, much smaller than the old coins, which was to be made of a combination of copper and nickel. The new cents were to be accepted at face value in exchange for both gold and silver, giving them an immediate advantage over the Large cents.

The idea of using nickel as a coinage medium was not new. It had

The one-dollar gold piece with Liberty Head type I design introduced in 1849.

This was the third variety of the gold dollar. It is the large-head Indian introduced in 1854. Note the small size of the head.

been utilized as far back as 200 B.C. However, nickel is far harder than copper, and it was many years before a copper-nickel alloy could be developed that was soft enough for conventional coining methods.

Nickel was more expensive than copper, so the mixture allowed for the striking of a one-cent piece that was intrinsically equal to the hated Large cents but less than half their weight. Nickel was also playing a part in politics, and Mint Director James Snowden was keenly aware of the fact.

Snowden was from Pennsylvania, where he had risen to the position of state treasurer. His appointment as mint director required

The three-dollar gold piece.

political support; thus, if he ever lost his job, there was always a chance that he could return to his home state as a politician. Since Lancaster Gap, Pennsylvania, a copper mining town, was also the site of a major nickel discovery, Snowden was anxious to help the "boys back home" who had been supporting him. If adding nickel to the cents could get him a few votes or financial support, he was more than happy to oblige.

The new coin utilized the Titian Peale eagle design that was used on the Gobrecht coins of 1836. However, this design was changed almost immediately to one using the Indian Head concept Longacre had developed for the gold pieces.

There is an interesting story connected with the new cents bearing the Indian Head design that appeared in the *American Journal of Numismatics* in 1906. The article was titled "The 'Emblem of Liberty' On Our Coins" and related a fanciful version of how the coin was created. The truth has already been shown—Longacre had used this design for many years. But according to the article (which has been quoted many times in recent years),

> The suggestion of the panache (i.e. "an Indian head with a feather head-dress, sometimes called a panache") is said to have come from a visit of a delegation of Indians from one of the tribes of the North-west, who came to talk with the 'Great Father' in Washington; and while in the East they were taken to see the operations of the Mint. At the time, as the story is told, Miss Sarah Longacre, the daughter of the Mint engraver, was present while the chiefs and their followers were going through the building, and attracted the attention of their leader. In a mood of sportiveness he

The Flying Eagle design was introduced in 1856 and used for three years. These coins circulated throughout the United States, though in relatively small numbers. Since the coin design had such a short life, some collectors consider these coins to be patterns. However, they were used as general-issue coins.

The Flying Eagle of 1857.

In 1858 there was a variation of the Flying Eagle design. This one has smaller letters.

The other variation of the 1858 cent, this one with large letters.

took his crown of feathers from his head and placed it upon hers. She was a child of five or six years of age, and as she stood for a moment wearing the novel head-dress, some one of the company made a sketch of the little maiden and her feathery cap, and in due time the design was engraved and used upon the coins, dies for which were then in preparation. Such is the story as told by a correspondent of a New York newspaper. Whether the tale is a true one the writer is unable to say; but certainly the device is far more appropriate to American coins than the conventional cap, which was originally given to the slave who had been freed by his Roman master, the awkward bonnet on our first gold coins, or the equally hideous turbans that so long disfigured the matronly heads on the silver pieces in the later years of the first half of the last century.

The reaction to the first of the smaller coins was tremendous. When the Flying Eagle design was released, Mint Director Snowden wrote to Treasury Secretary James Guthrie on May 25, 1857: "The demand for them is enormous. . . . We had on hand this morning $30,000 worth, that is 3,000,000 pieces. Nearly all of this amount will be paid out today. The coinage will forward, however, at the rate of 100,000 or more pieces per day and the demand will be met as well as we can."

In August 1857, *The Banker's Magazine* quoted an article in the *Philadelphia Bulletin* that described the scenes of people waiting at the mint for the new copper-nickel cents. The article, reprinted by Eric Newman in the October 1962, issue of *Numismatic Scrapbook Magazine,* read:

Every man and boy in the crowd had his package of coin with him. Some had their rouleaux of Spanish Coin done up in bits of

The reverse of the 1859 Indian Head cent. This coin was struck in copper-nickel and the reverse was used only one year.

The reverse of the Indian Head cent was changed in 1860 to a different design.

newspaper or wrapped in hankerchiefs, while others had carpet bags, baskets and other carrying contrivances, filled with coppers—"very cheap and filling," like boarding house fare.

The officiating priests in the temple of Mammon had anticipated this grand rush, and every possible preparation was made in anticipation of it. Conspicuous among these arrangements was the erection of a neat wooden building in the yard of the mint for the special accommodation of the great crowd of money-changers. This temporary structure was furnished with two open windows, which faced the South. Over one of these windows was inscribed the words "cents for cents," and over the other "cents for silver." Inside the little office were scales and other apparatus for weighing and testing coin, a goodly pile of bags containing the newly struck compound of nickel and copper, and a detachment of weighers, clerks, &c.

The bags containing the "nicks" were neat little canvas arrangements, each of which held five hundred of the diminutive little strangers, and each of which bore upon its outside the pleasant inscription "5." Just as the State House bell had finished striking nine o'clock the doors of the mint were thrown open, and in rushed the eager crowd—paper parcels, well filled hankerchiefs, carpet bags, baskets and all. But those who thought that there was to be a grand scramble, and that the boldest pusher would be first served, reckoned without their host. The invading throng was arranged into lines which led to the respective windows; those who bore silver had the post of honor assigned them and went to the right, while those who bore nothing but vulgar copper were constrained to the left.

These lines soon grew to an unconscionable length, and to economize space they wound around like the convolutions of a snake of a whimsical turn of mind. The clerks and the weighers exerted themselves to the utmost to meet the demands of all comers, and to deal out the little canvas bags to all who were entitled to receive them; but the crowd grew apace, and we estimated that at one time there could not have been less than one thousand persons in the zigzag lines, weighed down with small change, and waiting patiently for their turn.

Those who were served rushed into the street with their money bags and many of them were immediately surrounded by an outside crowd, who were willing to buy out in small lots at an advance of from thirty to a hundred per cent., and some of the outside purchasers even huckstered out the coin again in smaller lots at a still heavier advance. The great majority of those who came out "made tracks" with their bags of money, and not an omnibus went eastward past the mint for several hours that did not, like the California steamers, carry "specie in the hands of the passengers." Those who made their way homeward a-foot attracted the attention of passer-by by their display of specie bags, and we doubt much whether, in the history of the mint, there was ever so great a rush inside the building, or so animated a scene outside of it. It was, in effect, the funeral of the old coppers and of the ancient Spanish coins, and the giving of a practical working existence to the new cents.

In the course of a few weeks, the new coin will be plentiful enough at par, the Spanish coins will go out of the hands of the brokers just as they have already disappeared from ordinary circulation, and as regards the old cents there will be "nary red" to be seen, except such as will be found in the cabinets of coin collectors.

The fifth variety of Gobrecht quarters. Note the difference in the date.

The Gobrecht half-dollar.

No one could have anticipated the overwhelming demand for the new coins. In the first three years of their minting, ninety million of the copper-nickel cents were released. Still the demand persisted.

The only problem that arose was that the coins were not being evenly distributed. The public was desperate for cents in some cities and overwhelmed by the coins in others. In New York, for example, so many coins had entered circulation that the stores could no longer get rid of them in change during normal business hours. One New York firm received so many of the new cents that they made a temporary storehouse for them in a section of the second floor of the business. The stacks of coins grew higher and higher each day until the floor boards were overwhelmed by the weight and the cents went crashing through to the ground below.

When the Civil War began, the cents were being handled through brokers who discounted them three to five percent in the larger communities. However, the war also saw the hoarding of gold and silver, a fact that meant a new coin shortage would occur. Additional silver coins were being shipped to Canada, and this further depleted resources.

The Canadian situation was an interesting one. Canada was on the gold standard but accepted United States silver coins at face value and exchanged them for an equal face amount of gold. In the United States, the face value of silver was worth a reduced amount of gold. In addition, United States paper money was accepted in this country at face value when exchanged for silver but at a reduced rate for gold. For example, in January 1862, $100 in United States bank notes was equal to $100 in United States silver or $97 in United States gold.

The result of the different exchange rates between Canada and the United States was rampant speculation. Americans obtained bank notes, exchanged them for their face value in silver coin, crossed the border into Canada, and exchanged the silver for equivalent face value in gold. The gold was brought back into the United States and exchanged for paper money equal to a percentage greater than the face value of the gold. Thus, by starting with just $100.00 on the American side of the border, a speculator could make $103.00 with his first transaction, $106.00 with his second, and so on.

With silver and gold coins either being hoarded or sent over the border to Canada, the new cents were suddenly in demand again. They soon became the only coins available, and another financial crisis faced the nation.

During the coinage shortages of the 1830s, merchants solved the problem of small change with tokens. The Hard Times tokens and Jackson tokens had served as an alternative form of money for as long as was necessary. By the start of the Civil War, such an alternative was again required.

The types of tokens prepared by the Civil War era merchants were numerous and highly original. They ranged from small advertising pieces to money used by the traveling military salesmen known as sutlers to encased postage stamps that combined the federal mail system with private enterprise.

The tokens began appearing as change substitutes very early in the war years. One of the first was put out by a man who engaged in numerous businesses including the buying and selling of coins for collectors. The token read "Value Me As You Please" on one side and, on the other, there was an advertising message reading: "Alfred S. Robbinson, Banker, Numismatist & Notary Public. Dealer in Stocks, Bonds, Notes, Land Warrants, Uncurrent Money & All Kinds of American & Foreign Specie. Hartford Conn. 1861."

Business advertising was not the only form of promotion the manufacturers of tokens tried with their creations. Aaron White, another Connecticut resident, was determined to stop the use of paper money, which he felt threatened the nation's economy. His plea for the use of gold and silver in all business transactions was

When the Civil War was about to begin, there was widespread hoarding of gold, silver, and even copper coins. Merchants were unable to make change, so they returned to a practice that had been standard during the depression of 1837. They produced their own tokens that were passed as change. Sometimes the tokens were good only at a particular merchant. But when a merchant was highly respected in the community, other merchants would honor his tokens as legitimate coins. These represent a number of varieties of the tokens.

revealed on a token that stated: "Never Keep—A Paper Dollar 1837–1857." The back showed a sow who had rooted up a jar marked "$10." It has the words "Tollens" meaning *rooting;* "Sus" for *sow;* "Di Oboli," a reference to early Greek coins; and "Deux Sous" meaning *two sows.*

The inscription on White's tokens seems odd but not nearly so eccentric as the estate he left. He became convinced that the Civil War would bankrupt the United States; so during the war years, he regularly visited the mint, obtaining all the coins he could. When he died his estate was found to consist of, among other things, $350 in gold coins; 250 colonial copper coins; 100 silver dollars; 200 half-dollars; 60,000 copper cents; an equal number of the copper-nickel cents; and 5,000 bronze two-cent pieces (a coin to be discussed later in this chapter).

Tokens began appearing north and south, many of them made

from copper and bearing a design similar to that of the Flying Eagle cents. The coins bore various patriotic slogans. One Southern token bore the word "Dix" encircled by the motto: "If Anyone Attempts To Tear It Down—Shoot Him On The Spot." Northern slogans included "The Federal Union It Must And Shall Be Preserved" and "The Federal Government—A National Currency—Free Trade and Human Rights".

Most tokens passed as a cent. A few were meant to serve as specific commodities. Thus a token might have the value of a loaf of bread or perhaps twenty-five cents in bank bills.

Among the less known tokens were those used by the Civil War sutlers. The sutler's reputation made him the Civil-War equivalent to today's used car salesman. He was considered dishonest, greedy, the purveyor of overpriced, shoddy merchandise, and generally a man to take advantage of the war situation to get rich at the expense of the soldiers.

Sutlers were assigned to the military—one sutler per regiment. The position was a political one, and a man had to be recommended to it by the state governor, regimental officers, or others of great influence. Once a sutler was assigned to a regiment, he was the only person permitted to sell goods to the soldiers. Carrying a wide variety of necessity items and luxury goods, he followed the soldiers as they moved from place to place.

The soldiers maintained a love-hate relationship with the sutler. Sutler prices were marked up a minimum of 300 percent, and a 500 percent mark-up for merchandise was not uncommon. He carried books, food, tobacco, toilet articles, and almost everything else imaginable. The military authorities helped set the high prices because they received a kick-back in the form of a tax on every item sold. The more something cost, the more everyone but the soldiers prospered.

Soldiers relied heavily on the sutlers because their regular provisions gave them little more than the nccessities for survival. Army food was consistently tasteless and seldom varied. In 1861, a Union Army soldier was given sixteen ounces of hardtack or twenty-two ounces of flour or bread along with one and a quarter pounds of fresh or salted meat or three quarters of a pound of bacon. Later in the war, many of the men were given potatoes, hominy, beans or rice, and coffee for variety. Seasonings, seldom adequate, included vinegar, sugar, and salt. Each man prepared his own meal as best he could. It always tasted terrible, though some variety was possible. For example, hardtack might be softened in water, then fried in bacon fat to vary the taste.

Coffee came "in the raw." A soldier was given green coffee beans, which had to be roasted in whatever container the soldier could fashion from materials at hand. "Instant" coffee in paste form appeared later, and eventually it could even be obtained with milk and sugar.

The sutler's wares appealed to the soldiers because they brought relief from the monotonous meal of the day. If you had money you could buy canned goods imported from France, where the industry was quite advanced. You could buy canned fish, canned vegetables, and canned meats. You could also obtain pastry, cookies, and candy.

Part of the hostility towards the sutlers came from the way they operated. Sutlers sold on credit. A soldier bought whatever he wanted with no money down. The amount of the purchase and the name of the soldier were carefully recorded in the sutler's ledger. Most of the soldiers forgot just how much they were buying until the day the payroll was delivered. Then the sutler would take his ledger book and sit next to the paymaster. As a soldier's name was called, the sutler would stake his claim for the money owed him before the soldier received it. Many times a man gave most or all of his pay directly to the sutler, keeping himself broke for the next several days. Occasionally a man owed the sutler more than he earned, and his debts would haunt him through the next pay period.

To get an idea of how easily a man could lose his savings to the sutler, let's look at prices and income. A general naturally earned the most money—$200 a month. The lowest ranking soldier's income came nowhere near that figure; he earned just $7 a month in the Union Army. If the soldier wanted to write home to loved ones, he would have to pay the sutler $3 for a few envelopes and twenty-four sheets of writing paper. This was at the start of the war; paper cost a dollar a sheet toward the end of the violence, and a tiny bottle of ink ran $3. Regular correspondence could keep a man in debt throughout the conflict.

Perhaps the most popular items the sutler carried were patent medicines. They were so loaded with alcohol that everyone felt good after drinking them though the "medicine" did nothing permanent for whatever aches and pains a man might have. Often soldiers were quoted as endorsing a specific product. Lieutenant S. H. Fields of Company B, First Regiment, Heavy Artillery, was stationed in Washington's Fort Lincoln. He provided a testimonial letter to help advertise one of the patent medicines sold by the sutlers:

> Few are the living men who have suffered what I have with indigestion and piles. For two years I have suffered beyond expression. I have been on the sick list the greater part of my time, being unable to attend to duty as a Lieutenant. I had nearly given up, when one day the Captain came to my quarters, and told me if I would only take RUSH'S PILLS and SARSAPARILLA AND IRON, that you sent us, that I would soon be well again. I reluctantly consented thinking at the same time it was useless. I began taking it at noon; took some twice, and the PILLS at night; and I had not slept so well

for a year as I did that night; in the morning I felt better than I ever had since my stay at Fort Lincoln. I have now taken three bottles and a box of Pills, and, thanks be to God and your medicine, I am well. I relish my hard-tack; in fact, everything I can eat agrees with me; and, if ever one man felt grateful to another, I do to you. The boys (as we call the soldiers) think RUSH'S SARSAPARILLA and IRON saved my life, as well as that of the Captain. We want to keep some of the medicine on hand. Please find enclosed $3.50, and send three bottles of RUSH'S SARSAPARILLA and IRON and two boxes RUSH'S PILLS to your obliged friend.

The sutlers justified their high prices by stressing the many problems they endured. Everything they sold had to be transported by wagon from large communities that were often many miles from the camps. If a regiment had the misfortune to lose a battle before the sutler could flee, his wares might be captured by the enemy. Money was also lost when a man was transferred to a different regiment or killed in battle before he could settle his accounts. Yet most of the sutlers prospered with their businesses, and some became quite wealthy by war's end.

Sutlers had one problem in common with all merchants, though. The shortage of change made doing business extremely difficult. They tried making paper money, printing cash denominations on cards, and even issued their own tokens.

The sutlers' tokens were resented far more than tokens used by businesses in the various communities. A businessman in a city could issue a token and everyone would know how to value it. If he had a good reputation and his store had been in existence a few years, people knew he would always honor it. They used the token at its face value when doing business with other merchants in the same community, knowing the tokens would be honored because the issuer was respected. But a sutler was a transient individual. He was little known in the communities through which he passed and had no competition within a regiment. The tokens a sutler gave as change could only be used by the soldier to buy additional merchandise from the same sutler. As soldiers became entrapped by the tokens, resentment toward the sutler increased.

Periodically there were riots when sutlers cheated the men. Occasionally the food they sold was bad, and as many as half a regiment of men at a time might be sick from the spoiled goods. On occasion, the angered victims of such food poisoning had been known to attack their regiment's sutler, destroying his tent, stealing his ledger book, and carting off his wares.

Even as high a figure as General Ulysses S. Grant became so angered by the rapacity of the sutlers that he worked to stop their trade. During the march to Vicksburg he wrote:

Sutlers: In this connection, I would respectfully call your atten-

> tion to the present system of army sutlers. There is no article legitimately supplied by sutlers to officers and soldiers, which could not be furnished at a much less price by Quartermaster and Commissary Departments. Sutlers and their employes are now only partially subject to military authority and discipline, and it is not difficult for those who are so disposed to act the part of spies, informers, smugglers and contraband traders.
>
> The entire abolition of the system would rid the army of the encumbrance of sutler's stalls and booths in camp. It would relieve officers and soldiers of much of their personal expenses, and improve the discipline and efficiency of the troops in many ways, and particularly by removing from the camps, the profligate evil of drunkenness.

Sutlers continued plying their trade until 1866. However, the familiar Army post exchange lingers as a reminder of these men and their tokens.

The token that came closest to being a true money substitute originated with newspaperman Horace Greeley. In an article in the *New York Tribune* on July 9, 1862, he said that postage stamps should be used as small change. They were official government issues, accepted at face value just like coins and had never been criticized by the public. He felt that since the stamps would tear if carried loose, they could be pasted onto half a sheet of paper with the other half folded over them. Different numbers of stamps could be used to represent the denominations of coins worth less than a dollar.

Greeley's idea seemed excellent to many who read his column. Two days after it appeared, a Wall Street firm utilized a folded piece of parchment paper to provide the type of coin substitute suggested. A day later the *Chicago Tribune* picked up the idea and gave it full support. Even Congress, in less than a week's time, provided its endorsement. Postage stamps in sums totaling less than five dollars would be authorized legal tender equal to the coins that had disappeared from circulation.

The only criticism of the plan came from Postmaster General Montgomery Blair. He had been given no warning about the congressional endorsement and was not ready to supply stamps in the quantity that would be necessary. There was a sudden rush for postage stamps that resulted in a serious shortage at most post offices. Profiteers began selling their supplies at a 25 percent premium over face value.

The stamps were a mixed blessing for the public. While they solved the small-change problem, they were never meant to endure the abuse of being carried like currency. If they were pasted on good-quality paper they seemed to hold up fairly well, but many people tried to carry them loose. The stamps became hopelessly stuck together, torn and unrecognizable within a few days. The public immediately took them back to the post office, fully expecting to exchange them for good stamps. After all, bad paper money could be exchanged for fresh, so why not the stamps? However, not only was such an exchange against postal regulations, it also was not practical since the only clue to the denomination and quantity of stamps in a wad was the word of the person presenting them. They were too messy for the postal clerk to be certain.

New York merchants tried to avoid the problem of wear by placing loose stamps in envelopes on which they marked the value. But the stamps stuck together in the envelopes, and no one could be certain whether some of the stamps might be missing.

Congress finally decided that an alternative was necessary. It ordered that stamps be printed on large sheets of heavy paper without any glue. The public would buy the sheets, then cut off the number of stamps they needed for change. At least that was the idea. In reality, few people had the patience to cut the sheets carefully. They tore off the needed stamps, often ripping several in the process. Then they took the ones they had damaged back to the post office, demanding replacements. But the post office was not prepared to make such replacements.

During this period a man named John Gault came to the country's rescue with an invention that provided the most practical solution that had been proposed up to that time. He had created a holder for postage stamps, which he patented on August 12, 1862. The holder consisted of a round metal case into which a postage stamp could be inserted. The stamp was held in place by a thin, almost transparent mica cover. It would wear almost as well and as long as a coin, and though it cost the merchant a premium over the face value of the stamp, Gault felt it practical enough that no one would complain about the price. The cost could be recovered through slightly higher prices, and the coin shortage would be solved.

Merchants were delighted with the new stamp holders. They had been losing so much business from being unable to make change that the cost for the holders was of little concern. Even better was the fact that there was room on the cases for such advertising messages as "Ayer's Sarasparilla." Even Gault used his product, placing advertisements on the back of them reading: "Applications for Advertising on this currency to be addressed to Kirkpatrick & Gault, No. 1 Park Place, N.Y."

Success proved to be Gault's downfall. He quickly used up the supply of stamps he could find locally and began traveling to neighboring cities. But the Post Office decided that Gault was buying too many stamps for a business venture and was reducing the stock needed to move the mails. They began refusing to sell him any stamps.

Gault shifted his operations from Massachusetts to New York City, going into partnership with a man named Kirkpatrick. They made a slight modification in the case, dipping it in a tin solution to give it a silvered appearance (although the coating quickly wore off in circulation). He encased stamps worth from one cent to ninety cents and felt he could have made a million dollars from his venture had the Post Office allowed him to buy stamps in quantities equal to his orders. But even in New York he met Post Office hostility, a hostility that finally forced him out of business.

A limited number of postage stamp cases were made independently by the Scovill Manufacturing Company of Waterbury, Connecticut. This was primarily a button manufacturing company, but the manufacture of stamp cases fit in with the way their equipment was tooled. However, it seems that only a few were made by Scovill, and none were put into circulation. There is a chance that Gault may have worked for Scovill at one time and developed his stamp case idea there. But the early employment records for the company have been destroyed by fire, and this cannot be ascertained.

While Gault was having his troubles, the *New York Herald* ran an article by its Washington correspondent concerning the concept of postal currency as encouraged by Congress: He wrote, "Much difficulty is experienced in carrying out the law authorizing the issue of postage stamps for currency. The act appears to have been hastily drawn, without consultation with the Postmaster General. It inaugurates a conflict of authority between the Post Office and the Treasury departments. . . . The details in reference to the issue of stamps have not yet been arranged."

At the end of August 1862, the secretary of the Treasury had found a way to solve the change shortage and reduce the wrath of the Postmaster General. He decided to issue a new type of postage meant exclusively as money. This was "postage currency"—special stamps measuring 2¾ × 3⅜ inches that were printed on both sides of heavy paper. They were to be issued in denominations of five, ten, twenty-five, and fifty cents printed several to a sheet. There were perforations around each one at first, but later the perforations were dropped. The postage currency could be clipped in such a way that people could carry blocks worth $1 each.

Postage currency got its name from the designs printed on it. Each note bore portraits identical to those on the stamps of the same value. Thus, a five-cent note had the portrait of Thomas Jefferson found on the five-cent stamp. The twenty-five cent postage currency showed five portraits of Jefferson. Likewise, the ten-cent stamp's portrait appeared once on the ten-cent note and five times on the fifty-cent note. These notes became legal on March 3, 1863, their use limited to payments of less than a dollar.

On December 1, 1862, Postmaster Blair issued his official report on the use of regular postage stamps as change. The report stated:

> Postmasters were specially instructed to discontinue sales of stamps to persons evidently designing them for use as currency;

> but notwithstanding the precaution taken and the checks adopted . . . the demand has until quite recently been largely in advance of the daily manufacture . . . the majority of applications . . . from postmasters were only partially filled, generally but one-half the numbers asked for having been sent . . . the aggregate value of the postage stamps and stamped envelopes sold at 29 of the larger post-offices during the third quarter of 1862 was $1,400,937.48, and during the corresponding quarter of 1861 was $606,597.40, showing an excess in favor of 1862 or $794,340.08. . . . Nearly the entire excess . . . has been or is now in use as currency.

When postage currency was introduced the following year, many of the problems were eliminated. The *Springfield Republican* of January 29, 1863, was one of several papers that praised the new system: "There is a general agreement throughout the country to banish all private and corporate shinplasters and use only the government postage currency for change after the first of February. In Boston, already, none but those of the Parker House remain in circulation, and these are refused at many stores, and are being fast retired. . . . A few choice shinplasters may be temporarily retained in special localities, till sufficient of the postal currency works in to accomodate public wants. . . . There are large amounts of the postal currency in circulation, and most is hoarded that will come out as soon as the other sort is banished."

On March 3, 1863, Congress officially enacted legislation that would substitute paper money for change without using the postal currency. Section 4 of the act stated:

> And be it further enacted, That in lieu of postage and revenue stamps for fractional currency, issued or to be issued, the Secretary of the Treasury may issue fractional notes of like amounts in such form as he may deem expedient, and may provide for the engraving, preparation, and issue thereof in the Treasury Department building. And all such notes issued shall be exchangeable by the assistant treasurers and designated depositaries for United States notes, in sums not less than three dollars, and shall be receivable for postage and revenue stamps, and also in payment of any dues to the United States less than five dollars, except duties on imports, and shall be redeemed on presentation at the Treasury of the United States in such sums and under such regulations as the Secretary of the Treasury shall prescribe: Provided that the whole amount of fractional currency issued, including postage and revenue stamps issued as currency, shall not exceed fifty millions of dollars.
>
> SEC. 7. And be it further enacted, all banks, associations or corporations, and individuals issuing or reissuing notes or bills for circulation as currency after April first, eighteen hundred and sixty-three, in sums representing any fractional part of a dollar, shall be subject to and pay a duty of five per centum each half year thereafter upon the amount of such fractional notes or bills so issued.

Before we take leave of paper change and return to the subject of coins, there is a humorous incident worth telling concerning the fractional currency. For many years the portrait of a living person has not been placed on our paper money. The reason for this is an event involving the fractional currency that occurred toward the end of the Civil War.

The problem began when S. M. Clark, the chief of the First Division National Currency Bureau, was helping the government establish facilities for the printing of paper money. Previously, the American Bank Note Company had done most of the printing work and had control over the plates. However, the company charged the government what has been estimated to be four times the actual cost of producing the notes, and this was a highly lucrative situation the company did not want to end.

In an attempt to retain the account with the United States government—rather than have the government set up its own bureau of printing and engraving—the company decided to put Clark's portrait on the five-cent fractional currency note as a means of flattering him. It was hoped thereby that he would influence the Treasury Department to keep using the services of the American Bank Note Company.

The result was not expected. Congressmen were angered by the company's action, possibly because their images had not been used. Whatever the reason, on April 7, 1886, a law was passed making it illegal for a living person's portrait to appear on the nation's money.

The Civil War saw the introduction of a new coin for small change. On December 8, 1863, Mint Director Pollock proposed a coin of a new denomination—the two-cent piece. It would be made of bronze, a material that had recently come into use in European coinage. It was an alloy of copper, tin, and zinc and its use was proposed both for the one-cent piece (instead of the nickel alloy) and for a two-cent piece, which would be double the weight of the cent. Pollock stated, "This piece would be a great public convenience, and its coinage, in my opinion, should be authorized."

The new coin would be different from previous coinage in that it would bear a now familiar motto that had formerly not appeared on our coins. Apparently, the motto was first proposed on November 13, 1861, by M. R. Watkinson, a minister of Ridleyville, Pennsylvania. He wrote Secretary of the Treasury Chase:

> You are about to submit your annual report to Congress respecting the affairs of the national finances.
>
> One fact touching our currency has hitherto been seriously overlooked. I mean the recognition of the Almighty God in some form on our coins.
>
> You are probably a Christian. What if our Republic were now shattered beyond reconstruction? Would not the antiquaries of succeeding centuries rightly reason from our past that we were a

heathen nation? What I propose is that instead of the goddess of liberty we shall have next inside the 13 stars a ring inscribed with the words "Perpetual Union"; within this ring the all-seeing eye, crowned with a halo; beneath this eye the American flag, bearing in its field stars equal to the number of the States united; in the folds of the bars the words, "God, liberty, law."

This would make a beautiful coin, to which no possible citizen could object. This would relieve us from the ignominy of heathenism. This would place us openly under the Divine protection we have personally claimed. From my heart I have felt our national shame in disowning God as not the least of our present national disasters. . . .

Secretary of the Treasury Salmon P. Chase was apparently moved enough to write to Mint Director James Pollock on November 20 1861: "No nation can be strong except in the strength of God, or safe except in His defense. The trust of our people in God should be declared on our national coins. You will cause a device to be prepared without unnecessary delay with a motto expressing in the fewest and tersest words possible this national recognition."

Pollock considered the issue for more than a year. Then, in 1863 when minor design changes were made, Pollock suggested two mottoes, "God, our Trust" and "Our Country; our God."

Chase wrote a letter to Pollock on December 9 of that year, saying: "I approve your mottoes, only suggesting that on that with the Washington obverse the motto should begin with the word 'Our,' so as to read 'Our God and Our Country.' And on that with the shield, it should be changed so as to read, 'In God We Trust.' "

The mint director decided to use the motto "In God We Trust," placing it on the two-cent bronze coin introduced in 1864. Final authority had been given by the act of April 22, 1864 (see Appendix), so that the mint director could personally approve the motto.

The Confederacy was experiencing problems just like those of the Union. However, the story of the Confederate financial system is primarily the story of paper money. President Jefferson Davis and his cabinet relied on currency unbacked by gold or silver to see the Confederacy through the war. The result was a constantly increasing inflation and the near-collapse of government finances. However, this story is beyond the scope of this book.

There were two coins prepared by the Confederacy, and these are worth some discussion. Neither coin ever entered circulation, nor was there ever a serious plan to form a Confederate coinage. The Confederate government had captured the New Orleans branch mint but loyal federal employees had extensively sabotaged the equipment there.

According to existing records, the United States government operated the New Orleans mint until January 26, 1861, producing $265,000 in half-dollars and twenty-dollar gold pieces. Then, some

The two-cent piece, like the two varieties of three-cent coins, was an unwanted design. It was coined from 1864 to 1873. It was the first issue to use the motto "In God We Trust."

time following the appointment of A. J. Guirot as assistant treasurer of the Confederate States on March 11, 1861, the mint was used to turn out $59,820 in double eagles and $481,316 in half dollars. These coins were made from the standard United States coin dies rather than from dies specifically created for the Confederate government.

Confederate Secretary of the Treasury Christopher Memminger was assigned the task of determining whether the New Orleans mint could be operated economically. He determined that the cost of operation would exceed the income realized from the production of coins. Much as the South needed small change, it was impractical to pursue the matter further. On May 14, 1861, production was ordered suspended.

Before the mint was closed, there was a movement to create a coin that would be symbolic of the Confederacy. As early as March 6, 1861, the superintendent of the New Orleans mint had written to Memminger: "When the Government of the Confederate States assumes active control over the operations of this institution, I assume that it will require new dies, with new devices and inscriptions. To procure them will require time. Would it not be well to commence preparations for the new state of things?" Memminger replied, "I wish you could see some of the persons in New Orleans, who deal in engravings or designing, and procure some designs from them for the various coins and send them here immediately. I would suggest to them to design something new and appropriate to the South, leaving to the North the Eagle and its counterpart."

The mint superintendent, William Elmore, went to the best engravers he could find—in the Union. He received a design from the National Bank Note Company of New York as well as one from the firm of Gallier and Esterbrook, architects with offices in New Orleans. The latter design was described thus:

> The principal figure, the Goddess of Liberty, seated, holds in her right hand a staff surmounted by the Liberty cap: her left arm rests on a shield, and the left hand on the "Constitution." On the shield (there being no coat of arms yet adopted) is shown a portion of the flag on the Confederacy, unfurled; to the left of the figure will be observed sugarcane growing, a bale of cotton, a sugar hogshead, and a bale of tobacco; to the right, cotton in its various stages of growth, as also tobacco. On the reverse side is an endless chain composed of fifteen links; South Carolina, having taken the lead, occupies the top link, and the other links represent, right and left, the other States in the order of their secession; the remaining blank lines are an invitation to the border States to hasten to inscribe their names within the circle. The stars of the Confederate States are distinct; those of the border states are in the twilight, but visible, soon, we hope, to stand out as boldly as their neighbors. In the center is inscribed the monogram, composed of the letters C.S.A. Twenty dollars has been printed to represent the denomination of the coin. Of course, the design is adaptable to any denomination of our coin."

No patterns for this particular design concept have ever been discovered. There is a Confederate half-dollar in existence, though, so we know some work progressed on this.

The first widely known reference to the Confederate half-dollar occurred in 1879. At that time it was learned that a coin or coins existed bearing the Seated Liberty obverse used by the United States during that period and a unique Confederate States of America reverse featuring a shield and the Phrygian cap. The latter device dated back to ancient Rome, where the cap was given to slaves who had been granted their freedom. In modern times it has generally been called the Liberty Cap. The shield contained seven stars—one for each seceding state. There is a wreath of sugar cane and blooming cotton surrounding the shield.

E. Mason, Jr., a Philadelphia coin collector, wrote an article on the half-dollar in January 1879. The article was read by Dr. B. F. Taylor who had been chief coiner at the New Orleans mint during the Civil War. Taylor was then working as the secretary-treasurer of the Louisiana state Board of Health.

Taylor wrote Mason that he had commissioned A.H.M. Peterson, a die sinker and engraver, to prepare a new reverse for the Confederate half-dollar under consideration. Only the reverse would be changed. The obverse of the United States half-dollar was intended to be used from the start.

The reverse coin die that was developed did not fit the mint's normal coining press. Union sympathizers had damaged the press as well as defacing or destroying many of the dies.

Someone found an old hand press, so slow and cumbersome that the saboteurs had chosen to ignore it when vandalizing the mint. Four coins were struck on the press, and one coin was sent to Jefferson Davis, another to Professor Biddle at the University of Louisiana, the third to Dr. E. Ames of New Orleans; the last was kept by Chief Coiner Taylor.

Mason began exploring the story further. Jefferson Davis was still alive so he wrote him for more information. Davis replied: "I had a Confederate coin. It was in my wife's trunk when it was rifled by the Federal officers on board the prison ship on which she was detained at Hampton Roads before and after my confinement in Fortress Monroe. The coin, some medals and other valuables were stolen at that time. Whether the coin be the same which has been offered to you as a duplicate, I cannot say. It is, however, not true, as published, that it is now in my possession."

The reverse die of the Confederate half-dollar was purchased by J. W. Scott of New York's Scott and Company in 1879. He decided to file the reverses from 500 half dollars and restrike them with the die in his possession. These would be sold at what he hoped would be a handsome profit.

Scott advertised for genuine 1861 New Orleans ("O" mint mark) half-dollars to use for his restrikes. The following circular was sent out from the Scott & Company offices at 146 Fulton Street on October 17, 1879:

> It is with great pleasure we present you with the restrike half dollar subscribed for on the—ult., and hope it will meet your approbation. We regret the delay in forwarding, which was caused by the die breaking on the first trial. It then had to be set in a heavy steel band to prevent further damage. Before risking the die again on the hard silver we thought it advisable to strike the requisite number (500) in white metal with the following inscription for a reverse: 4 ORIGINALS STRUCK BY ORDER OF C.S.A. IN NEW ORLEANS, 1861 . . . REVERSE SAME AS U. S. (FROM ORIGINAL DIE, SCOTT). These will be sold in any quantity to those who subscribe to the silver Confederate piece, at 50 cents each. It was with difficulty that we procured the 500 half dollars of a special mintage on which the pieces have been struck by a new method over genuine 1861 N.O. mint U.S. half dollars, and in consequence they must rank high above ordinary restruck coins.
>
> The die (damaged only sufficiently to prevent restriking) is a very valuable and interesting relic, and is now for sale. Price, $50.
>
> Up to the 10th inst. we received orders for 567 pieces. The odd 67 subscribers have been supplied from a like number of patrons who ordered two copies. This we concluded would be the more equitable plan for all parties concerned. Amateurs who ordered

two will please remember that by this plan they certainly got one, whereas if they had drawn for chances they might have been left without any. We have received quite a number of orders since the 10th inst., all of which we are unable to fill unless some of our subscribers who get two will kindly return one, for which we will be pleased to pay $2.50.

A Confederate cent was also struck, again through the efforts of a Northern firm. Philadelphian Robert Lovett, Jr., received an order to prepare a one cent piece for the Confederate States of America early in 1861. He designed the coin, then struck a dozen pieces in copper-nickel, hiding them in his basement when he realized the Union government might be angry about his working for the enemy. The die and coins were eventually uncovered by Captain John Hazeltine of Philadelphia who, along with J. Colvin Randall, issued this notice to collectors on April 2, 1874:

> Having succeeded in discovering and purchasing the dies of the Confederate Cent, we, the undersigned, have concluded to strike for the benefit of Collectors a limited number, and in order to protect those gentlemen who had the nickel pieces, originally struck in 1861, we determined to strike none in that metal. Our intention was to strike five hundred in copper, but after the fifty-fifth impression the collar burst and the dies were badly broken. They are now in the possession of Mr. Hazeltine, and may be seen at any time at his store, No. 1343 Chestnut Street, Philadelphia.
>
> This history of this piece is probably known to most Collectors, but, for the information of those who are ignorant of the facts, we will state that the dies were made by Mr. Lovett, of Philadelphia, in 1861, who says that they were ordered in that year for the South, and that he struck but twelve pieces, but probably thinking that he might have some difficulty in reference to them (having made the dies for the South), he mentioned the matter to no one until a few months since, when he parted with ten pieces, struck in nickel, which he stated were all he had, having lost two pieces. One of the said lost pieces was the means of the dies and pieces being traced. Although the Southern Confederacy did not adopt this piece, it will always be considered interesting as the only coinage designed for the said Confederacy.
>
> Description.—Obverse, 1861; head of Liberty; inscription, "Confederate States of America"; reverse, a wreath of ears of corn and wheat, with a cotton bale at the bottom; in the centre, the words "1 Cent." The restrikes were struck by Peter L. Krider, No. 618 Chestnut Street, and we now offer them at the following prices:
>
> Gold, only seven struck, each $30.00
> Silver, only twelve struck, each 15.00
> Copper, only fifty-five struck, each 4.00
> Nickel, originals struck in 1861,
> only four left, each 20.00

All orders to be addressed to J. W. Haseltine, No. 1343 Chestnut Street, Philadelphia.

Several years later, at the Philadelphia convention of the American Numismatic Association, Captain Hazeltine spoke about the cents:

> I have been asked to say something about the so-called Confederate cent. A little circular issued by my self and Mr. Randall some years ago tells all the history of the striking of these pieces, but I do not think it mentioned how I obtained the dies. One day I was told by a gentlemen that a bartender in West Philadelphia had a Confederate cent. I doubted it. Mr. J. Colvin Randall (now deceased) was told the same. He conferred with me in reference to it, and we decided that if either of us obtained it we would share in any profit that would accrue from it. I saw the bartender and purchased the coin from him. It was in nickel, and he said he received it over the bar. I knew by the head on the obverse it was Mr. Lovett's work. I called on Mr. Lovett, and he denied ever having made the dies. Numerous times I called to induce him to give me some information about them, but he alway stuck to his story that he did not make them until one day, when he was slightly "in his cups," he pulled out a drawer in one of his cabinets, and I beheld a line of little Confederate cents. Of course I tackled him at once, and he then owned up and told me that he had eleven of them, but formerly there were twelve, he having lost one. He said he received the order to make them for the Confederacy through a well-known jewelry firm in Philadelphia (I think he said Bailey & Co.), but that his wife became timid about his delivering them for fear the United States Government might arrest him for giving assistance to the enemy, so he buried them in his cellar until long after the war was over, and even then he was afraid to show them. I purchased the dies from him, and, as you all probably know, did not strike any in nickel, considering them to a certain degree as originals, but we had three struck in gold, and I believe five in silver and fifty-five in copper, the dies breaking on the fifty-ninth piece, which is in existence showing the break in the die.

It would seem that the Confederate coinage, like the concept of a separate nation, died in the planning stages. The few coins and restrikes that do exist remain curious reminders of the bloody, abortive seccession attempt.

As the Civil War drew to a close, one other coin was authorized by Congress for the Union. On March 3, 1865, the three-cent nickel was approved as a way of appeasing the nickel-mine owners. There was no real purpose for the coin other than to insure a demand for the metal. John Wharton, a metallurgist who had built a nickel-mining works, handled the lobbying effort successfully. The new coin was 75 percent copper, 25 percent nickel, and weighed thirty grains. It's coinage continued twenty-five years; supposedly, it aided in the sale

The three-cent coin struck in nickel.

of postage stamps, though in reality, it was of little importance to commerce.

The design for the three-cent nickel was simple. The Liberty Head on the obverse had a flowing hair design capped with a tiara. The reverse had the Roman numeral III surrounded by a wreath. The coin passed into circulation with little public reaction one way or another. Only the following year did people become aroused by the new nickel coinage when the five-cent piece was introduced. Its story is told in the next chapter.

8

Years of Change

The years following the Civil War brought radical changes in American coinage. In 1866 the first five-cent piece made from nickel was introduced. The design was simple and unattractive. A shield, similar to the one found on the two-cent piece, formed the obverse. The reverse had stars spaced with arrows during the first year, and the same design with arrows omitted was used the second and succeeding years. The number *5* was in the center of the circle of stars and the words "United States of America" and "Cents" surrounded the stars. The new motto, "In God We Trust," was on the obverse, over the shield.

There were numerous critics of the new design. Perhaps the most interesting comment was made in the *American Journal of Numismatics* for August 1866, where the following statement was made: "Though collectors have long ceased to regard the true issues of the 'Government copper-head factory,' better known, perhaps, as the United States Mint, as of any value, they may be interested in the information that the ugliest of all known coins, the new five cent piece, is out, as oysters are served in some places 'in every style.' "

The most important law to be passed in the years immediately following the Civil War was the Mint Act of 1873. The changes in coinage it created caused havoc both financially and numismatically.

The most practical change in law in terms of organization affected the branch mints. The branch mints had, since their creation, been operating independently both of each other and the main Philadelphia mint. This caused problems with operating expenses and other matters. As a result, the proposal was made that the mint system

The Shield nickel five-cent piece was first struck in 1866. In 1867 there was a modification of the reverse, and the rays between the stars were eliminated.

become a bureau within the Treasury Department. The chief officer of the bureau would have the title of "Director of the Mint" and would serve under the secretary of the Treasury. The director would be a presidential appointee and would take precedence over all operating officers of the various branches.

The new bill had other provisions that proved extremely controversial, however. First was the abolition of the silver dollar, a coin that was no longer circulating to any degree. Unfortunately, this came at a time when silver production was increasing greatly within the United States, while international demand for the metal was dropping.

Germany, long a user of silver, switched to the gold standard in July 1873. Other European nations still used silver, but they were also considering a change. Demand was down almost everywhere, with the exception of China, where merchants insisted upon silver coins for international business. They were very particular about the coins they would use, though, and wanted only pieces of consistent weight and fineness. Usually this meant Spanish eight-real pieces, which, though fluctuating somewhat in value over the years, had maintained high standards for so long that they had become a widely used trading device.

Since silver deposits were being uncovered in ever-growing numbers, the mine owners and others with vested interests in silver decided that a special silver dollar should be struck for use in the Orient. This "Trade dollar" would be superior to any dollar produced in the United States and superior even to the Mexican mint issues. It would be of special help to the merchants on the West Coast, who could never seem to scrape together enough silver for direct dealings with the Orient. They usually had to work through the London silver market, where charges of several percent were added, effectively reducing the final buying power of the coins when they reached the East.

On February 10, 1873, a story appeared in the San Francisco newspaper the *Daily Alta California* describing a dispatch sent from Hong Kong by United States Consul Bailey with regard to the creation of a silver coin for the Orient trade. The dispatch was widely circulated by the silver interests in Congress who were trying to add a provision for the coinage of a Trade dollar to the 1873 coinage act. The article quoted Bailey as saying:

> For some time my attention has been drawn to the importance of closer and more direct banking facilities between the United States and China. The great and rapidly augmenting trade between the two countries would seem to demand new and cheaper channels for the immense sums of money floating to and fro. In other words, more direct and economical facilities by which the benefit of direct exchange and its lower rate would accrue more directly to Americans and to those engaged in commerce between Eastern Asia and the United States. As a natural consequence of such an improvement a certain percentage would be saved by which goods could be laid down in America cheaper than under the course pursued now. If this percentage be only a trifle, the total will show a heavy sum in the end.
>
> At present all the vast sums of money passing between America and Asia are paying enormous tribute to London.
>
> San Francisco, Shanghai and Hong Kong, facing each other on opposite sides of the Pacific, go round the world to pay each other in Lombard Street—an anomaly which, it seems to me, need not be, and which can and ought to be abrogated.
>
> It is a well known fact that the balance of trade between America and Europe (England predominating) is usually against the former. This deficit is made up by both North and South America sending bullion and specie to Europe. The United States imports from China and Japan and the Philippine Islands and East India, annually, to the extent of about approximately $50,000,000 in Mexicans. By far the greatest portion of this import is paid for by America in London. Thus, the United States annually adds to the debts already existing against her in Europe, the amounts of her imports from the East.
>
> For attending to this financiering of our commerce in the East, London banks and bankers charge as commission two percent on the amount drawn. The English banks in the East have—say ½ percent profit on the transaction for negotiating the paper.

Having thus lengthily quoted Consul Bailey, the writer of the article continued:

Mr. Bailey went on to show that the increase of percentage and commissions in London on American exchange from the Orient amounted to a tax on commerce of from 3 to 4 percent. He suggests that some powerful bank, or company of bankers, establish branches in the cities of China and Japan, with large credits and powers to draw on San Francisco, New York and other cities in the United States; thus relieving our Oriental commerce from paying tribute to London and facilitating exchange. He thinks that since the completion of the transcontinental railway in the United States; and the establishment of regular steam communication across the Pacific, there is no longer any need for continuing the financial system heretofore in vogue.

The coinage of a silver coin equal to the Mexican dollar, for use in China, he recommends as of great advantage to our commerce. This is thought would open a field for gold to follow in, and a market for our metals as well as an inducement to trade with us would be established.

The coinage act passed two days later, and the new Trade dollar became the only silver dollar produced by the United States. The act also ended the use of silver as a major force in finance. Silver retained legal tender status only in amounts not to exceed five dollars, a radical departure from the early days of United States silver coins. With the passage of this bill, the United States had effectively ended bimetallism and had gone on the gold standard.

On March 19, 1873, another San Francisco paper, the *Daily Evening Bulletin,* editorialized about the new coin:

Congress provided at the last session for the issue of a new silver

The Trade dollar was a special silver dollar, created strictly for trade with the Orient, was introduced in 1873 and continued through 1883.

> dollar which ought to be popular on this side of the country. It is only to be issued to depositors of bullion at their own request. The Mexican dollar has long been very popular, and has been extensively exported. The Chinese have sent immense sums of this currency to China, buying the coin at a premium over the American dollar. The Mexican dollar is worth 4¢ more than our gold dollar, but a premium of 5¢ has frequently been paid for the former for export.
>
> The new silver dollar, or trade-dollar, is to be .900 fine and to be worth 5¢ more than the gold dollar and one cent more than the Mexican dollar. The Mexicans have recently put a new stamp on their silver dollar and the Chinese are a little suspicious of it. If the new Mexican dollar can be crowded out by the new American dollar, which is of higher intrinsic value, a point will be gained.
>
> The value of silver bullion would be advanced if there was a large demand for the trade-dollar. But as it would not come into general circulation here as long as the old coin is abundant, the chief demand would be for export. If ten millions in trade dollars should be wanted within a short time, possibly the silver miners would find their account, whether by an advance of bullion or by sending the same to be coined into the trade-dollar.

The new Trade dollar was artistically of superior design to most of the other coins in circulation within the country. The *American Journal of Numismatics* described the new coin when it came out in 1873. An editorial commented: "A female figure [is] seated on bales of merchandise, holding in her left hand a scroll bearing the word 'Liberty.' At her back is a sheaf of wheat, expressing, with the bales of goods, the commercial character of the coin: her right hand extended holds the olive branch." The design was meant to be symbolic of peace and commerce.

The new Trade dollar was an immediate success in the Orient, and was frequently accepted without question. When merchants did check its quality, their approval would be indicated by a mark punched into the metal with a hand punch. This "chop mark" varied from merchant to merchant, and some Trade dollars have dozens of them added to their surfaces.

The Trade dollar also proved popular wherever there were coin shortages in the United States as, for example, in the many mining communities. One interesting commentary on the coin was written by William Wright, the editor of the *Territorial Enterprise* of Virginia City. Wright, using the pen name "Dan DeQuille," wrote a book entitled *The Big Bonanza* published in 1876. He talked of the Trade Dollar, saying:

> In Virginia City, as well as in all the towns and cities of the Pacific Coast, gold and silver coin is the only money in circulation. There are now in circulation at least two American coins almost unknown in other parts of the Union—the trade-dollar and the twenty-five

cent piece—as their coinage was not authorized until after greenbacks became a legal-tender, and had taken possession of the Atlantic states to the exclusion of all coin except copper and nickel.

The Trade-Dollar was coined for our trade with China and Japan. It was coined expressly to supersede the Mexican dollars in the countries named. It contains a trifle more silver than the Mexican dollar, and the Chinese were not long in ascertaining this fact. Now the American trade-dollar is in great demand in both China and Japan, and the old Mexican dollar is thrown completely into the shade. The Chinese and Japanese are great lovers of silver, and the American trade-dollar, being pure silver, is preferred by them to the coin of any other nation. The end—the final fate—of the trade-dollar, however is inglorious. It is sent to India by the Chinese for the purchase of opium. In India, the trade-dollars are sent to the Calcutta mint and are there made into rupees, stamped with the value on one side and on the other, outlandish heathen characters. Thus the silver of the big bonanza fills the opium pipe of the Chinese mandarin. The amount of American silver sent to India to pay for Opium is very great.

The Chinese in Nevada and in all other towns of the Pacific Coast industriously gather trade-dollars, which they send to the head men of their companies in San Francisco, by whom they are shipped to China. Persons who have but lately arrived from states where no coin is seen are astonished at the abundance of silver in Virginia City and delighted to be in a place where they may once again hear the almost forgotten jingle of gold and silver; though I once heard a New York lady say: "I never saw such a place. I hearing nothing but the jingle of money from one end of the town to the other. The people all go about jingling their money as though on purpose to show that they are able to pay their way."

The overseas enthusiasm was much stronger. A correspondent for the Hong Kong and Shanghai Banking Corporation, in a lengthy evaluation of the Trade dollar, commented: ". . . it is the best coin that ever has been imported, and, being produced at the fountainhead of silver, can be laid down more cheaply than any other dollar. The reliable character of the coin (for weight and purity) is a further consideration which must be favorably entertained."

In the early part of 1876, the decline in the silver market made it profitable to have Trade dollars coined at the mint, then placed into circulation along the Pacific Coast. The coins flooded the market and were spent everywhere, but the merchants suffered because banks could only accept them in amounts not exceeding five dollars. Soon the coins sold at a discount from face with the same disastrous effect both in California and the rest of the country.

Large-scale coinage of Trade dollars was stopped in February 1878. All future Trade dollars were prepared from specially polished dies and struck by what is known as the proof process. The coins were meant for collectors, not circulation, and very few were made.

The effect the Trade dollars had on commerce was devastating, especially since the silver in the coins was rapidly losing value in relation to gold. Intrinsically the coins were worth less than a dollar, and merchants had to sell their coins to speculators willing to take more than five at a time. The price they received was a discount well below their intrinsic worth. Members of the New York Mercantile Exchange reported on this problem on February 3, 1883, commenting:

> We are put to great inconvenience and pecuniary loss by a coin known as the trade dollar, which is not a legal tender payment of debts, and which, notwithstanding, is so largely received and recognized as a dollar by the community that we cannot without loss of trade individually refuse to accept it in payment, and which, being not taken on deposit by banks, and not accepted in payment of dues to the Government, we are compelled to sell at a discount.
>
> Some persons employing operatives make a practice of buying at a discount these coins and paying them at par value to their operatives, who again pay them to the retailers of goods, and these again pay them to us, and we, not able to deposit them or pay them in large amounts to our creditors, are compelled to sell them to brokers at a discount for legal money. It results that there is a continual loss falling upon us, and a corresponding profit reaped by such unscrupulous persons.

The legal-tender status had been revoked by Congress on July 22, 1876. The idea was to limit the coins to overseas trade. But since so many were circulating within the United States, the lack of a gradual withdrawal did immense harm. Eventually some merchants on the West Coast were receiving the coins at face, then selling them for as little as half face value to brokers who, in turn, distributed them to people buying merchandise from the men who had to broker them in the first place. It was a vicious circle.

It wasn't until February 1887 that Congress finally had the sense to recognize the redemption problem. On February 19, 1887, a bill was enacted stating: ". . . That for a period of six months after the passage of this act, United States trade-dollars, if not defaced, mutilated, or stamped, shall be received at the office of the Treasurer, or any assistant treasurer of the United States in exchange for a like amount, dollar for dollar, of standard silver dollars, or of subsidiary coins of the United States."

The Trade dollar story has an interesting sidelight. The two most valuable Trade dollars do not officially exist. They are the result of "private enterprise" at the mint.

Private enterprise had been exhibited at the Philadelphia mint a number of times over the years. Among other illegal activities, mint workers struck unauthorized coins and sold them for profit. The most notorious abuser of his mint position was Franklin Peale, an early chief coiner. He engaged in the private production of medals for outside sale, using the Mint's equipment, time, and manpower. His story is told in depth in Don Taxay's *The U.S. Mint and Coinage.*

The Proof Trade dollars struck from 1879 to 1883 were unquestionably legal, even though never intended for circulation. The coins, sold at a profit, could be struck as long as the regular coinage was permitted by law. Since it was only by an act of March 3, 1887, that the life of the Trade dollar was ended, proof issues could have been struck until that date. However, there are no records of any such coins being made after 1883.

One of the most thorough of the researchers into the question of the 1884 and 1885 Proof Trade Dollars, Walter Breen, is quoted by John Willem in his book *The United States Trade Dollar.* Breen wrote:

"There is not the slightest hint in the 1887 (or any other Director's Report) that any Trades were coined in 1884 or 1885. There is no account of any such in the Coiner's tables and reports for those years, or any others. There is no accounting for the bullion that must have been used for them. There is no record of any dies being made for Trades in those years. I conclude that the issue (which was not known before 1908, in spite of rumors) must have been a result of private enterprise at the Mint, in the Coiner's Department which had charge of the hubs and presses on which working dies were regularly made."

In March 1884, the editor of *Numisma* wrote about the Trade dollars which were no longer officially being struck as follows:

> Our critic at the Sandham sale recently, almost openly, insinuated that Trade Dollars have been quietly manufactured at the

In 1884 and 1885, Trade dollars were illegally coined. Ten of the 1884 Trade dollars were produced, as were five of the 1885 ones, one of which is shown. This is one of the most valuable of all United States coins. The coin shown here is currently valued in the neighborhood of a quarter million dollars or more.

Mint during the past year; in other words, not withstanding the positive assertions of the Mint authorities to the contrary, a Trade Dollar with the date 1884 does exist.

We hold that the plain but positive statement of the Mint officers on this point should be considered conclusive evidence, and they say that no Trade Dollars have been issued in the Philadelphia Mint, or in any Mint of the U. S. during the past year, or dated 1884.

But as doubts on this point may still exist in the minds of those who heard the report, we are authorized to make the following offers: $100 cash each for any number of United States Trade Dollars of 1884, coined at the Philadelphia or any other U. S. Mint; $25 to anyone who will show us such a dollar.

The coins were revealed, but not until 1908. Are they genuine? In a sense they are. The 1884 and 1885 Trade dollars undoubtedly originated in the mint. However, they were unauthorized and were made for private gain rather than being legitimate government proofs. But this has not stopped the collector's price from rising to over three hundred thousand dollars for the 1885 coin alone.

Criticisms of coin designs had long been a problem with which mint workers had to live. But in the 1870s the comments became so harsh and widespread that it was felt changes had to be planned. For example, the periodical *Galaxy* attacked the nation's coinage in a harsh article in its June 1876 issue, saying:

Why is it that we have the ugliest money of all civilized nations? For such undoubtedly our silver coinage is. The design is poor, commonplace, tasteless, characterless, and the execution is like thereunto. Our silver coins do not even look like money. They have rather the appearance of tokens or mean medals. One reason of this is that the design is so inartistic and so insignificant. That young woman sitting on nothing in particular, wearing nothing to speak of, looking over her shoulder at nothing imaginable, and bearing in her left hand something that looks like a broomstick with a woolen nightcap on it—what is she doing there? What is the meaning of her? She is Liberty, we are told, and there is a label to that effect across a shield on her right, her need of which is not in any way manifest. But she might as well be anything else as Liberty; and at the first glance she looks much more like a spinster in her smock, with a distaff in her hand. Such a figure has no proper place upon a coin. On the reverse the eagle has the contrary fault of being too natural, too much like a real eagle. In numismatic art animals have conventional forms, which are far more pleasing and effective than the most careful and exact imitation of nature can be. Compare one of our silver coins with those of Great Britain, France or Germany, and see how mean, slight, flimsy, inartistic and unmoneylike it looks. Our coins of forty or fifty years ago were much better in every respect, and looked much more like money, the reason being that they bore a head of Liberty which was bold, clear, and well defined in comparison with the weak thing that the Mint has given us for the last thirty years or so. The eagle too, although erring on the side of naturalness, was more suited in design to coinage. But still better were the coins struck at the end of the last century and the beginning of this one. The eagle was a real heraldic eagle, the head of Liberty had more character, and the whole work was bolder and better in every way. But even they had the great defect of being without significance in design. What is a head of Liberty? What distinctive character can be given to a head upon a coin which will make it much more like Liberty than anything else?

". . . The coins of the French republic bear a head supposed to typify the Republic. It has in its features and in its decorations some character and significance, and it is bold and stands out in good relief, as it should. But we can do better than to use such mere abstractions, no matter how bold the design, how high the relief, or how fine the workmanship. . . ."

The article went on to say that the ideal portraits for our coins would be busts of Washington and Franklin because:

. . . these two men represent the two elements of our population, the two great divisions of our country. One was a Virginia planter; the other, a Philadelphia printer, born in Boston, grew from a printer into a philosopher and a statesman. The proper place for Washington's head would be upon the gold pieces; for no one would dispute the appropriateness of placing that of the author of 'Poor Richard's Almanac,' and of the adage, 'A penny saved is a penny earned,' upon the silver coins representing fractional parts of a dollar, and upon the cents. Thus our gold and silver coins would be distinguished from each other in design, not as they now are by the mere difference between a meaningless head and a meaningless sitting figure, but by two noble portrait busts of which an American might be prouder than any European ever was in the effigy of king or kaiser. With this change and with a return to the old breadth of piece, and the heraldic eagle used in the beginning of this century (the two examples now before us are dated 1803 and 1805), we should have a coinage which instead of being as now the meanest in appearance and most insignificant of all that is known, would be the most beautiful and the most fraught with associations of historic interest and national pride. We commend the subject to the attention of the House, and hope that some member may be found who will take it up and bring it before the people.

Mint Director H. R. Linderman agreed with the critics that a change in coin design was needed. However, the mint's chief engraver, William Barber, and his son Charles were overworked and lacking in the artistic skills necessary to bring forth a radical change. He turned to the London mint for an employee, writing the director: "Could you find us a first class die-sinker who would be willing to take the position of Assistant Engraver at the Mint at Philadelphia. We would like a man who could produce a finished hub, and if he understood modeling and also bronzing it would make him more valuable to us. We could pay about $8 per day to a person of proper qualifications. If you know of such a one who would be likely to answer our purpose, I will be glad if you will place me in communication with him."

Because of its centuries of experience, the London mint was contacted. A great many skilled workers had been trained there, while the United States Mint was not even a hundred years old, and available talent was limited.

According to letters first reported in the February 1964 issue of *Numismatic Scrapbook,* London Mint Director C. W. Fremantle replied:

> My enquiries as to an Assistant Engraver lead me very strongly to recommend for the post Mr. George Morgan, aged 30, who has made himself a considerable name, but for whom there is not much opening at present in this country. I send a letter from him, to which you will of course reply as you may think best, but I may perhaps just say that looking to Mr. Morgan's real talent, I do not think that he wishes to make conditions which are in any way unreasonable, and that I am convinced you would not find in him any inclination to take undue advantage of such privilege in regard to private work &c as you may see fit to concede to him. I may add that he is personally agreeable & gentleman-like, & particularly modest and quiet in manner, so that he would be likely to make an agreeable colleague You will judge of his qualifications by the work he is sending you, & I can only say that I shall be sorry if we lose him from this country, while I make no doubt he will be a valuable acquisition to yours, both officially and as an artist. . . .

Morgan's letter provided some additional information about his background. He said: "I served an apprenticeship to the Die Sinking at Birmingham. From Birmingham School of Art I successfully competed for a Scholarship at South Kensington . . . during my Studentship I obtained Medals & Prizes for Models of Heads from Life . . . Figures from Life & Antique . . . Heads from Photographs and Flowers from nature."

Morgan was hired by the mint immediately. He was actually to replace William Barber who was going to retire due to both age and the fact that he was engaged in a lucrative side business involving misuse of mint facilities. He had his own private engraving firm, which engaged in private enterprise during business hours, wasting tax money. He planned to devote full time to this endeavor when he left the mint and Charles Barber would share an office with Morgan.

Morgan's first chance to prove what he could do came with the new silver dollar that was introduced in 1878. Both he and Charles Barber submitted possible designs. Morgan's utilized a classic design for the

Liberty Head while Barber created a design that seemed fat and rather dumpy looking.

Morgan, in a letter written in 1878, commented on the coin as follows: "I have taken one (a coin) to the mint today for reduction——I have entered as a student at the Academy of Fine Arts——where I am making a profile study from a Greek figure which I feel will be useful in finishing the head of Liberty. I shall endeaver to get studies in nature for the Eagle——I have been considering the wreath on the reverse of the Dime—although it could be improved by being more sharply & clearly defined, I have come to the conclusion myself that the wreath is too elaborate & complicated in so small a coin——I have therefore prepared a design of a wreath much simpler—but I think it without novelty."

The coin was in the Greek style but the model for Morgan's Liberty was quite modern for the day. Her name was Anna Williams, a Philadelphia school teacher. At first Miss Williams was modest about what she had done. An item appearing in the *Philadelphia Sunday Republic* shortly after the coin's release early in 1878 stated:

"The head of Liberty is chaste and beautiful, and, in an artistic sense, is considered the best executed head that has ever appeared upon United States coin. It is so well distributed as to be susceptible of easy work under the die, and altogether will certainly reflect credit upon both the designer and the Government. Like its predecessor of 1808, it was taken from life, and is a fair type of the beauty of one of our Philadelphia ladies, the model having been a young lady who is a

George Morgan designed the silver dollar introduced in 1878 and used through 1921.

George Morgan designed silver dollar, introduced in 1921.

teacher in one of the public schools in the Fifteenth Section, and who naturally objects to having her name published."

Apparently the attention Anna Williams received from the public went to her head. After a couple of years' anonymity, she decided to take advantage of her fame. At least this is the impression received if an article in the *American Journal of Numismatics* in 1882 is correct. It stated:

"It is announced that Miss Anna W. Williams, the Philadelphia lady whose portrait may be seen by any one who possesses or can borrow a "Morgan" silver dollar, has been engaged by a theatrical manager who proposes to make a 'star' of her. When the dollar was first issued the face was criticized considerably, as was also the figure of the 'scared hen' on the reverse; but there will now be an opportunity for the critics to see how they fancy the original. The lady certainly has a beautiful profile, if the likeness on the coin is good, and if successful will draw many of her portraits into her treasury."

Twenty years after the introduction of the Morgan silver dollar, Miss Williams was again the subject of an article, this time in the *New York Mail and Express,* which said: "Miss Williams is a decidedly modest young woman. She resides on Spring Garden Street, not far from the school in which for years she has been employed as instructor in philosphy and methods in the kindergarten department. She is slightly below the average height, is rather plump, and is fair. She carries her figure with a stateliness rarely seen and the pose of the head is exactly as seen on the silver dollar. The features of Miss Williams are reproduced as faithfully as in a good photograph."

The year 1878 was famous for more than just the Morgan silver dollar. It was also a year in which the United States had its first "goloid" coinage, a metal experiment the mint quickly abandoned.

The idea behind goloid was conceived by Wheeler Hubbell. He felt that if a combination of gold and silver could be used in a single coin, then both the gold and silver interests would be happy. Hubbell made a proposal to the House Committee on Coinage, Weights, and Measures during the 1877 debate over whether to use gold or silver as the standard for American coinage. He commented: "Let us have goloid, the combination of gold and silver which provides specie with an intrinsic value always equal to face. Gold is used to satisfy international markets, and silver is used to satisfy the silver interests who wanted to be certain the Treasury bought metal from their mines." The fact that such a compromise would make Hubbell, the owner of the goloid process patent, quite rich went unremarked.

While the debates were going on, Congress passed a bill authorizing a stable relationship between the price of silver and gold, a bill President Rutherford B. Hayes vetoed. Hayes commented:

> The silver dollar authorized is worth eight or 10 per cent less than it purports to be worth, and is made legal tender for debts contracted when the law did not recognize such coin as lawful money. The effect would be to put an end to the receipt of revenue in gold, and thus compel the payment of silver for both the principal and interest of the public debt. [The president continued:] It is my firm conviction that if the country is to be benefitted by a silver coinage, it can only be done by the issue of silver dollars of full value which will defraud no man. A currency worth less than it purports to be worth, will in the end defraud not only creditors, but all who are engaged in legitimate business and none more surely than those who are dependent on their daily labor for their daily bread.

While all this was going on, the Coinage Committee sent Philadelphia Mint Director H. R. Linderman a letter dated December 29, 1877, requesting a test of the goloid metal. The letter was quite specific as to the coins to be struck for the test:

> We want each dollar to contain 258 grains of the goloid metal, and in the same proportions for the half and quarter dollars. That is, the half dollar to have in it 129 grains of goloid and the quarter 64¼ grains, etc. Let the coins, if you please, have stamped these words: On the dollar, GOLOID ONE DOLLAR. 1G. 24S. .9 FINE. 258 GRAINS. On the half dollar, GOLOID HALF DOLLAR. 1G. 24S. .9 FINE. 129 GRS. On the quarter dollar, GOLOID QUARTER DOLLAR. 1G. 24S. .9 FINE, 64½ GRS.
>
> The committee would like to have these specimens in sufficient number for the convenience of members of Congress by the 10th of January next or as soon as practicable.

The instructions were forwarded to the coiners. Then, on January 3, 1878, Linderman received a letter reading: "Sir, Your instructions of the 31st of December ultimo, based on a request, under date of Dec. 27th, from Hon. Alexander H. Stephens, to have a pair of dies prepared from which to strike specimen dollars to illustrate the proposed 'goloid' coin, were daily received, and have been communicated to our Engraver, who will set to work immediately to prepare the dies, with the inscriptions and designs suggested: but he cannot promise to have them ready under three weeks from this date. When completed the specimens of the required weight and composition will

These are all varieties of the ten-dollar gold piece.

be struck and forwarded, together with a bill for the value of the metal contained in them."

The first goloid dollars were struck by Chief Coiner Oliver Bosbyshell on January 14, 1878. The design was the creation of mint engraver William Barber and the total effect was impressive. Unfortunately it did not result in the appearance Hubbell had hoped. Instead of being distinctly different from gold or silver, goloid took on a color almost identical to that of silver. Counterfeiters or corrupt workers could use all silver in the coinage and thus make a profit.

But, Hubbell was not to be defeated so easily. He felt that the composition could be altered by combining copper, and silver chloride dissolved in ammonia. Such a change would result in a color alteration that would make the coins practical.

On January 22, 1878, Linderman commented on the change in a note to Mint Superintendent Pollock:

> If I understand the matter correctly the directions which Mr. Hubbell gives 'to put a golden tinge face on the coin' is intended to be accomplished by the dissolution of the copper, the converting of the silver into a chloride, the dissolving of the chloride by ammonia, and the leaving of a slight film of gold on the surface of the planchet, and which of course, if it gives a gold coloring, will be confined to the surface of the coin and soon disappear under the ordinary attrition of circulation.
>
> I do not suppose for a moment that the melting of the metals as directed by Mr. Hubbell would secure a more thorough mixture of the same or homogeneity of the resulting mass than as prepared for

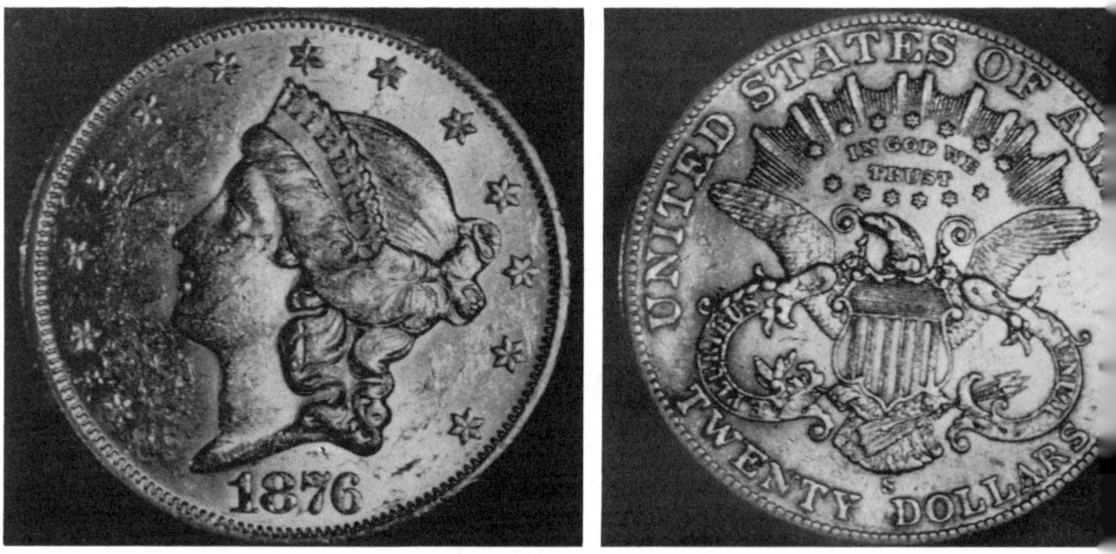

This is a variety of the twenty-dollar gold piece created by James Longacre.

the recent specimens struck and it will be likely to result in the burning out of more copper and the loss of more gold and silver from volatilization action than if all were melted together.

I need not enlarge upon these points as they are most thoroughly understood by the experienced assayer, melter and refiner of your Mint.

Linderman's predictions proved correct. However, the experimentation continued.

A new coin was added to the experiments. This was a four-dollar gold piece, known as a Stella because of the star on the design. It was conceived as a practical denomination by United States Minister to Austria John Kasson. The face amount would make it an international coin because it would be almost equal in value to the twenty-franc gold piece of France and the eight-florin coin of Austria.

Finally a last coin was added, this one being what was known as a

Examples of the four-dollar gold piece of 1879, also called a Stella. ***(Photo courtesy of Krause Publications.)***

Metric Dollar pattern by William Barber. This coin was under consideration for international trade and was made the same time as the four-dollar Stellas. (J-1617)

metric goloid piece. It was a combination of gold, silver, and copper in such proportions that the face value and intrinsic worth of the coins were identical. The acid-alkali content of the coins was altered to insure a change in color.

Despite the changes, the new coin was doomed to defeat. The ratio of silver to gold rose to eighteen to one at a time when Hubbell was planning for an intrinsic worth of sixteen to one. It became obvious that world fluctuation of silver values would create an unstable situation during which many of the goloid coins in circulation would be improperly valued. The Hubbell concept was abandoned.

The year 1878 saw another short-lived addition to United States coinage. This was the twenty-cent piece, another coin meant to placate the silver interests. No matter what the expressed motives, the real reason for the new coin was to increase silver purchases by the government.

The twenty-cent piece originally appeared on August 7, 1874, when patterns were produced at the Philadelphia mint. William Barber prepared the reverse design, but the obverse was done by the sculptor Joseph Bailly. A number of different designs were tried before the final adoption of the old Gobrecht concept that had been used for other denominations for so many years. This made them quite similar to the twenty-five-cent piece, a similarity that created problems of recognition and helped end the coin's life.

The similarity to the quarter was noted by mint officials. On April 5, 1875, while the coin was still in the design stages, Pollock wrote to Director Linderman: "I herewith enclose specimens of the twenty-

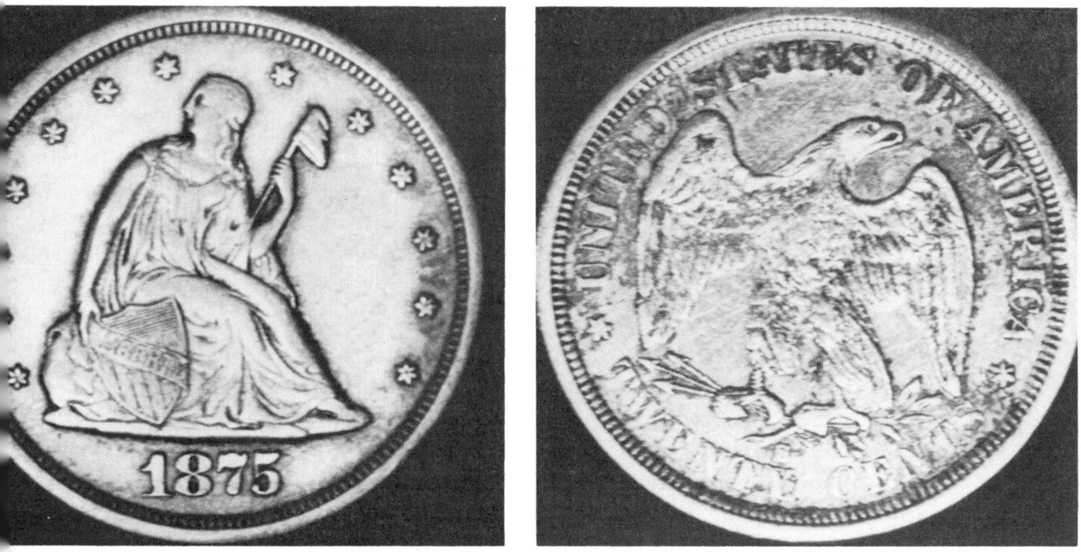

In 1875 another unusual denomination of coin was created. This is the twenty-cent piece, which was so similar to the quarter dollar that people complained that they couldn't tell how to make change accurately at first glance. The design was abandoned in 1878.

cent piece for your examination. Two in silver and two in copper are, as to design &c. in conformity with our present coinage. To distinguish these more readily from the Quarter dollar we have made the edge plain, not reeded. The other specimens, two each of silver and copper, are peculiar in design, very beautiful, but not conforming to our other coinage. . . ."

The reason for the twenty-cent piece's existence was never very clear. Senator John Jones of Nevada introduced the resolution authorizing the coin, but his reasons made little sense. He claimed the coin would prevent the problem of overchanging on merchandise sold for twelve and one-half cents, the value of the old Spanish bit. When someone bought an item priced at one bit, he would be given a dime in change if he paid with a quarter. He should have received a bit (Spanish real) or at least a dime and two cents. However there was a shortage of cents in the western states so they were seldom used as change. Somehow the twenty-cent piece was supposed to solve this problem, though it is impossible to fathom exactly how this would have occurred. Apparently the public also found the confusing denomination of limited use since it stayed in existence just four years.

Perhaps the most interesting coin of this period is the Liberty Head nickel of 1883. This coin seems rather innocuous in appearance, but it has one of the most colorful histories of any coin ever produced in the United States.

In 1879, Charles Barber became chief engraver of the Philadelphia mint, succeeding his father. Morgan was made assistant engraver, a change that amounted to a demotion.

Two years after becoming chief engraver, Charles Barber set to work designing a set of copper-nickel coins for possible use by the government. Most of the designs were ignored, but the five-cent piece was adopted in 1883. The design of the new "nickel" had a head of Liberty on the obverse and a large *V* in the center of the reverse. Surrounding the *V* was a wreath and the words "United States of America" and "E Pluribus Unum". Nowhere did the word "cents" appear on this coin.

When the new nickel came out, some people decided that it looked like a five-dollar gold piece. How they came to this conclusion is unclear. Certainly the coin lacked the word "cents" but the *V* on the reverse was in sharp contrast to the heraldic eagle on the reverse of the five-dollar coin currently in circulation. The head of Liberty was also different, the design on the five-dollar coin being similar to that found on the long-discontinued Large cents. Yet, somehow, a large number of people felt there was a similarity and decided to try to take advantage of this fact.

The most notorious of the individuals to take advantage of the supposed similarity between the new nickel and the gold half eagle was a man named Josh Tatum. He was a Boston hustler, who enjoyed earning money by any means short of honest work. He was also a deaf mute, a fact that would prove beneficial in his scheme.

Tatum went to a friend who was a pawn broker and jeweler. The friend had a machine that could gold plate objects, including coins. Together the men gold plated one thousand of the new Liberty Head nickels, which Tatum planned to pass as five-dollar gold pieces.

Tatum was extremely clever in passing the coins. He never told anyone that the coins were gold pieces, though he could easily have written a note to that effect when dealing with merchants. Instead he concentrated on cigar stores, walking in and purchasing a five cent cigar. He would lay the gold plated nickel on the counter and stand around, waiting to see what would happen. If the clerk recognized the coin for what it was and put it in his cash drawer, Tatum would walk out. If the clerk mistook the coin for a five-dollar gold piece, as happened the majority of times, Tatum would receive $4.95 in change.

The scheme was so successful that Tatum and his friend gold plated another five thousand of the nickels. Then Tatum began traveling between Boston and New York, spending three thousand of the coins and, in almost every case, receiving $4.95 in change. He always purchased a five-cent item, so he was technically never in violation of the law. However, word of what he was doing began reaching law enforcement officers, who eventually arrested him. They found one thousand gold-plated nickels on his person, further proof that the scheme was deliberate.

The Liberty Head nickel was introduced in 1883 without the word "cents" appearing on the reverse. This was the coin that was gold-plated and passed as a five-dollar gold piece. As a result, the design for the reverse was modified to include the word "cents."

Tatum was hauled before a judge and his trial was widely publicized. The attorney defending Tatum explained that his client had no malice in his heart. The poor man was unable to tell the clerks that the coin was a nickel, and so he had accepted the $4.95 change offered to him. What person facing the same circumstances would have done otherwise?

As to the gold plating of the coins, that act in itself was not illegal. It certainly may have misled the business people but a close examination of the coin would show it to be a five-cent piece and not a five-dollar gold coin.

The judge reluctantly agreed with the defense attorney. Although Tatum could not be proven guilty of a crime, the judge promised he would be thrown in jail if he ever passed a gold-plated nickel again.

Josh Tatum's stunt left us a non-numismatic legacy as well. When someone does something as a joke, it may be said that he is just "joshing."

Before the year 1883 was over, the government authorized a change in the nickel design. The word "cents" was added to the reverse so it would be impossible to pass a gold-plated nickel again.

The Liberty Head nickel series seemed destined to infamy. The issue began with a fraud and ended with an equally disreputable incident.

The year 1912 was to be the last time the Liberty Head design was used for the nickel. A new nickel was being prepared by sculptor James Earl Fraser that would depict the head of an Indian on one side and a buffalo on the other.

Although the Indian-Buffalo design was scheduled for production in 1913, it was taking longer to prepare than anticipated. On the chance that it would not be ready on time, the mint ordered 1913-dated dies for a Liberty Head nickel kept in a safe to which access was strictly limited. They would be used for coining only if the new design's delay became excessive.

The hubs for the new Indian-Buffalo design arrived at the Philadelphia mint on December 25, 1912. They were turned over to the chief engraver pending formal announcement of the government's acceptance of the new design. It wasn't until February 19, 1913, that approval came and production could begin, which it did two days later. At no time was it legal to strike 1913-dated Liberty Head nickels, though someone did just that.

There are several theories about how the 1913 Liberty Head nickels—five of which exist—came to be struck. One story calls them "setup" pieces. When the coiner is setting up the press, pressure and alignment are checked by taking impressions of the final coins. These are not full relief coins and are melted after inspection. But the 1913 Liberty Head nickels are each perfectly struck; this would not be the case had they been setup pieces.

Another possibility is that the coins were what are known as die trials. At one time, special die trials were run every few years that a coin was in existence. But when new procedures had been in operation for a long period of time, die trials were only made when the design was changed. A die trial would have been made for the Indian-Buffalo design but not for a coin that had been struck for more than twenty-four years.

One of the five 1913 Liberty Head nickels, which were never authorized and never legally produced. ***(Photo courtesy of Krause Publications.)***

Other stories about the coins' origin abound. Most state that the coins were legitimately produced, then ordered destroyed since the Indian-Buffalo dies had finally been approved. However, the truth is probably quite different.

The first mention of the existence of the 1913 Liberty Head nickels came in December 1919, when Samuel W. Brown of North Tonawanda, New York, advertised for the coins in the magazine *The Numismatist.* This is the publication of the American Numismatic Association, to which Brown had belonged since 1906. He stated in his advertisement that he would pay five hundred dollars for each 1913 Liberty Head nickel brought to him.

In January of 1920, Brown apparently had no sellers so he raised his bid for the coins to six hundred dollars each. This price remained during the next two months' advertisements.

The annual convention of the American Numismatic Association was held in August of that year, and Brown proudly displayed the coins that someone had supposedly sold him. A review of the display was printed in the October 1920 issue of *The Numismatist.* It stated:

> Samuel W. Brown of North Tonawanda, New York, was present for a short time on Monday. He had with him a specimen of the latest great rarity in U. S. coinage, the nickel of 1913 of the Liberty Head type. It was among the exhibits of the Convention, with a label announcing that it was valued at $600, which amount Mr. Brown announced he is ready to pay for all Proof specimens offered to him.
>
> An explanation of its rarity is that at the close of 1912, the Mint authorities not having received orders to use the dies of the Buffalo type nickel at the beginning of 1913, prepared a master die of the Liberty Head type dated 1913, and from this master die a few pieces, believed to be five, in Proof were struck. None of them are believed to have been placed in circulation.

The story obviously satisfied the Treasury Department as well as the public. The coins were never confiscated and have been extremely valuable for the owners. A 1913 Liberty Head nickel was one of the first coins to sell for over one hundred thousand dollars.

But the origin of the 1913 coins seems quite obvious when a study of Brown's past is made. He was hired by the Philadelphia mint on December 18, 1903. His first job was assistant curator of the mint's coin collection, a position he held until 1907. He quickly learned the value collectors place on rare coins, a fact underscored by his becoming Life Member No. 808 of the American Numismatic Association during this period. He later was mint clerk or storekeeper until he resigned in November 1913.

It is my contention that Brown used the dies, to which his job would have given him access, and made the five Liberty Head nickels himself. They probably served as a "retirement bonus" which he kept hidden until enough time had passed that he would not be suspect. The trust he was given even after the coins were sold can be seen in the fact that he later became a United States assay commissioner, a member of the North Tonawanda Board of Education, and even that community's mayor.

Even if the 1913 Liberty Head nickels could be proved to be genuine coins made for a legitimate reason during the period the 1913 Buffalo-Indian designs were uncertain, they would still not be legal. The mint regulations of July 1, 1887, include a statement that:

> The emission of impressions of experimental dies, whether in soft metal or in metal of the same weight and fineness proper to coins of the same denomination, is unlawful except in the case of pattern pieces of such denominations of coins as are coined for general circulation during the calendar year of its date.
>
> All impressions taken in copper, bronze, or other soft metal from an experimental die, are required to be destroyed as soon as the purpose for which it was struck is subserved.
>
> The above provisions, prescribed by the "General Instructions and Regulations in Relation to the Transaction of Business at the Mints and Assay Offices of the United States," approved by the secretary of the Treasury, have been in force since May 14, 1874.
>
> The striking of a piece in the semblance of a United States coin in a metal or alloy, or of a weight or fineness, other than prescribed by law, is a violation of section 5460 of the Revised Statues.
>
> The emission or offer for sale or exchange of an impression from any die of a coin of the United States, or of a proposed coin of the United States, but with a device or devices not authorized by law, whether such die has been prepared at the Mint of the United States, or elsewhere, is contrary to the provisions of Section 3517 and 5461, Revised Statutes.
>
> No impression from any coinage die of the United States struck in other metal than that authorized by law or of a weight and

fineness other than prescribed by law (Revised Statutes 3513, 3514, 3515), or pattern piece bearing a legend of a coin of the United States, and bearing a device or devices not authorized by law (Revised Statutes 3516, 3517, vide Mint regulations) should be in existence longer than required for the lawful purpose for which it was authorized to be struck.

Any emission, for private or personal use or possession, from the Mints of the United States or pieces of the character above specified has been in violation of the coinage laws of the United States.

As the nineteenth century came to a close, grand plans were made for changes in the designs of the dime, quarter, and half-dollar. A desire for change was expressed by Mint Director James Kimball in his 1887 annual report:

> The designs impressed upon the coins of any nation, ancient or modern, are accepted as an expression of the art of their time. But few citizens, who, with an artistic sense, have carefully scrutinized the current coins of this Republic, would consent to accept as a standard of excellence for their own day and generation almost any of the present compositions of statutory devices. The inferiority of our coinage to the same kind of work by almost every other advanced nation of the earth, as well as to the well-known work of numerous able designers in relief at home, seems to be perceived by all who have given attention to the subject, and to be keenly felt by many as unworthy of the development which the arts of sculpture and design have here attained. . . ."

The mint director's idea was to have a competition for new coin designs. But this seemed to violate the law passed in 1873 and 1874, which indicated that coin designs should originate at the mint. As a result, Kimball's supporters eventually pushed a bill through Congress so that, on September 26, 1890, the Treasury Department was authorized to change coin designs after twenty-five years. It also allowed outside artists to submit designs.

The Treasury Department decided to have a contest by invitation. Ten of the nation's best known artists were chosen. They were Herbert Adams, Kenyon Cox, Daniel French, Olin Warner Herbert, Will S. Low, Miller MacMonies, H. S. Mowbray, Charles S. Niehaus, Augustus Saint-Gaudens and J. Q. A. Ward.

The Treasury made every effort to cut expenses and expected the men to spend time on quality designs for which money would be paid only to the winning designer. As a result, the artists conferred among themselves, then sent the following reply to the government:

> The undersigned, having been invited to prepare designs for a new coinage for the United States, beg respectfully to state that the conditions of the competition as given in the circular letter of

> invitation are such as to preclude the possibility of any good result from it. The time given for the preparation of designs is too short and the compensation altogether insufficient, while no assurance is given as to who will make the awards.
>
> They beg to suggest the following terms of competition as such as they could accept:
>
> 1. The awards to be made by a jury of competent artists of standing in the profession, to be chosen by vote of the competitors, by presidents of the great art institutions or otherwise.
> 2. At least three months to be allowed for the production of sketch designs, and at least six months to be allowed for the production of completed models if these are to be insisted upon.
> 3. One hundred dollars to be paid out to each artist competing for each sketch design submitted, or five hundred dollars to be paid to each artist competing for each completed model accepted.
> 4. One thousand dollars in addition to the sum paid for competitive sketches or models finally accepted.
> 5. The obverse and reverse of any coin to be designed by the same artist and the reverse of the present half-dollar, quarter-dollar and dime to be abandoned.

The government officials immediately changed their plans. What happened next is best told by an article appearing in the summer 1891 issue of the *American Journal of Numismatics:*

> It was publicly stated, when these proposals appeared, that the inducements offered by the Government were not sufficient to elicit suggestions of value, much less complete designs for the purpose. Artists who might have given thought to the matter, complained that their time would be wasted, as they would receive nothing for their labor unless their models were accepted; and the result seems to have been, as was anticipated, a complete failure to produce anything that would unite beauty with utility and the practical necessities involved. When the Director of the Mint suggested to the engraver at Philadelphia that he get someone to assist him in some special work that was under way, he replied that he did not know of any one in the United States who was competent even to assist in this work. During the recent competition the celebrated sculptor, August St. Gaudens, who was one of the judges in the contest, told Mr. Leech that he knew of only four artists who were competent to do this class of designing, and that three of them were in France and he was the fourth. He could say this without egotism, for he made a special study of this subject before he attained celebrity as a sculptor. Admitting most willingly the pre-eminent genius of Mr. St. Gaudens as a sculptor, we fear that he can hardly be said to have shown equal talent for producing designs adapted to the coinage.
>
> We understand that the design favored by the latter gentleman was something after the rude but beautiful coinage of the Greeks. But these designs it would be impossible to follow, and Mr. Barber

said in a recent interview, that there was no machinery in existence to coin such pieces as cheaply and as quickly as was necessary. Doubtless American ingenuity could overcome this difficulty, but there are others which cannot be overcome. No three coins could be piled with stability; the third would inevitably fall; their high relief would not sustain the constant wear of circulation without soon being defaced, the protecting rim on our present coins not being compatible with such devices; their irregularity, and that is one of the chief features advocated by those who suggestions seem to have been sought, would prevent their use, and at the same time make an easy field for counterfeiters.

A correspondent of the *Boston Transcript* writes (July 31): " 'It is not likely that another competition will ever be tried for the production of designs for United States coins,' said Mr. Leech, the Director of the Mint, yesterday. 'The one just ended was too wretched a failure. Doubtless it was the first contest of the sort ever opened by any Government to the public at large. The result is not very flattering to the boasted artistic development of this country, inasmuch as only two of the three hundred suggestions submitted were good enough to receive honorable mention. . . . Anticipating a severe popular criticism, the chief engraver will do his utmost to render the five cameo pictures called for, as unexceptionable as possible, aesthetically speaking. No alteration is to be made in the gold coins, because they are really exquisite now and could hardly be improved upon. It is realized that the money of a nation is expressive of its art culture. (!) Therefore, lest posterity imagine the present generation to have been barbarous, it is desirable that our silver pieces should be as handsome as may be.'

" 'I have told our engraver,' said Mr. Leech to another reporter a few days ago, 'to prepare me a set of designs for the subsidiary coins to be submitted to Secretary Foster. I shall not do anything about the dollar for some time. There is no hurry about it, and the weather is too warm for us to worry ourselves about anything which does not require immediate attention. Our engraver at Philadelphia is the only competent person to prepare these designs, but it does not follow from the action I have taken that his work will be final. Of course, he receives no additional compensation for this. It is part of his regular work. I do not see any prospect of getting designs elsewhere in this country. We might get them in France. The French coin work is of the most artistic description. But the people of the United States would never forgive us if we went outside this country for our designs. To be sure, our designer is of an English family, but he is regularly in the employ of the Mint.' (He came at an early age we believe, to Philadephia, with his father, and upon the death of the latter was appointed to succeed him.)

"The fact seems to be proved from this attempt, that there are no American artists, outside the Mint, who are competent to furnish designs which it would be possible to follow. Whether the Mint officials can supply an acceptable device, under the limitations provided by statute, remains to be proved. We understand that Mr. Leech is glad that he tried the experiment of inviting outside

Charles Barber, the chief engraver of the mint, created new designs for the dime, quarter and half-dollar of 1892. These were basically identical. The one shown is for the dime.

The Barber design for the quarter dollar.

assistance, notwithstanding his regret at the failure of his efforts.

"The final decision in such matters, too often rests in the hands of those whose taste has not been numismatically educated, and it would therefore not be surprising if a design of much greater artistic merit than that which shall be finally adopted, should be rejected, possibly on the ground of utility, as has been the case heretofore. . . . Even a Cabinet officer, with his multifarious talents is not necessarily endowed with that discriminating taste in the choice of 'the fairest' and most beautiful, so happily possessed by the son of Priam. 'The judgment of Paris' in awarding the apple of discord received the approval of mortals, though Olympus

The obverse and reverse of the Barber design half-dollar. This type is also known as the Liberty Head design.

frowned: in like manner, the Secretary's ultimate decision, whatever it may be, will no doubt give popular satisfaction and incur the wrath of those who reign in the realm of art."

And so Charles Barber was given the opportunity to display his designing talents. The obverse of each dime, quarter and half dollar introduced in 1892 has a head of Liberty that can be considered functional at best. It is not up to the quality of the Liberty Head nickel and would prove greatly inferior to the designs which would be developed by artists outside the mint shortly after the turn of the century.

The reverse of the coin contains a heraldic eagle in a field of stars. It was a functional composition showing little artistic talent but displaying competence in the technical ability needed to create a coin that would be easy to handle.

Barber placed his initial on the neck of Liberty, an important fact to remember. He was an extremely jealous man, and as will be seen shortly, he would lie about such personal credit as the initial when he attacked our most popular coin, the Lincoln cent.

9

The Coinage of Augustus Saint-Gaudens

The Philadelphia mint workers were hampered by antiquated facilities, a situation that finally came to the attention of Congress in 1891. Secretary of the Treasury Windom explained that much of the old mint was cold and damp and requested that a new, more modern building be constructed.

Congress agreed with the request. Money for a new Philadelphia mint—the third to be built in that city—was authorized, and the structure was completed in the middle of 1901. It was located between Sixteenth and Seventeenth Streets and had the mint's first electrolytic refinery installed as a way to speed production and reduce manpower needs. Unfortunately it could do nothing to improve the quality of the workmen in the mint's employ.

One of the strongest critics of the Barber coinage was Theodore Roosevelt. He was a student of sculpture, especially the work of the ancient Greeks and Romans, and believed that coin design could be far superior to what the mint was producing. But he never realized how great an impact he could have on the nation's coins until he began working with the artist Augustus Saint-Gaudens to produce what became America's most beautiful gold pieces.

Roosevelt had his first direct contact with Saint-Gaudens back in 1903. Saint-Gaudens had created a massive sculpture honoring General William Sherman. The sculpture was placed at the Fifth Avenue entrance to New York's Central Park where it proved extremely impressive. It showed a woman, symbolizing Victory, walking beside the general, who was astride his horse. The future president was so impressed that he sent Saint-Gaudens a note, saying: "To my mind your Sherman is the greatest statue of a commander in existence. But I can say with all sincerity that I know of no man—of course of no one living—who could have done it. To make grim, homely, old Sherman, the type and ideal of a democratic general, and put with him an allegorical figure such as you did, could result in but one of two ways—a ludicrous failure or striking the very highest note of the sculptor's art. Thrice over for the good fortune of your countrymen, it was given you to strike this highest note."

Roosevelt didn't realize it at the time, but the Sherman monument was to have further involvement in his life. The reason was the face of Victory, which had been drawn from life. The model was the young Alice Butler, whom Saint-Gaudens had first spotted in Windsor, Vermont, the small town where she lived with her parents. Saint-Gaudens immediately noticed a heavy chin, the only flaw in what he felt to be a perfect face. She was tall, with a classic nose and curving, short upper lip that made her look as though she might have been the model for ancient Greek or Roman statues. He was anxious to work with her, knowing he could remold her single flaw so he would have a perfect, classical face.

Alice had heard of Saint-Gaudens, but his reputation did not please her. She knew he was one of the greatest artists of the day, yet she had also heard that he frequently had models pose in the nude for him. This was against her principles. However, he explained that he planned to drape her in yards of cotton fabric shaped to suggest an ancient Greek garment. She felt this approach was "proper" and agreed to pose.

In addition to using Alice Butler for his *Victory,* he also made several busts of her which were reproduced in bronze. Tiffany's, among others, sold the busts for ninety dollars each, a high price at the time. What the customers didn't realize is that the same bust would eventually be found on the ten-dollar gold piece.

When Roosevelt became president, the mint was expected to prepare a medal honoring the event. This had been a tradition for many years and Roosevelt resigned himself to it. Then he happened to have a few words with Frank Millet, a lithographer and war correspondent, who suggested that Roosevelt use an outside artist to design the medal. That way the president could have something of which he would be proud.

Roosevelt invited Saint-Gaudens to do the job, and the artist agreed. When it was done, Roosevelt told the sculptor:

> Really I do not know whether to thank most Frank Millet, who first put it into my rather dense head that we ought to have a great artist to design these medals, or to thank you for consenting to

undertake the work. My dear fellow, I am very grateful to you, and I am very proud to have been able to associate you in some way with my administration. I like the medals *immensely;* but that goes without saying, for the work is eminently characteristic of you. I thank heaven, we have at last some artistic work of permanent worth, done for the Government.

I don't want to slop over; but I feel just as if we had suddenly imported a little of Greece of the fifth or fourth centuries B.C. into America; and am very proud and very grateful that I personally happened to be the beneficiary. I like the special bronze medal particularly.

It is interesting to note that while the Roosevelt medal design was Saint-Gaudens', the execution was done by one of his assistants, Adolph Weinman. Both Weinman and another assistant, James Fraser, would eventually create coins themselves.

The obverse of the Roosevelt medal showed the President's portrait. The reverse displayed the image of an eagle that would be used again when Saint-Gaudens designed the gold coinage.

Roosevelt was intrigued with the idea of improving the coinage. He had seen that he could avoid using the mint for the creation of a medal. He wondered if he could also use an outsider to create a new coin. He asked the secretary of the Treasury to check the legalities and was delighted with the report that he could hire anyone he wanted.

As a result, he sent Saint-Gaudens a note on November 6, 1905, saying: "I want to make a suggestion. It seems to me worth while to try for a really good coinage; though I suppose there will be a revolt about it! I was looking at some gold coins of Alexander the Great today, and I was struck by their high relief. Would it not be well to have our coins in high relief, and also to have the rims raised? The point of having the rims raised would be, of course, to protect the figure on the coin; and if we have the figures in high relief, like the figures on the old Greek coins, they will surely last longer. What do you think of this?"

Saint-Gaudens replied:

You have hit the nail on the head with regard to the coinage. Of course the great coins (and you might almost say the only coins) are the Greek ones you speak of, just at the great medals are those of the fifteenth century by Pisanello and Sperandio. Nothing would please me more than to make the attempt in the direction of the heads of Alexander, but the authorities on modern monetary requirements would, I fear, "throw fits," to speak emphatically, if the thing was done now. It would be great if it could be accomplished and I do not see what the objection would be if the edges were high enough to prevent the rubbing. Perhaps an inquiry from you would not receive the antagonistic reply that would certainly be made to me from those who have the "say" in such matters.

Up to the present I have done no work on the actual models for the coins, but have made sketches, and the matter is constantly in my mind. I have about determined on the composition of one side, which would contain an eagle very much like the one I placed on your medal, with an advantageous modification. On the other side would be some kind of a (possibly winged) figure of Liberty striding energetically forward as if on a mountain top, holding aloft on one arm a shield bearing the stars and stripes with the word 'Liberty' marked across the field, in the other hand perhaps a flaming torch; the drapery would be flowing in the breeze. My idea is to make it a living thing and typical of progress. . . ."

Saint-Gaudens had had enough dealings with Charles Barber to know that the chief engraver tried to become involved with every coin design. Saint-Gaudens felt that he had to have total control, or he did not want to be involved with the designing at all.

Homer Saint-Gaudens, the son of the artist, commented on his father's letter to Roosevelt in the book *The Reminiscences of Augustus Saint-Gaudens,* which Homer edited. He said:

. . . my father . . . first purposed to model the cent with a flying eagle, the formal lettering treated in a new fashion, and to execute for the gold coins a full-length figure of Liberty mounting a rock, with a shield in her left hand and a lighted torch in her right, backed by a semi-conventional eagle, with wings half-closed. For one reason and another, the scheme proved impracticable. So, after months of confusion, he settled that the one cent should exhibit a profile head and the lettering; that the ten-dollar gold piece should carry the same head, with the inscriptions shifted, and the standing eagle; and that the twenty-dollar gold piece should exhibit the full-length figure of Liberty, without wings or shield, and the flying eagle.

To accomplish this result, my father altered and realtered the coins for a year and a half. The suggestion for the flying eagle he developed from the bird on the 1857 "White Cent." The conception of the standing eagle he drew from a design he had often used on such work as the Shaw Memorial, the medal struck to commemorate the inauguration of President Roosevelt, and the shield of the monument to President Garfield in Fairmount Park, Philadelphia. In all, he created seventy models of this bird, and often stood twenty-five of them in a row for visitors to number according to preference.

The profile head he modeled in relief from the favorite, but superseded bust of the Sherman "Victory," adding the feathers only upon the President's emphatic suggestion. Many persons regarded it with disfavor at the time because it was thought to have been posed for by an Irish maid, Mary Cunningham, when none but a "pure American" should have served for a model for our national coin. As a matter of fact, the features of the Irish girl appear only at the size of a pin-head upon the full-length Liberty, the body of which was posed for by a Swede, while the profile head, to which exception was taken, was modeled from a woman supposed to have negro blood in her veins. Who, other than an Indian, may be a "pure American" is undetermined. In reality here, as in all examples of my father's ideal sculpture, little or no resemblance can be traced to any model; since he was always quick to reject the least taint of what he called "personality" in such instances.

Finally he attacked the difficult problem of the inscriptions by placing upon the previously milled edge of the coin, in one case, the forty-six stars and, in the other, the thirteen stars with the "E Pluribus Unum." The motto "In God We Trust," as an inartistic intrusion not required by law, he wholly discarded and thereby drew upon himself the lightning of public comment. It is interesting to discover in regard to this that Secretary Salmon P. Chase received quite as severe a censure for placing the words upon this coin as was aroused by their removal.

Although a cent is mentioned by his son, Saint-Gaudens would produce only the two gold coins. He was dying of cancer during this period, and his illness slowed his work. His assistants had to handle everything but the initial design phase—the most creative aspect of the task. Since the cent was the least important coin, it was dropped for the moment, a fact which would result in the United States' eventually getting Victor D. Brenner to create the popular Lincoln cent.

At one point during the design of the gold coins, it was thought that the same bust of Liberty with Indian headdress could be used for both pieces. Samples were actually produced but only the ten-dollar coin eventually carried that image. The only twenty-dollar double eagle of the Indian headdress design known to exist is now valued at five hundred thousand to one million dollars.

The discussion of Roosevelt's wanting the Indian headdress refers to a letter the president sent Saint-Gaudens on November 14, 1905:

> I have summoned all the Mint people, and I am going to see if I cannot persuade them that coins of the Grecian type but with the raised rim will meet the commercial needs of the day. Of course I want to avoid too heavy an outbreak of the mercantile classes, because after all it is they who do use the gold. If we can have an eagle like that on the Inauguration Medal, only raised, I should feel that we would be awfully fortunate. Don't you think we might accomplish something by raising the figures more than at present but not as much as in the Greek coins? Probably the Greek coins would be so thick that modern banking houses, where they have to pile up gold, would simply be unable to do so. How would it do to have a design struck off in a tentative fashion—that is, to have a medal made? I think your Liberty idea is all right. Is it possible to

make a Liberty with that Indian feather head-dress? Would people refuse to regard it as a Liberty? The figure of Liberty as you suggest would be beautiful. If we can get down to bed-rock facts, would the feather head-dress be any more out of keeping with the rest of Liberty than the canonical Phrygian cap which never is worn and never has been worn by any free people in the world?"

The model for the bust, Alice Butler, mentioned earlier, was eventually a housemother's assistant at a Boston school. One of the pupils, Louise Hall Tharp, later wrote of Miss Butler in her book *Saint-Gaudens and the Gilded Era*. She said:

> When I was a student at the School of Fine Arts in Boston, I lived at the "Students' House" on the Fenway, a girls' dormitory sponsored by Emanuel Church and headed at that time by Miss Mary E. Libbey, a deaconess. Assisting Miss Libbey was Miss Alice Butler. Miss Butler's profile was so very beautiful that I finally plucked up courage to ask her if I might attempt a sketch. She was very nice about it, told me to go ahead, and in the course of conversation, said that she sat to Augustus Saint-Gaudens and that hers was the head on the ten-dollar gold piece. She said she had seen a bust that Saint-Gaudens made of her, for sale in an art store. She wanted to buy it for her mother, but it cost ninety dollars, which was more than she could afford.

On November 22, Saint-Gaudens made a suggestion to Roosevelt that was to have greater repercussions than either man could anticipate. He wrote: "I am now engaged on the models for the coinage. The law calls for, viz., 'On one side there shall be an impression emblematic of liberty, with an inscription of the word "Liberty" and the year of the coinage.' It occurs to me that the addition on this side of the coins of the word 'Justice' (or 'Law,' preferably the former) would add force as well as elevation to the meaning of the composition. At one time the words 'In God we trust' were placed on the coins; I am not aware there was authorization for that, but I may be mistaken. Will you kindly inform me if what I suggest is permissible."

Roosevelt was delighted with the idea of removing the religious inscription from coins. Although the original intent of the motto was to show respect for God, Roosevelt felt it did quite the opposite. He explained his position to William Boldly in a letter written two years later but lost to historians until it was auctioned in December 1975 by the American Auction Association of the California firm Bowers and Ruddy Galleries. The letter stated:

> When the question of the new coinage came up we lookt into the law and found there was no warrant therein for putting "IN GOD WE TRUST" on the coins. As the custom, altho without legal warrant had grown up, however, I might have felt at liberty to keep the

inscription had I approved of its being on the coinage. But as I did not approve of it, I did not direct that it should again be put on. Of course the matter of the law is absolutely in the hands of Congress, and any direction of Congress in the matter will be immediately obeyed. At present, as I have said, there is no warrant in law for the inscription.

My own feeling in the matter is due to my very firm conviction that to put such a motto on coins, or to use it in any kindred manner, not only does no good but does positive harm, and is in effect irreverence which comes dangerously close to sacrilege. A beautiful and solemn sentence such as the one in question should be treated and uttered only with that fine reverence which necessarily implies a certain exaltation of spirit. Any use which tends to cheapen it, and, above all, any use which tends to secure its being treated in a spirit of levity, as is from every standpoint profoundly to be regretted. It is a motto which it is indeed well to have inscribed on our great national monuments, in our temples of justice, in our legislative halls, and in buildings such as those at West Point and Annapolis—in short, wherever it will tend to arouse and inspire a lofty emotion in those who look thereon. But it seems to me eminently unwise to cheapen such a motto by use on coins, just as it would be to cheapen it by use on postage stamps, or in advertisements. As regards its use on the coinage we have actual experience by which to go. In all my life I have never heard any human being speak reverently of this motto on the coins or show any sign of its having appealed to any high emotion in him. But I have literally hundreds of times heard it used as an occasion of, and incitement to, the sneering ridicule which it is above all things undesirable that so beautiful and exalted a phrase should excite. For example, thruout the long contest, extending over several decades, on the free coinage question, the existence of this motto on the coins was a constant source of jest and ridicule; and this was unavoidable. Everyone must remember the innumerable cartoons and articles based on phrases like "In God we trust for the other eight cents"; 'In God we trust for the short weight"; "In God we trust for the thirty-seven cents we do not pay"; and so forth, and so forth. Surely I am well within bounds when I say that a use of the phrase which invites constant levity of this type is most undesirable. If Congress alters the law and directs me to replace on the coins the sentence in question the direction will be immediately put into effect; but I very earnestly trust that the religious sentiment of the country, the spirit of reverence in the country, will prevent any such notion being taken.

Roosevelt had a meeting with the secretary of the Treasury, then wrote to Saint-Gaudens on January 6, 1906: "I have seen Shaw about the coinage and told him that it was my pet baby. We will try it anyway, so you go ahead. Shaw was really very nice about it. Of course he thinks I am a mere crack-brained lunatic on the subject, but he said with great kindness that there was always a certain number of gold coins that had to be stored up in the vaults, and that there was no early objection to having those coins as artistic as the Greeks could desire. (I am paraphrasing his words, of course.) I think it will seriously increase mortality among the employees of the mint at seeing such a desecration, but they will perish in the good cause!

On January 9, 1906, Saint-Gaudens replied:

"All right, I shall proceed on the lines we have agreed on. The models are both well in hand, but I assure you I feel mightily cheeky so to speak, in attempting to line up with the Greek things. Well! Whatever I produce cannot be worse than the inanities now displayed on our coins and we will at least have made an attempt in the right direction, and serve the country by increasing the mortality at the mint. There is one gentlemen there, however, who, when he sees what is coming, may have "the nervous prostitution" as termed by a native here, but killed, no. He has been in that institution since the foundation of the government and will be found standing in its ruins." The gentleman to whom he refers was Charles Barber.

As time passed, Saint-Gaudens grew increasingly dependent upon his assistant, Henry Hering, to handle the production of the coins. Hering executed design changes under Saint-Gaudens' direction. Liberty was personified as a winged figure wearing a headdress and bearing a torch and shield. The torch and headdress were eliminated when it became apparent that the composition was awkward.

The reverse for the coin proved an equal problem. Seventy different eagle sketches were made before the final selection. Ironically, the design finally chosen was identical to that used on the inaugural medal.

The mint was concerned about how practical the new coin designs would be for bankers. Gold ten- and twenty-dollar coins would not be carried by the average person. These were times when you could go into a restaurant and have a full course roast beef dinner, including an appetizer of navy bean soup, a salad, corn on the cob, ice cream and coffee for just 60 cents. Coffee, alone, ran 15 cents per pound and eggs sold for a cent apiece. The gold pieces Saint-Gaudens was designing were meant for large business transactions, in which they would be stacked, several to a pile. If the surface were uneven, the coins wouldn't stack and the bankers would have serious problems.

The mint workers were also genuinely concerned about how quickly each coin could be made. A true high-relief coin could not be made with any speed at the mint. It would take several strikings to raise the design as high as the designer and Roosevelt wanted. But the mint needed a design that could be reproduced with one blow. Each additional strike necessary reduced production severely.

The mint had several problems with Saint-Gaudens' designs. Not only were they of unusually high relief, they also had to be reproduced on equipment that was forty years out of date.

Henry Hering discussed the problems he had encountered with the

The ten-dollar gold piece created by Augustus Saint-Gaudens.

mint's demands after the coins had become a reality:

> Owing to St. Gaudens' ill health I executed both coins under his direction, from his designs. Consequently, I was in charge of the work and engineered the proceedings at the Philadelphia Mint. I proceeded to make a model in very high relief, knowing perfectly well they could not stamp it in one strike, my object being to have a die made of this model and then have strikes made in order to see the various results.
>
> I took the model to the Philadelphia Mint and was introduced by the Director to Mr. Barber, who was the chief engraver. When he saw the plaster model of the $20 gold piece, which was about nine inches in diameter, he rejected it and said it was impossible for any mint to coin it. I told him my reasons for doing it and that we would have to experiment. After considerable discussion he finally decided to make the die.

It took nine strikes to get a perfect relief. The design was obviously unrealistic for coinage purposes, regardless of its beauty.

It was August 1907 when Saint-Gaudens died. Roosevelt became frantic to complete his new coins. He wanted to give the artist a memorial and didn't care what pressures had to be applied.

Hering was working on the coin design, trying to find ways to maintain its beauty while decreasing the number of strikes necessary to bring the coin to full relief. He also persuaded Roosevelt to order new mint machinery from France—machinery that could do a better job than the outdated equipment then in use.

Roosevelt finally convinced everyone involved with the new designs

The twenty-dollar Saint Gaudens gold piece. It is considered one of the most beautiful coins the United States has ever produced.

to get some coins struck for circulation at once. The result was three different types of coins. Trial strikes were made in ultrahigh relief. These were very close to the artist's original design. They were not stackable, though, and were meant to be given to dignitaries and various others rather than placed in circulation.

A slight modification of the high-relief coins, still requiring more than one strike, was also made. Eleven thousand of these coins were produced and they were distinguished by the use of a Roman numeral for the date.

Finally there were the 1907 coins with a relief modified by Barber. These are much flatter, though still among the most beautiful the nation has ever produced. They were stackable and easily entered circulation.

President Roosevelt felt he could relax. The nation had a magnificent new coin design and all seemed well. What he failed to realize was that his authorized removal of the motto "In God We Trust" was going to evoke greater controversy than anyone had thought possible.

Typical of the reactions was the one by the editor of the *United Presbyterian,* published in Pittsburgh: Roosevelt's reasons for removing the motto, he said, "would justify the striking of temperance laws and Sabbath laws from the statute-books of every State from the Atlantic to the Pacific. Because a good law is treated with disrespect by lawbreakers is no argument for its repeal. The principle advanced would justify the abrogation of the Ten Commandments. It is not so many years ago that one of the members of the United States Senate spoke of the Decalog as being an 'iridescent dream.' Would Mr. Roosevelt approve of the expunging of the Decalog because some men treat it with lightness and irreverence?"

Other publications echoed these sentiments. Many said that there was nothing wrong with letting the world know that we were a Christian nation when going about our public and business affairs.

Another Pittsburgh religious journal, the *Christian Advocate,* a Methodist publication, approved the president's action:

> On the whole, we believe he is right. At first thought some good people may not agree with him, but we believe that the more they consider the matter the more they will come to his way of thinking. At first we were unfavorably imprest by his action, but we have changed, and must now approve it. There is such a thing as making sacred things too common. Our religious faith should not be hidden in a napkin, but neither should it be too publicly and constantly paraded. It may thus be cheapened. Texts of Scripture may be degraded by unwise display, and being thrust into unseemly places and connections. There are suitable times and places for such things, and there are some unsuitable. Opinions may differ as to whether the coin of the country is a proper place for the beautiful motto in question, but we believe the majority of the people will approve the President's act, and that Congress will not restore the motto.

The *American Hebrew,* a New York publication, went further in an editorial that stated "the real question which should agitate the American people is not the restoration of God to its coinage, but to its life."

A study of the editorial policies of the newspapers, both religious and otherwise, reveals that perhaps the hostility had nothing to do with the motto. In most cases, the papers which backed Roosevelt when he ran for President also supported his change in the coin design. Only those papers which campaigned against him, for the most part, were critical of the change. The *New York Sun,* for example, went so far as to run an anonymous poem in its edition of November 17, 1907.

In God We Trust
Oh, no we don't
That is, we mustn't say so;
Such sentiment is out of date
At least so says the potentate
And He's the country and the State
  Our Teddy.

In God We Trust
Upon Our Coins!
Oh, sacrilegious people!

God is not needed in this nation!
We have the great Administration;
And He's enough for all creation
Our Teddy.

Members of Congress knew that the issue at hand was an important one. Many had strong feelings about the matter and others recognized the impact the controversy had on their home districts. They all saw that it was going to be necessary to pass a law concerning the motto.

Congressman J. Hampton Moore of Pennsylvania, a Republican and a friend of Roosevelt, decided that he had to sponsor a bill to restore the motto. He talked with the president about his feelings and the public mood. Roosevelt then stated:

"The Congressman says the House Committee wants to pass a bill restoring the motto to the coin. I tell him it is not necessary; it is rot; but the Congressman says there is a misapprehension as to the religious purport of it—it is so easy to stir up a sensation and misconstrue the President's motives—and that the Committee is agitated as to the effect of a veto. I repeat, it is rot, pure rot; but I am telling the Congressman if Congress wants to pass a bill reestablishing the motto, I shall not veto it. You may as well know it in the Senate also."

The bill to restore "In God We Trust" to American coins passed the House on March 8, 1908, and the Senate on May 13 of that year. Five days later Roosevelt signed it into law and, by July 1, the motto was appearing on the nation's coinage. It was only a minor setback, however. Roosevelt had still overseen the creation of the most beautiful coins ever produced in the United States.

In a speech given on December 15, 1908, Roosevelt summed up his feelings about Saint-Gaudens and the new coins. Speaking at the Corcoran Art Gallery, which was featuring an exhibit of the artist's works, he said:

> Saint-Gaudens gave us for the first time a beautiful coinage, a coinage worthy of this country, a coinage not yet properly appreciated, but up to which both the official and the popular mind will in the end grow. The first few thousands of the Saint-Gaudens gold coins are, I believe, more beautiful than any coins since the days of the Greeks, and they achieve their striking beauty because Saint-Gaudens not only possessed a perfect mastery in the physical address of his craft, but also a daring and original imagination. His full-length figure of Liberty holding the torch is his own conception. His flying eagle and standing eagle are each in its own way equally good. His head of Liberty is not only a strikingly beautiful head, but characteristically and typically American in that for the head-dress he has used one of the few really typical, and at the same time really beautiful, pieces of wearing gear ever produced inde-

pendently on this continent—the bonnet of eagle-plumes. The comments so frequently made upon this eagle-feather head-dress illustrate curiously the exceedingly conventional character of much of our criticism and the frequent inability to understand originality until it has won its place. Most of the criticism was based upon the assumption that only an Indian could wear a feather head-dress, and that the head of Liberty ought to have a Phrygian cap, or Greek helmet, or some classic equivalent. Now, of course, this was nonsense. There is no more reason why a feather head-dress should always be held to denote a Phrygian. The Indian in his own way finely symbolizes freedom and a life of liberty. It is idle to insist that the head or figure of Liberty shall only appear in the hackneyed and conventional trappings which conventional and unoriginal minds have gradually grown to ascribe to her. A great artist with the boldness of genius could see that the American Liberty should, if possible, have something distinctively American about her; and it was an addition to the sum of the art of all nations that this particular figure of Liberty should not be a mere slavish copy of all other figures of Liberty. So Saint-Gaudens put the American Liberty in an American head-dress. Up to the time of this coin the most beautiful American coin was the small gold coin which carried the Indian's head with the feather head-dress, but Saint-Gaudens' was the head of Liberty, the head of the American Liberty, and it was eminently fitting that such a head should carry a very beautiful and pure and characteristically American head-dress.

10

The Bigelow-Pratt Gold Pieces

The 1907 coins of Augustus Saint-Gaudens marked the height of innovative beauty for American coinage. The following year was also a time of innovation, but unfortunately, one of less artistic merit. This time the coins involved were the half and quarter eagles—the five-dollar and two-and-one-half dollar gold pieces.

One of the criticisms of the new twenty-dollar gold piece was the extremely high relief that made stacking so difficult. Dr. William Sturgis Bigelow, a friend of President Roosevelt, was aware of this problem and decided that the answer was simple—the design would be cut into the coin so that it became what is known as intaglio. The surface of the coin remains flat, with the design being cut into the metal instead of being raised above it.

Bigelow was not an artist, though, so he turned to Bela Pratt, a Boston sculptor, to complete the design. The influence of Roosevelt's artistic taste is obvious for the common obverse for both coins shows an Indian in full headdress. The reverse for both denominations uses the same eagle as is found on the ten-dollar coins of Saint-Gaudens, although it is cut into the gold instead of raised above it.

The new coins were a rather dull lot whose appeal was almost as limited as the appeal of the Saint-Gaudens' coins was strong. Perhaps the most famous correspondence concerning the designs was recorded in the February 1909 issue of *The Numismatist,* the publication of The American Numismatic Association. One of the active members, a numismatist and self-taught expert on medallic art, S. Hudson Chapman, sent the following letter to President Roosevelt, which was reprinted in the magazine.

These are the two-and-one-half-dollar gold pieces designed by Bela Lyon Pratt. Instead of a raised design, the coin has a design called incuse. This means that the design was cut into the coin.

The identical Pratt design used for the five-dollar gold piece.

It was the hope of every one that when our new coinage appeared we would have one of great beauty and artistic merit. But the new $5 and $2.50 gold pieces just issued totally lack these qualities, and not only those of beauty, but actually miss the practicability to which every effect of beauty in relief has been sacrificed.

The idea of Dr. William S. Bigelow, of Boston, to sink the whole relief below the flat surface of the coin causes it to appear like a design merely incised in the blank, and precludes entirely the effect of a miniature bas-relief.

The head of the Indian is without artistic merit, and portrays an Indian who is emaciated, totally unlike the big, strong Indian chiefs as seen in real life. The treatment of the head is crude and hard, with sharp, abrupt outlines, as if carved by a mere metal chaser; and on the reverse is a reproduction of the Saint-Gaudens' eagle, which represents not our national bird (the white-headed eagle—commonly but erroneously called the bald-headed eagle—which has no feathers on its feet), but resembles more closely the golden eagle, which is also indigenous to Europe.

The placing of the design below the surface of the plane, with deeply incised outlines, gives the effect of having been engraved into the metal, and can, therefore, be closely imitated by any metal chaser with the graver, without dies or moulds. And I am certain that if this had been suggested to the secret service officials it would never have been issued by the Treasury Department, and the issuance ought to be immediately stopped and the coins recalled, for every one will be in danger of the imitations.

The sunken design, especially the deeply sunken portion of the neck of the Indian, will be a great receptacle for dirt and conveyor of disease, and the coin will be the most unhygienic ever issued.

The principal claim put out for this coin, and which, according to the claim, would appear to be the most important any design can have, is that it will stack. But alas! even this is not obtained by this means, for I have before me a stack of twenty pieces—$100—the stack used by cashiers, and it is the most tottering stack of modern coins, rocking to a great degree, and when the table is jarred about four times the upper coins slide off.

They will fall when carried on a bank tray. It is well known that you cannot strike a lot of flat banks and get them perfectly true. As a connoisseur remarked to me: "Coins should be like a table, which we do not make with a flat bottom, but with feet to stand upon, and this result in coins can and has always been obtained by a flat rim."

And then the new coins, being thinner, as the metal is taken up by the full field, they do not make stacks equal in height to the old, and when mixed with the other issue cause the piles to be of unequal height; and the cashier cannot use the height of a stack as a test of count, but must sort this issue out.

The criticism from the bankers that the first model of the $20 and $10 pieces did not stack firmly should not cause the mint officials to throw all other considerations to the winds, for the firmness in stacking a coin, as stated above, could be obtained by the use of a sufficiently wide and high rim.

These coins will be a disgrace to our country as a monument of our present ideas of art as applied to coinage.

As compared with those of recent issues of European countries, not to mention the beautiful works of the ancient Greek coin engravers, it is an utterly miserable, hideous production, and let us hope that its issue will not be continued and that it will be recalled and remelted.

I would summarize the above objections as follows:

"First—Lack of beauty. The coinage of our country should be an example of beauty and art to all its citizens. Second—Ease with which it may be counterfeited. Third—Unhygienic. Its filth-bearing capacities. Fourth—Not forming stacks of equal heights."

Chapman continued, suggesting alternative means for selecting coin designs in the future. The letter was forwarded to the secretary of the Treasury and then to Bigelow who replied:

> Some of Mr. Chapman's criticisms are well founded, others less so. He says that "sinking the relief below the surface makes it look like an incised design and precludes the effect of a bas-relief." This is hardly correct, as Mr. Chapman can readily see for himself in photographs of the Egyptian sculptures. There may be at the Museum at Philadelphia some casts or originals of Egyptian wall-carving which will illustrate the principle. The bas-relief effect is accentuated and not diminished by the shadow of the sharp outline.
>
> He says the head of the Indian is "without artistic merit and portrays an Indian emaciated, totally unlike the big strong Indian chiefs as seen in real life." The answer to this is that the head was taken from a recent photograph of an Indian whose health was excellent. Perhaps Mr. Chapman has in mind the fatter but less characteristic type of Indian sometimes seen on the reservations.
>
> "The treatment of the head is crude and hard, with sharp, abrupt outlines, as if carved by a mere metal chaser." This doubtless refers to the feathers of the head-dress which were retouched in the die, the modeling of Mr. Pratt's design having been a little too delicate to hold its own in the reducing machine. I enclose a photograph from a plaster cast of Mr. Pratt's clay, which illustrates this point.
>
> The matter of the eagle was thoroughly threshed out at the time of the issue of the Saint-Gaudens' coin. That design proved to be an absolutely correct representation of the white-headed or American eagle, except that the head was, perhaps intentionally, a little small and the leg feathers a little heavy. Both these criticisms Mr. Pratt has met in the present design. Mr. Chapman says that the new American eagle has no feathers on its feet. This statement is true, but not exactly new.
>
> "The placing of the design below the surface of the plan with deeply incised outlines gives the effect of having been engraved into the metal [*sic*], and can, therefore, be closely imitated by any metal chaser by the graver without dies or moulds." This criticism can hardly be taken seriously. If a forger were going to engrave anything he would not waste his labor on a single coin. It would be as easy to engrave a die of any issue.
>
> "The sunken design will be a great receptacle for dirt and conveyor of disease, and the coin will be the most unhygienic ever issued." This remains to be seen. The question of hygiene has more relation to silver coins than gold, as they find their way into dirtier pockets. A dirty gold coin would be an anomaly. I have never

happened to see one.

What Mr. Chapman says in regard to the fact of the coins not stacking is perfectly true. I noticed it as soon as they were issued and called Mr. Leach's attention to it. It proved to be due to an accidental warping of the steel die in hardening. Mr. Leach tells me that it can and will be avoided in future.

"Coins should be like a table, which we do not make with a flat bottom, but with feet to stand upon, and this result in coins can and always has been obtained by a flat rim." This is true, and it is exactly the principle on which the present issue is made. The flat rim extends over the edge of the coin to the edge of the design.

The thickness of the coins after striking depends on the amount of metal displaced by the die. A stronger relief would give greater thickness. I agree with Mr. Chapman that it would be well if all the coins in circulation were of the same thickness.

Chapman insisted upon having the last word, though. In a return letter he stated:

The Egyptian wall-reliefs, from which, of course, I recognized Dr. Bigelow obtained his idea, do not equal in effect bas-reliefs where the surrounding surface is cut away to the level of the lowest part of the design. The first or general effect of the Egyptian wall reliefs is simply that they are wall-paintings with incised lines and slight modeling to help out or accentuate, and give the effect of shade on mural painting; and when viewed at an oblique angle are invisible.

Egyptian art, unlike the Greek, remained frozen in conventionalism and did not progress to the full free rendering of the round.

I am glad to hear from Dr. Bigelow on one phase of the subject, on which he has expert knowledge, that the health of the Indian is excellent. But, to me, his shrunken mouth and nostrils indicate a man below par in his physical condition.

He admits crude treatment in regard to head and eagle.

He thinks that the coin could not be easily imitated by incision, as a "man would make a die instead of a single piece." With this, I would beg to differ on account of actual experience, as I have met with several incised counterfeits. Recently I saw as small a denomination as a dime, which had been made by engraving on the piece of metal. The effect was that of a very much worn example. To make dies requires more time, mechanical applicances to use them, or, if moulds be used, furnaces to melt the metal, whereas a skillful engraver can make a copy rapidly on inferior alloy and without having the evidence against him of dies or moulds in his possession.

Chapman's letter was a needless exercise. The last year the coins were struck was 1929, and 1933 was the last year gold coins of any denominations were made in the United States.

11

The Lincoln Cent

Nineteen hundred and nine was not a good year for race relations in the United States. As blacks poured into the industrial north, residential segregation became a way of life in the major cities. For blacks, housing was likely to be overpriced, overcrowded, and so restricted that even a successful family had to remain in the ghetto.

In the South, lynchings of blacks for almost any reason were increasingly common. The Klu Klux Klan was being revived, and Klan ideas were influencing legislators in major cities around the country.

D. W. Griffith, a rising young filmmaker, was just a few short years away from producing *The Birth Of A Nation,* a three-hour spectacular that recreated the Civil War from a pro-Confederate viewpoint. The movie detailed the humiliation of the South during reconstruction and had black-hating audiences cheering Ku Klux Klansmen as they lynched Negroes on the screen. Riots broke out in many cities as groups anxious to see the film clashed with fellow citizens who wanted it closed because of its racist theme.

Most blacks felt helpless during these years. City, state, and federal government all seemed to be working against them. They felt that no one cared about them and were shocked when a new coin honoring Abraham Lincoln made its appearance. The new cent was called the "coin of freedom" and the "emancipation coin."

The Lincoln cent was to become the most popular coin the United States has ever produced, a fact one could have predicted from the wild demand for the coin on its first day of issue. The public was convinced the design would be changed almost immediately because it honored a president whose ideals seemed to have died with him. People felt that if they didn't get a coin the day it was issued, there would be no second chance. As a result, there were mob scenes wherever the cents were released. So many people rushed to the Wall Street subtreasury on the day of issue that ten officers sent to the scene to maintain order found themselves helpless and had to send for extensive reinforcements. Seven hundred thousand coins were issued the first two days, many of them immediately becoming treasured prizes which were hidden away with the family jewelry and other valuables.

The Lincoln cent was not to be short-lived, however. Over one hundred million were put into circulation that first year, and countless others were produced in the years that followed. Yet the excitement that greeted the coin's initial release would be repeated when scandals involving plastic and aluminum coins came to public attention during World War II and the 1970s.

The Lincoln cent was the creation of Victor David Brenner, the anglicized name of Viktoras Barnauskas who was born in Shavli, Lithuania, on June 12, 1871. (Lithuania was at that time ruled by Russia.) His father, who carved brooches, gravestones, rings, and other items, taught his son the art of die making and seal cutting.

When Brenner was sixteen he moved to Kovno, the country's capital, and became a seal cutter. He was hated by several business rivals jealous of his skill, and they schemed to ruin him. They convinced Brenner to take an assignment to make a seal for a government official, an action which was against the law. Only the government engraving bureau could legally take on such a task, a fact Brenner didn't know. Anyone else doing such work was guilty of counterfeiting.

Brenner was sentenced to transportation to Siberia but managed to flee to the United States. Here he became a die cutter and earned enough money to go to Paris for further study under Louis Oscar Roty. In Paris, he had his first chance to display his skills in the coin maker's art. He conducted a class in die cutting and coin and medal design during the period 1901–1902.

Nineteen hundred and nine was the 100th anniversary of Lincoln's birth. During the summer of 1908, Brenner, back in the United States and married to Anna Reeb, was asked to prepare a plaque and a medal in Lincoln's honor. By chance, he was given the commission during a period when he was sketching President Theodore Roosevelt in preparation for designing a Panama Canal service medal. Brenner suggested to the President that a more fitting Lincoln tribute would be a new coin in his honor.

Brenner was not concerned with the question of race relations or politics when he excitedly began work on a Lincoln coin design. He was interested in the artistic potential of the great president's face.

The artist did not have a specific coin in mind when he began the

Lincoln design, though he favored preparing a half-dollar. He produced a number of reverses to go along with the Lincoln-portrait obverse, including an eagle and a standing Liberty that was copied from the French two-franc coin.

On February 1, 1909, Brenner wrote to Mint Director Frank Leach:

> The model of this Eagle is improved by the engraving you gave me, and if my last Lincoln head is adopted, the Eagle could well (be) made for the other side. I think that a half-dollar would be more suitable for the Lincoln coin than a penny. In a day or so I shall send on to you a helmeted head of Liberty for one side of the cent or nickel, so that with the head I am to send, I think the models for the three coins would be accomplished, except the changing of the denominations and final finishing of detail in face and otherwise. I would also finish the Hubs so as to get all I want in the ultimate size. . . .

Brenner was anxious to get the coins adopted. He wanted them ready before President Roosevelt left office.

On February 9, Leach wrote to Treasury Secretary Franklin MacVeigh concerning Brenner's designs. One had a leafy twig with the word "One Cent" over it. This was surrounded by the words "United States of America 1908." It was a variation of the French coin, as was his second design, consisting of a walking woman carrying a scroll in one hand and leaves in the other. The walking woman's origin was not known at the time but Leach commented:

> In the matter of furnishing the designs for the proposed new one cent coinage, Mr. Victor Brenner is insistent upon introducing another design for the reverse side in place of the one first offered. It is necessary that we should have some other design than the one first submitted by him, for I have discovered that it is an exact copy of the design used by the Government of France on its two franc piece, the only difference being in the inscriptions. We should also refuse to adopt the second design offered, embracing a female figure, first, for the reason that there is a question as to its legality. This figure is supposed to symbolize Liberty, and to use it, it seems to me, would destroy our license to use the Lincoln head, so much desired, on the obverse side. The law does not provide for two impressions or figures emblematic of Liberty. Then, as this is the simplest coin we have it seems to me it should call for the plainest and most distinct design.
>
> Another objection, which is not so serious, being only a mechanical one, is that a figure on the reverse side of the coin, unless of the lowest possible relief, would interfere with securing the best results in producing the Lincoln portrait on the obverse side.

As the design work progressed, Brenner learned he would be

making a one-cent piece. Charles Barber was working on a half-dollar design and was not about to let someone else handle it. Barber also gave Brenner advice on the design to make it conform with engraving and reproduction demands of coinage. Since Brenner was skilled in this area, it seems likely this was just the jealous Barber's way of insuring he would influence the new coin's design even if he was not being allowed to create it.

One of Brenner's desires was to have his name imprinted on the Lincoln cent. This was not only unprecedented but would have been difficult to engrave. Mint Director Leach wrote of the matter on February 18, saying, "I notice that Mr. Brenner insists upon putting his full name on the obverse side. I am sorry to have to disappoint him in this matter, but after consultation with the Secretary of the Treasury upon the subject it was decided that only his initials could be permitted, and that in an unobtrusive way. . . ."

There were other modifications of the design for the new Lincoln cents. Most involved the placement of the motto, areas of blank space, and similar matters. Brenner was kept informed of each change and was consulted frequently. The mint personnel had been criticized for not cooperating fully with Saint-Gaudens and Bigelow during the designing of their coins, and the mint director was anxious to avoid a repetition of such charges.

When the coin was finally completed, Brenner's initials appeared on the reverse. They were so small and unobtrusive that they were almost invisible. The *Rochester Post-Express* stated indignantly: "Never before in all our coinage have the initials of the designers appeared on

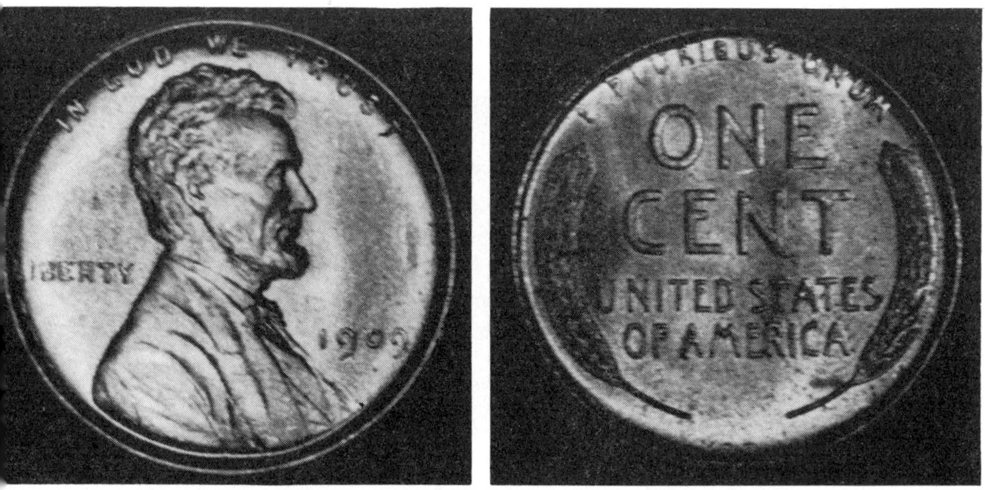

The Lincoln cent. The initials "V.D.B." for Victor David Brenner were placed at the very bottom of the reverse directly in line with the syllable "mer" of the word "America". They were barely visible but created such a furor with the mint officials that they were removed—and restored to the coin only after the chief engraver of the mint died. They were replaced at the bottom of the bust of Lincoln starting in 1917.

a coin. If one designer may put one initial on a coin, and the next put on three initials, the next will want his whole name to appear, and if on coins, why not logically on postage stamps, greenbacks, and bonds." The writer did not realize just what he was saying. Charles Barber had already placed his initial on coins and Brenner had wanted to use his full last name.

The *New Orleans Picayune,* an anti-Roosevelt paper, saw the initials as the start of a presidential power play. They were called "The first visible and outward emblem of the transmogrification of the republic into an empire."

On August 5, 1909, coin production was stopped and Barber was ordered to Washington. He was to remove the initials from the die, an action that would be difficult. This was further complicated by the desire to leave the letter *B* as a way of pacifying the artist. Barber said it would be simpler and two weeks faster if he could just remove all initials from the hub and leave the die alone. This was agreed upon.

Brenner was naturally upset with the changes. Not only had he been assured of the presence of his initials on the coins, he had also discovered that additional modifications had been made without notification or approval.

To make matters worse, the vending machine industry announced that the new cent was too thick for their coin detectors. Either the dies or the detectors had to be changed, a fact that Barber delighted in relating to all who would listen. However, this time Barber was not placated. The government informed the vending machine manufacturers that they would have to alter their equipment. The coin would not be changed further.

In February 1917, Charles Barber died and the mint lost its strongest opponent of change. Brenner's initials were quietly re-

The reverse used from 1909 to 1958. Note that the initials have been removed.

stored on the cents, this time on Lincoln's shoulder. It had taken eight years, but Brenner felt that justice had finally been achieved.

The next major problem with the Lincoln cent came during the years of the Second World War. Copper, once an almost worthless metal, suddenly assumed great value in the manufacture of military hardware. Since civilian needs had to be considered secondary to military requirements, a serious shortage of copper plagued the mint.

The mint officials recognized that a new material had to be found for use in manufacturing the Lincoln cent. Unfortunately, no experimentation could be done without congressional authorization for a metal change. This would normally not have been a problem but Congress was so concerned with war matters that civilian issues were set aside for weeks or months at a time.

Mint officials seemed to feel that Congress would eventually get around to dealing with the problem and would certainly authorize the use of a copper substitute. They saw no reason to delay their research, hoping to be ready to switch materials when the official word was given.

The logical alternatives to copper were metals such as tin, zinc, and nickel. But these metals were also scarce. The cent was legally composed of 95 percent copper and 5 percent zinc and tin. The exact amounts of tin and zinc could vary as long as they totaled the 5 percent set by law. In 1941, with tin in great demand, the mint reduced the percentage in the Lincoln cent from 1 percent (4 percent was zinc) to a trace of the metal with the remainder of the 5 percent required by law being zinc.

The following year the War Production Board suggested that a zinc alloy be used for the cents. Experiments were started, the New Jersey Zinc Sales Company supplying the rolled zinc needed for this purpose. Other experiments were made with widely varying metals, both officially and unoficially, so cents are known to have been made with brass, zinc, aluminum, copper, aluminum bronze, zinc and copper in different proportions, lead, antimony, and other metals. All were believed destroyed, though from time to time, following the war, there were reports of collectors discovering one or more of the experimental cents.

Word soon reached the mint that the amount of available zinc would be inadequate for coin production needs. New directions were taken. Paper coinage was considered, then rejected because it would not wear as long as metal coinage. Glass, and even plastic coinage, was then considered, and several firms were assigned to handle the testing. Among these were Durez Plastics and Chemical, Inc., of North Tonawanda, New York; The Patent Button Company of Tennessee, Inc.; Blue Ridge Glass Corporation of Kingsport, New Jersey; and Colt Patent Firearms Company of Hartford, Connecticut, to name just a few.

The mention of North Tonawanda is especially interesting since it was the home of the late Samuel Brown who was infamous in the story of the 1913 Liberty Head nickel. It was also in North Tonawanda, in 1943 at the Durez Plastic and Chemical Corp., that a child of one of the employees was found playing with a plastic coin. The incident was kept quiet, but word got out that the coin was part of secret experimental work being done for the mint.

In 1943, after the discovery of the plastic cent had been widely publicized, Mint Director Nellie Tayloe Ross finally admitted to the experimentation, which if not illegal, was certainly unauthorized. She said that all work had been handled under carefully controlled conditions and ignored the fact that at least one coin and possibly more, had escaped destruction.

In December 1942, New York Senator Robert Wagner finally got around to the question of coin manufacture. He introduced bill S. 2889 to "further the war effort by authorizing the substitution of other materials for strategic metals used in minor coinage, to authorize the forming of worn and uncurrent silver dollars into bars, and for other purposes," and asked "unanimous consent in connection with this bill that a memorandum may be printed in the record."

A summary of this extensive bill was made by New York Congressman Somers of the House Committee on Coinage, Weights, and Measures, which also considered the proposal. He said: "The purpose of this bill is to conserve the metals required for war production purposes which are now used in minor coins. The bill will permit the minting of minor coins in the denominations of one cent and three cents, which coins shall be of such metallic or other contents, weight, denominations, shape, and limitations of form and design as the Secretary of the Treasury by regulation may prescribe. In determining those physical properties the Secretary of the Treasury is directed to take into consideration the use of these coins in coin-operated devices. The authority contained in this bill is limited to the period between the date of enactment and December 31, 1946."

The bill was presented by Somers on December 10, 1942, after the mint had begun experimenting with the plastic coins. The fact that authorization was lacking made the mint's experiments illegal. However, this proved to be of little consequence. The plastic was found to be too brittle and was impractical for the vending industry.

During the course of debate, Somers was asked for specifics about the contemplated coin change. He said, "It is contemplated at the present time that they will be made of steel with a zinc coating." He emphasized that this would be strictly a temporary measure. Debate was intensive and fears were expressed that our minor coins would soon be worthless. But Somers stressed that copper was already almost worthless except for the unusual uses demanded by war. Then he presented the first word of mint experimentation to reach congressional ears:

> Let me simply restate what the mint told me. They said, "When it first became apparent that we would have a shortage of copper, we immediately experimented with other materials." They went to zinc because zinc is rather popular for similar coinage in other countries. They had just about completed their experiments with zinc and had brought a bill to my committee when the War Production Board said to them, "Gentlemen, zinc is now on the critical list."
>
> From that they went to plastics. They did some experimenting with plastics and found that they went on the critical list.
>
> They think now that the metal most readily obtainable at the moment, the one easiest to handle and the one that we can get the quickest, is steel. Consequently, they decided that they would use steel for the period of this bill, coating the steel with zinc for the purpose of protection, and use that for the penny and the three-cent piece.

The mention of plastics going on the critical list was actually a reference to urea and phenol, ingredients in the plastic considered for the coins. The three-cent piece was a proposed new coin that was never produced.

On December 18, 1942, the bill to alter the metallic content of the cents was passed. The experimental coins were destroyed or hidden away and remain little known to this day. The zinc-coated steel design was adopted for the 1943 gray cents, and copper was quickly returned to coins as soon as wartime shortage were alleviated.

As a result of the illegal experimentation and the controversy surrounding it, Nellie Tayloe Ross wrote a directive on May 26, 1947, saying:

> No official coinage dies, domestic or foreign, shall be used for striking experimental or trial pieces, except when the need for the use of such dies for that purpose is mandatory by reason of the requirements of the Engraver, the Superintendent of the Mint, or the Director of the Mint.
>
> Except when specifically authorized by the Director of the Mint in writing, no special coinage die bearing an official inscription, insignia or device, in whole or in part, of the United States or a foreign government or a United States Mint, or bearing a resemblance thereto, is to be used for striking experimental or trial pieces.
>
> Experimental and trial pieces of domestic or foreign coins shall be struck only by the Engraver from planchets furnished to him from the coining department upon receipt of written requisition for the specific number of pieces required, signed by the Superintendent of the Mint, and a record shall be kept of all such pieces, and such record shall include the date of, and the signed statement of the witnesses to, their final destruction.

The next change in the Lincoln cent came in 1959, the one

hundred and fiftieth anniversary of the emancipator's birth. Mint engraver Frank Gasparro produced a new reverse for the coin, showing the Lincoln Memorial in Washington, D.C., as seen from the front. The motto "E Pluribus Unum" is directly above the memorial and the words "United States of America" and "One Cent" surround both.

Oddly enough, Gasparro was born in Philadelphia in 1909, the year the Lincoln cent was created and the one hundredth anniversary of Lincoln's birth. He studied at the Pennsylvania Academy of Fine Arts and the Fleisher Art Memorial and joined the Mint in 1942.

The Lincoln Memorial was designed by Henry Bacon. Construction began on February 12, 1915, and the monument was dedicated on Memorial Day, 1922. The thirty-six columns represent the number of states in the Union in 1865. The statue of Lincoln was created by Daniel Chester French and is unusually detailed on the coin despite the fact that it is a tiny part of the Memorial reverse.

The change to the Lincoln Memorial design was accepted calmly by the general public. However, a few years later, a Lincoln cent with the new design was to cause a major scandal in government which at present is far from resolved.

The story began late in 1973 when the rising price of copper forced the mint to look to new materials for the production of Lincoln cents. Bureau of the Mint Director Mary Brooks proposed the manufacture of coins made from aluminum, and a test was made to see if this would be practical. The Philadelphia mint produced a reported 1,579,324 aluminum cents for experimental purposes. They were dated 1974, and none were meant for circulation. The vast majority remained in the mint, but an estimated twenty-four of the coins were sent to

The Lincoln Memorial reverse for the Lincoln cent.

Washington, entrusted to Frank MacDonald, a deputy director of the Mint Bureau.

In December 1973, fourteen aluminum Lincoln cents were taken to the House and Senate Banking committees. MacDonald and Mrs. Brooks wanted to convince the members to authorize the change in the metal. The fourteen cents were left with the legislators, who it was to be assumed, were honest individuals. MacDonald was later quoted by the *Wall Street Journal:* "We didn't require the congressmen to sign receipts or anything like that. That wasn't considered necessary. We simply left the coins in the custody of the committees."

There was nothing particularly controversial about the proposal for the change in metal, though it did not pass. A special-interest lobby composed of vending machine manufacturers worked against the bill because the new coins would not function properly in their equipment. In addition, the price of copper returned to a low enough level that making the coins of that metal again became practical.

The aluminum cents in the Philadelphia mint were all melted down. However, nine aluminum coins were left with members of the House Banking Committee, and five with the Senate Banking Committee. Senator Robert Taft, Jr., of Ohio was quoted in the *Wall Street Journal* as saying that he had had two of the coins on his desk, and then had lost them. When I attempted to check with Senator Taft about the matter, he asked Arizona Senator Barry Goldwater to write to me. That letter stated:

> Senator Taft asked that I respond to your letter as a matter of Senatorial courtesy. In speaking with an official at the Bureau of the Mint I was advised of the following:
>
> 1. The aluminum coins were formulated as a possible substitute to the copper pennies presently in use. This plan arose out of the copper shortage which was prevalent in 1973.
> 2. Aluminum coins were worked up and sent to the House and Senate Banking Committees for investigation. However, while investigations were being conducted, the copper shortage eased and it was decided to forgo plans for aluminum pennies.
> 3. At no time did the Bureau of the Mint ask for the return of the samples sent to the Congressional Committees and they feel there is no evidence of wrongdoing on anyones part. . . .

The statements may or may not be accurate. FBI Director Clarence Kelley wrote me as far back as November 24, 1975: "The FBI was instructed by the Department of Justice to consult with officials of the Bureau of the Mint about the disappearance of several prototype aluminum pennies in order to determine if there was any violation of the Federal statute governing theft of Government property. This matter is currently under investigation and therefore facts of this case cannot be discussed."

Obviously there was more concern than anyone was admitting. In fact earlier that same year, Frank MacDonald, then acting director of the mint, wrote to me to say:

"We appreciate your concern over the fourteen aluminum coins currently held by House and Senate Committees. You may be sure that appropriate steps are being taken to assure that these coins remain in the custody of the United States Government. Even while the proposed legislation was pending, all experimental aluminum pennies in Mint custody were ordered to be melted by the Director. The pieces provided to the Committees remain in their custody and will presumably be returned to the Bureau once the Committees no longer have any need for them."

What the acting director did not mention was the fact that the mint is dependent upon the banking committees for its funding. Public statements in any way critical of the congressmen, senators, and their staffs are highly unlikely to be made.

Prior to the MacDonald statement, the mint was actively trying to get the coins returned. Congressman Richard Ottinger of New York wrote a constituent: "My staff has been in touch with officials in the office of Ms. Mary Brooks, Director of the Mint, and I have been informed that she has requested that the coins be returned, but as of yet they are still outstanding. The Bureau of the Mint is, however, continuing its efforts."

While trying to run down the missing coins, I attempted to contact everyone involved with the scandal. Many of the comments were similar to the one made by Senator Lowell Weicker, Jr., of Connecticut who commented: "Neither I nor any of my staff members ever saw or possessed any of these coins. It is my understanding that only three members of the Senate Banking Committee have possessed these coins."

Tennessee Senator Bill Brock commented:

> I will attempt to answer your questions as best I can and provide what information I can. My records indicate that the date the Senate Committee on Banking, Housing and Urban Affairs considered the legislation to provide for the composition change was December 13, 1973. At this meeting of the full committee, which was to resume the markup of the bill that eventually became the Housing and Community Development Act of 1974, Senator Sparkman brought the Administration's request to our attention. I recall, there was no extended debate, only a brief explanation of the bill, before the Committee approved the measure by voice vote. To my knowledge, there were no representatives of the Bureau of the Mint or the Department of the Treasury present and no "samples" available.
>
> Personally, to this day, I have not seen an aluminum penny. I never had possession of any of the coins nor did any member of my staff. As to the present location of these coins, I am afraid I do not know.

Congressman Clair Burgener of California stated:

> I was a member of the House Committee on Banking and Currency during the 93rd Congress, for the years 1973 and 1974. During that time I was indeed a member of the Subcommittee on Consumer Affairs which handled legislation relating to the minting of U. S. coins. I do recall that one day Mrs. Mary Brooks, Director of the Mint, showed members of the Committee the pattern aluminum cents which you referred to in your letter. I did have the opportunity to look at them, but I never had any of them in my personal possession. The ones that were shown that day, to the best of my recollection, were taken from the room by Mrs. Brooks.
>
> At no time did I or any member of my staff have any of the coins in our own possession. I was told at the time that they had substantial value although, not being a coin collector or knowledgeable in the field, this meant little to me at the time. I have read, through newspaper accounts, that some of these coins are now missing. I deeply regret this, and hope that the chain of events surrounding the disappearance will be most carefully reviewed and examined, so that they can be returned to their rightful owner which, of course, is the people of the United States, through the U.S. Mint.

Congressman John Conlan of Arizona, a state where copper mining is a major industry, commented humorously: "I remember seeing the coins, handling them briefly and cursing them a bit. Beyond that, I don't have any idea what happened to them."

And Senator William Hathaway of Maine stated: "In the Fall of 1973 the Director of the Mint, Mary Brooks, visited my offices and left with me one of the sample aluminum pennies. To the best of my recollection a few days later a representative from the Mint came by the office and picked up the sample coin. No member of my staff possessed one of the coins at any time nor did I pass the coin on to anyone else. It is my understanding that the Mint has repossessed most of the coins made. If there are any left in public hands, I have no idea where they might be."

The majority of the fourteen aluminum cents are still missing. There are two logical answers to the mystery, neither of which reflects well on the people involved.

The least reprehensible answer is that the coins were simply lost or mislaid. It appears from the response to my queries that the committee members involved had some idea of the importance of such pattern coinage, but whether they knew the potential value—currently estimated at one thousand to thirty-five thousand dollars—remains unclear. Since the coins were identical to regular 1974 Lincoln cents except for the coloring, they might have been accidentally spent or casually tossed in a drawer and forgotten.

More likely, whoever has the coins has them knowingly. As has been shown by such coins as the 1913 Liberty Head nickels, there have been cases in our history when illegal coins kept long enough proved profitable to the people who owned them. There is a good chance that some of the aluminum cents rest in an honored place in a collection, safe deposit box, or similar repository. The owner may plan to bring the coins to the marketplace in a few years or to pass them on to his or her children, who will offer them for sale. By law they should be confiscated at that time, but what will actually happen remains to be seen.

12

The Buffalo Nickel and the Numismatic Art of the Frasers

The petty jealousies of artists and engravers have long been a factor in determining who will design our nation's coinage. Artists outside the mint have contributed coin designs, including that of our most beautiful coin, the Saint-Gaudens' twenty-dollar gold piece. But their work is usually limited to a single design which is often modified by mint workers. For this reason the story of James and Laura Fraser is one of the most unusual in United States coin history. They designed, separately and together, a total of five coins, with Laura a runner-up in a contest to develop a sixth. She was not given the assignment to design that coin only because of the prejudices of one of the committee members.

The best known Fraser coin was the Buffalo-Indian nickel introduced in 1913. James Fraser, the designer of the coin, was born in Winona, Minnesota, in 1876. He studied with sculptor Richard Bok while still in his early teens, after his family had moved to Chicago. Later he went to the Chicago Art Institute and eventually became the assistant of Augustus Saint-Gaudens.

It is interesting to contrast Fraser with both Saint-Gaudens and with another of Saint-Gaudens' assistants, Adolph Weinman, whose Walking Liberty half-dollar will be discussed later in the book. Weinman's design is in the classical style of his teacher's twenty-dollar coin. Fraser's design might be called "pure American." In fact, Weinman apparently scorned Fraser's nickel, at least as far as his son

Robert Weinman can recall. In a letter to me, Robert commented: ". . . I do recall his [Adolph Weinman's] disaffection for Fraser's nickel—I think he felt it was too 'homespun,' 'informal' for national currency. Or, maybe it was plain, old professional jealousy."

Fraser is best known for his sculpture *End Of The Trail,* the model for which was exhibited in Paris and earned him a one thousand dollar prize from the American Art Association. The year was 1898—before he had begun working with Saint-Gaudens. The sculpture shows an exhausted Indian, lance in hand, resting atop an equally tired horse. It was meant to show the Indian driven from his home, pushed to the Pacific Ocean, the "end of the trail," because he could no longer escape the advancing settlements of the white man.

The first full-scale model of *End Of The Trail* wasn't completed until 1910. Later a full size model, two and one half times life size, was exhibited at the Panama-Pacific International Exposition in San Francisco in 1915. It proved the most popular display at the Exposition and numerous pieces of jewelry, postcards, and other souvenirs utilized the design as a way to make money. Fraser was quoted as saying of the event: "I have been told more than $250,000 worth of prints and photographs were sold of the statute. Who got the money, I don't know. I do know I didn't get any of it. As a matter of fact, everyone knew of the statue, but no one seemed to know its sculptor. I'm afraid I was too busy to take advantage of how much it was liked."

The statue reveals Fraser's long interest in the Indian, an interest that ultimately led to the creation of the nickel. His earliest connection with coinage, though, was with the head of Victory used on the General Sherman statue discussed in the chapter on Saint-Gaudens. It was Fraser who handled the physical execution of the statue from Saint-Gaudens' design.

Charles Barber had been experimenting with designs for a new nickel as early as 1909. But it was not until two years later, on May 4, 1911, that the government became more serious about the coin. Oddly, it was the result of family pressure on Treasury Secretary Franklin MacVeagh, whose son wrote him: "A little matter that seems to have been overlooked by all of you is the opportunity to beautify the design of the nickel or five cent piece during your administration, and it seems to me it would be a permanent souvenir of the most attractive sort. As possibly you are aware, it is the only coin the design of which you can change during your administration, as I believe there is a law to the effect that the designs must not be changed oftener than every twenty-five years. I should think also it might be the coin of which the greatest numbers are in circulation."

The secretary realized that his son was right and decided to look into the possibility of obtaining designs for a new coin. Fraser learned of the matter and immediately contacted George Roberts, director of the Philadelphia mint. The men felt that a Lincoln Head design would be most appropriate, despite the fact that the cent already showed such a head. Fraser went so far as to prepare a very rough coin or medal showing the Lincoln head. It was struck in lead and treated with a copper wash followed by a silver wash. This lead piece is currently in the National Cowboy Hall of Fame and Western Heritage Center in Oklahoma City, Oklahoma.

On June 13, 1911, Fraser commented on the Lincoln Design in a letter to Roberts: "I think your idea of the Lincoln head is a splendid one and I shall be glad to make you some sketches as soon as possible and let you see them. I think they should be reduced to the actual size of the coin, otherwise we will not be able to judge them, even in the sketch period. I will have that done here, where I can watch the process. I have numerous sketches underway, some of which I hope may be of value."

A year earlier, on May 17, 1910, Congress had created the Fine Arts Commission. This was a group of experts in the arts whose members were to give advice relating to artistic matters in the District of Columbia. Daniel French, a sculptor and one of the members, learned of the Lincoln coin and liked the idea. In a letter to MacVeagh dated July 17, 1912, he wrote: "Mr. Fraser has also shown me the design containing the head of Lincoln, and I cannot help expressing the hope that this may be utilized for one of the other coins. It would seem a pity to lose so charming an example of medallic art and so striking a portrait of the man."

But the Lincoln head was not used at the time though Fraser eventually created a statue of Abraham Lincoln for the Lincoln Memorial Association in Jersey City, New Jersey.

Exactly why Fraser switched to the Indian Head design is uncertain. However, on September 19, 1911, the artist made reference to it in a letter to MacVeagh: ". . . The idea of the Indian and the buffalo on the same coin is without doubt, purely American and seems to be singularly appropriate to have on one of our national coins. You will see that the Indian is entirely different than any that has ever been used on a coin. Most of the heads have been caucasians with an Indian head-dress; in this case I have avoided using the war-bonnet and have made a purely Indian type."

Additional information about the Indian gradually came to light. Fraser had a composite face, utilizing features from the faces of Two Moons, Chief John Big Tree, and Iron Tail (the latter had been an opponent of Custer at the cattle of Little Big Horn). Chief Big Tree was in attendance at the 1966 annual convention of the Texas Numismatic Association. The following account of his presence at the convention appeared in *Numismatic News* on April 25, 1966.

> The limelight of the convention was shared by . . . Chief John Big Tree, one of the three Indians who posed for the Indian Head nickel. Clearly, the spry, witty, old chief stole the show.
>
> Chief John Big Tree, who posed as a model for the original

buffalo nickel, was commissioned by Falstaff Brewing Corporation of Galveston, Texas, to appear at the convention of the Texas Numismatic Association.

Chief John Big Tree, who claims to be 104 years old, is a full blooded Iroquois who now lives with his wife on the Onondaga Reservation near Syracuse, New York. He was one of three Indians selected to pose for the design of the buffalo nickel in 1912.

According to the chief, he was used as the model for the nose and forehead of the Indian nickel, while a Sioux modeled for the cheek and chin of the likeness and a Cheyenne for the hair and headdress.

Chief Big Tree says he was working in a Coney Island show when he was chosen to pose, "because of his classic features."

The buffalo on the nickel was not sketched in the wild as many people believe. Again Fraser went no farther than New York for his model. He chose Black Diamond who traveled the "prairies" of the Central Park Zoo. This honored creature was slaughtered two years after the coin was first issued. Black Diamond was twenty years old when he died, and his body yielded 750 pounds of usable meat as well as a thirteen-by-thirteen-foot hide that was turned into a robe. The slaughter brought $700, and the buyer made the head into a trophy.

On January 13, 1912, Fraser was notified that his design concept had been approved. However, by mid-summer, complications had arisen. Tests by manufacturers of vending machine equipment revealed that the new coins might not work as well as had been hoped.

The primary complaint came from the president of the Hobbs Manufacturing Company, which was making coin-operated equipment that would not work with the relief of the new nickel being prepared. Fraser commented on this in a letter dated December 1, 1912:

> . . . [Hobbs] asks me to reduce the size of the buffalo, inscription, etc., eight-one-hundredths of an inch which practically is one-tenth of an inch. I have carefully considered every space surrounding the buffalo and have changed them back and forth many times, arriving at this design only after the utmost care. So you see how radical any change approximating one tenth of an inch would be in the relation of the spacing in a coin of this size.
>
> Not only that but it is no sure thing that the coin detector will be a practical success. I suggested that the first rim of the nickel be used instead of a circle inside the fretwork and also to bring the second circle nearer the stars. This I am sure can be done.

Since there are no stars on the buffalo nickel, this idea obviously must have been discarded. There is as little known about this matter as there is about the Lincoln design, which had also been abandoned. The letter added:

> . . . I hardly think that the Government should be forced to

accept a design which is inferior to the present one when the machine could be changed without altering to any great degree its effectiveness, thus leaving the coin nearly in its present state. There would have to be a slight reduction even in the event of using the first rim of the nickel. In the future, this would eliminate the wide rim which, on the present coin, is wholly out of proportion to its size thereby adding to the difficulty in making the design. . . .

An experimental set of Buffalo-Indian Nickels was struck on January 7, 1913. They were rejected by Hobbs, and the dies ordered changed. Experimentation continued into February. By then the pressure from the single manufacturing firm seemed to be out of proportion to the problem. The government was in need of the new coin, and production had to be started. It was felt that the Hobbs Company could modify its equipment instead of insisting that changes be made in the coin only. Treasury Secretary MacVeagh, upset with the situation, wrote to the Mint Director saying that the requirements of the manufacturing company ". . . to sit, a clear space between the rim and the rest of the design and a radical change in the cheek of the Indian are, in my judgement, impossible to concede without the practical abandonment of the artistic qualities of the design."

MacVeagh also brought up a point that had been overlooked. The other manufacturers of vending machine equipment had found no problem in altering their machines to fit the new coin. It was only Hobbs that was protesting, and the Hobbs equipment wasn't even in full production. At the end of the letter, MacVeagh added: "If we should stop new coinage—which is always allowed every twenty-five years—for any commercial obstacles less than imperative, we should have to abandon a worthy coinage altogether. This would be a most serious handicap to the art of the Nation; for scarcely any form of art is more influential than an artistic coin, where the coin is widely circulated.

"You will please, therefore, proceed with the coinage of the new nickel."

There was to be one more change in the coin's design, however. By March 1913, it was seen that some of the lettering was wearing away with minimal circulation. The design was revised, changing the mound on which the buffalo stood, the relief, and similar minor matters. Three years later, the Indian Head was also revised and the relief of the word "Liberty" was increased.

Comments regarding the new coin were mixed. One newspaper writer even went so far as to say that he felt the buffalo was flawed by having a face that looked like a person's. The editor of *The Numismatist* said in the March 1913 issue:

The design is radically different from that of any five-cent piece that has ever been issued at the Mint, and is slightly concave on both

A side-by-side comparison of the two Buffalo nickel reverse designs. The one on the left became standard as a second design. The one on the right was the first variety and was used in 1913 only.

The Indian head from the Indian-Buffalo nickel.

sides, something like the present $10 and $20 pieces. Directly under the figure 3 of the date 1913 on the obverse is the letter *F* for the designer of the piece, James Earle Fraser of New York City. It is said that Mr. Fraser took as a model an Indian of the Cheyenne tribe who recently visited New York City. The bison was modeled after a specimen in the New York Zoological Garden.

Mr. Fraser, the designer, is reported as saying that the capital F below the date has met with the approval of the secretary of the Treasury, the director of the Mint, and also the National Art commission.

Already, it is said, the presence of this tiny letter has aroused a certain amount of criticism, similar to that which greeted the appearance of the letters V.D.B. on the Lincoln cent which resulted in their removal, doing an injustice to Mr. Brenner, its designer, and violating all precedents.

T. L. Comparette, curator of the Philadelphia mint's coin collection, stated: "It may not have been wise to place a type on each side of the small piece; a simpler reverse might have been better, the Indian head and the buffalo may be too softly modeled for coin types; perhaps inscriptions have been sacrificed to the types, so that the former are too small and the latter too large for the size of the field; but with all the faults that may be alleged against the new piece, one outstanding truth remains, that Mr. Fraser's designs are works of art, powerfully modeled, and strong."

The remaining coins created by the Frasers were half-dollars known as commemoratives, a subject to be discussed in a later chapter. Briefly, the commemorative half-dollars were official government issues, produced by the mints and printed in limited quantities for souvenir purposes. They were issued to commemorate special events between 1892, when the first-half dollar of this type was issued for the Columbian Exposition, and 1951, when the last of the coins was authorized—a half-dollar jointly honoring Booker T. Washington and George Washington Carver. The coins are all legal tender and can be spent, but they were meant as souvenirs and usually sold at a premium to benefit the sponsoring organization.

Laura Gardin was born on September 14, 1889 in Chicago. When she attended the Art Students' League in New York City some years later, one of her teachers was James Fraser. Commenting to Dean Krakel in his book *End of The Trail,* she said:

He was a great teacher. Jimmy had the rare quality of being able to recognize what someone else felt. He never liked to work in one specific manner. He encouraged individualism. Everyone loved him—especially me.

The year following our marriage we bought property in Westport. Our home was colonial in origin and we could date it back more than two hundred years. We designed our studio for our future together. It was 30 feet by 60 feet and a story and a half high. Big as it was, we kept it full most of the time. We loved it.

Alabama's centennial occurred in 1919. The state had been in the Union exactly one hundred years, its "time out" for joining the Confederacy overlooked by the celebrants. However, it was not until the following year that a coin was desired.

On May 10, 1920, Congress approved the creation of a half-dollar to celebrate the Alabama centennial. A committee was appointed by the state's governor to find a suitable design. However, the members of the centennial coin committee were unable to select anything they liked from the numerous sketches submitted by amateur and professional artists. On June 1, 1920, Mrs. Marie Owen, committee chairman, wrote Governor Thomas Kilby to tell him the committee had prepared its own design, saying that it should have:

> OBVERSE: A cut of the State Capitol occupying practically the whole of the center of the coin. The cut to show building crowning "Capitol Hill." The steps leading up from Dexter Avenue in right foreground.
>
> The three words "State of Alabama" just under the upper rim. The word "of" set just above the Dome of the building. An appropriate sized star at both right and left of building.
>
> The word "Centennial" in the shape of a crescent showing under the view of the cut and next to the two dates "1819–1919." These two dates to be in the same sized type as those used in "State of Alabama." "Centennial" should be in smaller type, if desired, to properly show off this line.
>
> In the design the State Flag should fly from the Dome, it consisting of a St. Andrews Cross, in red, on a square white field.
>
> REVERSE: "United States of America," and "Half Dollar" in same type to show immediately under and immediately above the outer rim of the coin. "In God We Trust" to show, in small type immediately under the inscription "United States of America" on the upper edge of the coin.
>
> The full center of the coin to be adorned with a bust profile of Monroe and Wilson, Presidents at the time of the admission of Alabama into the Union and at the time of the celebration of the one hundredth Anniversary. "Monroe" in small type and "Wilson" in a like sized type, to show immediately back of, and immediately in front of, respectively, the two faces.
>
> The date of coinage to be approximately put on this side of coin.
>
> Two relatively sized stars to show on this face opposite those on other face of coin.

The letter was forwarded to Mint Director Raymond Baker, who eventually sent it to the Commission of Fine Arts mentioned earlier. The sculptor member of the commission happened to be James Fraser, who disagreed with the proposal. He felt that it was never a good idea to show a building on a coin. He thought that such a design was lacking in artistic merit and was best avoided.

Fraser's criticism had weight with the Alabama committee. Mrs. Owen and her group modified the design and, in a letter dated June 23, 1920, stated that changes should be made. She commented:

"The obverse face of the coin should be the present cut of the State Seal, showing the Eagle holding the scroll in his beak, and standing on a shield. Immediately above the center of this design to be the word 'Alabama,' in a crescent around the face under the rim. Immediately below the cut of the Eagle should be '1819–1919,' in a corresponding position, just above the lower rim.

"The reverse of the coin to be the same as the original suggestion, that is the one showing a profile of Monroe and Wilson, Presidents respectively in 1819 and 1919. The issue date of the coin to be on this side."

The Commission of Fine Arts, after approving the changes, was required to find an artist to handle the execution of the commemorative half-dollar. Fraser, the sculptor member, was asked his opinion as to who could handle it most effectively. His choice was his wife Laura.

Laura accepted the commission, working independently of her husband despite his having seen to it that she got the opportunity to handle the execution. As she later commented to Dean Krakel: "Jimmy never did tell me what to do, he never superimposed his ideas, even, on another sculptor, and that is the reason that, when he taught at the Art Students' League where I first met him, the National Academy of Design accepted eighteen compositions done by his class, no two of them in any way similar, each the expression of an individual with no reflection of the teacher. That is because Jimmy was truly a great man, even at that early stage. And throughout our nearly forty years of married life, he never let anything interfere with my working."

Laura's execution of the coin is considered flawless by many art experts. She did modify the original design, though. Instead of the heads of the presidents, she placed the busts of the governors who served at the time of admission and the time of the centennial—Bibb and Kilby. It was the first time in our nation's history that the portrait of a living individual was used on a coin.

The one hundredth anniversary of the birth of Ulysses S. Grant occurred two years later. A commemorative half-dollar was authorized on October 17, 1921, but the bill was amended so that final approval was delayed until February 2, 1922.

The detail on the Grant coin is unusual. The reverse shows Grant's boyhood home in Point Pleasant, Ohio. It is surrounded by trees whose leaves seem almost real. The obverse bears the general's bust, the face seeming almost alive. A gold dollar was also issued with a similar design.

Laura Fraser's next venture into commemorative coin design occurred in 1925, when she prepared the half-dollar produced in honor of the one hundredth anniversary of Fort Vancouver. She was not the first artist selected for the design, however. Another artist, whose initials "S.B." on the first design are all that are known of him, prepared models for the coin, which were rejected by the Commission of Fine Arts in May of 1925. As an alternative, a letter to Mint Director Robert Grant suggested: "The Commission recommend that the work of making a satisfactory design and models for the Fort Vancouver souvenir coin be placed in the hands of Mr. Chester Beach, Sculptor, 207 East 17th Street, New York City, one of the most prominent sculptors and medalists of this country."

Beach, who was to design three commemorative coins of his own, was not available. Laura Fraser was the commission's second choice, and she was hired on June 15, 1925. The result is one of the most dramatic of the commemorative coins. The obverse shows a bust of Dr. John McLoughlin, who built Fort Vancouver. The reverse shows a close-up of a trapper holding a rifle and standing in front of the fort, which sits at the base of a mountain. The inscriptions are "Fort Vancouver Centennial" and "Vancouver Washington Founded 1825 by Hudson's Bay Company."

The reaction to the coin was highly favorable. One commission member, Louis Ayres, commented in a July 1 letter: "As far as I am concerned, I think she has done a splendid job and I had absolutely nothing to criticize. She has taken liberties with the reverse side of putting a trapper superimposing on the landscape, which the local committee gave as a requirement, thereby, I think, really making a medallic design out of a hopeless situation. The whole coin looks very interesting to me, and I think is mighty good."

On May 17, 1926, Laura and James Fraser joined together to produce the Oregon Trail Memorial half-dollar. Once again this was the second choice of the Fine Arts Commission. Chester Beach had been desired, but other commitments kept him from taking the assignment.

Each of the Frasers took one side of the coin—Laura handling the obverse and James designing the reverse. James created an Indian standing in front of a map of the United States. The figure is magnificent—lean and strong. However, he is draped with a robe that some critics feel is reminiscent of Greek coins rather than being uniquely American.

The reverse is a dramatic image of settlers traveling in a covered wagon towards the setting sun. The combination of designs is considered to be the most beautiful of all the commemorative coins produced within the United States.

A discussion of Laura Fraser's "near miss" in designing a regular-issue coin requires our going out of chronological order in this story of American coinage. It concerns the effort made to create a Washington quarter in 1932.

The story begins in 1931 when the Washington Bicentennial Commission and the Commission of Fine Arts convinced Congress to pass an act authorizing a new quarter. This was done on March 4 of that year. The Standing Liberty quarter, discussed in the next chapter, had been in existence far less than the minimum twenty-five years, so an act of Congress was essential.

The new coin, according to the joint commissions sponsoring it, was to have an obverse that "... shall bear a head of Washington based on the Houdon bust at Mt. Vernon." There would be a reverse of the artist's creation, though "... with the proviso that it shall be national in conception." A single sculptor would handle both the coin and a medal.

A number of sculptors, including Laura Fraser, were asked to submit designs. She had already won the competition to produce the Washington medal, and it was felt by the judges that she should handle the coin as well.

The Fraser design for the Washington medal utilized a profile bust of the late President. It was based on Jean Antoine Houdon's statue of George Washington, created for the Virginia legislature more than a century earlier. Houdon, a Frenchman, flourished around the time of the American Revolution. His busts of Washington, Jefferson, and Benjamin Franklin are considered among the best ever produced and provided the design basis for the coins honoring these men.

The following story of the Washington bust was told in the *Milwaukee Journal* and reprinted in the September 1932 edition of *The Numismatist:*

> The two hundredth anniversary of George Washington's birth is to have an eight-month celebration—from February 22 to Thanksgiving Day, 1932. By the time it is over all Americans will be familiar with the appearance of the famous bust of Washington which the French sculptor, Houdon, came over from France to make. The United States commission for the celebration has chosen it to be the official "likeness" of Washington, to be used in books, pictures, on stamps and special coins.
>
> The Houdon bust, modeled from life and regarded as having remarkable vigor and power, was made during a particularly peaceful and happy period in Washington's life. The War of the Revolution was over and he had retired to his beloved Mount Vernon, to develop its lawns and orchards, its "bolling green" and terraces; to plant and dig and experiment with fertilizer, grass and grains; to hunt, go to funerals, arrange marriages and plan improvements for the navigation of the Potomac. He had not yet been called from this happy retirement to become President of the new Government, and was free to indulge his natural bent toward the practices of a country gentleman's life.
>
> The bust was made at the instance of the Legislature of Virginia, which resolved, in the year following the close of the Revolution, "that measures be taken for procuring a statue of General Washington, of the finest marble and best workmanship." Houdon was chosen for the work, and Benjamin Franklin, who was our representative in France at the time, arranged for the sculptor's journey to America.
>
> Washington records the arrival in his diary of Sunday, October 2, 1785:

"After we were in bed (about eleven o'clock in the evening), Mr. Houdon, sent from France by Doctr. Franklin and Mr. Jefferson to take my bust, in behalf of the State of Virginia, with three young men assistants, introduced by a Mr. Perin, a French Gentleman of Alexandria, arrived here by Water from the latter place."

Houdon was a gifted and cultivated Frenchman, then approaching the height of his fame and talents. The son of a domestic in the employ of a courtier, he early carried off the Prix de Rome and spent ten years in the Eternal City. When he came to Washington he was already famous for his "Morpheus," his "St. Bruno" and for busts of Catherine II, D'Alembert, Moliere, Prince Henry of Prussia, Buffon, Mirabeau, Voltaire and many others.

The courtier strain helped him to land on his feet in difficult places. Thus when he was denounced to the convention during the French Revolution for creating a statue of St. Scholastica, he immediately transformed the saint into a presentment of 'Philosophy.' When Napoleon came into power Houdon was taken into favor and made a nude statue of him (now in Dijon), as well as a bust, and likewise busts of the Empress Josephine and Marshall Ney, and the colossal reliefs intended for the column of the Grand Army at Boulogne. Napoleon rewarded him with the Legion of Honor. The Napoleonic days were still in the future, however, when he arrived at that unseemly hour of 11 o'clock and wakened General Washington from his slumbers.

The sittings for the Washington bust were made in the midst of many activities on the part of the industrious host, and one marvels how he ever found time to sit still.

The reverse of Laura Fraser's Washington medal shows a standing Liberty holding a sheathed sword in one hand and a torch in the other. Her head is topped with a spiked crown and an eagle rests on her right shoulder. A motto reads: "Proclaim Liberty Throughout All the Land."

It was a foregone conclusion of the judges that Laura Fraser would also design the coin. Her bust of Washington faithfully reproduced the classic by Houdon as required by the rules of the competition. Almost everyone involved with the selection of the final design agreed that hers should be chosen. The one exception was Treasury Secretary Andrew Mellon who had the power to overrule everyone else. He was biased against Laura Fraser and had no intention of letting her design be used for the coin.

To show the attitude of the members of the commission, which declared Laura Fraser's design the best, it is worth quoting a letter from Fine Arts Commission Chairman Charles Moore:

> . . . the model selected for recommendation to you is distinguished above those submitted by other sculptors. Simplicity, directness, and nobility characterize it. The design has style and elegance. The composition, from the medalist's point of view of

spacing and balance, is entirely satisfactory. The Commission believe that this design would present to the people of this country the Washington whom they revere.

The selection of the model for the reverse was based on its universality as an emblem of the United States. The general conception is the one universally accepted by the people of this country. This fundamental conception has been worked out by the artist in a truly heraldic fashion. The eagle is exceptionally well rendered. It has vigor. It has sculptural quality. The emblematic characteristics get proper emphasis. . . .

Laura Fraser's creation was in direct competition with that of John Flanagan. It is interesting to note that Flanagan, a medalist, had been a student of Augustus Saint-Gaudens and once produced a highly regarded bust of his late teacher.

The Flanagan design for the Washington quarter was quite different from the Houdon bust and theoretically did not qualify. But Mellon was insistent that the Flanagan design be used. However, before the coin could be struck, Mellon left office and was succeeded by Ogden Mills. On the chance that Mills would be more reasonable, Moore sent him a letter on March 31, 1932, repeating the reasons why the coin by Flanagan should be rejected:

The face of Washington is weak. It should be strong, as shown in the Houdon life mask at Mount Vernon. The arrangement of the hair is not only unnatural but also it detracts from the strength of the head.

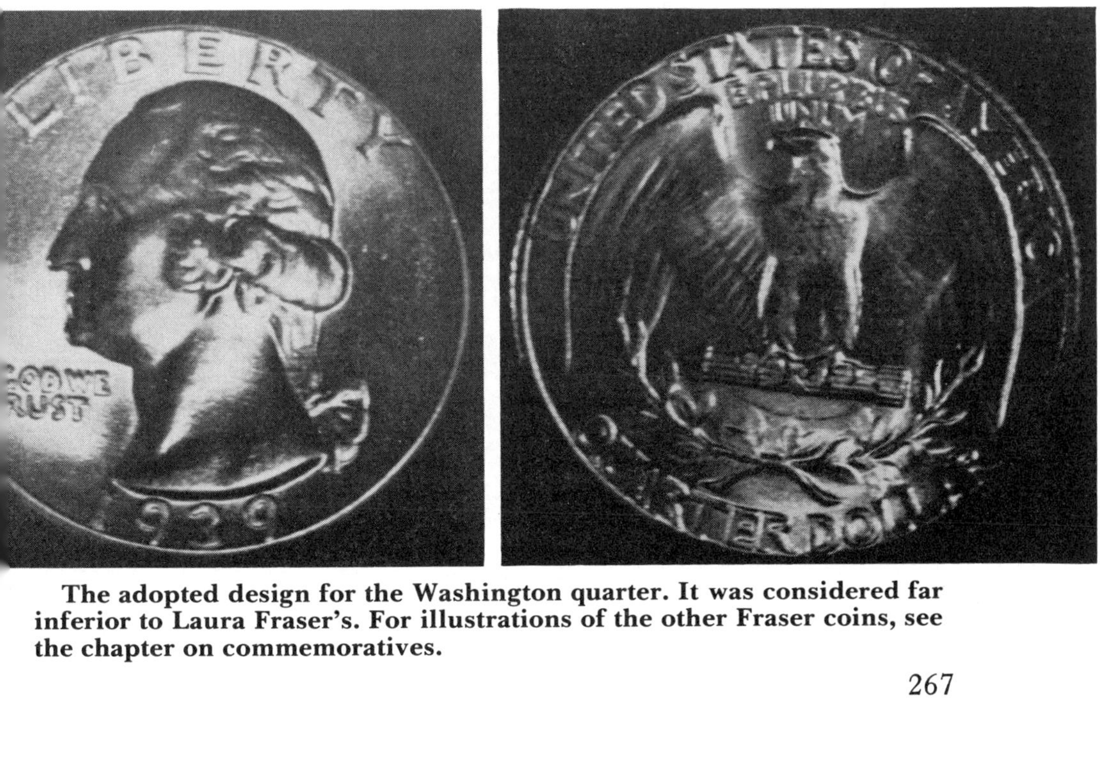

The adopted design for the Washington quarter. It was considered far inferior to Laura Fraser's. For illustrations of the other Fraser coins, see the chapter on commemoratives.

> The eagle on the reverse is not a good eagle in itself, and it is lacking symbolic quality. It does not represent the dignity and power which an emblem of the United States should have. Moreover, the balance is not good. The model shows emphasis on nonessentials and subordinates details.
>
> The Commission has in mind that in reducing these models to the actual size of the coin, some details now visible will be lost, and, on the other hand, other details will be increased. Emphasis, balance, simplicity and dignity are essential in medallic art, and the Commission are confident that in the coin itself these essentials would be lacking.
>
> For these reasons the Commission find the models submitted unacceptable and advise their rejection. They do not reach the standard of design which should characterize the coinage of the United States. It is these standards which the Commission is solicitous that the national coinage should attain. . . .

Unfortunately both for Laura Fraser and the quality of United States coinage, the Flanagan design was selected by the new Treasury secretary, who stated: "My predecessor in office, Honorable A. W. Mellon, gave thought and attention to the models submitted in the competition and finally selected the particular model in question. In the light of your suggestions, I gave further thought to the matter and certain changes have been made by the artist, prompted by these considerations. I have given further consideration to the subject and am constrained to adhere to the decision of my predecessor, and I select that model."

With those words, Laura Fraser's chance to design a regular-issue coin came to an end. But despite the defeat, she and her husband made a greater contribution to the coinage of the United States than any other artist not directly connected with the United States Mint.

13

America's "Obscene" Quarter

The year 1916 marked a period of radical change both for the nation and its coinage. The restraints of the Victorian Era were being overthrown, and women were seeking new freedoms. Many women demanded the right to vote while others rebelled against past restraints in more radical ways. Some entered bars, demanding to be served even though they were without escorts. Others dared to smoke cigarettes or even learned to fly the newly invented airplane.

The business world was also feeling the impact of women who were boldly leaving the home and seeking jobs once held only by men. In most such cases poverty was the compelling motive rather than a desire for liberation. Women needed to earn their way in the world and were demanding the chance to do so.

An anonymous British writer commented in the pages of the *New York American:* "About the average American woman of the middle-classes there can be no doubt at all. She is incomparably the smartest, most elegant and beautiful thing that exists under Heaven.

"It is not of the women of fashion I speak, though many are lovely enough. It is the ordinary, everyday-go-to-work girl who takes her lunch at Child's, runs to catch a trolley-car, jostles you in the subway, and patronizes what you call the cinematograph theatre and she calls the 'movies.' It is, in fact, the goddess of the typewriter, the fairy of the newspaper office, the grace of the telephone that I sing."

But despite the movement to liberate women, American morals were still quite strict. One of the more exciting new fashions for women was an imitation of the Salvation Army uniform, for example. That is why the nation was so shocked when the United States government issued a new twenty-five cent piece that was—obscene!

By 1916, the rather dull coinage of Charles Barber had been in circulation long enough for the designs to be changed. A new dime, quarter, and half-dollar were planned, all to be made by artists working outside the mint. According to a letter from Mint Director Robert Woolley to Charles Barber dated March 3, 1916, ". . . selections have been made from a large number of designs submitted for the proposed new subsidiary silver coins. The models submitted by Mr. Adolph Weinman have been chosen for the Half Dollar and the Dime, and the designs submitted by Mr. Hermon MacNeil have been determined upon for the Quarter Dollar . . ."

MacNeil, a sculptor who had lived in College Point, New York since 1900, had an impressive background. Not only was he a member of the National Academy of Design, the New York Municipal Art Association, the National Academy of Arts and Letters, the president of the National Sculpture Society, and a member of other prestigious organizations, he had also produced several medals. The latter achievements included a medal created for the Pan-American Exposition held in Buffalo in 1901 which should have served to warn the government what type of design MacNeil might create. That medal shows the famous Black Diamond, the same buffalo Fraser had used for the nickel, walking beside a totally nude woman representing Liberty.

MacNeil was first approached about designing the coins early in 1916; he made it clear to Director Woolley that he understood the requirements of coinage. On January 4th of that year he wrote:

> . . . I have a very clear understanding of the necessities of coin designing through the courtesy of Messrs. Barber and Morgan, who were very cordial indeed. Amongst other information Mr. Barber gave me a typewritten copy of the law regarding coin designing which reads:—"Sec. 18. Devices and legends upon coins. Revised Statues, 3517. Inscriptions. That upon the coins of the United States there shall be an impression emblematic of liberty, with an inscription of the word "Liberty" and the year of the coinage, and upon the reverse shall be the figure or representation of an eagle, with the inscriptions "United States of America" and "E Pluribus Unum" and a designation of the value of the coin, and inscription, "In God We Trust."

The designs MacNeil created were dramatically different from anything previously used on United States silver coinage. The obverse had the standing figure of Liberty, a shield in hand, facing the east. The reverse had a flying eagle as its main design element. The coin was considered perfect by almost everyone who saw it and the mint director's annual report for 1916 commented that:

> The design of the 25-cent piece is intended to typify in a measure

The reverse design for the Standing Liberty quarter used in 1916 and part of 1917.

> the awakening interest of the country to its own protection.
>
> The law specified that on the obverse of the coin not only the word "Liberty" but a representation of Liberty shall be shown. In the new design Liberty is stepping forward to the gateway of the country, and on the wall are inscribed the words "In God We Trust," which words also appear on the new half dollar, mentioned above. The left arm of the figure of Liberty is upraised, bearing the shield in the attitude of protection, from which the covering is being drawn. The right hand bears the olive branch of peace. On the field above the head is inscribed the word "Liberty," and on the step under her feet "1916." The reverse of this coin necessitates by law a representation of the American eagle, and is here shown in full flight, with wings extended, sweeping across the coin. Inscription: "United States of America" and "E Pluribus Unum" and "Quarter Dollar" below. Connecting the lettering above an outer circle are thirteen stars.

The model for the coin was well publicized, but the publicity may have been undeserved. She was originally reported to be one Dora Doscher according to the following article in the May 1917 issue of *The Numismatist:*

> From a recent newspaper article by Marguerite Norse we extract the following facts regarding Miss Dora Doscher, who posed for Mr. Hermon A. MacNeil while designing the female figure that appears on our new quarter dollar, and who is now referred to by her friends as "the Girl on the Quarter":
>
> Miss Doscher is 22 years of age, and is 5 feet 4½ inches in height.

Through her own efforts she has developed from a half invalid child to a most perfect type of American womanhood. Her days are spent in artistic and intellectual pursuits. She is a lecturer, scenario writer and trained nurse. At the first intimation of war she enrolled in the Red Cross service and stood from that day ready for a moment's call. She presents an attractive appearance in the Red Cross uniform.

Mr. MacNeil's "Liberty" on the new quarter is indeed a beautiful piece of work. The idea conceived by the artist is highly expressive of national sentiment. The figure comes down a flight of steps in an attitude of welcome to the world. In one extended hand she holds a laurel branch of peace, on the left arm she carries a shield. Though she offers peace first she is prepared to defend her honor and her rights. The design suggests a step forward in civilization, protection and defence with peace as the ultimate goal.

As for the coin girl, her pride is just what you would expect to find in a wholesome, ambitious young woman upon whom the honor had been placed.

Dora Doscher later married a man named Baum and lived to be eighty-eight. She posed for numerous artists as well as having a theatrical career using the stage name Doris Doree. Later she began writing a column called "Beauty, Health, Physical Culture and Psychology" for the New York World in the late 1920s. She was interested in the subject because she had both polio and a bad back while young and managed to overcome both problems.

Dora Doscher Baum also had a radio program on New York City's WOR Radio and was the star of several silent movies. In addition, she was once president of the Women's Auxiliary of the American Naturpathic Association.

The story about Dora Doscher was shockingly challenged in 1972. An article appeared in the September 19, 1972, edition of the Newburgh, New York *Evening News* which said that another woman, who died four months later, was the real model for the coin. The article, written by Robert Curran, stated:

The Liberty Girl, whose beautiful face and figure adorned United States quarters minted from 1916 to 1932, is alive and well at 92 years of age and still believes America is the grandest country of all.

Mrs. Irene MacDowell, who posed for the 25-cent piece 56 years ago, maintains an avid interest in world events but points out that contemporary women's liberation doesn't interest her.

For years the Liberty Girl symbolized peace and freedom in a growing America. Of the United States today she says: "In spite of all the talk you can't find another country that has the liberty we have. I think we're very lucky to be Americans."

The Liberty Quarter shows Mrs. MacDowell as the Liberty Girl descending a flight of steps. She is holding a laurel branch of peace [*sic*] in one hand and a shield in the other.

She posed for 10 days for sculptor Hermon A. MacNeil who competed with 50 other artists seeking to design the 25-cent piece.

At the time, Mrs. MacDowell, a former Broadway actress, wore white, sheet-like drapery and she described her dress for the quarter as "a kind of classical robe." She joked that she was fully dressed.

The coin was minted during President Woodrow Wilson's term.

MacNeil, one of the country's leading sculptors, included Mrs. MacDowell as the Liberty Girl in a memorial statue. Mrs. MacDowell believes that the statue is now in Albany.

The famous Liberty Girl is an alert and remarkably lucid conversationalist today, who likes to watch television late at night and read the newspapers to keep up with what's happening.

She lives in a spacious New Windsor country home not far from Newburgh with her husband George, 90, daughter Louise and son-in-law, Harry Wagner.

Mrs. MacDowell has a strong long love of her country and its traditional stance of liberty.

"Some of the young don't feel that way but they don't know what it's all about. I guess they're trying to find their way," she comments.

No one except her friends and relatives ever knew that she was the person who posed for the Liberty Quarter, because no articles on the national level ever appeared about her.

The Liberty Girl believes clean country living is one of the reasons for her good health.

One flaw in the well-known, artistically-designed quarter of which she is so prominent a part, is that it wears easily. The piece is somewhat difficult to find in the exchange of money these days.

Mrs. MacDowell has one of the quarters in fairly good condition but she would like to obtain another one—not worn as much.

On the coin, the word "Liberty" is inscribed, along with "In God We Trust" and sculptor MacNeil's Roman "M" initial on the right. The other side shows an American Eagle.

But the outstanding characteristic of the coin is the beautiful woman on it, Mrs. MacDowell.

The article also contains an interesting item about the times: "Do times change? Mrs. MacDowell joked that at the time she posed for the famous quarter, a shopper could buy a pound of steak for 25 cents—a far cry from today's prices."

Which story is true? There is a good chance that Mrs. MacDowell's is. However, with both women and the sculptor now dead, positive proof of the model's identity may never be uncovered.

While the new coin was beautiful to the casual observer, a person taking a closer look discovered something quite startling. By the standards of the day, it might be concluded that Miss Liberty was obscene. Not only was there a vast expanse of thigh peeking through the drape, she also had one breast completely bared.

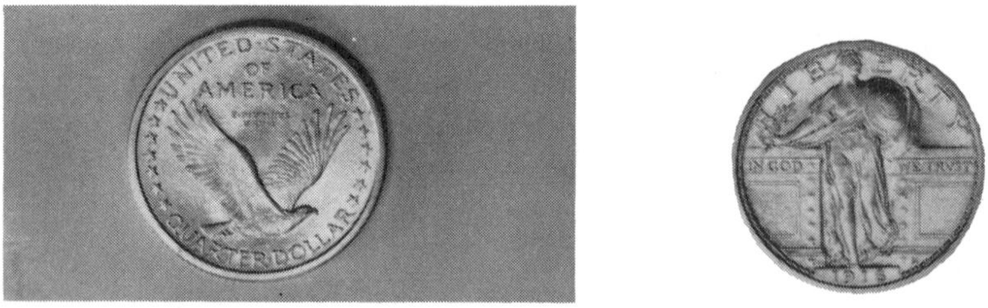

The "obscene" Standing Liberty quarter of 1916. The design was modified by the middle of 1917. ***(Photo courtesy of Krause Publications.)***

The public was outraged. Complaints poured into Washington from all over the United States. One imagines that small boys went racing out behind the barn with a handful of the new quarters and a magnifying glass.

Official Washington handled the crisis in typical bureaucratic fashion. Since a large number of people had approved the design and creation of the coin, no one wished to admit a mistake had been made in allowing such blatant immodesty to be cast in the nation's coinage. As a result, the coin design was ordered changed, but no one said a word about the charges of lewdness that had been made. Instead they concentrated on altering the relief of the design, the eagle on the reverse and other minor points. MacNeil, in an interview with the press, stated: "Making a relief for a coin is very different from making one for any other purpose. There is much to be considered. Especially must there be no crevices in which germs and dirt may collect. Uncle Sam is very particular about this."

In April, 1917, Congress began debating the authorization for modifying the coin design. While everyone knew the reason was primarily because of Miss Liberty's "over-exposure," officials never discussed it.

Instead, Congress talked about the fact that the design prevented the coin from being stacked when counted by bankers. Senator Warren skeptically commented about the stacking problem mentioned by Senator Owen: "After the experience we had some years ago with the St. Gaudens coin that would not stack and we have to provide for a new die, I would like to ask the author of the bill how it happens that a model is accepted and adopted as the law of the land before it is known whether the coins will stack?"

Senator Owen replied, "It was found after they had actually made them that they did not stack well and for that reason it became of some importance to change the die. I do not know how it occurred in the first place, but they have to change the position of the eagle in order to prevent the coins from toppling when stacked."

Treasury Secretary W. G. McAdoo made a proposal for changing the new quarter which was sent to Congressman William Ashbrook, the chairman of the Committee On Coinage, Weights and Measures. The letter, as read into the Congressional Record, stated:

The modification of the reverse used from the last half of 1917 on.

The modified Standing Liberty quarter with both breast and thigh covered.

I have the honor to submit for your consideration a draft of an act to authorize the modification of the design of the current quarter dollar in accordance with a specimen submitted by Mr. Hermon A. MacNeil, the sculptor whose designs were accepted on May 23, 1916 for the quarter dollar now being issued.

The modifications proposed are slight, the principal one being that the eagle has been raised and three of the stars placed beneath the eagle. On the reverse the lettering has been rearranged and the collision with the pinions of the wings obviated. These changes together with a slight concavity will produce a coin materially improved in artistic merit and not interfere in any way with its practical use.

I am sorry to have to ask for this change, but since the original dies were made the artist has found that they are not true to the original design and that a great improvement can be made in the artistic value and appearance of the coin by making the slight changes the act contemplates.

No changes in the coin's design could be made without the passage of a law stating what they would be. After much debate and design experimentation, Congress passed the following bill:

Monetary Legislation (Public Law No. 27—65th Congress)

An ACT providing for the modification of the designs of the current quarter dollar.

Be it enacted by the Senate and House of Representatives of the United States of America in Congress assembled, That for the purpose of increasing the artistic merit of the current quarter dollar, the secretary of the Treasury be, and is hereby, authorized to make slight modifications in the details of the designs in accordance with sketches submitted by the sculptor whose models were accepted under date of May twenty-third, nineteen hundred and sixteen, and now being used in the execution of the coins.

No changes shall be made in the emblems or devices used. The modifications shall consist of the changing of the position of the eagle, the rearrangement of the stars and lettering, and a slight concavity given to the surface. Such changes shall be made and completed on or before July first, nineteen hundred and eighteen.

Approved July 9, 1917.

When the changes were made, an unspoken, unauthorized addition was also prepared. Chain mail now covered the previously naked breast, and the drape had been lowered on her thigh. The coin had abandoned eroticism for less exciting symbolism.

14

The Coins of Adolph Weinman

Adolph Weinman was the last of the coin designers to work with Augustus Saint-Gaudens, and his creations—far more than those of Fraser—reflect Saint-Gaudens' classical taste. Weinman's creation of the Walking Liberty half-dollar and Mercury dime are among the highlights of numismatic achievement in the United States.

The commission to design the new coins came about as a result of the same contest that Hermon MacNeil successfully entered. Weinman, another competitor, was selected to prepare the dime and half-dollar.

Weinman was born in Karlsruhe, Germany in 1870 and came to the United States at ten years of age. He attended public schools and became an apprentice wood and ivory carver at the age of twenty. In addition to his regular work, he attended classes at Cooper Union, where he studied modeling and drawing. Later he worked for a number of sculptors including Saint-Gaudens.

In 1905, Augustus Saint-Gaudens was commissioned to prepare the medal commemorating Theodore Roosevelt's inauguration. Unable to finish the work, he referred the medal to Weinman, explaining to the new president: "I cannot do it [The inauguration medal], but I have arranged with the man best fitted to execute it in the country (Mr. Adolph Weinman). He has a most artistic nature, extremely diffident. He would do an admirable thing. He is also supple and takes suggestion intelligently. He had made one of the great Indian groups at St. Louis that would have interested you if brought to your attention. He is so interested that he begged me to fix a price. I named two hundred and fifty dollars."

On March 3, 1916, Chief Engraver Charles Barber was informed that Weinman had been selected to design the new coins. Each would be a radical departure from tradition. However, little is known as to why he made the design selections he did. To learn more about this, I asked one of the late artist's sons, Robert Weinman, a successful sculptor in his own right. Robert responded:

> Why AAW elected to depict his figure of Liberty (Columbia?) as he did on the 1916 half-dollar—I can't tell you. I can guess that being in competition with his peers, he turned in a virtuoso performance to dazzle the competition and to show those clods at the Mint what could be done on a coin. My surmise.
>
> He must have admired antique Greek & Roman coins because he had a small collection of base-metal copies, as well as one of the molds of same. Any designer in his right mind would have to admire same. He had assisted St. Gaudens for some time as a young man (1900? 1905?), & St. Gaudens influenced a whole school because of the success of his work.

The mint director's report for 1916 had extensive praise for the new coin. The report says: "The dime and half dollar are the work of Mr. Adolph A. Weinman. The design of the half dollar bears a full-length figure of Liberty, the folds of the Stars and Stripes flying to the breeze as a background, progressing in full stride toward the dawn of a new day, carrying branches of laurel and oak, symbolical of civil and military glory. The hand of the figure is outstretched in bestowal of the spirit of liberty."

The director's praise was not matched by others who saw the half dollar, however. A writer for the *New York Sun,* having studied the new coins said:

> Not the design on the coins, but the number of them in the pocket, is the matter of gravest concern to all except numismatists, but a change in the coinage interests all amateurs of the decorative arts. The treasury will confer a new series of dimes, quarters and half dollars on us this summer, regardless of the storm that broke over the revisers of the gold pieces. The printed description of the new dies suggests that they will make money more lively than ever before.
>
> The halves and quarters are to bear full length Liberties "striding" and "stepping." On the larger of the two the flag is to be "flying to the breeze." No more heads for the new pieces; they will typify hustle, that great accomplishment of those who are noisy about their work. Liberty is to hold aloft laurel and oak branches, symbolic of civic and military glory; had Chautauqua's most highly remunerated philanthropist continued in a post of eminence no such horrid slap at pacifism would have been tolerated. But the lady of the quarter will bear an olive branch, for the mollification of coatroom boys who, according to our visitors from afar, score a lower reward for their unsolicited services.

The Walking Liberty half-dollar, which many people considered the most beautiful regularly circulated coin. Note that the inspiration is quite similar to that of the Saint-Gaudens twenty-dollar gold piece.

The dime will show the fasces, the honored symbol of unity and power, backing a Liberty adorned with a winged cap. The money flies away. But does anybody nowadays count a dime as money? Does it not occupy the ignoble place of the cent in that California of which the Native Sons never cease to boast?

Let us await the new tokens with suspended judgement. The half dollar has fallen into unexplained unpopularity. Why do the people reject it, seeking instead two twenty-five cent pieces? It is a good coin. Let the cashiers worry; the proceeding designers of new coins forgot that they should "stack." May art join hands with utility in the Wilsonian issue!

The eagle was also attacked. One critic wrote in the Numismatist the year after the coins were released: "Mr. Weinman's eagle has long legs and wears feather chaps; and from the shoulder joints to end of tail extremity long; wing, if folded would reach leg and the tail; end of wings rounded and the feathers impossible; and the left wing is an impossible position leaving it artistic but not natural."

The Mercury dime was also a radical departure from the tradition of mediocrity in coin design. The design was explained by Weinman in a letter to editor of *The Numismatist,* F. G. Duffield, dated November 17, 1916:

In response to your letter of November 14, requesting a word of explanation as to my reasons for selecting a winged female head for the design of the obverse, the fasces for the reverse of the new dime, permit me to say that the law on the coinage of the United States stipulates that on all subsidiary coins there shall appear upon

> the obverse a figure or representation of Liberty. Hence the head of Liberty, the coin being obviously too small in size to make the representation of a full-length figure of Liberty advisable.
>
> The wings crowning her cap are intended to symbolize liberty of thought.
>
> As to the reverse of the dime, the law does not stipulate what is to appear upon this side of the coin, while it does specifically state that upon the reverse of the quarter dollar and the half dollar shall appear the figure of an eagle.
>
> I have selected the motive of the fasces and olive branch to symbolize the strength which lies in unity, while the battle-ax stands for preparedness to defend the Union. The branch of olive is symbolical of our love of peace.

As can be seen from the designer's explanation, the idea that the head is supposed to be Mercury, messenger of the gods, is incorrect. It was meant to be Liberty, and the common term "Mercury dime" is actually a misnomer.

The model for the Mercury dime was Elsie Viola Kachel Stevens, the wife of the famous poet, Wallace Stevens. She was apparently selected by chance. The Stevenses rented an apartment at 441 West 21st Street in New York in 1909 and Weinman was their landlord for seven years. Weinman made a bust of Elsie Stevens in 1913, and it was that bronze bust which eventually became the basis for the obverse of the dime.

Holly Stevens, daughter of Wallace and Elsie Stevens, comments on her mother's posing for Weinman in a letter. "Presumably she posed for Mr. Weinman as a favor; she was not a professional model and, as a matter of fact, was somewhat shy. She was also beautiful. To the best of my knowledge she did not pose for the figure on the half dollar, but the head is hers. Weinman did a bust that we had when I was a child; it

The Mercury dime of Adolph Weinman. The model was the wife of the poet Wallace Stevens.

disappeared sometime between 1958 and 1963, as I discovered after my mother's death in February 1963."

To learn who posed for the body of Liberty in the half-dollar, I checked with Robert Weinman, who told me: "I dimly remember an 8 by 10 print of AA working on some relief—or coin—model whilst a model, swatched in a sheet or light blanket, posed on a stand. Whether or not this was for that model or some other project—I no longer recall. Come to think of it, the pose was similar. I believe it was more bowed down. Anyway, I suspect the model for the half was whatever model he was using at the time.

Perhaps the best evaluation of the dime came from Howland Wood, a New York collector, quoted in *The Numismatist:*

> The new dime by Adolph A. Weinman is without doubt the finest example of our new coinage which was begun in 1907 with the advent of the $20 and $10 gold pieces. Before commenting on any of the new pieces it is but fair to consider the limitations and difficulties that beset the designer. Artistic rendering and a superabundance of lettering do not go hand in hand towards the best results. Our artists at the start are handicapped by having to place on the coin "United States of America," "E Pluribus Unum," "Liberty," "In God We Trust," the date and the denomination. In other words, six separate mottoes or legends. Consequently, the artist cannot strive for simplicity, and, despite his best endeavors, one or both sides of the coin are bound to be chopped up with a lot of discordant elements. According to the requirements of a modern utilitarian coinage, the designer is precluded from employing or arriving at the best effects in modelling; for both the upper and lower planes of the relief must be considered. High relief and certain effects cannot be employed, and, despite everything the artist may strive for, a certain mechanical technique must be used. Mr. Weinman, notwithstanding all these handicaps, has produced on the side bearing the head a most pleasing and artistic conception—dignified, simple. The head of Liberty in her Phrygian cap ornamented with wings gives us on our new coins the most artistic conception yet arrived at. The two mottoes are kept subordinated. The word "Liberty" has been so treated as to blend itself into the general design in the best possible manner. The reverse has undoubtedly been sacrificed for the other side. Although good, it is open to criticism. At the first glance it is hard to tell which is right side up, as the olive branch and the lictor's fasces are so interwoven as to make the whole a confused jumble. Far better results could have been obtained if the spray had been much more simplified, and rendered with only a few leaves, and not placed so closely around the fasces. In itself the idea of this design is good; the rendering only could have been improved upon. Undiluted praise should be given to Mr. Weinman, and we trust that the

other two denominations of the silver coins will equal if not exceed in merit the new dime.

As the year 1916 drew to a close, the United States had achieved the highest state of coin design ever witnessed before or since in American coinage. The work of Weinman as well as that of MacNeil and Saint-Gaudens reached new heights in beauty and medallic art.

15

The Peace Dollar

The year was 1920. The war in Europe was over and the world was attempting to bury its dead and rebuild its cities. The violence had been called the war to end all wars, and optimism reigned throughout the United States. The country was going to move forward into a new era of growth and prosperity.

At the American Numismatic Association Convention of 1920, Farran Zerbe, a well-known coin dealer, suggested that a new coin be struck to commemorate the signing of the various peace treaties. Others in the association agreed and a committee was formed to approach Congress with the idea.

Representative Albert Vestal, chairman of the House Committee on Coinage, Weights and Measures, worked with the ANA, Mint Director Raymond Baker, and Charles Moore of the Commission of Fine Arts to prepare a bill that would authorize a silver dollar to commemorate the end of the war with Germany. A number of sculptors were asked to compete, including such experienced coin makers as Victor D. Brenner, Hermon MacNeil, Chester Beach, and Adolph Weinman. However, it was a lesser-known contestant, Anthony De Francisci, who was awarded the commission to design the coin.

Anthony De Francisci was born in Italy on June 13, 1887. He came to America at the age of sixteen and was naturalized in 1913. He received his training at the Art Students League in New York, the Cooper Union Institute, and the National Academy of Design, and worked with the great sculptors Herman MacNeil and Adolph Weinman, among others, before going off on his own in 1917.

De Francisci's work, unlike that of some with whom he worked while learning, was not in the classic mold. He wanted a fresh approach to the bust of Liberty, something that related neither to the ancient concepts nor to the early figures found on American coins. In fact, his departure in style was so radical that the *Wall Street Journal* later called the new coin "Our 'Flapper' Silver Dollar."

The model for the head of Liberty was the artist's wife, the former Teresa Cafarelli, who was born in a remote Italian village and brought to the United States at the age of three. She was introduced to her future husband by her brother, a fellow art student, and the couple found they had mutual interests. They were married when she was twenty-one and her new husband entered the competition to design the new coin.

Teresa later commented: "My husband didn't think he had a chance in the competition going up against all those famous sculptors. But they were paying $100 for the designs, and I guess he figured we could use the money—so he went ahead and did it."

The artists were given very short notice. Competition for the design was held on November 19, 1921, and they were given three weeks to submit sketches to the Fine Arts Commission. The approved sketches had to be made into coin models within four days after that.

De Francisci developed a concept of a young, vibrant Liberty. His wife formally wore her hair up but her husband had her stand by a window, letting the breeze blow it into a more casual design. He had no thought of winning the $1,000 prize but figured he would take the $100 given to each of the contestants submitting a design. So sure was he that winning would be impossible that he made several one-dollar bets with friends that he would lose. When he actually won, he had to pass out fifty of the new silver dollars to those with whom he had made the bets.

In a 1922 interview with a reporter for the *Duluth Tribune,* the artist confided: "You will see that the Liberty is not a photograph of Mrs. De Francisci. It is a composite face and in that way typifies something of America. I did not try to execute an 'American type' or a picture of any woman. I wanted the Liberty to express something of the spirit of the country—the intellectual speed and vigour and virility America has, as well as its youth. I had nothing of the magazine-cover idea."

A frequently repeated story about Teresa is that she had loved the Statue of Liberty ever since she first saw it when entering the United States. The head of Liberty for which she posed was supposed to represent the head of the statue, a fact that reportedly delighted her. Don Taxay, in his book *The U.S. Mint and Coinage,* quotes a letter from Teresa to her brother Rocco in which she said: "You remember how I was always posing as Liberty, and how broken-hearted I was when some other little girl was selected to play the role in the patriotic exercises in school? I thought of those days often while sitting as a model for Tony's design, and now seeing myself as Miss Liberty on the new coin, it seems like the realization of my fondest childhood dream."

Teresa later claimed such stories were inaccurate. In May 1974, she was the guest of honor at the Greater New York Convention of the American Israel Numismatic Association. During this time, when she turned seventy-six years of age, she was interviewed extensively in the press. Not only did she claim she couldn't remember such posing as a child, she also said that such posing would have been out of character for her. Since she was just three when she saw the statue, she doubted it could have had much of an impact on her.

There were two reverses for the coin for which Teresa posed. The approved design showed an eagle holding a broken sword and an olive branch. The rejected design, which committee members later claimed to prefer despite the rejection, showed the eagle breaking a sword on which it was standing.

President Warren Harding approved the models for the obverse and reverse of the new coin on December 19, 1921. Teresa, in a letter to her parents, commented:

> . . . All the designs submitted were carefully gone over by President Harding himself, who took a great interest in the work. Last Saturday he was about to approve Anthony's design, when he noticed an extra dimple in the chin of Liberty. "It is not exactly a dimple," he explained to the President, "but only an artistic touch, which seems to indicate the presence of one."
>
> The President, however, maintained that he preferred a dimpleless Liberty, because the dimpled variety did not exactly express peace, so Anthony resubmitted the design, minus the dimple. The

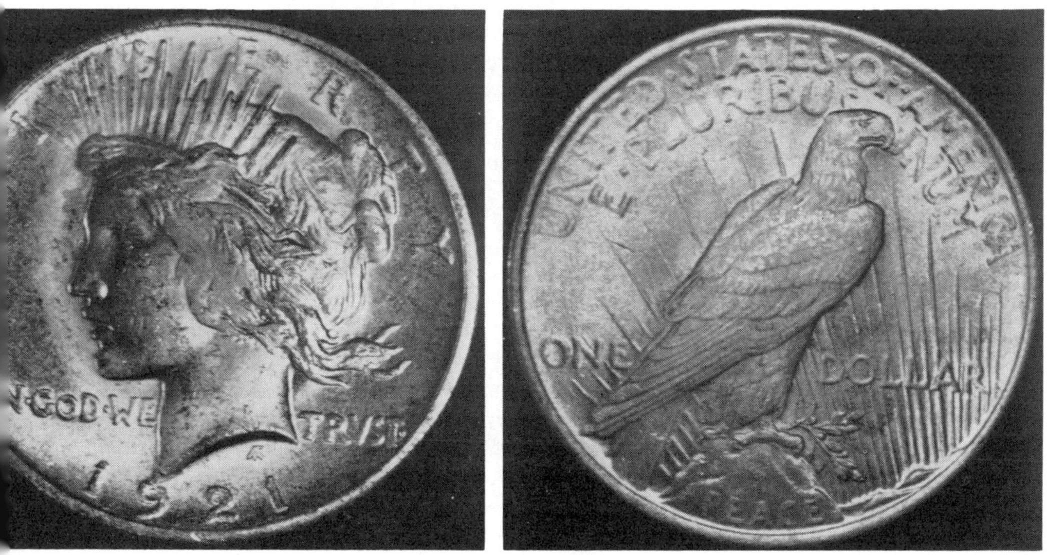

The Peace dollar.

new coin is symbolic of peace, liberty and the Disarmament conference. On one side of the coin is the well known profile of Liberty, together with the numerals 1921 and "E Pluribus Unum" in the usual position. On the reverse side is an eagle, with folded wings, perched upon the top of a mountain, with the rising sun in the distance. Above the eagle's head are the olive branches of peace, while a broken sword, symbolic of the end of the war, is clutched in its talons. Just beneath the eagle is the word "Peace," while crowning the top of the coin are the words "United States of America."

There was some criticism of the approved reverse design. Some people felt that the broken sword symbolized defeat rather than triumph. The artist disagreed but yielded to pressure and eliminated that particular design element. The eagle's talons were left holding just the olive branch.

The introduction of the new coin brought widespread criticism as well as acclaim. One Philadelphia newspaper wrote:

> Liberty is growing younger. Take it from the new "Peace Dollar" put in circulation yesterday. The young woman who has been adorning silver currency for many years never looked better than in the "cartwheel" which the Philadelphia Mint has just started to turn out. The young lady, moreover, has lost her Greek profile. Hellenic beauty seems to have been superseded by the newer "flapper" type.
>
> A sculptor of genius would have put into that face some quality of divinity. He would have suggested divine wisdom, courage, ardor and severe confidence in the triumph of freedom.
>
> Looked at in this way, the head on the new coin is merely that of a fairly attractive girl of 17 . . . whose immature chin and half-open mouth merely suggest the expression of her kind. If words were issuing from her lips they would hardly take the elegant languor of "Line's bizzay!" They would more probably be "Say, lissen!"

A Syracuse paper made so bold as to say:

> The old dollar had a solemn and serious look. The new one seems sissified by comparison. One had dignity, the other has prettiness, and if one wanted to be critical it might be added that while the old dollar had sentiment the new one has sentimentality.
>
> The two leading differences are in the eagle, and the Goddess of Liberty. The old eagle was a scrapper. He looked as if he were on the alert to start something any time, and between whiles, to scream to his heart's content. The 1922 version of the American bird of freedom looks anything but free. He looks out of luck. He has wings furled and is sitting, gazing into vacancy with the cheerless and pepless attitude of a wet barnyard fowl waiting for the weather to clear. There are some who say that he even wears pants, but that is an illusion. The real eagle does have thick foliage on his legs, all

the way to his claws, which, when in a standing position gives something of a trousered effect.

The coin, released at the end of 1921, had an extremely high relief, almost like the early Saint-Gaudens design. This made striking difficult, and the coins coming from the mint had varying surfaces, according to the pressure used when coining. This was a circumstance that Chief Engraver George Morgan felt he couldn't tolerate. He wrote to De Francisci about a change he was making for the coins dated 1922: "In changing the date to 1922 I took the opportunity of making a slight change in the curvature of the ground. I anticipate at least 20 tons less pressure will be required to bring up the design. This could double the life of the die. I send you an early strike of the 1922."

De Francisi was outraged by the change. He protested to the Commission of Fine Arts but to no avail. The die was changed, and the new coin continued to be struck until silver dollars were discontinued in 1935.

On August 3, 1964, President Lyndon Johnson authorized the striking of Peace dollars for the first time in almost thirty years. He signed legislation which would permit the coining of the silver dollars at the Denver mint. A total of 45 million were planned, all of them to be identical in design to the earlier De Francisci coins. It was felt that the silver-dollar production would begin by the following year at the latest.

Silver dollars dated 1964 were struck by the mint, then melted. The story was succinctly told in a release from the Bureau of the Mint ten years later. The 1974 release, issued when there was talk of people owning illegal examples of the coin, stated:

> In 1965, in response to a Treasury request, Congress appropriated $600,000, an amount sufficient to manufacture 45 million silver dollars. To carry out the expressed intent of the Congress, the Treasury recommended to the White House that the United States Mint be authorized to begin production. It was on this recommendation that announcement was made by The White House on May 15, 1965, that production could begin.
>
> Some trial strikes were produced at the Denver Mint as a prelude to the resumption of manufacturing this denomination for the first time since 1935. The Peace Dollar design was utilized, and because of the delayed-dating arrangement then in effect, the year of coinage shown on the coin was 1964. These coins contained 90 per cent silver.
>
> Members of the Congress, however, who by reason of their committee assignments, and having a direct and responsible interest in the United States coinage, strongly urged the Treasury not to proceed with the production of these dollars, due to the fast approaching shortage of silver. The Treasury Department determined, therefore, that the Mint would not produce any dollar coins at that time.

All of the trial strikes for this proposed 1964 dollar were ordered destroyed under the strict supervisory and accounting procedures required by Mint regulations. None reached the final stage of being counted, bagged and issued by the Mint's cashier as finished coins. Should anyone have such trial Mint-struck pieces in his possession, they are the property of the United States which is entitled to recover since the pieces were never issued.

There is a chance that a 1964 silver dollar will one day make an appearance. It is likely that someone in the mint may have given more than thought to spiriting some of these coins from the grounds. But unlike the 1913-dated Liberty Head nickels, it is doubtful that such coins could ever be sold on the open market without being confiscated by Treasury Department agents.

16

The Jefferson Nickel

In 1936, the United States government realized that the Buffalo nickel would soon have been in circulation for twenty-five years. It was decided to make a definite change, following the pattern established by the Washington quarter of 1932, discussed in the chapter on James and Laura Fraser. A new coin would be designed with a head commemorating Thomas Jefferson, again to be based on a Houdon statue. Artists were requested to submit designs according to the following specifications:

> The subject matter must contain on the obverse of the coin an authentic portrait of Thomas Jefferson. On the reverse side the subject matter will be a representation of Monticello, Jefferson's historic home near Charlottesville. In addition to the words required by law to appear on the coin, the coin may contain the inscription "MONTICELLO," in order to identify the architecture. The coinage laws require that there shall appear upon the obverse side of the coin the word "LIBERTY" and the date "1938," and "UNITED STATES OF AMERICA," and the denomination "FIVE CENTS." The coin should also contain the motto "IN GOD WE TRUST." None of the legends are to be abbreviated and should be all in capital letters.

The quality of entries varied greatly. Jefferson's appearance ranged from sickly thin to obese. The reverses had complex designs in many cases, including one which showed eagles perching on the roof of Monticello. Some entrants ignored the rules entirely and used an ear of corn, among other devices, for the reverse.

The winner of the contest and its one-thousand-dollar prize was

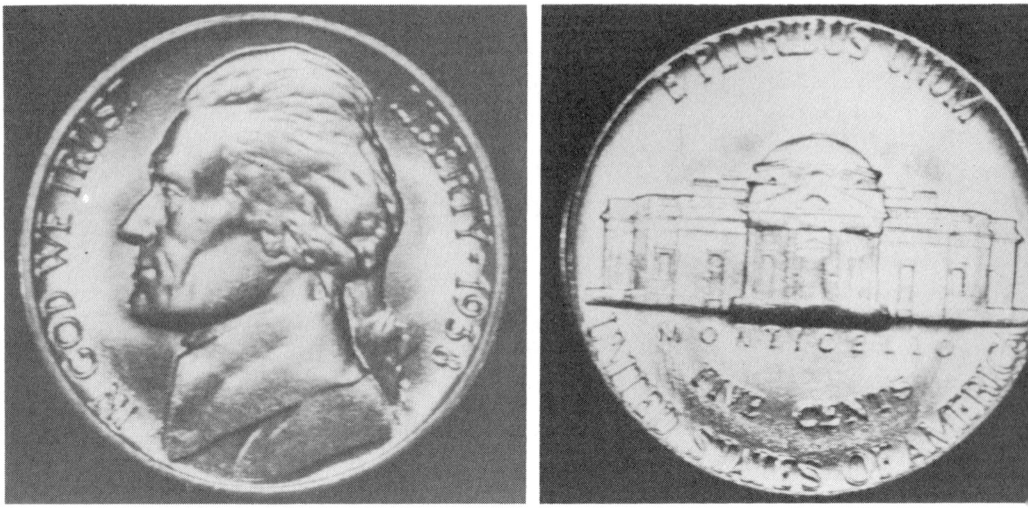

This is the Jefferson nickel, modeled after Houdon's bust of Jefferson.

In 1942 nickel was considered more valuable to the war effort than silver. As a result, a new coin was made containing 56 percent copper, 35 percent silver and 9 percent manganese. These coins were identified by a mint mark placed over the rendition of Monticello. In this case the coin was made in San Francisco. All other coins that were made from nickel have the mint mark in the right corner of Monticello. During this period, the Philadelphia mint, for the first time, placed a mint mark on the coins. Coins made by the Philadelphia mint had a large P. In the case of the coin shown here, the mint was San Francisco and the large S is obvious. Throughout the rest of the history of the Philadelphia mint, its coins were identified by having no mint mark whatsoever. All branch mint coins have always carried a mint mark.

Felix Schlag. His design used the Houdon bust of Thomas Jefferson, which was greatly admired by artists. In the publication *Sculpture by Houdon: A Loan Exhibition*, author H. H. Arnason states that:

> The marble Jefferson in Boston is a superb interpretation of the third President of the United States. Jefferson is shown in modern dress, his face tilted upward and angled slightly to the right. The hair is dressed in a manner similar to that of Washington, worn rather long at the sides. The eyes are large and cut unusually deep, shadowed under heavy brows in a manner which gives them an exceptional sense of vitality. The lean symmetrical face, with its sharply aquiline nose, compressed lips and jutting chin is the perfect reflection of the intellectual man of affairs that we know Jefferson to have been. It is at the same time a face of great sensitivity and the face of an aristocrat.

The original reverse design showed a side view of Monticello with a large tree to the left. This was the reverse that won the prize. However, before the coin went into production, the reverse was altered so there is a full front view of the home, totally devoid of the landscaping shown on the first design. In addition, the word "Monticello" was added just below the structure.

In the end, the Jefferson nickel proved to be a technically sound, artistically boring design. It represented a return to less inspired motifs than those that motivated the earlier works of MacNeil, Weinman, and Saint-Gaudens.

17

The Roosevelt Dime

The task of creating the Roosevelt dime was removed from public hands and returned to the chief engraver of the mint, John Sinnock. The coin, created in late 1945, was to honor Franklin Roosevelt, who had died earlier in the year. Roosevelt was the originator of the March of Dimes, and this coin seemed a fitting memorial to him.

For many years it was thought that Sinnock's creation was totally original. It was believed to have been based on photographs and other items unrelated to anyone outside the mint.

The original design preparation of the Roosevelt dime was rather crudely done. Gilmore Clarke, chairman of the Commission of Fine Arts, said that it needed more dignity. It also needed more detail because of the design's weakness, which made the face seem lifeless.

The final changes resulted in a strong design that was as bold and detailed as those of the earlier quarter and nickel based on Houdon creations. This design was thought to be original until an article appeared in the *Washington Post* (reprinted in the newspaper *Coin World* of June 18, 1975). That article, written by Jacqueline Trescott, stated that the dime portrait was copied from the work of black artist Selma Burke. The president sat twice to Burke in 1943 in preparation for her making a bronze portrait plaque of him. That plaque hangs in the Recorder of Deeds Building in Washington, D.C.

The article says:

> Take out a dime. It's lost the financial power that once bought a chocolate soda, a bus ride or a phone call. But a dime remains a work of art.

Its profile of Franklin D. Roosevelt—cheekbones high, jaw taut and mouth closed—was done by one of the century's most prolific black artists.

In 1943, Burke won a national competition to sculpt a likeness of Roosevelt for the new Recorder of Deeds building here. The profile was later adopted for the dime, but before it was unveiled, all the Roosevelts had to approve.

"And they all came to my New York studio, one by one. Finally Eleanor called, and she visited the studio on January 10, 1945," Burke recalled (She calls herself Burke).

"My sister brought the family silver to make breakfast. We had scones, all that jazz. Mrs. Roosevelt was wearing a red suit with fox pieces that my Siamese cat leaped at. I had to put them (the fox pieces) away," she continued.

"I uncovered the profile, and Mrs. Roosevelt said, "Oh, it's well done, but you've made him too young." I replied, "I've not done it for today but for tomorrow and tomorrow." She just answered, "Well, the head's too high."

FDR's profile wasn't changed for the Deeds building but Burke says, "Someone did lower the head a little for the dime."

Trescott continued in the same article: "The three-foot-six by two-foot-six profile used for the dime was unveiled by Harry S. Truman in 1945 and is still located in the recorder of Deeds building in Washington, D.C.

"Though she was not involved in the use of the FDR plaque for the Roosevelt dime, Burke was aware the Mint made an impression from her creation. Mint engraver John R. Sinnock designed the coin which appeared first in 1946."

The reverse of the dime, unquestionably Sinnock's creation, shows a torch of Liberty between sprays of oak and laurel. It is quite similar to the concept previously used on the reverse of the Mercury dime.

The Roosevelt dime.

An earlier reverse idea, rejected by Sinnock, showed a hand gripping the torch and the plants. There were also designs showing a half figure of Liberty with a branch of peace and flaming lamp of freedom; a woman, perhaps Liberty, standing near an olive tree and looking up at a flaming torch; as well as several other designs, all more complex than the one finally selected.

Although the coin was never very exciting, some hostility was generated by the fact that the designer's initials were seen below the neck of Roosevelt on the coin's obverse. The initials "J.S." were believed by some to stand for Joseph Stalin, the Russian dictator. Roosevelt was frequently criticized for his extremely liberal views of government, and ultra-rightists believed that the coin had Stalin's initials to show the Russians' influence in the post-war United States.

18

The Franklin Half-Dollar

Of all the men honored by our nation's coinage, none was so controversial as Benjamin Franklin, the famous inventor, printer, and statesman. School children are frequently taught sayings that appeared in Franklin's *Poor Richard's Almanac*—sayings that Franklin frequently quoted simply without attribution rather than having created them all himself.

As a newspaperman, Franklin is well known for starting the *Pennsylvania Gazette,* a paper sometimes considered a model for modern journalism. Yet this paper was also the first publication in the United States to use "sex-and-violence" as a sales tool. For example, one issue had the following item:

> Friday Night last, a certain St–n–c–tt–r was, it seems, in a fair way of dying the Death of a Nobleman; for being caught Napping with another Man's Wife, the injur'd Husband took the Advantage of his being fast asleep, and with a Knife began very dilgently to cut off his Head. But the instrument not being equal to the intended Operation, much struggling prevented Success; and he was oblig'd to content himself for the present with bestowing on the Aggressor a sound Drubbing. The gap made in the side of the St–n–c–tt–r's Neck, tho deep, is not thought dangerous, but some People admire, that when the Person offended had so fair and suitable an Opportunity, it did not enter into his Head to turn St–n–c–tt–r himself.

The following week another interesting item appeared:

We hear, that on Tuesday last, a certain C–n–table having made an Agreement with a Neighboring Female, to Watch with her that Night; she promised to leave a Window open for him to come in at; but he going his Rounds in the dark, unluckily mistook the Window, and got into a Room where another Woman was in bed, and her Husband it seems lying on a Couch not far distant. The good Woman perceiving presently by the extraordinary Fondness of her Bedfellow that it could not possibly be her Husband, made so much Disturbance as to wake the good man; who finding somebody had got into his Place without his Leave, began to lay about him unmercifully; and 'twas thought, that had not our poor mistaken Galant, call'd out manfully for Help (as if he were commanding Assistance in the King's name) and thereby raised the Family, he would have stood no more Chance for his Life between the Wife and Husband, than a captive L---- between the two Thumb Nails.

Franklin's far-ranging interests included the field of numismatics. On May 10, 1785, for example, he wrote to John Jay to express his opinions about some medals that Congress was planning to strike:

The forming of dies in steel to strike medals or money, is generally with the intention of making a great number of the same form.

The engraving those dies in steel is, from the hardness of the substance, very difficult and expensive, but, once engraved, the great number to be easily produced afterward by stamping justifies the expense, it being but small when divided among a number.

Where only one medal of a kind is wanted, it seems an unthrifty way to form dies for it in steel to strike the two sides of it, the whole expense of the dies resting on that medal.

It was by this means that the medal voted by Congress for M. de Fleury cost one hundred guineas, when an engraving of the same figures and inscriptions might have been beautifully done on a plate of silver of the same size for two guineas.

The ancients, when they ordained a medal to record the memory of any laudable action, and do honour to the performer of that action, struck a vast number and used them as money. By this means the honour was extended through their own and neighboring nations, every man who received or paid a piece of such money was reminded of the virtuous action, the person who performed it, and the reward attending it, and the number gave such security to this kind of monuments against perishing and being forgotten, that some of each of them exist to this day, though more than two thousand years old, and, being now copied in books by the arts of engraving and painting, are not only exceedingly multiplied but likely to remain some thousands of years longer.

The man who is honoured only by a single medal is obliged to show it to enjoy the honour, which can be done only to a few and often awkwardly. I therefore wish the medals of Congress were ordered to be money, and so continued as to be convenient money, by being in value aliquot parts of a dollar.

Copper coins are wanting in America for small change. We have none but those of the King of England. After one silver or gold medal is struck from the dies, for the person to be honoured, they may be usefully employed in striking copper money, or in some cases small silver.

The nominal value of the pieces might be a little more than the real, to prevent their being melted down, but not so much more as to be an encouragement of counterfeiting.

Franklin received his medallic honor in 1933 when John Sinnock designed a medal for him. The design so impressed Mint Director Nellie Tayloe Ross that she felt it should be used on a coin as well. However, the only coin soon to be available for redesign was the Walking Liberty half-dollar, which could be changed no earlier than 1941. As it turned out, it was 1947 before the mint's chief engraver was asked to modify the medal design for a new coin.

When the Franklin half-dollar was introduced to the public, Ross made a speech explaining her part in the coin's production. She said:

You may be wondering how it came about that the portrait of Benjamin Franklin found its place upon the fifty-cent piece together with a replica of the Liberty Bell. For several years I had harbored the hope that, during my tenure in the Mint, these two features might be incorporated in design for one of our coins. From time to time, letters have come in to my office urging the use of Franklin's portrait on the one-cent piece, probably because of his identity with the maxim "A penny saved is two-pence clear," often misquoted "A penny saved is a penny made." You will agree, I believe, that the fifty-cent piece, being larger and of silver, lends itself much better to the production of an impressive effect.

During the war it appeared for a time that the addition of one or more denominations might be required to ease the demand for one-cent pieces, the enormous production of which, under pressure of demand, was straining the coinage capacity of the Mint. The necessity did not materialize. In order to be ready, however, for any contingency, we assigned to our highly skilled sculptor in the Mint, Mr. Sinnock, the task of evolving a new design, to embody a likeness of Franklin and a representation of the Liberty Bell. That design was in readiness for the fifty-cent piece. I mention with sorrow that Mr. Sinnock's death occurred one year ago.

When, after the war, the extraordinary pressure of work upon the Mint had eased, we determined that the half dollar should be given a 'new look,' it having worn its old attire since the year 1916. We resolved that the figure of Liberty with her flowing robes on the obverse, and the eagle on the reverse, should give place to Franklin and the Liberty Bell, assuming, of course, the approval of the secretary of the Treasury. This, happily, was readily forthcoming with his expression of pleasure in the choice of the design.

I point out that the new fifty-cent piece is unique in one important respect. On it, the eagle is for the first time given a subordinate position on any of the silver coins of denomination above the dime. The coinage law under which we operate and which was enacted in 1873 provides that each of these silver coins must bear the figure of an eagle or representation thereof; ambiguous language that, you will agree. What could be a representation of an eagle but an eagle itself? We tried to persuade ourselves that the eagle was supposed to represent strength and freedom and that the Liberty Bell would suffice as a representation thereof. But in the end we decided that discretion was the better part of valor and we had better put it on to assure conformity with the law. Accordingly, Mr. Roberts, our capable sculptor at the Mint, very cleverly and with pleasing effect, we think, added a small eagle at the right of the bell to balance with E PLURIBUS UNUM on the left of it.

The subordination of the eagle on this particular coin is an interesting coincidence, inasmuch as Benjamin Franklin—Dr. Allen reminded me—condemned in strong and picturesque language the use of the eagle as a United States emblem. He called it a bird of prey, of bad moral character, a coward, lazy. The turkey, he contended, was more worthy and, being a distinctly American bird, would be a more suitable emblem.

Benjamin Franklin is also on record as disapproving the use of portraits on coins. Royal heads he had in mind apparently. He advocated the substitution of proverbs profitable for human reflection. Renowned for wisdom as Dr. Franklin was, he no doubt had some of the weaknesses to which most human flesh is prone; even a little vanity perhaps. Had he known in his day that 150 years hence his image would be placed on a coin of this, his native land, to whose service his life was consecrated, we may assume I believe, that he would not have been seriously displeased.

The speech continued with a discussion of Franklin's achievements and his attitude towards thrift. She then returned to the discussion of the new coin:

About the Liberty Bell on the reverse of the coin. I am deeply impressed with its significance to us as a country, as a symbol, at this juncture of the world's history. To me it is soulstirring thought that on this coin it will go out to the four corners of our country into the heads of practically every American. As one largely responsible for its being on the coin I express the ardent hope that it may be a constant reminder to us all how blest we are to live in this land of liberty; how blest we are that our forefathers had it in their minds and souls to establish in this new country, a free government, though it should cost them their lives, and to hand it down as such to their children of succeeding generations. So brilliant in mentality were those early statesmen who laid the foundation of this government, so forceful of character were they, and sound in integrity, it seems as if Heaven must have endowed them for that special purpose.

We do well to remember that this precious freedom, bequeathed us by them, is ours, to have and to hold, if we jealously safeguard it and stand ever ready to defend it at any cost.

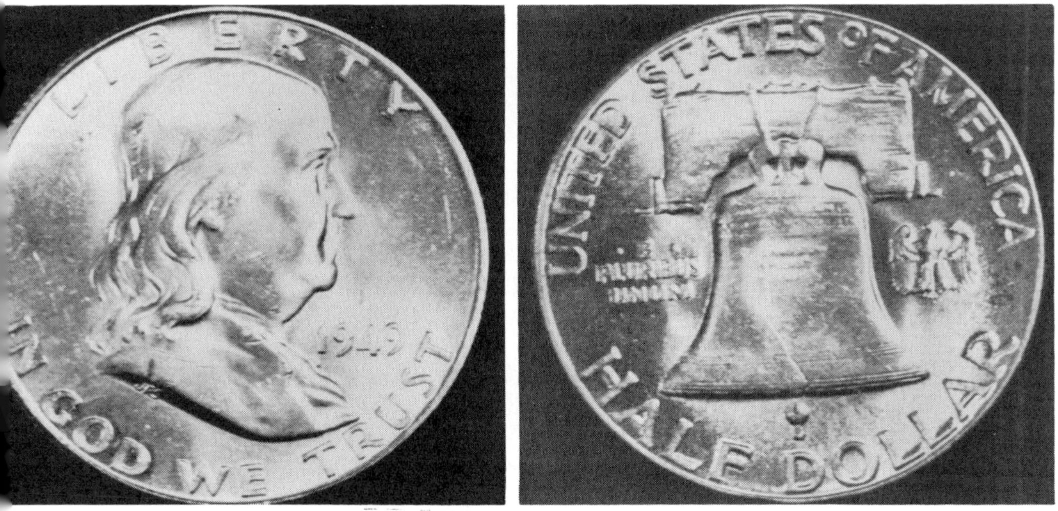

The Franklin half-dollar.

> No condition in this world can be assumed to be static; not even this blessed state of freedom we enjoy, unless it is safeguarded. We know that right now there are forces on the march, which are bent upon undermining the order under which we live. They would put an end, if they could, to this system of ours that exalts the dignity of the individual citizen and respects his right to make for himself a place in the sun, according as his talents and industry make possible; that permits every person to choose his own religion, and manner of worship, and to speak aloud his views on any subject, so long as he does no harm to his fellow men.

The speech discussed the concept of freedom and then returned to the new half-dollar.

"Again referring to the coin. On its face it bears, as do our other coins, the words 'In God We Trust.' Thus do we as a nation proclaim to the world our recognition that human wisdom has its limitations. Right now our statesmen are grappling with problems, thrust upon them by postwar conditions, which are challenging their powers of brain and soul. There are many facets to those problems which make decisions so difficult they seem almost to defy human wisdom. The world's woe cannot be ignored by this strong, highly-favored nation. The general recognition of that fact, which is evident, is a tribute to the character of the American people. . . ."

It is interesting to note that Ross was not speaking for all the parties involved with the creation of the new coin when she praised it so highly. The Commission of Fine Art's members strongly disliked the design and said so in a letter to her!

> However, the Commission are not satisfied with the model of the reverse. The eagle shown on the model is so small as to be

insignificant and hardly discernible when the model is reduced to the size of a coin. The Commission hesitate to approve the Liberty Bell as shown with the crack in the bell visible; to show this might lead to puns and to statements derogatory to United States coinage.

The Commission disapprove the designs.

For a coin as important as the fifty-cent piece, the Commission recommend a limited competition, in which some of the ablest medallists of the country would be invited to participate. What St. Gaudens, Fraser, Weinman, and MacNeil have accomplished in producing notable designs for coins that are acknowledged as works of art could be repeated in this instance.

But Ross had no intention of letting anyone prevent her from having the design she wanted. The Commission was an advisory group and had no real power. She ignored their complaints and went ahead with the design she favored.

In November 1963, President Kennedy was tragically assassinated. An immediate move to honor him with a new half-dollar was made, an effort which is the subject of the next chapter. However, what is important for this discussion is the fact that there was a last-minute decision to not make any 1964-dated Franklin half-dollars.

According to a number of different sources, 1964-dated Franklin half-dollars do exist. One "reliable source" said a total of seventy were made. Another person told me that he had received a 1964 Franklin half-dollar from his bank. The coin was of a new design with the date split so that "19" was on one side of the coin and "64" was on the other.

To date I have been unable to locate anyone who owns a 1964 Franklin half-dollar, although I have been in contact with a number of people who claim to have seen one. If the dies for the new coins did exist, it would obviously pay a mint employee with access to them to strike one or more coins for later sale. This is probably what happened with the 1913 Liberty Head nickels, so why should not history repeat itself, assuming the nickel conjecture is correct?

The truth is that 1964-dated Franklin half-dollars, if they exist, are counterfeits. According to former Chief Engraver Gilroy Roberts who, more than anyone, should know the facts: "No Franklin half dollars with a 1964 date could have been struck by the U. S. Mint because no dies with this date were made."

A check with mint officials revealed much the same story. One man, however, claimed there was a newly designed Franklin coin he had received, though he (conveniently) no longer had it when I requested he send me a photograph. The answer came from Roy Cahoon, former assistant director of the mint for public services:

"We made no experiments with the Franklin design in 1964. It was discontinued in 1963, as you know, upon passage of the December 30, 1963, legislation authorizing the Kennedy half-dollar," said Cahoon. "If an alteration of the design had been contemplated, it would have been for some other reason than just a rearrangement of the date to resemble the 'split' figure you describe. There was no trouble with the striking of the piece with the date figures in the right field, which would have given rise to changing the position of the figures."

It is obvious that the Franklin half-dollar series ended with the coins dated 1963. Since no dies were made for new coins, 1964-dated Franklin halves which may one day appear will undoubtedly be counterfeits.

19

The Kennedy Half-Dollar

The overwhelming sense of loss many Americans felt upon hearing the news of the assassination of President Kennedy resulted in the desire to pay tribute to his life and achievements. Streets, apartments, and even the Florida space center all took on his name. More important from the standpoint of coin history, the government decided to introduce a new coin to honor the late president.

It was shortly after word of the assassination reached Washington that the mint's chief engraver was contacted by telephone concerning a Kennedy coin. In an interview quoted in the June, 1972, issue of *COINage Magazine,* Roberts commented: "I remember that phone call like it was yesterday. It was the Mint Director, Eva Adams, telling me that a portrait of John Kennedy was needed for a new coin. At the moment, no one had yet decided which coin to put the portrait on. Mrs. Kennedy didn't want to replace George Washington on the quarter even though the quarter design was due for a change. In preparation for a quick congressional review, the Treasury decided on the half dollar."

The Kennedy coin was to be a rush job. Roberts had six weeks to prepare the coin.

Roberts was fortunate in that he had met Kennedy several times while preparing a portrait medal of the president. The medal design had been approved by both the president and Mrs. Kennedy, and it was that design which Roberts decided to bring to the new coin.

The work was begun without authorization from Congress. The authorization was necessary because the Franklin half-dollar had been in circulation less than the required twenty-five years. However, that authorization was considered a foregone conclusion, and Roberts was asked to proceed without regard to this minor technicality.

On December 13, 1963, the House Committee on Banking and Currency prepared a bill to authorize a new coin. The committee reported: ". . . a large number of communications [have been received] from citizens urging that a coin of one denomination or another be minted to bear the likeness of the late president, and many members of the House . . . have introduced bills or resolutions for this purpose. The committee considered and adopted H. R. 9413. . . . The director of the mint informs us that the total cost of converting to the new 50 cent piece will be less than $1,000, as the patterns are already in possession of the mint and new dies must be made in any case, and only the cost of making a master die will be involved."

The House passed the bill on December 17, although with a surprising amount of opposition. Many congressmen felt that the country was rushing to pay tribute to Kennedy much faster than was warranted. But the bill moved to the Senate, where on December 18, the late Senator Everett Dirksen, whose voice was as famous as his legislative skills, spoke about the coin:

> I suppose times have changed. New philosophies abound. This is, after all, the decade of deficits.
>
> There is a belief that we can spend ourselves rich. Balanced budgets are old-fashioned. Why mind a rising public debt, since we owe it to ourselves?
>
> Thrift is for children with piggy banks. And frugality is old hat.
>
> So, in the decade of deficits, perhaps Mr. Franklin's idea that "a penny saved is two pence clear, a pin a day's a groat a year" is considered modern twaddle.
>
> It seems to me that if Ben Franklin must go—and it distresses me—I should shed a tear for him and for Poor Richard. When the federal deficit for fiscal year 1964 and the projected deficits for 1965 and 1966 are announced, let us ponder that it was Franklin who said:
>
> "Get what you can, and what you get, hold.
>
> "Tis the stone that will turn all your lead to gold."
>
> So as we make this change, I say "Good-by Benjamin Franklin, apostle of thrift and frugality. Evidently you are not so popular in this age of the deficit."

The bill passed Congress, and on December 30, 1963, Public Law 88-256 was officially enacted by the Eighty-eighth Congress:

> An Act to provide for the coinage of 50-cent pieces bearing the likeness of John Fitzgerald Kennedy.
>
> Be it enacted by the Senate and House of Representatives of the United States of America in Congress assembled, that in lieu of the coinage of the 50-cent piece which shall bear on one side the

likeness of the late President of the United States, John Fitzgerald Kennedy, and on the other side an appropriate design to be prescribed by the Secretary of the Treasury.

Approved December 30, 1963.

Gilroy Roberts described how the work on the coin progressed. Writing in the August 1965 issue of *Coins Magazine* he stated: "Starting back with the original plastilene model of President Kennedy's portrait, which he had approved, the coat was deleted and the periphery was changed to bring the head nearer center and to decrease the size of the circle in relation to the portrait. The background was reshaped to provide the required depressed field necessary for proper coinage. The inscription and date required by law were established."

The new coin was produced as a trial strike. A sample was shown to Mrs. Kennedy and Attorney General Robert Kennedy on December 17. Roberts later stated that Mrs. Kennedy was favorably impressed with the coin ". . . but felt it would be an improvement if the part in the hair on the portrait was less pronounced and more accents were added. . . . Mrs. Kennedy's suggestions were carried out on the intermediate size, and another trial die was made for the obverse," said Roberts. This was the design that was used for the coin.

Mrs. Kennedy and the attorney general would have preferred to see more design varieties. They thought it might be good to have a full figure or half figure of the late President and would have liked to see how such a design might appear. There wasn't enough time, however.

The Kennedy half-dollar with the original reverse. ***(Photo courtesy of Krause Publications.)***

The work on the reverse was handled by Frank Gasparro, who is now chief engraver of the mint, but at that time assistant to Roberts. The work was completed on schedule, and on February 11, 1964, the coin was officially introduced in ceremonies at both the Denver and Philadelphia mints.

Roberts had been a student of John Sinnock, who created the Roosevelt dime, and there is in his half-dollar some similarity to their work. He appreciated some of the earlier coins, such as those of Saint-Gaudens, but felt the designs were inappropriate. He felt that low relief is the most economical and efficient way for a country to make its coinage.

In the *COINage Magazine* interview, Roberts summed up his philosophy about coin art:

> A work of art should be something you'd like to possess. If it's grotesque, or has gross political connotations or an ugly meaning, it loses its beauty and then it's contrary to my belief. That's why I tried to talk Robert Kennedy out of depicting the President giving a speech to a crowd—we weren't trying to make a political poster out of the design, just a simple but pleasing likeness of a guy everybody loved because of his bright personality.
>
> Too, I think the nearness of a portrait to the person being portrayed should far outshine the artist who produced it. You should look at it and say, "Oh, that's so-and-so" instead of saying "That's the work of so-and-so." When you see a bust of George Washington done by Houdon, you know Washington must look like that. I really believe in the old saying, "A work of art is a thing of beauty and a joy forever." Art should have an appeal, an attractiveness that makes you want to be around it. That's what I tried to put into the Kennedy portrait.

20

Clad Coinage and the Eisenhower Dollar

In 1964, the government again faced the problem of rising metal costs. This time silver, not copper, was the metal in question. Dimes, quarters, and half-dollars would soon be worth more intrinsically than their face value. An alternative had to be found.

The problem was not a simple one. Vending machines of one sort or another effect all our lives. Whether we buy a candy bar in an office building, place a coin in a turnstile, use a parking meter, or engage in any one of a thousand other activities, we are involved with vending machines. These units have coin detectors. At the time of the proposed change, the detectors were balanced for the silver coins. If the metal content of the coins was to be changed, either vending machines all over the country would have to be modified (at astronomical cost) or a metal would have to be used that would "feel" the same as silver to the coin detectors.

The answer to the problem was the creation of a copper-nickel coin. The copper would be in the center with the nickel clad on top and bottom. The metal was laminated by an E. I. DuPont Company process called explosive binding, and the result is a laminated coin that will not split, even when subjected to great stress.

The experimentation with different metals resulted in the creation of a new "coin" as well. This was the Martha Washington "coin," a design having Martha's profile on the obverse along with her name, the word "Virginia," and the date 1759. This special dating was meant

Perhaps the most unusual coins to come out of the period when both the metallic content and the designs were being changed is this Martha Washington coin. It was one of several patterns made to test the new clad coinage. It was deliberately dated 1759 as a security measure. This specimen is in the Smithsonian Institution collection. ***(Photo courtesy of Krause Publications.)***

to reduce the chance of someone's passing or selling the coins should he obtain one illegally.

The reverse of the coin shows a two-sided view of Mount Vernon framed by shade trees. The name "Mount Vernon" is below the structure, and a legend ringing the design reads "Home of the Washington Family." These coins were never meant for circulation or seriously considered as a permanent design for any denomination.

The last major change in United States coinage occurred with the introduction of the Eisenhower dollar—clad silver coins being reserved for collectors, who paid a premium to the mint for special sets. The coin jointly honors the president and the United States space program. It was sponsored by Congressman Bob Casey of Texas, who had been trying for a space commemorative coin for several years.

Referring to July 20, 1969, the day the astronauts landed on the moon, Casey commented in an article in the July, 1971, issue of *Coins Magazine:*

> For me—and thousands of my constituents who labored long and hard at NASA's Manned Spacecraft Center in Houston (MSA)—it was a particularly satisfying process.
>
> In my district live the astronauts, the scientists, the technicians, and the janitors at MSA—and together, we shared one common goal: to see America first in space. Together, we shared the joys of our early successes, and the sorrow brought by our tragedies. And we did it openly, as a free society should, for the world to see.
>
> [Casey continued:] Eleven days after that great moment of lunar touchdown, I introduced in the 91st Congress by bill, H. R. 13238—to provide for the minting of a new half-dollar coin bearing

the official symbol of the *Apollo XI* flight, and the inscription, "We Came In Peace For All Mankind." While I held little hope in my heart that this bill would gain favorable approval by the House Banking and Currency Committee, in view of the relatively-new Kennedy half-dollar, I could think of no better way to commemorate that great event. Neither could I think of a more readily accessible token for those millions of people over the world who applaud our efforts and our success in space. I shared the vigorous view of every foreign visitor I encountered that we should make more positive capital out of our tremendous success, and I knew that such a coin would be an excellent goodwill emblem for the United States.

At the same time, efforts were being made to honor former President Eisenhower through minting of a new silver dollar, and this moved eventually to the House floor for action. A vigorous battle was going on between the pro and anti silver interests. While I have personal beliefs about what a silver dollar ought to contain, I saw an opportunity to bring honor and credit to the United States for an unsung achievement too long ignored. And on October 15, 1969, I offered on the Floor of the House an amendment to the Eisenhower "silver" dollar legislation.

"What could be more appropriate," I argued, "than that the reverse of this coin should also honor a great momentous feat in history which began under his Administration."

It was President Eisenhower, who in 1958, signed into law the act creating the National Aeronautics and Space Administration, and launched us into the great space race with Russia to reach the moon.

The artist assigned to produce the new coin was Frank Gasparro, the mint's chief engraver. Gasparro had long admired President Eisenhower and had made a special trip to New York City on June 20, 1945, just to see the general appear in a motorcade along Fifth Avenue. He watched as the General raised his arms in a salute of victory and was so impressed that he returned home and sketched the war leader's portrait from memory. His design was meant for a medal, but he had no money to take it through the various steps needed for completion.

"One of the things that impressed me so much about Ike, as an artist, was his neck. He had a massive neck—thick and strong, and when it came to doing the dollar portrait I concentrated on the neck as one of the most important parts of the design. His face was broad but dominated by that tremendous smile. His face had strong character in it, and his eyes were honest and unflinching," Gasparro explained in an interview. "It's a joy to do a portrait of such a man."

Congressman Casey had definite ideas about the reverse of the new dollar coin. He commented:

. . . I offered my amendment, requiring the Apollo XI eagle, and

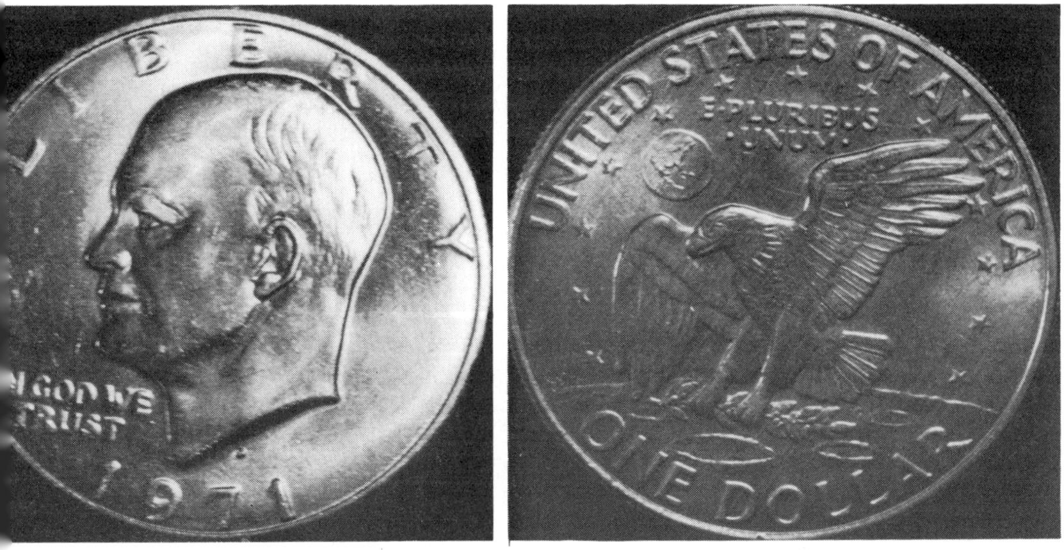

The Eisenhower dollar with original reverse.

that the reverse also carry the inscription: "We Came In Peace For All Mankind."

It was a considerable jolt, needless to say, when my longtime friend, Representative Leonor Sullivan—a great lady, and a colleague whom I consider an expert on coinage—advised me the law also required other points. She informed me, for example, that the reverse must also carry: "United States of America," and if that were not enough, it was also required that there be on the reverse "E Pluribus Unum," and it would be somewhat crowded with what I proposed. With the great gentleness for which she is known, she inquired through the presiding chairman if I would be agreeable to accepting an amendment that the reverse be "emblematic" of the motif of Apollo XI, thereby giving the engraver some latitude in inscribing his design.

I would, and I did, and we passed the bill requiring that the reverse of this new coin carry a design "emblematic of the symbolic eagle of Apollo XI landing on the moon."

On the final coin, an eagle clutching an olive branch of peace is shown landing on the moon. The message is conveyed symbolically, Congressman Casey's motto having been abandoned. In addition, the earth has been placed in the upper left of the coin to act as an effective balance for the coin design.

Despite the fact that the new coin was cupro-nickel, it proved immensely popular. Many former soldiers who served under "Ike" during World War II have kept them as souvenirs of the leader. They have been used in tie clasps, money clips, jewelry, and on occasion, for making change.

21

The Coin Designs of the American Revolution Bicentennial

When the United States celebrated the two-hundredth anniversary of the start of the American Revolution, the art of numismatics shared in the event. New reverse designs were used on the dollar, half-dollar, and quarter, each prepared by a private citizen unconnected with the United States Mint.

The planning for the new coins began on October 18, 1973, when the Ninety-third Congress passed Public Law 93-127 authorizing changes in the designs. Then an announcement went out to the news media, stating:

"The National Sculpture Society on behalf of the Department of the Treasury invites competition for new designs for the reverse side of the dollar, half-dollar and quarter-dollar coins to be struck by the United States Mint.

"Eligibility: Open to all sculptors who are citizens of the United States and WHO ARE CAPABLE OF EXECUTING A PLASTER MODEL compatible with the coining process. Members of the panel of judges and sculptors of the U. S. Government are not eligible."

The announcement described the method for presentation of designs and the method to be used to keep each design's creator anonymous until after the judging. It continued:

> Plaster models submitted at the request of the Treasury Department which meet such requirements and specifications will be purchased for the sum of $750 each by the Treasury Department.

FINALISTS: The National Sculpture Society jury will select no more than six plaster models suitable for coinage reduction and submit them to the Secretary of the Treasury.

The final selections of the new designs for the reverse side of the coins by the Secretary of the Treasury will be made after recommendations submitted from a committee composed of the Director of the Mint; the Chairman of the Senate Committee on Banking, Housing and Urban Affairs; the Chairman of the House Committee on Banking & Currency; the Chairman of the Advisory Committee on Coins and Medals of the American Revolution Bicentennial Commission; and the Fine Arts Commission.

If no submitted design is found by the Secretary of the Treasury to be satisfactory aesthetically or technically for the coining process, no contract will be awarded.

AWARD: A contract award of $5,000 will be given to the designer of each of the final designs selected by the Secretary of the Treasury.

The initial judges in the contest were also announced. They

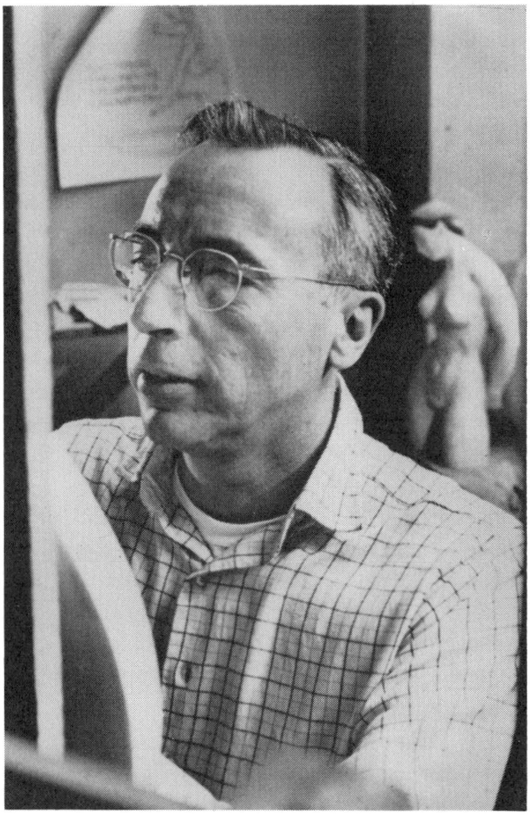

When new coin designs were sought from the general public, five individuals were chosen to make the final selection. Shown here is Robert Weinman, the president of the National Sculpture Society.

The sculptor Adlai Hardin.

included Robert Weinman, the son of Adolph Weinman who designed the Mercury Dime and Walking Liberty Half Dollar. Weinman was President of the National Sculpture Society. Additional judges were: Gilroy Roberts, chief engraver of the Philadelphia mint from 1948 through 1964 and, at the time of the contest, chief sculptor of the privately owned Franklin Mint; Adlai Hardin, a sculptor; Elvira Eliza Clain-Stefanelli, curator, Division of Numismatics at the Smithsonian Institution; and Julius Lauth, Vice President and Art Director of the Medallic Art Company of Danbury, Connecticut.

Numerous entries, both amateur and professional, were submitted to the judges. The backgrounds and ages of the entrants were extremely varied. To learn more about them, I contacted several of the semi-finalists.

Brydon Stewart of Yakima, Washington, commented shortly after winning the $750-prize:

> I am presently involved in preparing the first public showing of my work. Also, an acute case of starvation forced me to drop school this Quarter, and embark upon yet another sojourn into the working

Gilroy Roberts, chief sculptor of the privately owned Franklin Mint. He was formerly chief engraver of the United States Mint and the creator of the obverse of the Kennedy half-dollar.

world. My present occupation is that of a flagman for a crop-dusting company. When the weather is good, we're in the wheatfields 10–14 hours a day; and when the weather is NOT good, we spend nearly as much time waiting for it to get better. So my time these days IS limited. But the job can be exciting: on Easter Sunday one of the Stearmans crashed into a sprinkler line not more than 20 yards away from me. Had he been a couple of feet lower, he would have crashed into ME! (The pilot, by the way, miraculously survived, and with nothing more than a bruised shoulder and a fractured ego; although the airplane, which tumbled end-over-end into a rocky ravine, was completely demolished. True to the spirit of the holiday, it was a day of miracles!).

Stewart, twenty-seven years old at the time he entered, produced a quarter-dollar design which showed the American eagle winging through the environs of the moon. He said:

For several weeks I was obsessed with the notion that I had to

Julius Lauth, the Vice-president and art director of the Medallic Art Company.

"improve" my original design: it seemed too simple (the very thing that made it effective!). Also, it wasn't commemorative enough of the Revolution. The eagle, soaring free above the dates 1776–1976 expressed definitely, it seemed to me, our greatest achievement as a nation; i.e. remaining INDEPENDENT after 200 years and thus becoming the longest-lived single republic in history, but I realized that the selection committee, and the public, would want something less abstract, something more concretely depicting a Revolutionary theme, and probably also something depicting the nation's MATERIAL progress in 200 years. So for some time I tried to work in a nuclear energy symbol . . . but the circling electrons took on the aspect of a CAGE, which I thought was a nice editorial comment, but a "cage" also from a design standpoint. The consequent cluttering of the design was simply unworkable. Finally, a few days before Thanksgiving, it occurred to me to change the disk of the sun to that of the moon. Of course here the spectre of chauvinism raised its ugly head (the moon as 51st State?), but this was not my intention. Landing men on the moon was unquestionably our nation's greatest MATERIAL achievement in 200 years and is anyway

Elvira Eliza Clain-Stefanelli, curator of the, Division of Numismatics of the Smithsonian Institution.

an achievement not so much of one nation or group of individuals as of—as the astronaut said—"mankind." Also a moon would work better from a design standpoint: the modeling of the lighted side of the moon would have been convex, and the dark side concave, which would have resulted in a stunning three-diminsional effect. (Plus I had a nice visual pun going in the fact that the "quarter" moon matched the "quarter" dollar.) Also a moon in crescent phase would have read better as "moon" because the required shallow relief would make the disk of a full moon too flat, and in the small size of the final rendering on a coin, most surface detail would be obliterated. Nevertheless, when the selection committee asked me to render the moon full-phase ("Render moon as Moon," they said), I meekly complied. I wanted too badly to win the $5,000. (My financial situation at that time was desperate—in fact I was starving—literally!) It was the worst mistake I made, and the most valuable lesson learned, in my participation in the competition. That is, NEVER TO COMPROMISE MY ARTISTIC JUDGMENT, FOR WHATEVER REASON. Even if I had won, I would still reproach myself for giving in as I did.

Dean McMullen, another runner-up, lived in Portland, Oregon at the time of the coin-design contest and worked as a promotional designer. McMullen's background was more extensive than that of Stewart. He was forty-one when the contest occurred and had already successfully completed other medal designs. He won the Captain Cook Festival medal design competition sponsored by the Kona, Hawaii, Jaycees in 1967 and designed their medals in 1968 and 1969 as well. His other medal designs included the reverse of the 1971 Freightliner twenty-fifth Anniversary medallion and the Goldendale, Washington, one-hundreth anniversary commemorative dollar trade token in 1972. McMullen's design for the bicentennial coin was based on a quarter dollar and featured thirteen stars representing the colonies, and an eagle and the lunar lander.

McMullen's approach was to "doodle" possible designs, then extract portions of each and vary the results. "In evaluating the first design," he wrote me:

> I realized it was better suited to being a medal with all the detail and relief possibilities medal work allows. The final choice on the other hand was a comparatively simple statement with better relief relationships to the existing obverse designs with which it would be used. Probably the term "concept" rather than "design" would be a better choice of words in this case as I learned of the competition only one month prior to the deadline. I really had to hustle and ended up with the lettering and 50 stars from the first design with a superimposed second piece of paper showing the lander, 13 stars, eagle, etc., and yet another piece of paper on which the 13 stars were changed from a 5 pointed style to 6 pointed. The sketch as submitted was in the end a composite of 3 levels of illustration. (I had no time left to refine my concept further).

The three winners were Jack Ahr of Arlington Heights, Illinois, who designed the Colonial drummer boy for the quarter, Seth Huntington of Minneapolis, Minnesota, whose Independence Hall design was for the half-dollar; and Dennis Williams of Columbus, Ohio, whose Liberty Bell and moon design was chosen for the dollar coin. Ahr ran Jack Ahr Design and Sales Company. Huntington headed the custom art department of Brown and Bigelow in Minneapolis; and Williams, the youngest at twenty-two, was a student majoring in sculpture at Columbus College of Art and Design.

The selection resulted in a certain amount of controversy. A charge was made that the drummer boy on Ahr's coin was deliberately modeled after the drummer on Archibald Willard's famous painting *The Spirit of '76*. However, the artist said his son, in junior high school, had served as the model.

Then William Smith, another artist, said that Ahr's concept was an imitation of Smith's design for the United States eight-cent stamp *Rise of the Spirit of Independence*. According to *Coin World* of August 28,

This is the Kennedy half-dollar with Bicentennial reverse. ***(Photo courtesy of Krause Publications.)***

The Bicentennial Washington quarter with the special reverse. ***(Photo courtesy of Krause Publications.)***

The Eisenhower Bicentennial dollar with the special reverse. ***(Photo courtesy of Krause Publications.)***

1974, Smith made his charge in a letter to Mint Director Mary Brooks stating, ". . . recognizing that there have been countless drawings and paintings of colonial drummers, I make no claim, of course, to exclusive rights to the subject matter, but Mr. Ahr has copied my drawing. . . ."

In the end it was decided that the charges were probably groundless. Both the Smith and the Ahr designs resembled the Willard painting, yet neither was a copy and the drummer boy concept has been a popular one in art for many years.

On May 3, 1974, Mary Brooks commented about the new coins in a speech at the Greater New York Coin Convention:

In honor of our Bicentennial, the backs of three coins are going to have new designs evocative of our 200 year history.

A Colonial drummer. Independence Hall. The Liberty Bell and moon. These all have deep significance to Americans. They form the new designs that will appear on the reverses of 1776-1976 quarters, half dollars, and dollars, respectively. When in circulation, these coins will reach out to every citizen. Hopefully, the history embedded in these new designs will serve as reminders of our rich national heritage and continuing dedication to freedom and self government.

[Mrs. Brooks continued]: To borrow an excuse used on television, due to circumstances beyond our control, the time limit in which we had to conduct the competition was severely limited.

This made for a hectic period for the office—and for the artists. One hard-pressed young student from Yakima, Washington, Brydon Stewart, one of the 12 semi-finalists, called frantically one day to let us know he didn't have postage money to get his plaster to Philadelphia and had to take a collection from among his friends to raise the fees.

My staff then was as antsy about the arrival of his model as he was. On the closing date, his model hadn't arrived with the morning mail. The afternoon mail came and went. We were heartsick. Then about two hours later a special delivery box appeared. Yes. It was his. And we all heaved a sigh of relief.

I didn't want the competition limited only to successful, professional medallic artists. So, among others, at the time of the launching we mailed the rules to art schools, public and private, throughout the country. I also traveled around the nation for three weeks doing television interviews about the competition.

Naturally, I was delighted when so many art students, as well as their professors, submitted entries. I wish I could report to you on the background of each artist and on each design—but the number makes this impossible.

When I looked through the nearly one thousand sketches, I was struck by the recurring combination of an astronaut and a patriot to tell the story of our 200 years. In fact, this design concept was a favorite of mine.

An artist from my own state of Idaho, John Collias, was the first runner-up to the 12 semi-finalists. He entered a beautiful example of a Revolutionary War soldier and a helmeted spaceman facing each other across a backdrop of the Liberty Bell.

In case of a disqualification of one of the semi-finalists, I asked him to prepare a plaster model of his design. Later, while sitting in my Idaho dentist's chair, I learned my dentist had been his source of supply for the plaster. Since then I've wondered whether I, too, may have a part of that supply nestling somewhere in a tooth. . . .

The bicentennial coin designs were used only for the year 1976. Despite public clamor to either retain the new reverses or have new commemorative designs produced, the mint returned to the previous designs for the coinage of the succeeding years.

22

America's Commemorative Coinage

This chapter of our study of American coinage is concerned with the series of commemorative coins produced between 1892 and 1954. These coins were never meant to be circulated, although they were legal tender. They were designed as souvenirs and, as will be shown, became a profit-making business for the sponsors quite by chance.

The number of commemorative coins issued is extremely large, and the scope of this book is such that only a few can be mentioned in any detail. Some were already mentioned in the chapter on James and Laura Fraser. But altogether there were 157 varieties consisting of 142 half-dollars (48 varieties with different years and mint marks providing the large total), a quarter-dollar, silver dollar, nine gold dollars (6 different types), 2 two-dollar-and-fifty-cent gold pieces and 2 fifty-dollar gold pieces.

The first of the commemorative coins relate to the Columbian Exposition, which opened in Chicago in May 1893. It was a world's fair, and the sponsors were determined to make it the most dramatic ever conceived. Bonds were sold to raise money, but the amount collected was far less than the board of directors desired. They made an appeal to Congress for a five-million-dollar grant, but Congress would only consider providing such a sum as a loan. Finally, through a series of proposals, debates, and amendments, Congress agreed to authorize the melting of two and one-half million dollars in obsolete silver coins for recoining into half-dollars commemorating the event. Congress also enabled the board of directors to sell these to the public for double face value—one dollar each—to raise the necessary capital. As a result of that precedent, all subsequent commemorative coins have been sold to make money for the sponsoring organization even though they are legal tender at face value and are official government issues.

The city of Chicago fought long and hard to obtain the right to hold the World's Columbian Exposition. It was an event honoring the four hundredth anniversary of Columbus's discovery of America, and was only the second world's fair held in the United States. The previous one was in Philadelphia.

Chicago had to vie with New York, St. Louis, and Washington, D.C., for the right to have the exposition. When the competing cities lost to Chicago, their area newspapers greatly criticized the selection site and delighted in reporting problems and delays with the fair's opening. The only thing that could be accomplished by October 21, 1892, was the dedication of the grounds; the actual opening occurred several months later than would have been ideal for honoring the discovery of America.

The site for the exposition was a 686-acre section of land on Lake Michigan that had been set aside twenty years earlier for use as a public park. The park was never built. The land was left wild instead, covered with oak trees, swamps, and sand dunes. When construction was completed, the massive new buildings were extremely impressive. One hundred and fifty buildings were constructed in all to serve the reported twenty-eight million people who went to see the exposition. At its conclusion, most of the buildings were removed. One of the few reminders of those days is the Fine Arts Building, which today has been converted to the Museum of Science and Industry.

One of the most popular entertainments at the exposition was a giant amusement ride invented by a man named Ferris. According to *Harper's Weekly* of July, 1893:

> . . . Whether the visitor approaches the fair from the lake or by the Illinois Central Railway, the huge wheel is about the first thing to catch the eye. The top of the wheel is 265 feet above the ground, as the wheel itself is 250 in diameter and the bottom of it is 15 feet above ground. This huge plaything, a gigantic merry-go-round running vertically instead of horizontally, is a splendid point of observation, from which a visitor can take bearings and arrange plans for seeing the fair. The wheel is something like 825 feet in circumference, and as it requires ten minutes for each revolution, the passengers have plenty of time in which to see what lies about them.
>
> As the wheel ascends, a better view may be had of Chicago and the prairies beyond than from any of the tall buildings in town; and as the wheel descends, there is the fair—the White City—stretched in front, the lake beyond, and the busy Midway Plaisance right underneath. There are 36 cars attached to the periphery of the wheel, the attachment being by an axle in the top of the car, which, swinging freely and having its weight at the bottom, always remains parallel with the earth. As each car holds 40 (persons), the total capacity of the wheel is 1,440 passengers.

Candor compels the confession that one does not step into the cars of the wheel without some trepidation. It is an engineering novelty. Nothing like it was ever built or attempted before.

There was another important amusement at the exhibition, which provided the visitor a chance to see and experience electricity. A writer for *Harper's Weekly* commented: "The very ground on which the exposition is built will vibrate to the hum of electrical machinery, and at night the air will blaze with bright light springing into being through forces set at liberty by the subtle fluid. Illumination in ample quantity for the fifteen buildings will be furnished by 5,000 arc lamps of 2,000 candle power each."

There was also an exhibit of Thomas Edison's inventions. The *Harper's Weekly* report stated: "It will show a large variety of incandescent lamps, and a most interesting collection of the uses and abuses to which the famous phonograph may be put. The most startling features of his display will be his illustrations of the wonders of his kinetograph and the telephone combined . . . he can reproduce, visually and audibly, a theatrical performance many miles from the scene of the actual production. Let us say that he selects a performance at a theatre in St. Louis; he will confidently undertake to represent the same performance in Chicago, at a distance of 280 miles from the scene, and this synchronously with the actual performance at St. Louis."

One of the more highly criticized events at the exposition was an area called The Streets Of Cairo. This was a "sinful" area filled with exotic dancers from the Middle East. The most notorious was Little Egypt who dared to expose her midriff while she performed the sensuous belly dance. Many of the other "Middle Eastern" dancers were actually American girls wearing heavy make-up.

The half-dollar commemorating the Columbian Exposition was authorized by an act of August 5, 1892. The coins were to be of the same weight and fineness as regular half-dollars and were to have the same legal-tender status.

Charles Barber decided to use what was supposedly the most accurate rendering of Columbus's features known. This was a portrait that had been painted in 1512 by Lorenzo Lotto and had won a silver medal for its quality. Barber did not have access to the painting, though, so he sent for a bronze medal produced by Enrique Lopez Lorensis that supposedly was an exact copy of the Lotto rendering. Unfortunately the medal did not arrive, and Barber had to use other sources, which were not of the same quality. The *American Journal of Numismatics* (1893), declared: "As a work of art it certainly is a great disappointment. . . ."

The reverse design had not been decided upon when F. W. Peck, finance chairman of the Columbian Exposition, came up with the idea of showing the ship *Santa Maria* atop two hemispheres. Several officials liked the idea and ordered plaster models to be made. The

This coin commemorated the World's Columbian Exposition held in Chicago, Illinois, in 1893. The exposition celebrated the 400th anniversary of Christopher Columbus's discovery of America. It was designed by Charles Barber, with the reverse design being handled by George Morgan. The coins were authorized on August 5, 1892.

jealous Barber was not going to let an outsider create coins, especially when that person was not even an artist. He had one of his controlled tantrums, and the officials allowed George Morgan, assistant engraver at the mint, to handle the work. His design is quite similar to Peck's, but at least it was done by the "proper" person.

The women's rights movement was becoming strong about the time the exposition was to be held. Earlier world's fairs had done little for women but the Columbian Exposition was going to be different. It even had a Board of Lady Managers, who took an active part in all aspects of the event. Since one coin was being made to honor Columbus, the women insisted that another coin be issued to honor his financial backer—Queen Isabella.

Movement for the adoption of the new coin began in January. Mrs. Potter Palmer, a member of the Board of Lady Managers and the wife of a Chicago millionaire, asked the Appropriations Committee of the House of Representatives to provide ten thousand dollars for souvenir quarter dollars. On March 3, 1893, the government passed an act stating:

> . . . and ten thousand dollars of the appropriation for the Board of Lady Managers shall be paid in souvenir coins of the denomination of twenty-five cents, and for that purpose there shall be coined at the Mints of the United States silver quarter-dollars of the legal weight and fineness, not to exceed forty thousand pieces, the devices and designs upon which shall be prescribed by the Director of the Mint, with the approval of the Secretary of the Treasury; and said silver coins shall be manufactured from uncurrent subsidiary silver coins now in the Treasury; and all provisions of law relative to the coinage, legal tender quality, and redemption of the present subsidiary silver coins shall be applicable to the coins herein authorized to be issued.

Mrs. Palmer had no intention of letting the mint handle the quarter her group had won the right to produce. The mint was male dominated, and there were plenty of women artists with the skill to handle the coin design. She immediately went to New York, where Caroline Peddle was commissioned to handle the creation of the quarter.

What developed was predictable. Barber and Morgan would have been hostile to any outsider and were doubly so to a woman. And Caroline Peddle had the added drawback of knowing nothing about coin production. She constantly questioned Mint Director Bosbyshell about the production aspects, how many words had to be put on the coin, what mottoes were needed, and numerous other matters. Then she produced a coin with far greater inscription than was realistic. Barber, upon seeing it, took great delight in writing:

"You no doubt have seen that it is quite impossible to put all the reading matter furnished by Mrs. Potter Palmer on a coin as small as a 25¢ piece, and therefore the question arises how much shall be used, that is to what extent is the Director of the Mint willing to comply with the request of the ladies, and it is more to ascertain this point that I submit the designs than anything else." The artist had designed an obverse having a full figure of the queen. Barber, however, felt that just her head would be preferable. One should remember that this was a time when Barber had produced a series of coins with nothing but the bust of Liberty on the obverse. He was certain a full figure had no place on the coin. This idea was later proven to be nonsense when MacNeil's Standing Liberty proved to be one of the most effective coin designs ever created. Ironically, it replaced the Barber coins in 1916.

The reverse of the coin was to show the Woman's Building at the exposition. But Barber hated the idea of using any building on a coin because of problems with the relief: "The Woman's Building is particularly unsuitable. To follow the suggestion of the ladies and use a section of the building would, I fear, leave the design so uncertain that none could tell what building it was intended for, there being no striking feature in the building. The building being a long rather low structure, I fear to use it in its entirely. It would look a mere streak across the coin."

Barber pressured the women's group concerning the reverse design, eventually convincing them to let him do it. This greatly upset Peddle, who at first wanted to abandon the entire project since she would not be granted the artistic freedom she expected to have. However, she was finally convinced to settle for the obverse and forwarded a model for approval by the mint.

Barber moved in for the kill when he got the Peddle design. He had gotten his way with the reverse and knew it would take little effort to win complete artistic control. After studying the obverse model, he wrote Bosbyshell:

> I do not know whether this model is a likeness of Queen Isabella or not. I mean whether Miss Peddle had a profile portrait to model from, or whether she was obliged to make a profile from a full-faced portrait. It does not seem to matter much, as I reckon the likeness will answer just as well. Again, is the drapery over the head enclosed by a hand and falling over the shoulder, a mantilla, and if so, ought it not to be of lace, thus greatly enriching the design?
>
> To criticize closely, how small the top of the head drawing a straight line around the forehead above the ears and how large the neck, drawing a line back from just under the chin. I point these matters out not in a hypercritical way, but to anticipate criticism that may come. Personally, I'm not ready to fall in love with the model. It does not strike me as artistic, certainly not strong, and if placed on a coin will fall far short of the Columbia half dollar. It is crudely modeled, not nearly sufficiently defined, and leaves entirely too much for our engravers to work out.

The result of Barber's complaints is not really known. Both he and Peddle submitted designs for the obverse, and the one selected is in Barber's style. There are no records that conclusively prove it to have been Barber's design, but most experts feel it was his.

It is interesting to note that the obverse shows a crowned head of Isabella. Peddle had left off the crown because it was felt that the

The Isabella quarter was designed by Charles Barber for sale at the World's Columbian Exposition. It was created as a result of pressure by the Board of Lady Managers. The image displayed is that of a kneeling woman with a spindle and distaff, a symbol of industry in Columbus's time.

United States should not so honor a monarch. It was thought preferable to show her without the crown so she appeared more as a person of influence who helped Columbus rather than a head of state.

The reverse of the quarter is symbolic. A kneeling woman holds the implements for spinning—a woman's industry. The legend reads, "Columbian Quar. Dol.—Board of Lady Managers."

The *American Journal of Numismatics* was not pleased with Barber's quarter. After the coin's release, it editorialized:

> Of its artistic merit, as of the harmony which is reported to have prevailed at the meetings of those Managers, perhaps the less said the better; we do not know who designed it; but in this instance, as in the Half Dollar, the contrast between the examples of the numismatic art of the nation, as displayed on the Columbian coins, on the one hand, and the spirited and admirable work of the architects of the buildings, for instance, on the other, is painful. If these two coins really represent the highest achievements of our medallists and our mints, under the inspiration of an opportunity without restrictions, the like of which has never been presented hitherto in the history of our national coinage, we might as well despair of its future, and should be forced to believe that the merely mechanical side of the art of coining was all that was thought worthy of attention. We are not ready to admit this to be true. Not to speak of St. Gaudens, and Lafarge among the living, and Hunt and Richardson among the dead, artists confessedly at the head of the various departments of the fine arts to which they have devoted themselves, the architecture of the Exposition buildings, as we have remarked above, and the skill and taste with which the grounds and

waterside have been laid out . . . prove that there does exist in America an artistic instinct . . . an appreciation of beauty as well as of utility, a genius to design and an ability to execute works not less eminent in the world of art than [achievements of engineers, inventors, mechanics] . . . we shall search in vain in our national coinage for evidence to sustain our confidence.

The figure on the reverse is mournfully suggestive of the old anti-slavery token, "Am I not a woman and a sister."

When the exposition was over, most of the quarters were sold, and only a relatively small number of half-dollars had been purchased, despite the fact that both sold for one dollar each. Half-dollars continued to be sold after the exposition, and a number of them were spent at face value to help meet pressing expenses.

It is interesting to note that people eventually tired of owning the small quarter dollars. They began spending them, and as a result, few remain in the same condition as when they were first placed for sale.

In 1900, the Paris Exposition was held and for it, the mint authorized the creation of a dollar coin to honor the French leader Lafayette. This was to coincide with the erection of a monument to the general created by Paul Bartlett. The monument was a gift from the American people and was paid for, in part, by fifty thousand dollars collected in the form of pennies donated by school children around the country. Further expenses were to be defrayed by sale of another half-dollar—later changed to a dollar—coin. According to an act approved March 3, 1899:

Lafayette Monument: For the purpose of aiding in defraying the cost of a pedestal, and completing in a suitable manner the work of erecting a monument in the city of Paris to General Lafayette, designed by the Lafayette Memorial Commission, as a feature of the participation of the United States in the Paris Exposition of nineteen hundred the Secretary of the Treasury shall be, and is hereby authorized to purchase in the market twenty-five thousand dollars worth of silver bullion, or so much thereof as may be necessary for the purpose herein provided for, from which there shall be coined at the mints of the United States silver dollars of the legal weight and fineness to the number of fifty thousand pieces, to be known as the Lafayette dollar, struck in commemoration of the erection of a monument to General Lafayette, in the city of Paris, France, by the youth of the United States, the devices and designs upon which coins shall be prescribed by the Director of the Mint, with the approval of the Secretary of the Treasury, and all provisions of law, relative to the coinage, and legal tender quality, of the present silver dollars shall be applicable to the coins issued under this Act, and when so coined, there is hereby appropriated from the Treasury the said fifty thousand of souvenir dollars, and the Secretary of the Treasury is authorized to place the same at the disposal of the Lafayette Memorial Commission, a commission

The Lafayette dollar, prepared to mark the erection of a monument to General Lafayette in Paris. The statue was erected during the Paris Exposition of 1900. The statue was designed by Charles Barber and paid for by American students' contributions of coins. ***(Photo courtesy of Krause Publications.)***

organized under the direction and authority of the Commissioner-General for the United States to the Paris Exposition of nineteen hundred.

Charles Barber was assigned the task of creating the commemorative dollar, and he became the first coin designer to use Houdon's bust of Washington as a model. This bust would later be the model for the Washington quarter as was discussed in the chapter on the Frasers. He also utilized a Washington portrait from a medal by Du Vivier. This head, plus one of Layfayette taken from a French medal engraved by Caunois, formed the obverse of the coin.

For the reverse Barber used the mounted figure of Lafayette in a pose similar to the one utilized by Bartlett on his statue. The inscription reads: "Erected by the Youth of the United States in Honor of Gen. Layfayette–Paris–1900."

Barber had the honor of designing the first commemorative gold dollar as well as the first to be struck in silver. The gold coin was prepared for the Louisiana Purchase Exposition which was officially authorized on March 3, 1901.

The Louisiana Purchase Exposition made the Columbian Exposition seem rather small. It was held on 1,272 acres of land in the Forest Park section of St. Louis beginning on April 30, 1904.

The exposition was meant to glorify the new mechanical wonders of the world. One hundred and sixty gasoline-, electric-, and steam-powered motor cars were on display, as were a number of dirigibles or blimps. There were exhibits showing wireless telegraphy and other scientific marvels only recently invented.

The gold dollar commemorative was authorized by Congress on June 28, 1902. It was decided to issue two designs rather than one. The first coin honored Thomas Jefferson, president when the

The gold dollar was the first commemorative gold coin that the United States struck. The obverse shows the head of Thomas Jefferson as produced by Charles Barber of the United States Mint. The dollars were issued in conjunction with the Louisiana Purchase Exposition, which was held to honor the 100th anniversary of the purchase of the Louisiana Territory. A variation of this coin shows a head of President William McKinley. Jefferson was president when the Louisiana Territory was purchased, and McKinley was president when the Louisiana Purchase Exposition plans were passed into law on March 3, 1901.

The gold dollar for the Lewis and Clark Exposition. These coins commemorated the 100th anniversary of the explorations of both the Oregon Territory and the Louisiana Territory by Meriwether Lewis and William Clark. The exposition was held shortly after the Louisiana Purchase Exposition but, unlike the latter, was not international in scope. ***(Photo courtesy of Krause Publications.)***

Louisiana Territory was purchased. The bust was copied from a medal made by John Reich, an assistant engraver at the mint during Jefferson's presidency. It lacks the quality of design achieved on the Jefferson nickel based upon the Houdon bust.

The second coin showed President McKinley who had been assassinated the previous year (1901). A common reverse was used to make the pair of coins semi-legal. Officially, only one obverse and reverse design had been authorized. It was probably a violation of the law for the mint to make the two different designs, but nobody pressed the issue since the common reverse was used.

Another gold commemorative dollar was created by Barber for sale in 1904 and 1905. This time the Lewis and Clark Exposition was the subject, and the coin was a unique undertaking in that it was the first American coin to have two portrait busts, one on each side. The obverse showed Meriwether Lewis and the reverse showed William Clark. Neither portrait is of very high quality, though they were apparently based on the excellent likenesses painted many years earlier by Charles William Peale.

The gold dollars were sold for double face value with the proceeds used to pay for a memorial to Sacagawea, the Indian wife of Toussaint Charbonneau. Charbonneau was a French guide for the expedition, and his wife acted as an interpreter with the various Indians they encountered. The memorial was erected in Portland, Oregon.

The most dramatic of the gold commemoratives were struck in 1915 for the Panama-Pacific Exposition, held to mark the opening of the Panama Canal. There were gold one-dollar pieces, quarter-eagle gold commemoratives, and fifty-dollar gold pieces, both round and octagonal, in addition to the commemorative half-dollar.

The Congressional act relating to the coinage, passed January 16, 1915, stated: ". . . That the Secretary of the Treasury shall cause to be coined at the United States mint at San Francisco not exceeding three thousand gold coins of the denomination of $50 each, ten thousand gold coins of the denomination of $2.50 each, twenty-five thousand gold coins of the denomination of $1 each, and not exceeding two hundred thousand silver coins of the denomination of 50 cents each, all of legal weight and fineness; said coins to be struck in commemoration of the Panama Pacific International Exposition. . . ."

An unusual first for the exposition was the location of machinery

This is the half-dollar prepared in honor of the Panama-Pacific Exposition, which celebrated the completion of the Panama Canal.

The gold dollar, gold two and one-half-dollar, and gold fifty-dollar coins were prepared for the same exposition. Charles Barber produced the half-dollar and two and one-half dollar gold pieces, Charles Keck produced the dollar coin, and Robert Aitken produced the fifty-dollar coin. Normally the coins were sold at double face value to insure a large profit for the organization sponsoring the event commemorated. However, because of the high price of the fifty-dollar gold pieces ($100.00 each), the sponsor of the Panama-Pacific International Exposition decided that if someone bought both the round and octagonal fifty-dollar gold pieces for a total of $200.00, then a two and one-half-dollar gold piece, one dollar gold piece and a fifty-cent silver coin would be given free. The entire set came in a custom case. ***(Photo courtesy of Krause Publications.)***

for the physical production of the new coins. The act stated:

> . . . That the 50-cent silver coins herein authorized may, in the discretion of the Secretary of the Treasury, be coined or finished and issued from the machinery to be installed as a part of the exhibit of the United States mint at said exposition, and for the purpose of maintaining the exhibit as an educative working exhibit at all times the coins so minted may be remelted and reminted. All of said 50-cent silver coins herein authorized not issued to and at the request of said Panama-Pacific International Exposition, whether the same are coined as a part of said working exhibit or coined at the mint in San Francisco, shall be remelted upon the official closing of said exposition. . . ."

The exposition also had the largest display of coins ever assembled for such an event. The display provided a visual history of money and had been prepared by numismatist Farran Zerbe. Zerbe's background included a term as president of the American Numismatic Association, and he had been an active proponent of the Peace dollar. According to a contemporary account entitled "The Coin Outlasts The Throne" by Frank Morton Todd published in 1921 in Volume IV of *The Story of the Exposition:*

There are about 20,000 original specimens of what man at the main stages of his evolution and in all known countries has used as money, and the whole collection represented a one time value of at least $50,000,000. . . .

> There were clay tablets of accounts from Nippur, constituting a record of values measured in labor, love, stock, and grain. There were implement-shaped metal pieces from China, meant to be the fixed price of the article represented, for even in ancient times people befuddled themselves with the supposition that government could fix prices permanently—a knife-shaped coin, for example, standing for the price of a razor, but without power to enlarge or diminish itself in response to the ever changing relation of razor supply and demand. A similar idea and use of such original token money was found among the Aztecs, indicating either some early connection between the peoples of the two continents or else a mere, common coincidence of fallacious ideas.
>
> There were "plugs" of brick tea, stamped by the Russian Government, notched so they could be broken into small change, and circulated among the peoples of Tibet; long black strips of licorice-soaked tobacco, pierced so they could be strung for necklaces, made in Petersburg, Virginia, and circulated as money in certain South Pacific islands, where they would buy more than anything else you could take there; a slab of copper two feet long, a foot wide, and an inch or so thick, which was once eight dollars in Sweden; and gold coins of some Indian state that were no larger than a pinhead. There was leather money, paper money, shells, wampum of all descriptions, rubber money, condensed milk money, bone, fiber, clay, coal, glass, cloth, and pasteboard, and there were linen notes, and iron coins in the shape of fish hooks and musket balls. There were Russian platinum coins minted when platinum was so little valued it was thought only good to make jitneys with. There was every kind of wildcat note, including the money of John Law and his Mississippi Bubble. There were interesting historical and financial documents—checks of many presidents, from Washington to Lincoln. There was a check for half a cent, and a photograph of the Government voucher for $40,000,000.00 in payment for the French interests in the Panama Canal. There were notes redeemable in rum. And there were private coinages such as the 50-dollar slugs of California, beaver coins of Oregon, Mormon issues of Utah, and the Bechtler coins of the South.

There were coins here that showed something about the art, architecture, mythology, religion, sports, and pleasures of every period of Greece in her glory, and Rome in her fall. The deterioration that followed the universal tragedy of a dead empire was reflected in the barbarous crudities of the coins of the Dark Ages. There was siege money in all its variety; the devices of besieged cities to carry on business in spite of war. It told sometimes of lost causes, of nations going down; it suggested civilizations destroyed and forgotten.

The coins for the Panama-Pacific Exposition were primarily done by artists outside the mint. The Commission of Fine Arts was asked to submit a list of different designers from which the names Evelyn Longman, Robert Aitken, Paul Manship, and Charles Keck were selected. Only the Keck and Aitken designs would be used, though, the half dollar and Quarter Eagle designs eventually being taken over by Barber.

Robert Aitken was assigned to do the fifty-dollar gold piece. In a letter to acting Mint Director T. P. Dewey, written January 23, 1915, he explained his design for both the round and octagonal coins, which included the goddess Minerva on the obverse and the owl on the reverse. Aitken stated:

> . . . in order to express in my design the fact that this coin is struck to commemorate the Panama-Pacific Exposition, and as the Exposition stands for all that Wisdom and Industry have produced, I have used as the central motive of the obverse the head of the virgin goddess Minerva. She is the goddess of wisdom, of skill, of contemplation, of spinning and of weaving, of horticulture and agriculture. Moreover she figures prominently upon the seal of the State of California. This head will make a beautiful pattern in the circle and the use of the Dolphins on the octagonal coin do much to add to its charm, as well as express the uninterrupted water route made possible by the Canal.
>
> "Upon the reverse I use the owl, the bird sacred to Minerva, also the symbol of wisdom, perched upon a branch of western pine, behind which is seen the web of the spider, suggesting industry. . . .

Charles Keck's one-dollar coin proved a radical departure from anything ever attempted on an American coin. It pictured the average man—a canal worker's head topped with a cap. It was jokingly referred to as a "baseball player" design but has been greatly admired by medallic art experts for its effective use of space on a small surface.

There is a definite question as to whether the two-and-one-half-dollar gold piece designed by Evelyn Longman was of poor quality. It is quite possible that Barber killed it because he didn't want an outsider, and a woman at that, handling the details. He was undoubtedly jealous of the men who produced the one-dollar and fifty-dollar coins, also, but could do nothing about them.

According to Longman:

> . . . the head only of the eagle is shown on the side symbolic of the Nation, that its value may be noted at a glance. The dollar sign universally used in the United States has been used in preference to the letter *D*. On the reverse, a cluster of fruit is shown symbolic of California, the greatest fruit growing state in the Union, and in a larger sense symbolic of the general fruition and achievement of the Panama-Pacific exposition. . . .

The references to California are added because the exposition was held in San Francisco.

Barber took over the design. His obverse shows Columbia riding sidesaddle on a mythical creature called the hippocampus. This creature has a dolphin's tail and the body and forefeet of a horse. Columbia is holding a caduceus. The obverse design was meant to represent commerce through the canal and the fight against yellow fever. The reverse has an eagle with upraised wings.

In theory, the Longman work was rejected because she became ill and was unable to finish in the time remaining. However this is questionable, because if illness was the only problem, there is no reason why Barber couldn't have worked from her concept instead of developing a radically different design for the coin.

A coin depicting the William McKinley Memorial in Niles, Ohio (his birthplace) was struck in 1916. The coin was supposed to be a silver dollar, but McKinley had been so concerned with the gold standard

The William McKinley Memorial gold dollar. This coin made President McKinley the first person to have his portrait appear on two different United States coins. It was issued to honor the memorial erected at his birthplace in Niles, Ohio. The designer of the McKinley bust was Charles Barber, and the reverse of the coin, showing the memorial, was designed by George Morgan. Barber was chief engraver of the mint at this time, and Morgan his assistant. ***(Photo courtesy of Krause Publications.)***

when he ran for president, it was felt that a gold coin struck in his honor would be more fitting.

The McKinley Memorial gold dollar marked the second time President McKinley appeared on a coin. He was also modeled on the Louisiana Purchase Exposition gold dollars. But though Charles Barber designed both coin portraits of McKinley, the Memorial gold dollar seems the better likeness. Because of his double use of the design, Barber made McKinley the first president to appear on two different coins.

The reverse of the McKinley coin shows the Niles, Ohio, Memorial. It was designed by George Morgan and is far below the quality of Morgan's other work, such as the silver dollar he created.

The final gold coin to be discussed is the two-and-one-half-dollar gold piece struck to honor the Sesquicentennial of the American Independence. The coin, along with a fifty-cent piece, was authorized on March 3, 1925. Sponsors of the bill originally wanted a one-and-a-half-dollar commemorative coin and a paper-dollar commemorative but the current secretary of the Treasury, Andrew Mellon, was against such creations.

John Sinnock, chief engraver of the United States Mint and the creator of both the Roosevelt dime and the Franklin half-dollar, was asked to prepare the designs. He made the obverse of the gold coin—the last gold commemorative struck by the United States—with a draped figure of Liberty standing on a globe. She holds the "torch of freedom" in her right hand and a scroll representing the Declaration of Independence in her left hand.

The reverse of the gold piece shows Independence Hall. The image is encircled by the words "Sesquicentennial of American Independence—2½ Dollars."

The obverse of the half-dollar shows the dual portraits of Presidents George Washington and Calvin Coolidge facing right. The reverse has an extremely detailed version of the Liberty Bell—much the same design as would appear on the reverse of the Franklin half-dollar, which Sinnock was to create more than twenty years later.

There is some controversy over who really designed the half-dollar. While there is no question that John Sinnock did the final work, some experts feel that it was modeled after original designs by John Frederick Lewis. This remains a debatable point.

The remainder of the coins are of limited historic importance other than to those sponsoring the events. A brief description of each coin and its background will be found accompanying the following illustrations. Despite the "commemorative" label of the bicentennial designs, commemorative coins ended production in 1954 when the last of the Booker T. Washington/George Washington Carver pieces were issued. Current mint hostility towards the commemorative concept coupled with the fact that many of the early issues had to be remelted due to lack of buyer interest makes it unlikely that such coins will appear again in the near future.

23

The Susan B. Anthony Dollar

They might be called the odd couple. One was a two-dollar bill, a denomination few Americans had seen in recent years except for those found at racetracks. The other was a new dollar coin, smaller and more unusual than any coin previously issued. They appeared three years apart but their stories were intricately interwoven.

In 1975, the U. S. Treasury Department realized that the American public could utilize paper money at a denomination larger than a dollar and smaller than the five-dollar bill. The two-dollar bill seemed to fit this picture because it would cut the demand for one-dollar notes almost in half. It was a denomination that could easily be utilized in most transactions. A projection of use from the 1976 fiscal year through the 1981 fiscal year indicated a savings of $35 million, according to Secretary of the Treasury William Simon, who stated:

> A Bicentennial design was selected to help maximize public acceptance and interest, though the new note is not simply a commemorative issue. The Treasury plans to issue 400 million notes per year to assure sufficient volume as a circulating medium and intends the $2 notes become a permanent part of our currency.
>
> At these levels of production the $2 note will provide great convenience to the American people by accommodating the decreased purchasing power of $1 bills due to world wide inflation since 1966 and allowing the public to carry fewer $1 bills.

The women's liberation movement was interested in the new paper money and questioned whether or not a woman would be included. One proposal was for the use of the portrait of Susan B. Anthony, the pioneer women's suffragette. Ms. Anthony, who was born in 1820, was educated as a schoolteacher. She then became involved in the temperance movement, where she discovered that men had no interest in seriously working with women delegates. She had to form her own organization, the Women's State Temperance Society of New York (1852), in order to actively pursue her beliefs.

The shock of sex discrimination in organizations such as the temperance movement had a profound effect on Susan B. Anthony. She became an activist in the fight for human dignity and freedom. She worked for the American Anti-Slavery Society prior to the Civil War and founded the Women's National Loyal League to help free blacks after the war began. After the war was over, she became a pioneering leader of the women's suffrage movement, attempting to obtain the right for women to vote, hold land, receive equal pay for equal work, and otherwise achieve full acceptance in American society.

When the two-dollar bill was under consideration, many Americans felt that Susan B. Anthony should be honored with her portrait on the paper money. American women have been notoriously absent from money of all types, though women represented as the character "Liberty" have appeared since the earliest coinage. A few women have appeared on specialized notes, such as the use of Lucy Pickens on some of the $100 Confederate notes during the Civil War. But these were not official U. S. Government issues; such money had only used the portraits of men. However, the Treasury Department statement concerning the new paper money emphasized the fact that the two-dollar bill would not represent the first break with this male tradition. In answer to the question, "Why was not a portrait of a minority member or a woman chosen for the face of the new bill?" the Department spokesperson replied:

> In response to the recommendations that a new $2 currency note should have a Bicentennial theme, it was determined that the Signing of the Declaration of Independence epitomized the birth of our Nation and was therefore the most appropriate vignette for the back design.
>
> Thomas Jefferson is universally recognized as the author of the Declaration of Independence and, accordingly, the use of his portrait on the face design was judged most suitable in the relationship with the back vignette. The fact that the Jefferson portrait had been used on the earlier $2 U. S. Note contributes to the desirable familiar association by the public of a currency portrait and denomination.
>
> Other possible subjects for the face portrait were considered, including Martin Luther King and Susan B. Anthony. None of the alternative choices are as appropriately and consistently associated with the Bicentennial theme as is Thomas Jefferson.

The reason behind the elimination of Susan B. Anthony from the two-dollar bill seemed acceptable to some, but others felt it was unfair.

Some critics said that the Declaration of Independence was enhanced by the addition of the Constitutional Amendment allowing full rights to women through gaining the vote. Such individuals saw the honoring of only men as a denial of part of our history which the Bicentennial should have celebrated. However, despite such arguments, the bill went through as originally designed.

The two-dollar bill was an immediate hit with collectors and an immediate flop with everyone else. Merchants complained that the bills had no two-dollar slot in their cash drawer and that their clerks often confused the two-dollar with the twenty-dollar bills. The public shunned them for other reasons, one of which was that they were "unlucky."

Numerous superstitions grew up around the idea of a two-dollar bill, but few people were aware of their origins. For example, the two-dollar bill once meant that a pregnant woman would have twins if she or her husband received one in change. This superstition arose during the mid-1800s in poor communities, primarily in the South. Twins were so expensive to feed and clothe that overburdened and underpaid individuals had tremendous fear of such a phenomenon. Thus they shunned the two-dollar bill.

In some parts of the United States, the two-dollar bill was the price of a prostitute. It was shunned because, if a man was carrying it, it meant he was going to use such a woman. A woman carrying it meant that she *was* a prostitute. Naturally these assumptions had no basis in reality, but the people avoided them anyway.

Some two-dollar bills are found with the corners torn off. Supposedly the bad luck of the bills could be canceled by tearing off a corner. This created a triangle, which was a symbol of good luck. When all four corners were gone, some people refused the bills and others accepted them as being "defused" of danger.

Kissing a two-dollar bill was another way to avoid the danger. This superstition dated back to primitive times when some people spat into the cooking pot to make certain the food was safe. Human saliva contains enzymes, and these enzymes actually destroyed aspects of the food which could be dangerous to eat. Since some people got sick when they ate food prepared in pots in which no one had spat, the idea of touching an object with saliva was considered to be good luck. Kissing the two-dollar bill, with the kiss planting the saliva on the potentially dangerous item, solved the "danger" problem.

All the superstitions were old, and few if any government officials ever thought they might have an influence on modern acceptance of the new two-dollar bill. They were wrong. Few two-dollar bills circulated and the problem of expensive one-dollar notes was as great as ever.

In 1979, a new theory was tried. If a dollar coin were created, the dollar bill might be phased out and the coin would circulate along with the previously introduced two-dollar bill.

Frank Gasparro, Chief Engraver of the United States Mint, was asked to create the new dollar coin, which would be smaller than and shaped differently from any previous dollar coin used by the United States. Previous dollar coins had been large and heavy. They were difficult to carry in change. It was felt that size and weight had been a major factor in their failure to circulate over the years. Therefore, the new dollar would be slightly larger and thicker than a quarter, with eleven sides within the circular outer ring.

Gasparro had been thinking about the design of a new coin for many years. He had already handled the creation of the Lincoln Memorial reverse for the Lincoln cent, the Kennedy half-dollar reverse, and both sides of the Eisenhower dollar. However, his one hope was that he could produce a coin in the classic United States tradition. This would be a coin which had a head of Liberty in a somewhat more sophisticated style than the ones used on some of the nation's earliest copper and silver money.

Reproductions of the proposed design for the new dollar were released to the general public, and reaction to the photographs was rapid. The people who had opposed using the portrait of Jefferson on the two-dollar bill were even more vehement in their hostility this time. There were also protests from other special interest groups, all of which felt it was time to use a woman from history, preferably Susan B. Anthony.

Gasparro was disappointed when he learned that the design he had developed over the years would not be used on the new coin. However, he never argued with the change, according to a statement he made to Ed Reiter, a writer for *Coins Magazine.* In the February, 1979, issue, Gasparro was quoted as saying:

"I have a job. I can't dictate. I'm like the fella in Congress who gets a lot of letters. He's got to do what the people want him to do. It's not a hard attitude; you've got to live with the times.

"I am very, very happy that so many numismatists wanted that Liberty design. I'd been working on that since 1968, and I'm glad so many people liked it. But it's not a disappointment that it won't be used on the coin. It's like a job well done—and now you move on to the next. I never look back on what I've done; I always look forward to what I'm going to do next."

Finding images of Ms. Anthony was difficult. She was photographed several times over the years but nothing was found at the age Gasparro chose to use for the engraving of the coin. A half-dozen images were uncovered, only two of which actually served as models and neither of which related to the age he sought. As the engraver explained to Reiter.

"What I made here is a combination of all the portraits, putting her at the age when she was at her height, about fifty—which was hard, because I had no picture of her when she was fifty."

The coin took numerous trials to produce. Most of the designing was done in the afternoon, evenings and on weekends. Gasparro devoted three months to the project. "I had the most trouble with the nose and the mouth," the engraver explained to Reiter. "The chin was no problem. As Miss Anthony got older, her features started drying in. She was just as strong as ever, but her nose got longer, her eyebrows came in more and her chin became recessed. But she still held that strength and dominance that I feel is so important to a portrait."

U. S. Mint officials were determined that the Anthony dollar would go directly into circulation instead of being hoarded as had happened with the first of the Kennedy half-dollars. The Treasury decided to strike and stockpile the coins, releasing them simultaneously on July 2, 1979. This timing was to allow the release to coincide with a new one-dollar Americana Series postage stamp. The stamp issue was not of Susan B. Anthony but the dollar value was the same.

As of April 1, 1979, a total of 71,800,000 Anthony dollars had been struck and stockpiled with a few being released to industry. Vending machines had to be modified for the coins, and companies such as Bell Telephone utilized blanks for testing in case a dollar slot were to be added to pay telephone units. In addition, several thousand coins were released early to banks for employee training. However, none of these were to be placed in the hands of the general public.

On June 4, 1979, an employee of the Michigan National Bank was arrested for the early release for sale of the Anthony dollars. The employee was responsible for approximately 2,000 dollars received by the bank for use in training employees in handling and wrapping the new coins. Such training in advance of the release of a new issue is normal procedure but the bank employee was not authorized to release the coins. To make the matter more serious, the bank official allegedly sold the coins to a dealer from Westchester, Indiana, who was attending the Central States Numismatic Society Convention in Dearborn, Michigan. This dealer reportedly purchased a thousand of the coins for $1.50 each and 300 for two dollars each. He did not attempt to profit from the purchase but sold 345 of the coins to customers and friends at cost as novelty items. The remaining 955 were turned over to the Secret Service.

At this writing, the bank official is awaiting the judicial process. Total penalty could include five years in jail and a $5,000 fine for his action. The coins that ended in circulation have no special premium value because they are no different from the millions of coins released all over the United States on July 2.

The final acceptance of the millions of Anthony dollars has yet to be determined and may take several years to know. The Mint is spending $600,000 promoting the coin use to avoid the problems which occurred with the two-dollar bill. Retailers were encouraged to hold special Susan B. Anthony sales, and various groups were encouraged to hold parties and bingo games in which the Anthony coins were prizes.

If the coin does become popular in the years ahead, cost for production of money will drop as the two-dollar bill becomes more practical for merchants. The coins cost three cents each and are expected to last up to fifteen years each. A paper dollar costs 1.8 cents but has a maximum life expectancy of only eighteen months.

And so the newest United States coin has entered circulation. It is hoped that it will be the more acceptable partner of the odd couple of American money. However, several years of use will pass before anyone is certain what the outcome will be. In the meantime, American coinage has finally honored a woman of historical importance rather than utilizing another representation of the mythical Liberty.

Appendix: Coinage Laws

1

On April 2, 1792, a number of laws establishing the coinage system of the United States were passed. The following sections are among the most important of those acts:

> SECTION 1. Be it enacted by the Senate and House of Representatives of the United States of America in Congress assembled and it is hereby enacted and declared, That a Mint for the purpose of a national coinage be, and the same is established; to be situate and carried on at the seat of the Government of the United States, for the time being: And that for the well conducting of the business of the said Mint there shall be the following officers and persons, namely,—a Director, an assayer, a chief coiner, an engraver, a treasurer.

The second section authorized the director to hire necessary workmen subject to presidential approval. The third section listed the duties of each office. The fourth ordered all officers and the clerk to take an oath promising to perform their duties properly. The fifth authorized the positions of treasurer, assayer, and chief coiner and stated that each must post bonds of ten thousand dollars.

The sixth section authorized salaries for the officers. These ranged from $2,000 for the Mint Director to $1,200 per year for the engraver. The seventh arranged for an accounting to both the Treasury and Congress, and the eighth ordered mint construction.

> SEC. 9: And be it further enacted, That there shall be from time to time struck and coined at the said Mint, coins of gold, silver, and copper, of the following denominations, values, and descriptions, viz. Eagles—each to be of the value of ten dollars or units, and to contain two hundred and forty-seven grains and four eighths of a

The Illinois Centennial half-dollar features a portrait of Lincoln that duplicates the face of the Lincoln statue unveiled in Springfield, Illinois, in August 1918. This coin has an unusual history. Fifty-eight more coins than the one hundred thousand officially authorized were produced. Many went unsold and were placed in bank vaults, where they stayed until the Great Depression. At that time, the coins were put on the market at less than cost to help shore up the finances of struggling banks.

grain of pure, or two hundred and seventy grains of standard gold. Half-eagles—each to be of the value of five dollars, and to contain one hundred and twenty-three grains and six eights of a grain of pure, or one hundred and thirty-five grains of standard gold. Quarter Eagles—each to be of the value of two dollars and a half dollar, and to contain sixty-one grains and seven eighths of a grain of pure, or sixty-seven grains and four eighths of a grain of standard gold. Dollars or Units—each to be of the value of a Spanish milled dollar as the same is now current, and to contain three hundred and seventy-one grains and four sixteenth parts of a grain of pure, or four hundred and sixteen grains of standard silver. Half-Dollars — each to be of half the value of the dollar or unit, and to contain one hundred and eighty-five grains and ten sixteenth parts of a grain of pure, or two hundred and eight grains of standard silver. Quarter Dollars—each to be of one fourth the value of the dollar or unit, and to contain ninety-two grains and thirteen sixteenth parts of a grain of pure, or one hundred and four grains of standard silver. Dismes—each to be of the value of one tenth of a dollar or unit, and to contain thirty-seven grains and two sixteenth parts of a grain of pure, or forty-one grains and three fifth parts of a grain of standard silver. Half Dismes—each to be of the value of one twentieth of a dollar, and to contain eighteen grains and nine sixteenth parts of a grain of pure, or twenty grains and four fifth parts of a grain of standard silver. Cents—each to be of the value of the one hundredth part of a dollar, and to contain eleven penny-weights of copper. Half Cents—each to be of the value of a half a cent, and to contain five penny-weights and half a penny-weight of copper.

SEC. 10. And be it further enacted, That, upon the said coins respectively, there shall be the following devices and legends, namely: Upon one side of each of the said coins there shall be an impression emblematic of liberty, with an inscription of the word Liberty, and the year of the coinage; and upon the reverse of each of the gold and silver coins there shall be the figure or representation of an eagle with this inscription, "United States of America" and upon the reverse of each of the copper coins, there shall be an inscription which shall express the denomination of the piece, namely, cent or half cent, as the case may require.

SEC. 11. And be it further enacted, That the proportional value of gold to silver in all coins which shall by law be current as money within the United States, shall be as fifteen to one according to quantity in weight of pure gold or pure silver; that is to say, every fifteen pounds weight of pure silver shall be of equal value in all payments, with one pound weight of pure gold, and so in proportion as to any greater or less quantities of the respective metals.

SEC. 12. And be it further enacted, That the standard for all gold coins of the United States shall be eleven parts fine to one part alloy; and accordingly that eleven parts in twelve of the entire weight of each of the said coins shall consist of pure gold and the remaining one twelfth part of alloy; and the said alloy shall be composed of silver and copper in such proportions not exceeding one half silver as shall be found convenient; to be regulated by the Director of the Mint, for the time being, with the approbation of the

This coin commemorates the centennial of the state of Maine. It was designed by Anthony de Francisci, who would later become famous for his Peace dollar. It was the second coin to honor a state centennial.

This is the Pilgrim Tercentenary half-dollar, struck to honor the 300th anniversary of the landing of the Pilgrims at Plymouth. It was designed by Cyrus Dallin, who had an excellent reputation for his creation of sculpture relating to the Pilgrims. Coins were issued in 1920 and 1921.

President of the United States, until further provision shall be made by law. And to the end that the necessary information may be had in order to the making of such further provision it shall be the duty of the Director of the Mint, at the expiration of a year after commencing the operations of the said Mint, to report to Congress the practice thereof during the said year, touching the composition of the alloy of the said gold coins, the reasons for such practice, and the experiments and observations which shall have been made concerning the effects of different proportions of silver and copper in the said alloy.

SEC. 13. And be it further enacted, That the standard for all silver coins of the United States, shall be one thousand four hundred and eighty-five parts fine to one hundred and seventy-nine parts alloy; and accordingly that one thousand four hundred and eighty-five parts in one thousand six hundred and sixty-four parts of the entire weight of each of the said coins shall consist of pure silver, and the remaining one hundred and seventy-nine parts of alloy; which alloy shall be wholly of copper.

SEC. 14. And be it further enacted, That it shall be lawful for any person or persons to bring to the said Mint gold and silver bullion, in order to their being coined; and that the bullion so brought shall be there assayed and coined as speedily as may be after the receipt thereof, and that free of expense to the person or persons by whom the same shall have been delivered, shall upon demand receive in lieu thereof coins of the same species of bullion which shall have been so delivered, weight for weight, of the pure gold or pure silver therein contained: Provided nevertheless, That it shall be at the mutual option of the party or parties bringing such bullion, and of the Director of the said Mint to make an immediate exchange of coins for standard bullion with a deduction of one half per cent from the weight of the pure gold, or pure silver contained in the said bullion, as an indemnification to the Mint for the time which will necessarily be required for coining the said bullion, and for the advance which shall have been so made in coins. And it shall be the duty of the Secretary of the Treasury to furnish the said Mint from time to time whenever the state of the Treasury will admit thereof, with such sums as may be necessary for effecting the said exchanges, to be replaced as speedily as may be out of the coins which shall have been made of the bullion for which the monies so furnished shall have been exchanged; and the said deduction of one half per cent shall constitute a fund towards defraying the expenses of the said Mint.

SEC. 15. And be it further enacted, That the bullion which shall be brought as aforesaid to the Mint to be coined, shall be coined and the equivalent thereof in coins rendered, if demanded, in the order in which the said bullion shall have been brought or delivered, giving priority according to priority of delivery only, and without preference to any person or persons: and if any preference shall be given contrary to the direction aforesaid, the officer by whom such undue preference shall be given, shall in each case forfeit and pay one thousand dollars; to be recovered with costs of suit. And to the

This coin was issued to mark the centennial of Missouri's becoming a state. A Frontiersman, complete with coonskin cap, appears on the coin. Although originally intended to honor Daniel Boone, the design apparently was not accurate and instead was meant to represent all of the early frontiersmen. It was designed by Robert Aitken, who was also involved with the Panama-Pacific International Exposition coins.

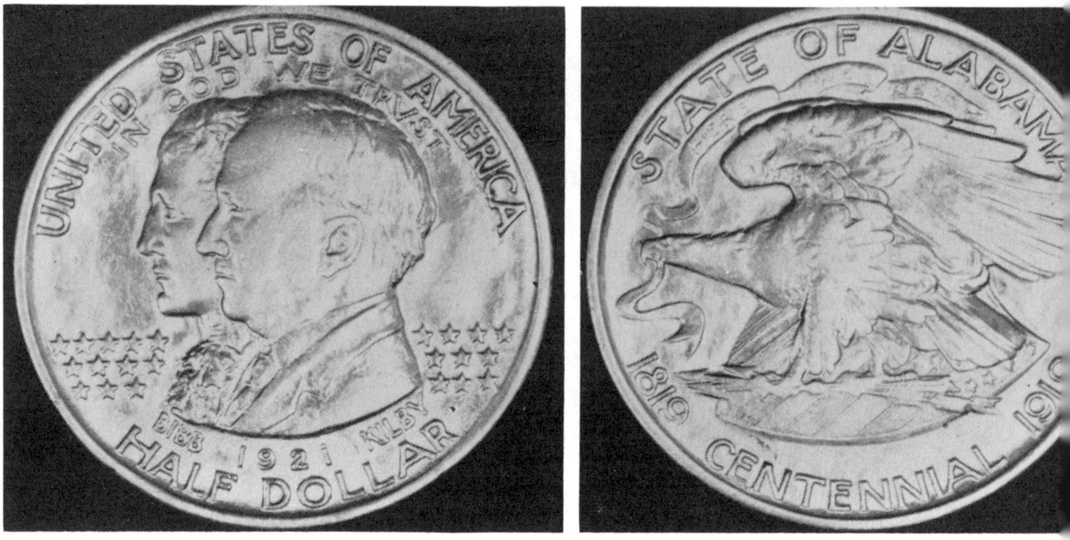

This coin marked the centennial of Alabama's admission to statehood. It was designed by Laura Fraser and was the first coin ever issued in the United States to show a living individual. The man is Thomas Kilby, who was governor when the coin was issued. The other image is that of William Bibb, who was the first governor of Alabama.

end that it may be known if such preference shall at any time be given, the assayer or officer to whom the said bullion shall be delivered to be coined shall give to the person or persons bringing the same, a memorandum in writing under his hand, denoting the weight, fineness and value thereof, together with the day and order of its delivery into the Mint.

SEC. 16. And be it further enacted, That all the gold and silver coins which shall have been struck at, and issued from the said Mint, shall be a lawful tender in all payments whatsoever, those of full weight according to the respective values herein before declared, and those of less than full weight at values proportional to their respective weights.

SEC. 17. And be it further enacted, That it shall be the duty of the respective officers of the said Mint, carefully and faithfully to use their best endeavours that all the gold and silver coins which shall be struck at the said Mint shall be, as nearly as may be, comformable to the several standards and weights aforesaid, and that the copper whereof the cents and half cents aforesaid may be composed, shall be of good quality.

SEC. 20. And be it further enacted, That the money of account of the United States shall be expressed in dollars or units, dismes or tenths, cents or hundredths, and milles or thousandths, a disme being the tenth part of a dollar, a cent the hundredth part of a dollar, a mille the thousandth part of a dollar, and that all accounts in the public offices and all proceedings in the courts of the United States shall be kept and had in conformity to this regulation.

This coin honored the 100th anniversary of the birth of President Ulysses Grant. It was designed by Laura Fraser, and the design was repeated on a gold dollar commemorative in addition to the half-dollar commemorative.

2

On May 8, 1792, Congress authorized the use of copper for coinage. Copper coins were considered a necessity by the government rather than "real money" like gold and silver pieces. The public felt the same way, and the chapter on the Large cent includes the numerous ways people used copper coins other than as a circulating medium.

> SEC. 1. "Be it enacted . . . That the Director of the Mint, with the approbation of the President of the United States, be authorized to contract for and purchase a quantity of copper, not exceeding one hundred and fifty tons, and that the said Director, as soon as the needful preparations shall be made, cause the copper by him purchased to be coined at the Mint into cents and half cents, pursuant to "the act establishing a mint, and regulating the coins of the United States"; and that the said cents and half cents, as they shall be coined, be paid into the Treasury of the United States thence to issue into circulation.
>
> SEC. 2. And be it further enacted, That after the expiration of six calendar months from the time when there shall have been paid into the Treasury by the said Director, in cents and half cents, a sum not less than fifty thousand dollars, which time shall forthwith be announced by the Treasurer in at least two gazettes or newspapers, published at the seat of the Government of the United States, for

This coin commemorates the 100th anniversary of the promulgation of the Monroe Doctrine, which was meant to prevent foreign influence in both North and South America. John Quincy Adams, who is shown on the coin, advocated an anticolonial attitude towards foreign governments. The governments were not to establish further colonies in the New World. James Monroe, the other man shown on the coin, insisted that foreign countries not become involved in the affairs of South America.

This coin marks the 300th anniversary of the settlement of New Netherland and the Middle States in 1642. The settlement was made by the Dutch West India Company, the Huguenots and the Walloons. The Huguenots immigrated from France, and the Walloons were French-speaking natives of southern Belgium. Both groups had a common bond in that they followed the Protestant teachings of John Calvin. This coin was issued in 1924 and was designed by George Morgan, who was chief engraver of the United States Mint at the time. It was to be his last coin design. He died in January of the following year (1925).

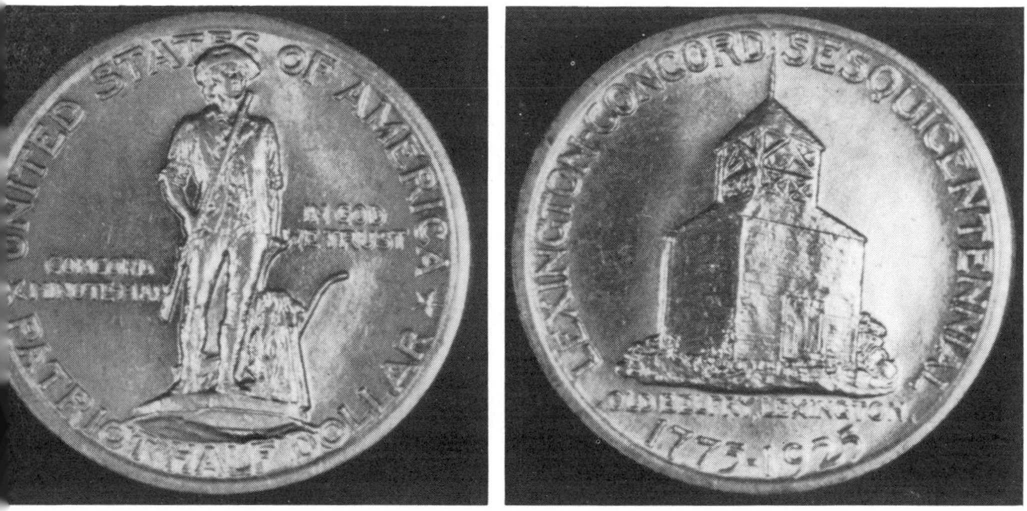

This coin honors the 150th anniversary of the battle of Lexington and Concord. It was designed by Chester Beach and features the statue *The Minute Man,* which was erected in Concord, Massachusetts. Interestingly enough, Beach was just twenty-three years of age when he designed this coin.

Stone Mountain, Georgia has a monument to Confederate soldiers. The carving of a monument to General Lee, General Jackson, and President Jefferson Davis was begun by Gutzon Borglum, who also designed the half-dollar. However, due to disputes and various funding problems, the Stone Mountain work was continued by Augustus Lukeman and, later, by Walter Kirkland Hancock. The coin was authorized in 1924.

The commemorative half-dollar for the California Diamond Jubilee. This day honored the seventy-fifth anniversary of California's admission to statehood. The obverse of the coin shows a prospector panning for gold. The reverse shows a grizzly bear. The coin was authorized in 1925. (Photo Courtesy of Krause Publications.)

This coin commemorates the 100th anniversary of the founding of Fort Vancouver. It was created by Laura Fraser and was a modification of a design by an unknown sculptor discussed in the chapter on the works of Laura and James Fraser.

the time being, no copper coins or pieces whatsoever, except the said cents and half cents, shall pass current as money, or shall be paid, or offered to be paid or received in payment for any debt, demand, claim, matter or thing whatsoever; and all copper coins or pieces, except the said cents and half cents, which shall be paid or offered to be paid or received in payment contrary to the prohibition aforesaid, shall be forfeited, and every person by whom any of them shall have been so paid or offered to be paid or received in payment, shall also forfeit the sum of ten dollars, and the said forfeiture and penalty shall and may be recovered with costs of suit for the benefit of any person or persons by whom information of the incurring thereof shall have been given.

3

On January 14, 1793, the weight of copper coins was changed so: ". . . That every cent shall contain two hundred and eight grains of copper, and every half cent shall contain one hundred and four grains of copper; and that so much of the act, entitled "An act establishing a Mint, and regulating the coins of the United States," as respects the weight of cents and half cents, shall be, and the same is hereby repealed."

4

The circulation of foreign coins within the United States was a serious problem. Dependence upon coinage of uncertain weight, fineness, and legitimacy caused tremendous difficulties for merchants and public alike. It was important for the United States to be self-sufficient in the area of coinage, but for the first few years, this was impossible. Thus the necessity for a law that would regulate the value of foreign coins. On February 9, 1793, an act was passed stating:

Section 1. Be it enacted . . . that, from and after the first day of July next, foreign gold and silver coins shall pass current as money within the United States, and be a legal tender for the payment of all debts and demands, at the several and respective rates following, and not otherwise, viz: . . . Spanish milled dollars, at the rate of one hundred cents for each dollar the actual weight whereof shall not be less than seventeen pennyweights and seven grains; and in proportion for the parts of a dollar. Crowns of France, at the rate of one hundred and ten cents for each crown, the actual weight thereof shall not be less than eighteen pennyweights and seventeen grains, and in proportion for the parts of a crown.

Sec. 2. Provided always, and be it further enacted, That at the expiration of three years next ensuing the time when the coinage of gold and silver, agreeably to the act, entitled "An act establishing a

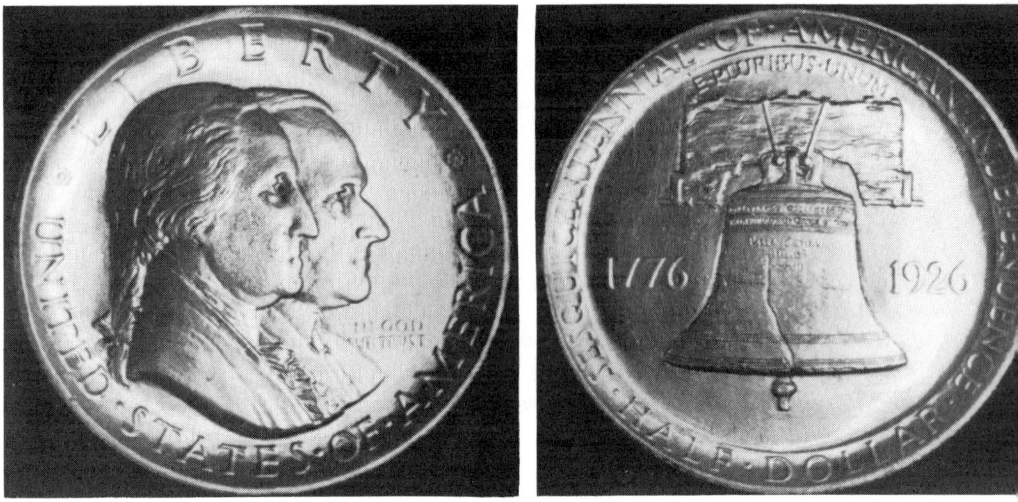

This coin was authorized to honor the 150th anniversary of the signing of the Declaration of Independence (1926). It was created by John Sinnock, though it may have been modeled after a design originated by John Lewis. The Liberty Bell depicted on the reverse of the coin is almost identical to the design Sinnock used for the Franklin half-dollar, which went into circulation in 1948.

A Dollar Coin Sinnock designed at the same time he did the silver coins. The coin shows Independence Hall in Philadelphia and a standing figure of Liberty.

Mint, and regulating the coins of the United States," shall commence at the mint of the United States, (which time shall be announced by the proclamation of the President of the United States,) all foreign gold coins and all foreign silver coins, except Spanish milled dollars and parts of such dollars, shall cease to be a legal tender, as aforesaid.

This coin commemorated the blazing of the Oregon Trail. It is the only coin ever designed by a husband and wife and is considered one of the most beautiful of all the commemoratives produced over the years. It was authorized in 1926.

> SEC. 3. And be it further enacted, that all foreign gold and silver coins, (except Spanish milled dollars, and parts of such dollars,) which shall be received in payment for monies due to the United States, after the said time, when the coining of gold and silver coins shall begin at the Mint of the United States, shall previously to their being issued in circulation, be coined anew, in conformity to the act, entitled "An act establishing a Mint and regulating the coins of the United States."

5

In June 1834, two changes in the coinage laws were enacted by Congress. The first, on June 25, changed the legal-tender status of foreign coins circulating within the United States. The second, three days later, changed the gold-silver ratios. The acts, in part, read:

> That from and after the passage of this act, the following silver coins shall be of the legal value, and shall pass current as money within the United States, by tale, for the payments of all debts and demands, at the rate of one hundred cents the dollar, that is to say, the dollars of Mexico, Peru, Chile, and Central America, of not less weight than four hundred and fifteen grains each, and those re-stamped in Brazil of the like weight of not less fineness than ten ounces fifteen pennyweights of pure silver, in the troy pound of

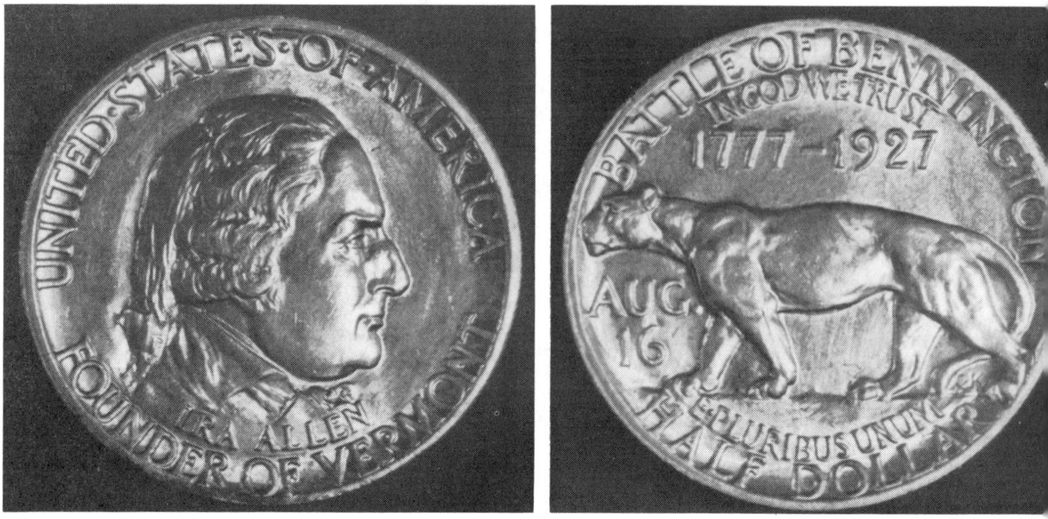

Charles Keck designed this coin to honor the 150th anniversary of the battle of Bennington, which resulted in an independent Vermont. The coin features Ira Allan, the brother of Ethan Allan. He then organized the Green Mountain Boys to protect the land from attack from New York during the Revolutionary War. Ira was more statesman than fighter and was involved in the various conventions that led to the state's independence.

twelve ounces of standard silver: and the five franc pieces of France, when of not less fineness than ten ounces and sixteen pennyweights in twelve ounces troy weight of standard silver, and weighing not less than three hundred and eighty-four grains each at the rate of ninety-three cents each.

That the gold coins of the United States shall contain the following quantities of metal, that is to say: each eagle shall contain two hundred and thirty-two grains of pure gold, and two hundred and fifty-eight grains of standard gold: each half eagle one hundred and sixteen grains of pure gold, and one hundred and twenty-nine grains of standard gold: each quarter eagle shall contain fifty-eight grains of pure gold, and sixty-four and a half grains of standard gold; every such eagle shall be of the value of ten dollars; every such half eagle shall be of the value of five dollars; and every such quarter eagle shall be of the value of two dollars and fifty cents; and the said gold coins shall be receivable in all payments, when of full weight, according to their respective values; and when of less than full weight, at less values, proportioned to their respective actual weights.

SECTION 2. And be it further enacted, That all standard gold or silver deposited for coinage after the thirty-first of July next, shall be paid for in coin under the direction of the Secretary of the Treasury, within five days from the making of such deposit, deducting from the amount of said deposit of gold and silver one-half of one per centum: Provided, That no deduction shall be

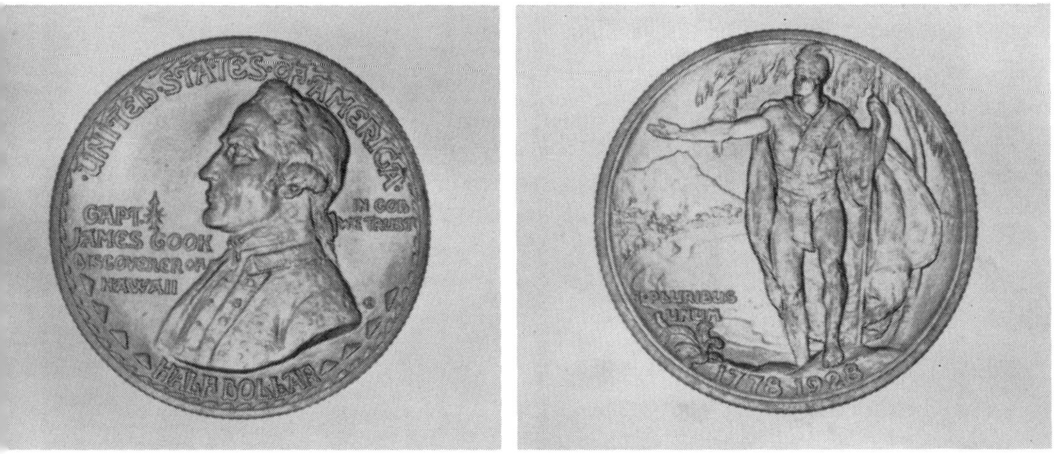

The Hawaiian Sesquicentennial half-dollar commemorated the 150th anniversary of Hawaii's discovery by Captain James Cook. The design was originated by Juliett Fraser of Honolulu (no relation to James and Laura Fraser) and was later altered by Chester Beach. At the bottom of the coin are eight tiny volcanoes, representing the eight largest volcanic islands. (Photo courtesy of Krause Publications.)

This coin commemorates the 300th anniversary of the founding of Maryland. The obverse shows Cecil Calvert, Lord Baltimore. It was created by Hans Schuler. The coin, authorized in 1934, was the first of Franklin Roosevelt's administration.

made unless said advance be required by such depositor within forty days.

SEC. 5. And be it further enacted, That this act shall be in force from and after the thirty-first day of July, in the year one thousand eight hundred and thirty-four.

This coin commemorated the 100th anniversary of the independence of Texas. It was designed by Pompeo Coppini, a transplanted New Yorker living in Texas. The reverse depicts Victory and the Alamo. During the ten year period that Texas was an independent republic, one of the leaders, Mirabeau Lamar, had hoped to make it an empire stretching to the Pacific coast. Had he succeeded, it might have rivaled the United States for power.

The 1934 Daniel Boone half-dollar, commemorating the 200th anniversary of his birth. The coin was designed by Augustus Lukeman, the second man to work on the Stone Mountain Memorial in Georgia.

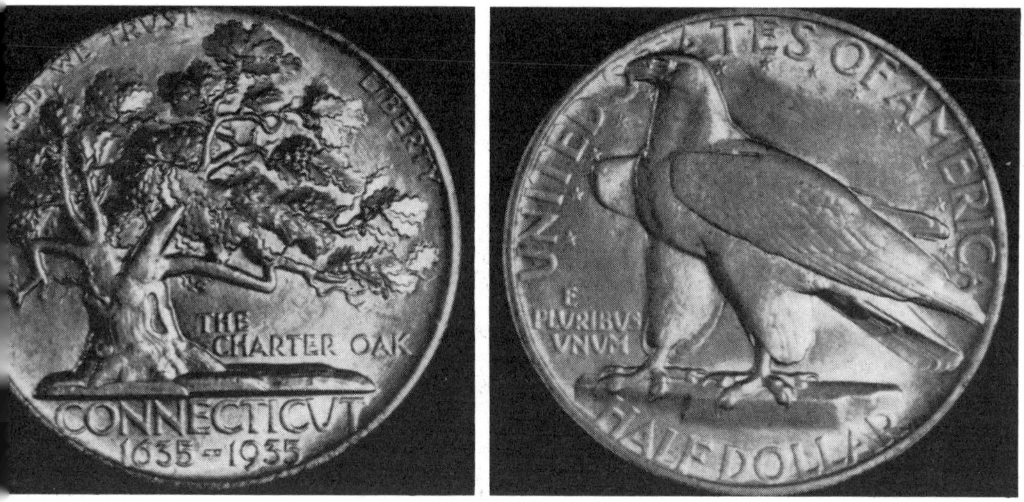

This coin commemorates the 300th anniversary of the founding of Connecticut. The obverse depicts the Charter Oak Tree in which the statute, or charter, of the colony was hidden when it was learned that it conflicted with the wishes of the king of England.

6

On January 18, 1837, the United States Congress made several major changes in the coin laws. Although these were quite extensive, only the high points will be quoted here.

> SECTION 8. And be it further enacted, That the standard for both gold and silver coins of the United States shall hereafter be such that of one thousand parts by weight, nine hundred shall be of pure metal, and one hundred of alloy; and the alloy of the silver coins shall be of copper; and the alloy of the gold coins shall be of copper and silver, provided that the silver do not exceed one-half of the whole alloy.
>
> SEC. 9. And be it further enacted, That of the silver coins, the dollar shall be of the weight of two hundred and six and one-fourth grains; the quarter dollar of the weight of one hundred and three and one-eighth grains; the dime, or tenth part of a dollar, of the weight of forty-one and a quarter grains; and the half dime or twentieth part of a dollar, of the weight of twenty grains, and five-eighths of a grain. And that dollars, half dollars, and quarter dollars, dimes, and half dimes, shall be legal tenders of payment according to their nominal value, for any sums whatever.
>
> SEC. 10. And be it further enacted, That of the gold coins, the weight of the eagle shall be two hundred and fifty-eight grains; that of the half eagle one hundred and twenty-nine grains; and that of the quarter eagle sixty-four and one-half grains. And that for all sums whatever, the eagle shall be a legal tender of payment for ten

This coin commemorates the 100th anniversary of the admission of Arkansas into the Union. It was designed by Edward Burr and executed by Emily Bates. It was authorized in 1934 but dated 1936. It was actually issued from 1935 through 1939.

dollars; the half eagle for five dollars; and the quarter eagle for two and a half dollars.

SEC. 11. And be it further enacted, That the silver coins heretofore issued at the Mint of the United States, and the gold coins issued since the thirty-first day of July, one thousand eight hundred and thirty-four, shall continue to be legal tenders of payment for their nominal values, on the same terms as if they were of the coinage provided for by this act.

SEC. 12. And be it further enacted, That of the copper coins, the weight of the cent shall be one hundred and sixty-eight grains, and the weight of the half-cent eighty-four grains. And the cent shall be considered of the value of one hundredth part of a dollar, and the half cent of the value of one two-hundredth part of a dollar.

SEC. 13. And be it further enacted, That upon the coins struck at the Mint there shall be the following devices and legends: upon one side of each of said coins there shall be an impression emblematic of liberty, with an inscription of the word Liberty, and the year of the coinage: and upon the reverse of each of the gold and silver coins, there shall be the figure or representation of an eagle with the inscription United States of America, and a designation of the value of the coin; but on the reverse of the dime and half dime, cent and half cent, the figure of the eagle shall be omitted.

SEC. 33. And be it further enacted, That copper bullion shall be purchased for the Mint, from time to time by the treasurer, under instructions from the Director; that the cost shall be paid from the fund hereinafter provided for; and that the copper bullion shall be of good quality, and in form of planchets fit for passing at once into the hands of the chief coiner.

A second design of the same coin. While the first coin shows the heads of Liberty and an Indian chief, the second shows Senator Joseph Robinson, an important politician of the time.

SEC. 35. And be it further enacted, That it shall be the duty of the treasurer of the Mint to deliver the copper coins, in exchange for their legal equivalent in other money, to any persons who shall apply for them; Provided, That the sum asked for be not less than a certain amount, to be determined by the Director, and that it be not so great as, in his judgement, to interfere with the capacity of the Mint to supply other applicants.

SEC. 36. And be it further enacted, That the copper coins may, at the discretion of the Director, be delivered in any of the principal cities and towns of the United States, at the cost of the Mint for transportation.

SEC. 37. And be it further enacted, That the money received by the treasurer in exchange for copper coins shall form a fund in his hands, which shall be used to purchase copper planchets, and to pay the expense of transportation of copper coins; and that if there be a surplus, the same shall be appropriate to defray the contingent expenses of the Mint.

7

On March 3, 1835, Congress approved "An Act to establish branches of the Mint of the United States." That Act read:

Be it enacted, &c., That branches of the mint of the United States shall be established as follows: one branch at the city of New Orleans, for the coinage of gold and silver; one branch at the town of Charlotte, in Mecklenburg county, in the State of North Carolina, for the coinage of gold only; and one branch at or near

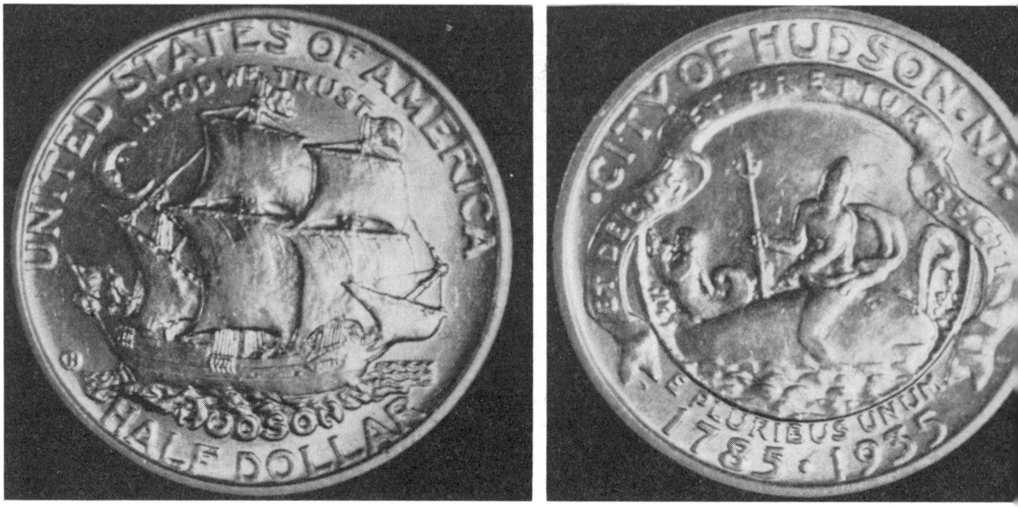

This coin commemorates the 150th anniversary of the founding of Hudson, New York. It was designed by Chester Beach and honors Henry Hudson, an English navigator who sought a northwest passage to the Orient in 1607. He did not find it, but he did find New York and sailed up the river that is now named after him. However, he called it the North River rather than being so bold as to give it his own name.

Dahlohnega, in Lumpkin county, in the State of Georgia, also for the coinage of gold only. And for the purpose of purchasing sites, erecting suitable buildings and completing the necessary combinations of machinery for the several branches aforesaid, the following sums, to be paid out of any money in the treasury not otherwise appropriated, shall be, and hereby are, appropriated: for the branch at New Orleans, the sum of two hundred thousand dollars; for the branch at Charlotte, fifty thousand dollars; for the branch at Dahlohnega, fifty thousand dollars.

SECTION 2. And be it further enacted, That, so soon as the necessary buildings are erected for the purpose of well-conducting the business of each of the said branches, the following officers shall be appointed upon the nomination of the President, and by and with the advice and consent of the Senate: One superintendent, one treasurer, one assayer, one chief coiner, one melter, and one refiner. And the superintendent of each mint shall engage and employ as many clerks and as many subordinate workmen and servants as shall be provided for by law; and the salaries of the said officers and clerks shall be as follows:

For the branch at New Orleans, to the superintendent, the sum of two thousand five hundred dollars; to the treasurer, the sum of two thousand dollars; to the chief coiner, the sum of two thousand dollars; to the assayer, melter, and refiner, the sum of two thousand dollars each; to two clerks, the sum of twelve hundred dollars each; to the subordinate workmen and servants, not exceeding twenty in number, such wages and allowances as are customary and reasonable, according to their respective stations and occupations. And for the purpose of paying the said salaries, wages, allowances, and the incidental expenses of the said branches of the mint, for the year one thousand eight hundred and thirty five, the following sums, to be paid out of any money in the treasury not otherwise appropriated, be, and the same hereby are, appropriated: for the branch at New Orleans, the sum of thirty-five thousand dollars; for the branches at Charlotte and Dahlohnega, the sum of fifteen thousand dollars each.

SEC. 3. And be it further enacted, That the officers and clerks to be appointed under this act, before entering upon the duties thereof, shall take an oath or affirmation, before some judge of the United States, faithfully and diligently to perform the duties thereof, and shall each become bound to the United States of America, with one or more sureties, to the satisfaction of the Director of the Mint and the Secretary of the Treasury, with condition for the faithful and diligent performance of the duties of their offices.

SEC. 4. And be it further enacted, That the general direction of the business of the said branches of the Mint of the United States shall be under the control and regulation of the Director of the Mint at Philadelphia, subject to the approbation of the Secretary of the Treasury; and for that purpose it shall be the duty of the said Director to prescribe such regulations and require such returns

This coin commemorates the California-Pacific International Exposition of 1935-36. In a sense, it makes amends for the absence of a coin commemorating the Panama-California Exposition of 1915 held in San Diego. That particular exposition never had a commemorative because it was greatly overshadowed by the Panama-Pacific International Exposition of the same year. The California-Pacific International Exposition was also held in San Diego and cost approximately twenty million dollars to erect. The coin was designed by Robert Aitken.

This coin marks the 400th anniversary of the opening of the Old Spanish Trail by Cabeza de Vaca. It was designed by L. W. Hoffecker, and the models were made by Edward Senn. Issued in 1935, the coin depicts the states of Texas, Louisiana, Mississippi, Alabama, and Florida, all of which lay on the de Vaca's route. Interestingly enough, the designer of the coin is one of the few coin artists who have also been interested in coin collecting as a hobby. Hoffecker was eventually named president of the American Numismatic Association.

periodically and occasionally as shall appear to him to be necessary for the purpose of carrying into effect the intention of this act in establishing the said branches; also, for the purpose of discriminating the coin which shall be stamped at each branch, and at the mint itself; also, for the purpose of preserving uniformity of weight, form, and fineness, in the coins stamped at each place; and, for that purpose, to require the transmission and delivery to him, at the Mint, from time to time, such parcels of the coinage of each branch as he shall think proper, to be subjected to such assays and tests as he shall direct.

SEC. 5. And be it further enacted, That all the laws and parts of laws made for the regulation of the mint of the United States, and for the government of the officers and persons employed therein, and for the punishment of all offences connected with the mint or coinage of the United States, shall be, and the same are hereby, declared to be in full force in relation to each of the branches of the mint by this act established, so far as the same shall be applicable thereto.

8

On February 21, 1857, the mint withdrew foreign coins from

This coin celebrates the 300th anniversary of the founding of Providence, Rhode Island. The coin shows Roger Williams in a canoe signaling his friendship to an Indian on the shore. The coin was designed by Abraham Carey and John Benson.

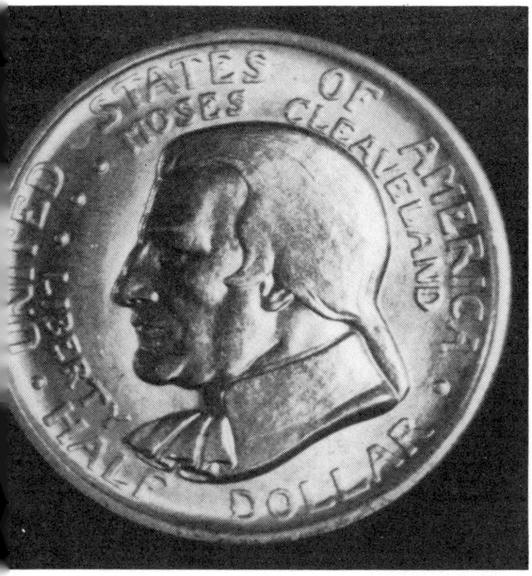

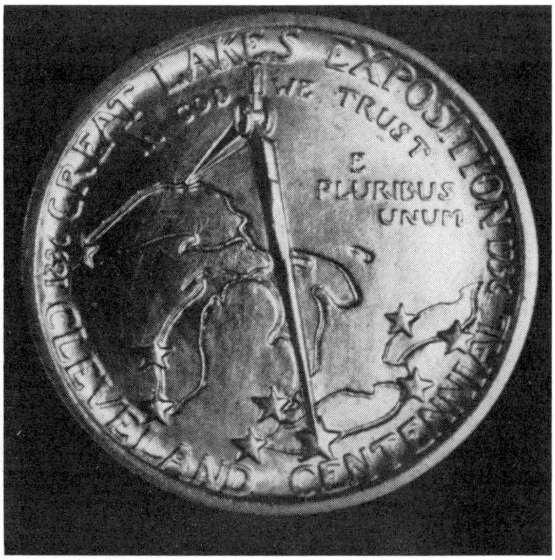

This coin, designed by Brenda Putnan and authorized in 1936, commemorates the Great Lakes Exposition held in Cleveland, Ohio, in connection with that city's 100th anniversary. The obverse shows Moses Cleaveland, for whom the city was named. Because of its closeness to the automobile manufacturing cities, the exposition was generously funded with a budget of twenty-five million dollars. It covered 150 acres and had four million people in attendance during 1936 and 1937, even though two other expositions were being held in the country at the same time.

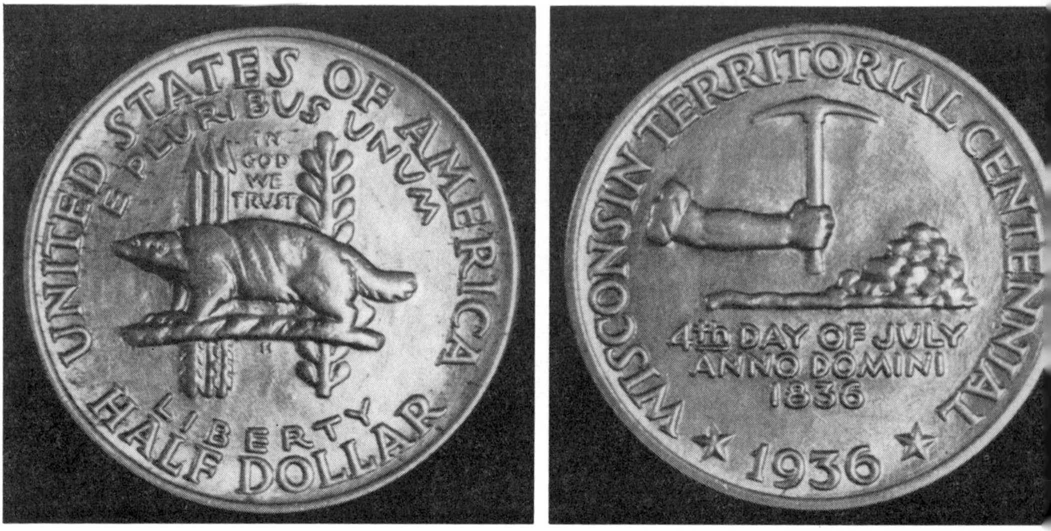

This coin commemorates the 100th anniversary of the opening of the Wisconsin Territory. The obverse depicts a badger, the state animal. The reverse, showing an arm holding a pickaxe over a pile of lead ore, is identical to the territorial seal. The coin, authorized in 1936, was prepared by David Parsons (a University of Wisconsin art student) and Benjamin Hawkins of New York.

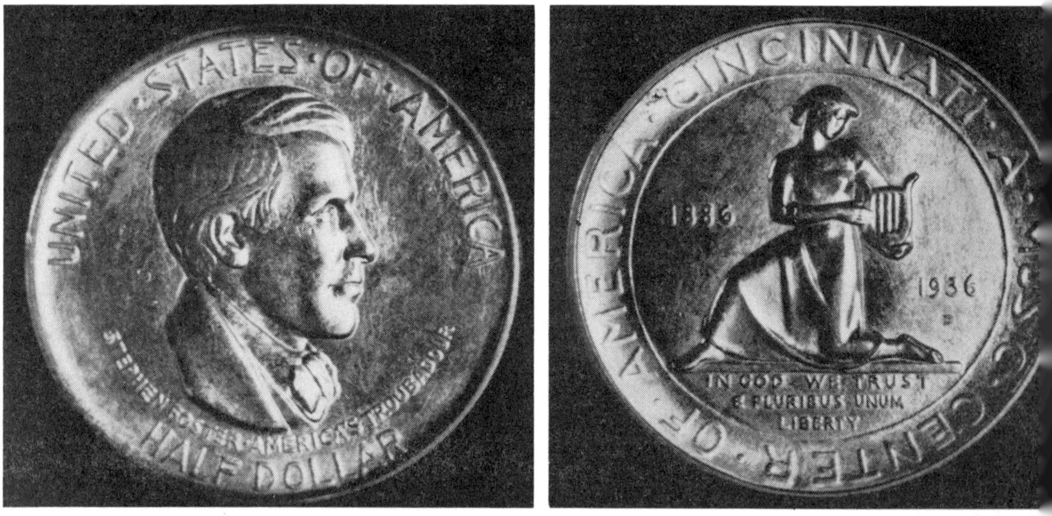

This coin commemorates the 50th anniversary of the Cincinnati, Ohio music center. The coin depicts Stephen Foster on the obverse and a figure of the goddess of Music holding a lyre, on the reverse. Cincinnati was host to a major music festival in 1873 and continued holding one every two years. The city's Conservatory of Music dates back to 1867, and there is also a College of Music located there.

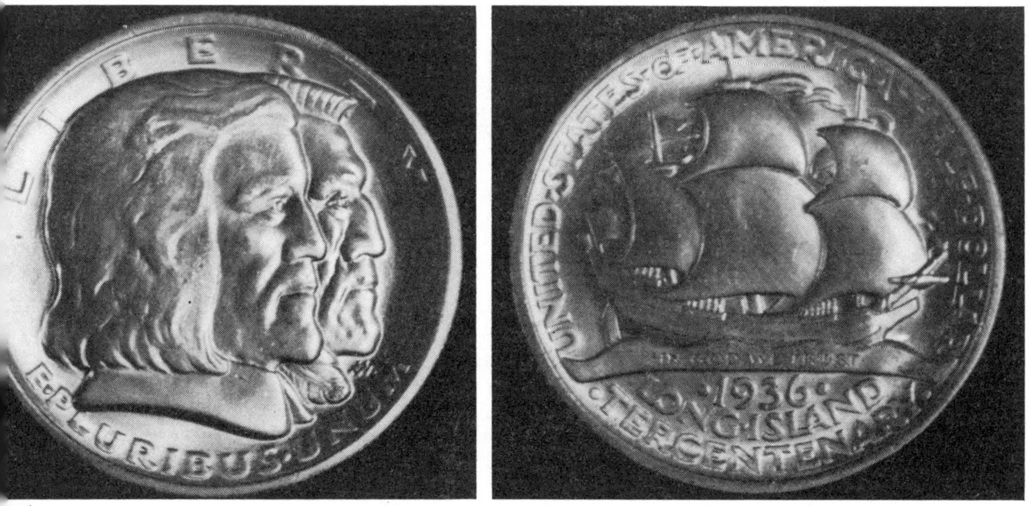

This coin commemorates the 300th anniversary of the settling of Long Island, New York. The coin was designed by Howard Weinman, one of the sons of Adolph Weinman, the designer of the Walking Liberty half-dollar and the Mercury dime. The coin features a Dutch pioneer and an Indian on the obverse. It was authorized in 1936.

circulation as legal tender and authorized the new copper-nickel cent. The law stated:

> Be it enacted . . . That the pieces commonly known as the quarter, eighth, and sixteenth of the Spanish pillar dollar, and of the Mexican dollar, shall be receivable at the Treasury of the United States, and its several offices, and at the several post-offices and land-offices, at the rates of valuation following,—that is to say, the fourth of a dollar, or piece of two reals, at twenty cents; the eighth of a dollar, or piece of one real, at ten cents; and the sixteenth of a dollar, or half real, at five cents.
>
> Sec. 2. And be it further enacted, That the said coins, when so received, shall not again be paid out, or put in circulation, but shall be recoined by the Mint. And it shall be the duty of the Director of the Mint, with the approval of the Secretary of the Treasury, to prescribe such regulations as may be necessary and proper, to secure their transmission to the Mint for recoinage, and the return or distribution of the proceeds thereof, when deemed expedient, and to prescribe such forms of account as may be approximate and applicable to the circumstances; Provided, That the expenses incident to such transmission or distribution, and of recoinage, shall be charged against the account of silver profit and loss, and the net profits, if any, shall be paid from time to time into the Treasury of the United States.
>
> Section 3. And be it further enacted, That all former acts authorizing the currency of foreign gold or silver coins, and declaring the same a legal tender in payment for debts, are hereby

This coin, designed by Walter Rich in 1936, commemorates the 300th anniversary of the founding of York County, Maine.

repealed; but it shall be the duty of the Director of the Mint to cause assays to be made, from time to time, of such foreign coins as may be known to our commerce, to determine their average weight, fineness, and value, and to embrace in his annual report a statement of the results thereof.

SEC. 4. And be it further enacted, That from and after the passage of this act, the standard weight of the cent coined at the Mint shall be seventy-two grains, or three twentieths of one ounce troy, with no greater deviation than four grains in each piece; and said cent shall be composed of eighty-eight per centum of copper and twelve per centum of nickel, of such shape and device as may be fixed by the Director of the Mint, with the approbation of the Secretary of the Treasury; and the coinage of the half cent shall cease.

SEC. 5. And be it further enacted, That the Treasurer of the Mint, under the instruction of the Secretary of the Treasury, shall, from time to time, purchase from the bullion fund of the Mint the materials necessary for the coinage of such cent piece, and transfer the same to the proper operative officers of the Mint to be manufactured and returned in coin. And the laws in force relating to the Mint and the coinage of the precious metals, and in regard to the sale and distribution of the copper coins, shall, so far as applicable, be extended to the coinage herein provided for: Provided; That the net profits of said coinage, ascertained in like manner as is prescribed in the second section of this act, shall be transferred to the Treasury of the United States.

SEC. 6. And be it further enacted, That it shall be lawful to pay out the said cents at the Mint in exchange for any of the gold and silver coins of the United States, and also in exchange for the former copper coins issued; and it shall be lawful to transmit

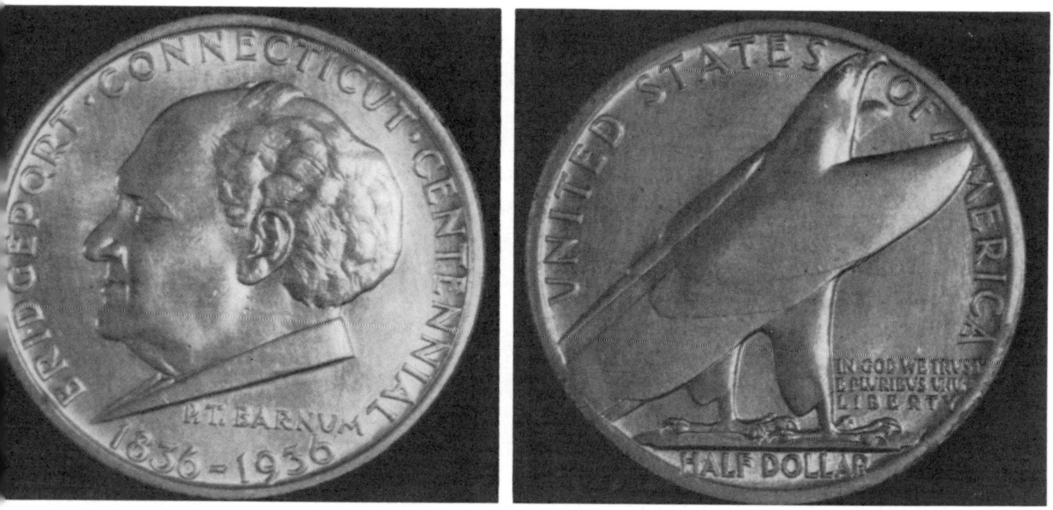

This coin commemorates the 100th anniversary of the incorporation of Bridgeport, Connecticut, as a city. Oddly enough, the coin features a head of Phineas T. Barnum, who was once mayor of that city. He became famous for his shows. Among his stable of performers were "General Tom Thumb" and the "Swedish Nightingale," Jenny Lind, one of the most famous singers of the day. He eventually teamed with James Bailey to form the Barnum and Bailey circus. The coin was designed by Henry Kreiss.

This coin celebrates the 150th anniversary of the granting of the city charter of Lynchburg, Virginia. The coin, designed by Charles Keck, features a bust of Carter Glass, who was a leading newspaperman, state senator, Congressman, and eventually secretary of the Treasury under President Wilson. Later he was elected United States Senator from Virginia. In 1933, three years before this coin was authorized, Glass co-authored the act establishing the Federal Deposit Insurance Corporation, which insures bank deposits so that a repeat of the bank failures of the Depression will not be possible.

This coin, designed by Trygve Rovelstad, honors the 100th anniversary of the city of Elgin, Illinois. It features a head of a bearded pioneer, and the reverse shows the pioneer memorial erected in that city.

parcels of the said cents, from time to time, to the assistant treasurers, depositaries, and other officers of the United States, under general regulations proposed by the Directors of the Mint, and approved by the Secretary of the Treasury, for exchange as aforesaid. And it shall also be lawful for the space of two years from the passage of this act and no longer, to pay out at the Mint the cents aforesaid for the fractional parts of the dollar hereinbefore named, at their nominal value of twenty-five, twelve-and-a-half, and six-and-a-quarter cents, respectively.

SEC. 7. And be it further enacted, That hereafter the Director of the Mint shall make his annual report to the Secretary of the Treasury, up to the thirtieth of June in each year, so that the same may appear in his annual report to Congress on the finances.

9

The Flying Eagle cents, discussed in the chapter on Civil War coinage, are of great importance in that they represent a radical change in the size and composition of the one-cent piece. An interesting historical document relating to this coin was written by Mint Director James Ross Snowden on February 9, 1856. It was uncovered by Walter Thompson who wrote of it in the *Numismatic Scrapbook Magazine* of September 1960. Snowden stated:

I received yesterday your favor of the 6th inst. inviting the

This coin marks the 250th anniversary of the chartering of the city of Albany, New York. It was created by Gertrude Lathrop, and shows Peter Schulyer and Robert Livingston shaking hands with Governor Thomas Dongan in 1686. The coin was authorized in 1936.

expression of my views upon the resolution of inquiry, adopted by the Senate, "Whether the smaller Spanish coins may not be removed from circulation or have a value established by law to accord with their intrinsic value and to avoid fractional parts of a cent."

I have heretofore given this subject a careful attention, and as a convenient mode of presenting my views of the importance and expediency of removing the small Spanish coins from circulation, I insert a copy of a letter I addressed to the Secretary of the Treasury on the 9th of November, 1853. It is as follows: "My attention for some months past has been called to the fact that one of the greatest hindrances to our furnishing the country with a wholesome and abundant silver currency of our own stamp is the existence of a large quantity of worn-out Spanish coin which are worth much less than their current value. From data obtained by a circular letter a few years ago, it was rendered pretty certain that the amount of those coins in circulation in the United States was about five millions of dollars. I estimate the amount of those Spanish coins now in circulation at about that sum. For the purpose of bringing this miserable currency to the melting pot, I recommend that a larger price per piece be paid for these coins than is paid for large coin and other bullion. In connection with an increase of price it would be of great service if we had the aid of the Post Office Department either through its head or through the agency of the Postmasters of the principal cities. It is only a few years since that those coins were taken at the city Post Offices, by fixed regulations at 23, 11 and 5 cents respectively, and, it was only the scarcity of our own silver change that restored them to their original nominal

This coin commemorates the opening of the San Francisco-Oakland Bay Bridge. It was designed by Jaques Schnier and authorized in 1936. Near the right front paw of the bear is the letter "S," which stands for the San Francisco mint.

valuation. If they were discredited to the amounts above stated and an offer made to pay 123 or 124 cents per ounce for them, we would have a fair prospect of ridding the community from a depreciated and troublesome currency which would be supplied by our own quarters, dimes and half dimes now so few, by issuing from the Mints. If you sanction this suggestion and authorize one to increase the price for these fractional parts of a dollar, I will make further investigations and ascertain whether we can go as high as 124 cents per ounce, which leaves only a margin of one cent per ounce to cover the expense of coinage. But as the object in view is to accomplish a great public benefit it may well be considered whether we may not go very nearly to the margin which the new coin will not permit."

To this letter the Secretary of the Treasury the next day replied by stating that he thought favorably of the proposition to adopt some measures for withdrawing the small Spanish silver coins from circulation but that, in his opinion, it would not be judicious to do so at this time, not until we can supply its place with our own.

As we have now issued upwards of twenty (20) millions of dollars of silver coins since the passage of the Act of March 3, 1853, the objection stated no longer exists, although at that time of some force.

The supply of the new silver coin is now large and our means of increasing it any reasonable extent undoubted. So that the only question which now presents itself is as to the mode of excluding from circulation the objectional currency.

This coin commemorates the sesquicentennial of the founding of Columbia, South Carolina. It was created by A. Wolfe Davidson in 1936.

I would respectfully suggest the following remedies as a means of accomplishing the object in view.

1. That a law be passed declaring the value of Spanish quarters, eighths and sixteenths of a dollar to be 20 cents, 10 cents and 5 cents respectively and be receivable at that rate only at the Treasury of the United States and at the different Post Offices. That when received they should not be paid out again but be transmitted to the Mint for coinage. The gain or loss on the coinage to be charged or credited, as the case may be, to the Treasury of the United States or the Post Office Department.

The manner of keeping these accounts and the transmission of them be required may be regulated by the Director of the Mint with the approbation of the Secretary of the Treasury.

2. That the price paid at the Mint per ounce for the Spanish quarters, eighths and sixteenths of a dollar, may at the discretion of the officers above named be replaced at a higher rate than for other silver purchased under the Act of March 3, 1853.

3. That a new cent be authorized either by a reduction in the weight of the present cent, or be composed by such metal or alloy and of such weight as the Director of the Mint with the approbation of the Secretary of the Treasury may prescribe. Such cent to be legalized by proclamation of the President of the United States, as was done in 1796 by President Washington under an Act of Congress.

The cents thus authorized to be paid out under the same regulations as are now prescribed for the present cent and in addition thereto that the Spanish coins before mentioned will be received at their nominal value in exchange for the new coinage. The cents issued to be exchanged in like manner for the new cent.

This coin commemorates the 300th anniversary of the landing of Swedish pioneers in Delaware. The coin was designed by Carl Schmitz and features the ship *Kalmar Nyckel,* which means "Key of Kalmar," a city in Sweden.

The half cent to be discontinued as useless and unnecessary.

The proposition to change the present cent is important in this connection because in consequence of the advance in the price of copper the present cent could not be exchanged for the small coins named at this nominal value without a considerable loss to the government—hence the necessity of reducing the intrinsic value of the present cent. This would, however, for other and obvious reasons, be advantageous as it would relieve the community from the present cumbrous and inconvenient cent and supply one better suited for circulation.

In a communication attached to my annual report for the year, 1854, I presented a project for a law "relating to the coinage of cents," with some remarks upon the subject to which I beg to refer you. But I am not now satisfied that the alloy therein recommended is the best for the purpose in view. Since that time further experiments have been made and I incline to the opinion that the introduction of an alloy of nickel may be advantageously used. I would prefer that the alloy and weight should be left optional in the manual herein before stated; especially as further experiments are now in progress and which were interrupted by the dismantled condition of the Mint during the repairs recently being made but now nearly completed. The adaption of the new metal aluminum to this object is also under consideration and the assayers of the Mint are making experiments in relation to it.

No valid objection can be made to the proposition now recommended, for, after all, the cent circulates because of the stamp of the government upon it, and not because it has any special or known intrinsic value.

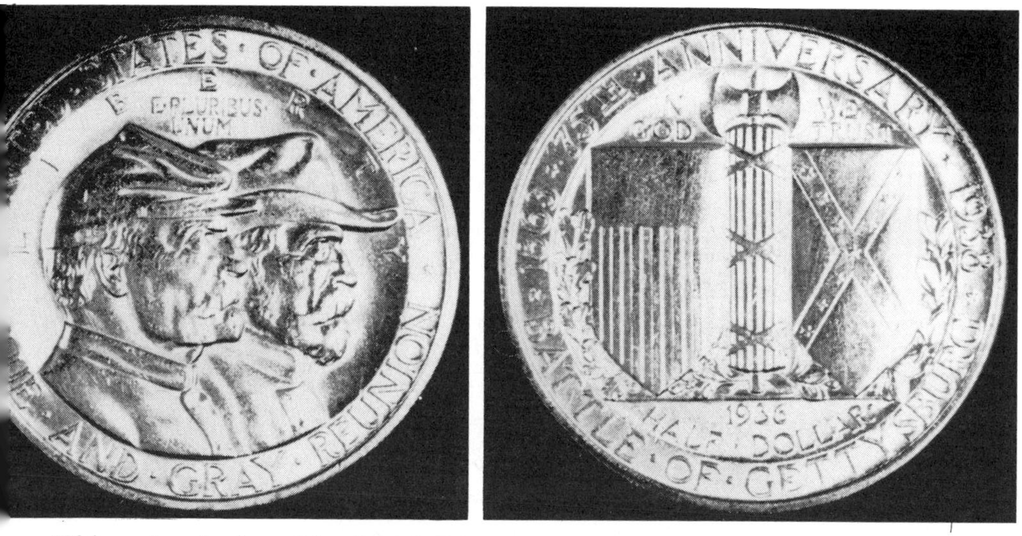

This coin, designed by Frank Vittor, commemorates the seventy-fifth anniversary of the battle of Gettysburg, which was staged in 1863. A Union and a Confederate soldier are depicted on the obverse.

This coin, designed by William Simpson and his wife Marjorie, commemorates the 200th anniversary of the founding of the city of Norfolk, Virginia, as a borough—as well as the 300th anniversary of the original Norfolk land grant. The coin was authorized in 1937.

I may add that the removal of the smaller Spanish silver coin from circulation will, in my judgment be much sooner and better accomplished by a conciliatory than by a compulsory process. Indeed, it may be regarded as certain that a stringent enactment, positively forbidding the circulation of these coins would be

This coin, designed by William Simpson, honored the 350th anniversary of the founding of the colony on Roanoke Island, North Carolina. It shows the head of Sir Walter Raleigh, who laid the groundwork for the colony but never actually set foot on American soil.

generally evaded or disobeyed. The Spanish American coinage, thoroughly domesticated here by long use, has taken a deep root in our petty trading; and even its vexatious fractions making halves and quarters of a cent, are patiently carried out and faithfully added up in the columns of store books and ledgers. Strange today, that while they are not known in Spain, and are supplanted by other issues in Spanish America, they find their only home, with their royal effigy and coarse execution in this land of republicanism and of high mechanic art. But the genial voice of the people now decides them to be a nuisance, which the legislation of Congress and the activity of the Mint may and should abate.

If the remedies herein suggested meet with your approval, I can, if you desire it, prepare and transmit to you a few sections of a bill, which, if passed into a law, will accomplish the object of removing from circulation the Spanish coins in question, and provide for a smaller and more convenient cent than the cumbrous and unsightly coin which is now used.

10

On July 17, 1862, the first of the acts making postage issues legal tender was passed. The measure stated:

> Be it enacted . . . That the Secretary of the Treasury be, and he is hereby, directed to furnish to the Assistant Treasurers, and such

This coin, again designed by William Simpson, was authorized in 1937 to commemorate the seventy-fifth anniversary of the battle of Antietam, which took place in 1862. It features General George McClellan and General Robert E. Lee on the obverse.

designated depositaries of the United States as may be by him selected in such sums as he may deem expedient, the postage and other stamps of the United States, to be exchanged by them, on application, for United States notes; and from and after the first day of August next such stamps shall be receivable for all dues to the United States less than five dollars, and shall be exchanged for United States notes when presented to any Assistant Treasurer or any designated depositary selected as aforesaid in sums not less than five dollars.

SECTION 2. And be it further enacted, That from and after the first day of August, eighteen hundred and sixty-two, no private corporation, banking association, firm, or individual shall make, issue, circulate, or pay any note, check, memorandum, token, or other obligation, for a less sum than one dollar, intended to circulate as money or to be received or used in lieu of lawful money of the United States; and every person so offending shall, on conviction thereof in any district or circuit court of the United States, be punished by fine not exceding five hundred dollars, or by imprisonment not exceeding six months, or by both, at the option of the court.

Less than a year later, on March 3, 1863, paper "change" was authorized. The bill providing for fractional currency stated:

SECTION 4. And be it further enacted, That in lieu of postage and revenue stamps for fractional currency, and of fractional notes, commonly called postage currency, issued or to be issued, the Secretary of the Treasury may issue fractional notes of like

This coin commemorates the 250th anniversary of the founding of the city of New Rochelle, New York. It was designed by Gertrude Lathrop and authorized in 1936. It shows John Pell, who was granted the rights to the land.

amounts in such form as he may deem expedient, and may provide for the engraving, preparation, and issue thereof in the Treasury Department building. And all such notes issued shall be exchangeable by the assistant treasurers and designated depositaries for the United States notes, in sums not less than three dollars, and shall be receivable for postage and revenue stamps, and also in payment of any dues to the United States less than five dollars, except duties on imports, and shall be redeemed on presentation at the Treasury of the United States in such sums and under such regulations as the Secretary of the Treasury shall prescribe: Provided, that the whole amount of fractional currency issued, including postage and revenue stamps issued as currency, shall not exceed fifty millions of dollars.

Sec. 7. And be it further enacted, all banks, associations, or corporations, and individuals issuing or reissuing notes or bills for circulation as currency after April first, eighteen hundred and sixty-three, in sums representing any fractional part of a dollar, shall be subject to and pay a duty of five per centum each half year thereafter upon the amount of such fractional notes or bills so issued.

11

On April 22, 1864, a law was passed creating the two-cent piece and allowing bronze to be used in the manufacture of the Indian Head cent. It stated:

Be it enacted . . . That, from and after the passage of this act, the standard weight of the cent coined at the mint of the United States shall be forty-eight grains, or one-tenth of one ounce troy; and said cent shall be composed of ninety-five per centum of copper, and five per centum of tin and zinc, in such proportions as shall be determined by the Director of the Mint; and there shall be, from time to time, struck and coined at the mint a two-cent piece, of the same composition, the standard weight of which shall be ninety-six grains, or one-fifth of one ounce troy, with no greater deviation than four grains to each piece of said cent and two-cent coins; and the shape, mottoes, and devices of said coins shall be fixed by the Director of the Mint, with the approval of the Secretary of the Treasury; and the laws now in force relating to the coinage of cents and providing for the purchase of material and prescribing the appropriate duties of the officers of the mint and the Secretary of the Treasury be, and the same are hereby, extended to the coinage herein provided for.

SECTION 4. And be it further enacted, That the said coins shall be a legal tender in any payment, the one-cent coin to the amount of ten cents, and the two-cent coin to the amount of twenty cents; and it shall be lawful to pay out said coins in exhange for the lawful currency of the United States (except cents or half cents issued under former acts of Congress,) in suitable sums, by the treasurer of the mint, and by such other depositaries as the Secretary of the Treasury may designate, under general regulations proposed by the Director of the Mint and approved by the Secretary of the Treasury; and the expenses incident to such exchange, distribution, and transmission may be paid out of the profits of said

This coin, designed by Adam Pietz in 1946, commemorates the 100th anniversary of Iowa's admission to statehood. The coin was the first commemorate to be issued following the stoppage of the series during World War II.

coinage; and the net profits of said coinage, ascertained in like manner as is prescribed in the second section of the act to which this is a supplement, shall be transferred to the Treasury of the United States.

SEC. 5. And be it further enacted, That if any person or persons shall make, issue, or pass, or cause to be made, issued, or passed, any coin, card, token, or device whatsoever, in metal or its compounds, intended to pass or be passed as money for a one-cent piece or a two-cent piece, such person or persons shall be deemed guilty of a misdemeanor, and shall, on conviction thereof, be punished by a fine not exceeding one thousand dollars, and by imprisonment for a term not exceeding five years."

12

On June 8, 1864, the problems of the private mints and counterfeit coinage were handled:

Be it enacted . . . That if any person or persons, except as now authorized by law, shall hereafter make, or cause to be made, or shall utter or pass, or attempt to utter or pass, any coins of gold or silver or other metals or alloys of metals, intended for the use and purpose of the United States or of foreign countries, or of original design, every person so offending shall, on conviction thereof, be punished by fine not exceeding three thousand dollars, or by imprisonment for a term not exceeding five years, or both, at the discretion of the court according to the aggravation of the offence.

13

There was one additional law regarding paper "change", this one passed on June 30, 1864.

SECTION 5. And be it further enacted, That the Secretary of the Treasury may issue notes of the fractions of a dollar as now used for currency, in such form, with such inscriptions, and with such safeguards against counterfeiting, as he may judge best, and provide for the engraving and preparation, and for the issue of the same, as well as of all other notes and bonds, and other obligations, and shall make such regulations for the redemption of said fractional notes and other notes when mutilated or defaced, and for the receipt of said fractional notes in payment of debts to the United States, except for customs, in such sums, not over five dollars as may appear to him expedient; and it is hereby declared that all laws and parts of laws applicable to the fractional notes engraved and issued as herein authorized, apply equally and with like force to all the fractional notes heretofore authorized, whether known as postage currency or otherwise, and to postage stamps issued as currency; but the whole amount of all descriptions of notes or stamps less than one dollar issued as currency shall not exceed fifty millions of dollars.

14

The new copper-nickel coins were introduced as the Civil War came to a close. The first, a three-cent piece, was authorized March 3, 1865.

Be it enacted . . . That as soon as practicable after the passage of this act, there shall be coined at the Mint of the United States a three-cent piece, composed of copper and nickel in such proportions not exceeding twenty-five per centum of nickel, as shall be determined by the Director of the Mint, the standard weight of which shall be thirty grains, with no greater deviation than four grains to each piece, and the shape, mottoes, and devices of said coin shall be determined by the Director of the Mint, with the approval of the Secretary of the Treasury. And the laws now in force relating to the coinage of cents and providing for the purchase of material and prescribing the appropriate duties of the officers of the Mint, and of the Secretary of the Treasury be, and the same are hereby, extended to the coinage herein provided for.

"SECTION 3. And be it further enacted, That the said coin shall be

This coin, designed by Isaac Scott Hathway, was authorized in 1946 to commemorate the life of Booker T. Washington, the former slave who established a major educational institution in Tuskegee, Alabama, and greatly advanced educational opportunities for blacks throughout the United States.

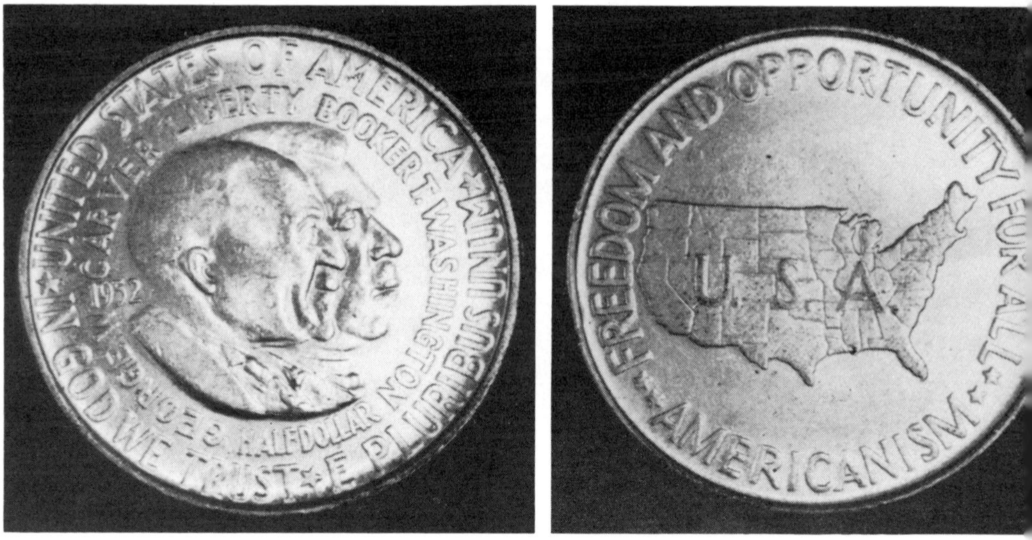

This coin is a joint commemorative for both Booker T. Washington and George Washington Carver. It was designed by Isaac Hathway and was issued from 1951 to 1954. George Washington Carver, born at the end of the Civil War, was head of the agricultural department of Tuskegee Institute. He worked with Booker T. Washington to make the school world-famous for its research. Carver carried on experiments that resulted in hundreds of new uses for sweet potatoes, peanuts, and soy beans. Prior to his reseach, the plants were considered to be "junk" foods having minimal nutritional value.

a legal tender in any payment to the amount of sixty cents. And it shall be lawful to pay out said coins in exchange for the lawful currency of the United States, (except cents or half-cents or two-cent pieces issued under former acts of Congress,) in suitable terms by the Treasurer of the Mint and by such other depositaries as the Secretary of the Treasury may designate, and under general regulations approved by the Secretary of the Treasury. And under the like regulations the same may be exchanged in suitable sums for any lawful currency of the United States; and the expenses incident to such exchange, distribution, and transmission, may be paid out of the profits of said coinage, and the net profits of said coinage, ascertained in like manner as is prescribed in the second section of the act entitled 'An act relating to foreign coins, and the coinage of cents at the Mint of the United States,' approved February twenty-first, eighteen hundred and fifty-seven, shall be transferred to the Treasury of the United States: Provided, That from and after the passage of the act, no issues of fractional notes of the United States shall be of a less denomination, than five cents, and all such issues of a less denomination at that time outstanding, shall, when paid into the Treasury or any designated depositary of the United States, or redeemed or exchanged as now provided by law, be retained and cancelled.

SEC. 5. And be it further enacted, That, in addition to the devices and legends upon the gold, silver, and other coins of the United States, it shall be lawful for the Director of the Mint, with the approval of the Secretary of the Treasury, to cause the motto 'In God we trust' to be placed upon such coins hereafter to be issued as shall admit of such legend thereof.

SEC. 6. And be it further enacted, That the one and two cent coins of the United States shall not be a legal tender for any payment exceeding four cents in amount; and so much of the laws of the United States heretofore enacted as are in conflict with the provisions of this act, are hereby repealed."

On May 16, 1866, the five-cent copper-nickel coin was created:

Be it enacted . . . That, so soon as practicable after the passage of this act, there shall be coined at the Mint of the United States a five-cent piece composed of copper and nickel, in such proportions, not exceeding twenty-five per centum of nickel, as shall be determined by the Director of the Mint, the standard weight of which shall be seventy-seven and sixteen hundredths grains, with no greater deviation than two grains to each piece; and the shape, mottoes and devices of said coin shall be determined by the Director of the Mint, with the approval of the Secretary of the Treasury; and the laws now in force relating to the coinage of cents, and providing for the purchase of material, and prescribing the appropriate duties of the officers of the Mint and the Secretary of the Treasury, be, and the same are hereby, extended to the coinage herein provided for.

SEC. 3. And be it further enacted, That said coin shall be a legal tender in any payment to the amount of one dollar, and it shall be lawful to pay out such coins in exchange for the lawful currency in the United States, (except cents, or half cents, or two cent pieces, issued under former acts of Congress) in suitable sums, by the treasurer of the Mint, and by such other depositaries as the Secretary of the Treasury may designate, and under general regulations approved by the Secretary of the Treasury. And under the like regulations the same may be exchanged in suitable sums for any lawful currency of the United States, and the expenses incident to such exchange, distribution, and transmission may be paid out of the profits of said coinage; and the net profits of said coinage, as ascertained in the manner prescribed in the second section of the act entitled "An act relating to foreign coins and the coinage of cents at the Mint of the United States," approved February twenty-first, eighteen hundred and fifty-seven, shall be transferred to the Treasury of the United States: Provided, That from and after the passage of this act no issues of fractional notes of the United States shall be of a less denomination than ten cents; and all such issues at the time outstanding shall, when paid into the Treasury or any designated depositary of the United States, or redeemed or exchanged as now provided by law, be retained and cancelled.

SEC. 5. And be it further enacted, That it shall be lawful for the Treasurer and the several assistant treasurers of the United States to redeem in national currency, under such rules and regulations as may be prescribed by the Secretary of the Treasury, the coin herein authorized to be issued when presented in sums not less than one hundred dollars.

15

On February 12, 1873, there was enacted a general revision of the coinage laws resulting in several important changes quoted below:

Be it enacted . . . That the Mint of the United States is hereby established as a Bureau of the Treasury Department, embracing in its organization and under its control all mints for the manufacture of coin, and all assay-offices for the stamping of bars, which are now, or which may be hereafter, authorized by law. The chief officer of the said Bureau shall be denominated by the Secretary of the Treasury. He shall be appointed by the President, by and with the advice and consent of the Senate, and shall hold his office for the term of five years, unless sooner removed by the President, upon reasons to be communicated by him to the Senate.

SECTION 13. That the standard for both gold and silver coins of the United States shall be such that of one thousand parts by weight nine hundred shall be of pure metal and one hundred of alloy; and the alloy of the silver coins shall be of copper, and the alloy of the gold coins shall be of copper, or of copper and silver; but the silver shall in no case exceed one-tenth of the whole alloy.

SEC. 15. That the silver coins of the United States shall be a trade dollar, a half-dollar, or fifty-cent piece, a quarter dollar, or twenty-five-cent piece, a dime, or ten-cent piece; and the weight of the trade dollar shall be four hundred and twenty grains troy; the weight of the half-dollar shall be twelve grams (grammes) and one-half of a gram, (gramme;) the quarter-dollar and the dime shall be respectively, one-half and one-fifth of the weight of said half dollar; and said coins shall be a legal tender at their nominal value for any amount not exceeding five dollars in any one payment.

SEC. 17. That no coins, either of gold, silver, or minor coinage, shall hereafter be issued from the mint other than those of the denominations, standards, and weights, herein set forth.

SEC. 18. That upon the coins of the United States there shall be the following devices and legends: Upon one side there shall be an impression emblematic of liberty, with an inscription of the word "Liberty" and the year of the coinage, and upon the reverse shall be the figure or representation of an eagle, with the inscriptions "United States of America" and "E Pluribus Unum," and a designation of the value of the coin; but on the gold dollar and three-dollar piece, the dime, five, three and one cent piece the figure of the eagle shall be omitted; and on the reverse of the silver trade-dollar the weight and the fineness of the coin shall be inscribed; and the Director of the Mint, with the approval of the Secretary of the Treasury, may cause the motto "In God we trust" to be inscribed upon such coins as shall admit of such motto: and any one of the foregoing inscriptions may be on the rim of the gold and silver coins.

SEC. 21. That any owner of silver bullion may deposit the same at any mint, to be formed into bars, or into dollars of the weight of four hundred and twenty grains, troy, designated in this act as trade-dollars, and no deposit of silver for other coinage shall be received; but silver bullion contained in gold deposits, and separated therefrom, may be paid for in silver coin, at such valuation as may be, from time to time, established by the Director of the Mint.

SEC. 25. That the charge for converting standard gold bullion into coin shall be one-fifth of one per centum; and the charges for converting standard silver into trade-dollars for melting and refining when bullion is below standard, for toughening when metals are contained in it which render it unfit for coinage, for copper used for alloy when the bullion is above standard, for separating the gold and silver when these metals exist together in the bullion, and for the preparation of bars, shall be fixed, from time to time, by the Director, with the concurrence of the Secretary of the Treasury, so as to equal but not to exceed, in their judgement, the actual average cost to each mint and assay-office of the material, labor, wastage, and use of machinery employed in each of the cases aforementioned.

SEC. 27. That in order to procure bullion for the silver coinage authorized by this act, the superintendents, with the approval of the Director of the Mint, as to price, terms, and quantity, shall purchase such bullion with the bullion fund. The gain arising from the coinage of such silver bullion into coin of nominal value exceeding the cost thereof shall be credited to a special fund denominated the silver profit fund. This fund shall be charged with the wastage incurred as hereinafter provided. The balance to the credit of this fund shall be from time to time, and at least twice a year, paid into the Treasury of the United States.

SEC. 28. That silver coins other than the trade-dollar shall be paid out at the several mints, and at the assay-office in New York City, in exchange for gold coins at par, in sums not less than one hundred dollars; and it shall be lawful, also, to transmit parcels of the same, from time to time, to the assistant treasurers, depositaries, and other officers of the United States, under general regulations proposed by the Director of the Mint, and approved by the Secretary of the Treasury; but nothing herein contained shall prevent the payment of silver coins, at their nominal value, for silver parted from gold, as provided in this act, or for change less than one dollar in settlement for gold deposits: Provided, That for two years after the passage of this act, silver coins shall be paid at the mint in Philadelphia and the assay-office in New York City for silver bullion purchased for coinage, under such regulations as may be prescribed by the Director of the Mint, and approved by the Secretary of the Treasury.

SEC. 29. That for the purchase of metal for the minor coinage authorized by this act, a sum not exceeding fifty thousand dollars in lawful money of the United States shall be transferred by the Secretary of the Treasury to the credit of the superintendent of the Mint at Philadelphia, at which establishment only, until otherwise provided by law, such coinage shall be carried on. The superintendent with the approval of the Director of the Mint as to price, terms and quantity, shall purchase the metal required for such coinage by public advertisement, and the lowest and best bid shall be accepted, the fineness of the metals to be determined on the Mint assay. The gain arising from the coinage of such metals into coin of a nominal value, exceeding the cost thereof, shall be credited to the special fund denominated the minor coinage profit fund; and this fund shall be charged with the wastage incurred in such coinage, and with the cost of distributing said coins as hereinafter provided. The balance remaining to the credit of this fund, and any balance of profits accrued from minor coinage under former acts, shall be, from time to time, and at least twice a year, conveyed into the Treasury of the United States.

SEC. 30. That the minor coins authorized by this act may, at the discretion of the Director of the Mint, be delivered in any of the principal cities and towns of the United States, at the cost of the Mint, for transportation, and shall be exchangeable at par at the mint in Philadephia, at the discretion of the superintendent, for any other coins of copper, bronze, or copper-nickel heretofore authorized by law; and it shall be lawful for the Treasurer and the several assistant treasurers and depositaries of the United States to redeem, in lawful money, under such rules as may be prescribed by the Secretary of the Treasury, all copper, bronze, and copper-nickel coins authorized by law when presented in sums of not less than twenty dollars; and whenever, under this authority, these coins are presented for redemption in such quantity as to show the amount outstanding to be redundant, the Secretary of the Treasury is authorized and required to direct that such coinage shall cease until otherwise ordered by him.

SEC. 37. That in adjusting the weight of the silver coins the following deviations shall not be exceeded in any single piece: In the dollar, the half and quarter dollar, and in the dime, one and one-half grains; and in weighing large numbers of pieces together, when delivered by the coiner to the superintendent, and by the superintendent to the depositor, the deviations from the standard weight shall not exceed two-hundredths of an ounce in one thousand dollars, half-dollars, or quarter dollars, and one-hundredth of an ounce in one thousand dimes.

SEC. 38. That in adjusting the weight of the minor coins provided by this act, there shall be no greater deviation allowed than three grains for the five-cent piece and two grains for the three and one cent pieces.

16

On March 3, 1875, a law was enacted authorizing the twenty-cent piece. The law stated:

> . . . That there shall be, from time to time, coined at the mints of the United States, conformably in all respects to the coinage act of eighteen hundred and seventy-three, a silver coin of the denomination of twenty cents, and of the weight of five grams.

The twenty-cent piece was discontinued just thirty-eight months after it began. On May 2, 1878, a new law stated:

> . . . That from, and after the passage of this act, the coinage of the twenty cent piece of silver, by the Government of the United States be, and the same is hereby prohibited. And all laws in conflict with this act are hereby repealed.

17

On February 19, 1887, the Trade dollar was ordered to be redeemed by the government to eliminate its use in domestic commerce. The order stated:

> . . . That for a period of six months after the passage of this act, United States trade-dollars, if not defaced, mutilated, or stamped, shall be received at the office of the Treasurer, or any assistant treasurer of the United States in exchange for a like amount, dollar for dollar, of standard silver dollars, or of subsidiary coins of the United States.

18

On September 26, 1890, the three-cent nickel, dollar gold piece and three-dollar gold piece were also discontinued according to a law that stated:

. . . That from and after the passage of this act the coinage of the three-dollar gold piece, the one-dollar gold piece, and the three-cent nickel piece be, and the same is hereby, prohibited, and the pieces named shall not be struck or issued by the Mint of the United States.

19

On April 24, 1906, the branch Mints were affected by new coinage legislation:

Be it enacted . . . That sections thirty-five hundred and twenty-eight and thirty-five hundred and twenty-nine of the Revised Statutes be, and the same are hereby, amended so as to read as follows:

SECTION 3528. For the purchase of metal for the minor coinage authorized by this act a sum not exceeding two hundred thousand dollars in lawful money of the United States shall, upon the recommendation of the Director of the Mint, and in such sums as he may designate, with the approval of the Secretary of the Treasury, be transferred to the credit of the superintendents of the mints at Philadelphia, San Francisco, Denver, and New Orleans, at which establishments, until otherwise provided by law, such coinage shall be carried on.

20

On May 18, 1908, reaction to President Roosevelt's having the motto eliminated from Saint-Gaudens' coins resulted in an act stating:

> . . . That the motto "In God we trust," heretofore inscribed on certain denominations of the gold and silver coins of the United States of America, shall hereafter be inscribed upon all such gold and silver coins of said denominations as heretofore.

21

On October 18, 1973, Public Law 93-117 was passed. It was meant to provide for the bicentennial reverses for the dollars, half-dollars, and quarter dollars and stated:

> Be it enacted by the Senate and House of Representatives of the United States of America in Congress assembled, That the reverse side of all dollar, half-dollar, and quarter dollar coins minted for issuance on or after July 4, 1975, and until such time as the Secretary of the Treasury may determine, shall bear a design determined by the Secretary to be emblematic of the Bicentennial of the American Revolution.
>
> SECTION 2. All dollar, half-dollar, and quarter-dollar coins minted for issuance between July 4, 1975, and January 1, 1977, shall bear "1776–1976" in lieu of the date of coinage; and all dollar, half-dollar, and quarter-dollar coins minted thereafter until such time as the Secretary of the Treasury may determine shall bear a date emblematic of the Bicentennial in addition to the date of coinage.
>
> SEC. 3. Until the Secretary of the Treasury determines that the

mints of the United States are adequate for the production of ample supplies of coins and medals, any facility of the Bureau of the Mint may be used for the manufacture and storage of medals and coins.

SEC. 4. Notwithstanding any other provision of law with respect to the design of coins, the Secretary shall mint prior to July 4, 1975, for issuance on and after such date, 45 million silver-clad alloy coins authorized under section 101(a) of the Coinage Act of 1965, commemorating the Bicentennial of the American Revolution, of such design, in such denomination, and containing such quantities of such other metals as he determines appropriate. In addition, the Secretary shall coin and issue not more than an additional 15 million such coins, if he determines such coins are needed to meet public demand. Coins minted under this section may only be distributed by the Secretary as proof or uncirculated coins at such prices as he may determine. The Secretary is authorized, by regulation, to limit the number of silver coins minted under this section which any one person may purchase. Coins minted under this section shall be treated as pieces subject to the one hundred and fifty million piece limitation contained in section 101(d) of the Coinage Act of 1965, and shall be subject to such limitation. Receipts from the sale of coins under this section shall be conveyed into the Treasury as miscellaneous receipts.

SEC. 5. In connection with the operations of the Bureau of the Mint, the Secretary of the Treasury is authorized to manufacture and distribute numismatic items. Proceeds from the sale of numismatic items shall be reimbursed to the current appropriation for the cost of manufacturing and handling of such items.

Bibliography

Americanization Department, Veterans of Foreign Wars of the United States. *America, Great Crises in our History Told by Its Makers.* 12 vols. Chicago: Americanization Department, 1925.

American Numismatic Association. *Selections from* The Numismatist: *United States Coins.* Racine, Wis.: Whitman Publishing Company, 1960.

Ashbaugh, Don. *Nevada's Turbulent Yesterday: A Study in Ghost Towns.* Los Angeles, Calif.: Westernlore.

Bancroft, George. *History Of The United States.* Vols. 1–6. New York: D. Appleton and Co., 1887.

Basler, Roy; Pratt, Marion; and Dunlap, Lloyd. *The Collected Works of Abraham Lincoln.* 8 vols. New Brunswick, N.J.: Rutgers University Press, 1955.

Benton, Thomas. *Thirty Years' View: A History of the American Government for Thirty Years.* Vol 2. New York: D. Appleton and Co., 1856.

Bishop, Joseph Buckland. *Theodore Roosevelt and His Time.* Vol. 1. New York: Charles Scribner's Sons, 1970.

Blaine, James G. *Twenty Years of Congress: Lincoln to Garfield.* Vol. 2. Norwich, Conn.: Henry Bill Publishing Co., 1886.

Boorstin, Daniel J. *The Americans: The Colonial Experience.* New York: Random House, 1958.

———. *The Americans: The National Experience.* New York: Random House, 1965.

———. *The Americans: The Democratic Experience.* New York: Random House, 1973.

Bowers, Claude G. *Jefferson and Hamilton: The Struggle for Democracy in America.* 10th impression. Cambridge, Mass.: The Riverside Press, 1927.

Boykin, Edward, ed. *Living Letters From American History.* New York: Halcyon House, 1934.

Bruff, J. Goldsborough. *Gold Rush: The Journals, Drawings and Other Papers of J. Goldsborough Bruff.* Edited by Georgia Read and Ruth Gaines. New York: Columbia University Press, 1949.

Carothers, Neil. *The Fractional Money.* New York: John Wiley & Sons, 1930.

Caughey, John. *California.* 2nd ed. Englewood Cliffs, N.J.: Prentice-Hall, 1953.

Commager, Henry Steele, ed. *Documents of American History.* 3rd edition. Crofts American History Series, edited by Dixon Ryan Fox. New York: F. S. Crofts & Co., 1947.

Commins, Saxe, ed. *The Basic Writings of George Washington.* New York: Random House, 1948.

Crosby, Sylvester. *The Early Coins of America and the Laws Governing Their Issue.* Chicago: Argonaut, Inc., 1967.

Current Literature 43 (1907).

Current Literature 44 (1908): 68–70.

Del Mar, Alexander. *The History of Money in America.* New York: Burt Franklin, 1969.

Elliot, Russell. *The History of Nevada.* Lincoln, Nebr.: University of Nebraska Press, 1973.

Elson, Henry William. *History of the United States.* Vols. 1–5. Norwood, Mass.: The MacMillan Co., 1905.

Fitzpatrick, John, ed. *The Writings of George Washington: From the Original Manuscript Sources,* 1745–1799. Vols. 31, 32, and 33. United States Government Printing Office, 1931.

"Free Coinage of Silver and Gold at the U.S. Mint, The." *The Numismatist,* December 1940, p. 860.

Gatewood, Willard Jr. *Theodore Roosevelt and the Art of Controversy.* Baton Rouge, La.: Louisiana State University Press, 1970.

Greever, William. *The Bonanza West.* Norman, Okla.: University of Oklahoma Press, 1960.

Hafen, Leroy, and Rister, Carl. *Western America.* Englewood Cliffs, N.J.: Prentice-Hall, Inc., 1970.

Hammond, Bray. *Banks and Politics in America.* Princeton, N.J.: Princeton University Press, 1957.

Harbauth, William H., ed. *The Writings of Theodore Roosevelt.* Indianapolis, Ind.: Bobbs-Merrill Co., 1967.

Harper's Weekly 51 (1907): 1787–1788.

Hind, C. Lewis. *Augustus Saint-Gaudens.* The International Studio. New York: John Lane Co., 1908.

Hindle, Brooke. *David Rittenhouse.* Princeton, N.J.: Princeton University Press, 1964.

Johnson, William. *The Forty-Niners.* New York: Time-Life Books, 1975.

Julian, Robert. "Beginning of U.S. Coinage." *Coins Magazine,* June 1974, p. 40.

Jullian. R. W. "The Cent Coinage of 1794–1795." *The Numismatic Scrapbook,*

January 25, 1975, p. 6.

———. "A Cent Coinage of 1793." *The Numismatic Scrapbook,* December 24, 1974, p. 60.

———. "The Cent Coinage of 1795." *The Numismatic Scrapbook,* March 25, 1975, p. 6.

———. "A Cent Coinage of 1797." *The Numismatic Scrapbook,* April 25, 1975, p. 84.

The Kensington Collection Auction Catalogue of the American Auction Association. Bowers and Ruddy Galleries, 1975.

Krakel, Dean. *End of the Trail: Odyssey of a Statue.* Norman, Okla.: University of Oklahoma Press, 1973.

Labaree, Leonard, and Bell, Whitefield Jr., ed. *The Papers of Benjamin Franklin.* Vol. 1–20. New Haven, Conn.: Yale University Press, 1964.

Lindeman, Jack, ed. *The Conflict of Convictions.* Radnor, Pa.: Chilton Book Co.

Literary Digest, 1907, p. 788.

Miller, Ronald. *Shady Ladies of the West.* Los Angeles, Calif.: Westernlore, 1974.

Morris, Anne Cary, ed. *Morris Diary and Letters.* New York: Charles Scribner's Sons, 1888.

Morrison, Samuel Eliot. *The Oxford History of the American People.* New York: Oxford University Press, 1965.

———. *The European Discovery of America: The Northern Voyages.* New York: Oxford University Press, 1971.

Nevada: The Silver State. American Guide Series. Portland, Ore.: Binfords and Mort.

Nevins, Alan. *The American States during and after the Revolution: 1775 to 1789.* Reprints of Economic Classics. Clifton, N.J.: Augustus M. Kelley, Publishers.

New York Times, November 15, 1907.

New York Times, December 8, 1907.

The Numismatist, August 1971, pp. 115–1124.

Oberholtzer, Ellis Paxson. *Robert Morris: The Patriotic Financier.* New York: MacMillan Company, 1903.

Obojski, Robert. "A Continental Currency." *The Numismatic Scrapbook,* June 1975, p. 20.

Oliver, Frederick Scott. *Alexander Hamilton: An Essay on American Union.* New York: G. P. Putnam's Sons, 1907.

Olmstead, Roger. *Scenes of Wonder and Curiosity.* Berkeley, Calif.: Howell-North, 1962.

Padover, Saul K. Arr. *The Complete Jefferson.* New York: Tudor Publishing Co., 1943.

Porkhill, Forbes. *The Wildest of the West.* Stage Book.

The Paramount Journal, April-May 1974. Englewood, Ohio: Paramount International Coin Corporation, 1974.

Porter, Kirk, and Johnson, Donald. *National Platforms: 1840–1860.* Urbana, Ill.: University of Illinois Press, 1970

Randall, J. G., and Donald, David. *The Civil War and Reconstruction.* 2nd ed. Boston: D. C. Heath and Co., 1961.

Reinders, Robert, *End of an Era: New Orleans 1850–1860.* Gretna, La.: Pelican Publishing Co., 1964.

Reiter, Ed. "Silver Dollar Model." *Colliers,* December 28, 1907, p. 54.

Roosevelt, Theodore. *Gouverneur Morris.* Boston: Houghton Mifflin Co., 1898.

———. *The Rough Riders and Men of Action.* New York: Charles Scribner's Sons, 1929.

Saint-Gaudens, Homer, ed. *The Reminiscences of Augustus Saint-Gaudens.* Vol. 2. New York: Century Co., 1913.

Sherman, John. *John Sherman's Recollections.* Vol. 1. New York: Werner Co., 1895.

Slabaugh, Arlie. *United States Commemorative Coinage.* Racine, Wis.: Western Publishing Co., 1975.

Smith, George Winston, and Judah, Charles. *Life in the North during the Civil War.* Albuquerque, N.M.: University of New Mexico Press, 1966.

Smyth, Albert Henry, ed. *The Writings of Benjamin Franklin.* 10 vols. New York: Haskell House, 1970.

Starkey, Marion. *Lace Cuffs and Leather Aprons: Popular Struggles in the Federalist Era.* New York: Alfred A. Knopf, 1974.

Stern, Phillip Van Doren, ed. *Soldier Life in the Union and Confederate Armies.* Bonanza Books.

Swiggett, Howard. *The Extraordinary Mr. Morris.* New York: Doubleday, 1952.

Syrett, Harold, and Cooke, Jacob, ed. *The Papers of Alexander Hamilton.* New York: Columbia University Press, 1961.

Taxay, Don. *Counterfeit, Mis-Struck and Unofficial U. S. Coins.* New York: Arco Publishing Co., 1963.

———. *An Illustrated History of Commemorative Coinage.* New York: Arco Publishing Co., 1967.

———. *The U. S. Mint and Coinage.* New York: Arco Publishing Co., 1966.

Tharp, Louise Hall. *Saint-Gaudens and the Gilded Era.* Boston: Little, Brown and Co., 1969.

This Fabulous Century: 1900–1910. New York: Time-Life Books, 1969.

Trowbridge, Richard. "Heritage Revisited." *The Numismatic Scrapbook,* June 1975, p. 12.

Van Doren, Carl. *Secret History of the American Revolution.* New York: Viking Press, 1941.

Ver Steeg, Clareance. *Robert Morris: Revolutionary Financier.* New York: Octagon Books, 1972.

Walther, Donald. *Gouverneur Morris: Witness of Two Revolutions.* New York: Funk and Wagnalls Co. Literary Digest Books.

Wheeler, Keith. *The Townsmen.* New York: Time-Life Books, 1975.

Young, Eleanor. *Forgotten Patriot Robert Morris.* New York: MacMillan Co., 1950.

Index